EARLY MODERN TALES OF ORIENT

Early Modern Tales of Orient is the first volume to collect together these travellers' tales and make them available to today's students and scholars. By introducing a fascinating array of accounts (of exploration and diplomatic and commercial ventures), Kenneth Parker challenges widely-held assumptions about early modern encounters in the Orient.

The documents assembled in *Early Modern Tales of Orient* have extraordinary resonance for us today. Many of the discourses which, in part, emerged from those early encounters – such as Islamophobia, English nationalism and the Catholic/Protestant divide – are still active in contemporary society. This volume sheds a unique light on the development of a very English interest in 'the exotic'.

Kenneth Parker is Professor Emeritus of Cultural Studies and formerly Head of the Cultural Studies Graduate Centre, University of East London, UK.

EARLY MODERN TALES OF ORIENT

A critical anthology

Edited by Kenneth Parker

London and New York

First published 1999
by Routledge
2 Park Square, Milton Park, Abingdon, Oxon, OX14 4RN

Simultaneously published in the USA and Canada
by Routledge
270 Madison Ave, New York NY 10016

Routledge is an imprint of the Taylor & Francis Group

Transferred to Digital Printing 2007

Typeset in Garamond by Routledge

British Library Cataloguing in Publication Data
A catalogue record for this book is available from the British Library

Library of Congress Cataloging in Publication Data
Early Modern Tales of Orient: a critical anthology/
edited by Kenneth Parker
Includes bibliographical references and index.
1. Middle East–description and travel. 2. Travellers' writings, English–Middle
East–History. 3. British–travel–Middle East–History. I. Parker, Kenneth, 1932–.
DS49.7.E17 1999 98–54316
915.604'15–dc21 CIP

ISBN 0–415–14756–5 (hbk)
ISBN 0–415–14757–3 (pbk)

For Gabrielle – again

CONTENTS

CONTENTS

ACKNOWLEDGEMENTS

It has been my singular good fortune to have been the beneficiary, over the years, of unstinting support and excellent advice (not always heeded) from scholars of great eminence as well as willingness to share their knowledge: Anne Barton; Catherine Belsey; J. M. Coetzee; John Drakakis; Dorothy Driver; Rod Edmond; Terence Hawkes; Margaret Healy; Thomas Healy; Giuliana Iannaccaro; Javed Majeed; Alessandra Marzola; Michael Neill; John Noyes; Anthony Parr; Jonathan Sawday; Bill Schwarz; Alan Sinfield; Kian Soheil; Couze Venn; Allesandro Vescovi; Susan Wiseman. I am also increasingly aware of indebtedness to a new generation of scholars beginning what promises to be brilliant careers: Catarina Albano; Anita Biressi; Rachel Holmes; Bernhard Klein; Heather Nunn; Philippe Parker. Four people do, however, require especial mention: Jerry Brotton, with whom I have been trading intellectual as well as geographical territories (wholly to my advantage) for the past few years; Benita Parry, who, from the time of our first encounters growing up in apartheid South Africa, insisted upon the need to take account of the nuances of the politics of postcolonial theories and practices; Maurice Pope, classical scholar, whose encyclopedic knowledge is allied to an amused patience to ensure that (at the very least) translations from the Latin are not only accurate, but also elegant. Last, but not least, Gabrielle, not simply for her vast knowledge of things French, but because, above all, but for whom…

I am delighted to acknowledge the support of the Humanities Research Board of the British Academy, via its Research Leave Scheme, by which means it became possible to find the time to do the work, initially in the fusty conviviality of the North Library, more recently in the elegant surroundings of the Rare Books section of the newly built British Library, to whose curators and staff much thanks.

INTRODUCTION

Travellers' tales

The 3rd Earl of Shaftesbury, Anthony Ashley Cooper (1671–1713), commenting on the ubiquity of the genre, observed, in 1710, that travel books 'are the chief materials to furnish out a library...[and are] in our present days, what books of chivalry were to our forefathers'. Contrasting reader responses of his times with what he saw as the credulity of that of his forefathers, he concluded that 'for our faith, indeed, as well as our taste... I must confess I can't consider reading it, without astonishment'.[1] Since Shaftesbury was one of the three figures (the others were Hume and Burke) with whom Terry Eagleton[2] begins his explorations into the category of the aesthetic in post-Enlightenment Europe, the Earl's observation about the reading practices of his own time deserves serious attention on at least two counts. Firstly, because that interest in travellers' tales offers evidence of interest in other places and peoples, about which the publication of specialist texts on cosmography at that time provides testimony. Secondly, that such an interest runs parallel with the reading of what was probably the largest single genre at that time: sermons and other texts with the objective of moral improvement.

Because of that ubiquity of the genre (as well as for other reasons to be adduced later on), travellers' tales present particularly acute problems for critical and cultural theories. Because of the hybrid nature of the form, these tales belong neither simply to the inventions of fiction, nor to the 'facts' of scientific 'discovery', neither to the public world of official discourse nor to that of the private one of diary, autobiography and letter that marked literary production in early modern England. Indeed, publication of these tales occurs not only in a key moment in the destabilization of feudal political hegemony and the emergence of mercantile capitalism; they coincide, as well, in that moment of the destabilization of generic categories which Michael McKeon has characterized as one of the distinctive features of the transition from Christian pilgrimage to 'scientific' travel in European cultural history.[3] If books telling the story of Christian pilgrimage during the previous centuries were not readily available in print in the vernacular might offer one explanation why travel writers make such scant reference to such precedent stories (especially those having to do with the Crusades). McKeon is right to warn that:

> No single factor could account for the sheer proliferation not only of actual journeys, nor even of their published accounts, but of an entire spectrum of printed, first-person narratives, some recognizably 'true', some apparently or obviously

fabricated, and all preoccupied with the question of their own historicity and how it might be authenticated.

(p. 101)

An earlier generation of scholars[4] had sought to do so, but the challenge for literary and cultural theorists is to assess the contribution of tales told by ecclesiastics, diplomats, merchants and scholars, as well as tourists to the phenomenon now commonly referred to as 'Orientalism' and (almost inevitably) associated with the name of Edward Said.

'Orientalism'

In his 'Introduction' to *Orientalism. Western conceptions of the Orient* (1978),[5] Said observes that, by the use of the term 'Orientalism' he means several things which, he insists, are interdependent. Firstly, that 'Orientalism' is not only an academic tradition; it is also 'a style of thought based upon an ontological and epistemological distinction between "the Orient" and (most of the time) "the Occident"'. Secondly, it was that binary distinction between West and East, Said contends, which laid the foundations for accounts, theories and subsequent practices by which the former sought to achieve hegemony over the latter in a moment of history which, he insists, is historically specific. It is out of these two that Said derives, and proposes, a third meaning:

> Taking the late eighteenth century as a very roughly defined starting point Orientalism can be discussed and analyzed as the corporate institution for dealing with the Orient – dealing with it by making statements about it, authorizing views of it, describing it, by teaching it, settling it, ruling over it: in short, as a Western style for dominating, restructuring, and having authority over the Orient.

(p. 3)

To such an extent, Said goes on to say, that

> no one writing, thinking, or acting on the Orient could do so without taking account of the limitations on thought and action imposed by Orientalism. In brief, because of Orientalism the Orient was not (and is not) a free subject of thought or action. This is not to say that Orientalism unilaterally determines what can be said about the Orient, but that it is the whole network of interests inevitably brought to bear on (and therefore always involved in) any occasion when the peculiar entity 'the Orient' is in question.

(p. 3)

Said's formulation has itself been (and continues to be) a subject for critical attention.[6] Since he has, himself, responded, at various times, to commentaries of his general thesis (invariably, with considerable generosity) – notably in his talk 'Orientalism Reconsidered' at the 1984 Essex Sociology of Literature conference[7] – that debate will not be explored here. Instead, this project, by a reading of early modern English travellers' tales, seeks to ascertain if the objective of 'dominating, restructuring, and having authority over the Orient' in the centuries of European colonial expansion and imperialist domination can apply in the same ways, and for the same reasons, in the preceding period: that of chiefly

Portuguese, French, Italian, Dutch and English encounters. In that attempt recall one further Said observation, this time from *The World, the Text, and the Critic*, that 'texts have ways of existing that even in the most rarefied form are always enmeshed in circumstance, time, place, and society – in short, they are in the world, and hence worldly'.[8]

The validity of such a thesis needs to be tested not only against the texts of the time in which they were written, and which they write, but also in the present in which they are being read. That dominant phrase in the present seems to be that binary formulation 'The West and the Rest'. That phrase is itself freighted with a massive baggage to do with the power of the West – not only over peoples and places, but over discourses as well. One feature of that binary is – to reiterate the Said observation – that, while Orientalism does not unilaterally determine what can be said about the Orient, the limitations imposed take place 'inevitably'. But if that is the case, how then to account for resistance on the part of those who are not free subjects of thought and action? Reading of these tales of early modern encounters will reveal that it is the travellers, not those amongst whom they travel, who are not the free subjects of thought and action. It is the travellers who are dis-oriented.

Travellers are dis-oriented for two main reasons. Firstly, with Constantinople becoming part of Muslim Turkey (1453) there was a great need as well as considerable urgency for European powers to acquire knowledge about the languages and cultures of the peoples of this new imperial power. Not only for commercial, but especially for philosophic and religious reasons. Islam was the enemy; Turks the embodiment of that enmity;[9] Persians (as will be shown later) the potential foil. Speedily therefore there developed the need to know, if not your enemy, then certainly those with whom you were in contention. And not only Turks and Persians. If you were English then also very often French and Italian and, above all, the Portuguese encountered in foreign places. And then there were also others living in Ottoman lands: not only those others who defined themselves as Christians (Armenians; Greeks, etc.), but also Jews. If the victory of the combined forces of the Christians over the Turks at the Battle of Lepanto (1571) made the Mediterranean at least a relatively safe place for Christian rivalries to be played out in, fear of Ottoman expansion was probably not fully laid to rest until the signing of peace accords with the Holy Roman Empire, with Poland and with Venice at Carlovitz (1699) and with Russia (1700). This explains why this account of travellers' tales ends round about that date.

But that them-and-us binary, with the Turks as the embodiment of everything that is the antithesis to Christianity, was never as clear-cut as some present-day accounts of that 'West' versus 'East' story would have it. The evidence is there in the output from early modern European scholars. Furthermore, as Jerry Brotton has so splendidly excavated in the case of Francesco Berlinghieri, they could not automatically and unequivocally be attached to the 'West'. That Florentine scholar dedicated his remarkable world map not to (for instance) one of the Medici but to Muhammad II (also known as Mehmed, Mehmet, Mahmud and Mahomet), popularly referred to as the 'scourge of Christendom', as follows: 'To Mehmed of the Ottomans, illustrious prince and lord of the throne of God, emperor and merciful lord of all Asia and Greece, I dedicate this work'.[10]

Numbered within the ranks of these European scholars were several Englishmen: William Bedwell (1561–1632); John Selden (1584–1654); the Greaves brothers, one of whom, John, was Professor of Astronomy in Oxford, who wrote a treatise on Arab astronomy and mathematics; Edward Pococke (1604–91), who lived in Aleppo, where he studied Arabic, Hebrew, Syrian and Ethiopic, and who (when back in England) wrote not only essays on Arabic history and language, but also the first book to be printed in Arabic type in England (1636).[11] The contribution made by these English Arabists, written about some half a century ago by A. J. Arberry,[12] has recently been splendidly assessed by G. J. Toomer and G. A. Russell.[13] While Toomer as well as some of the contributors to the Russell volume[14] tell the story of the foundations of the study and teaching of Arabic in the Universities of Cambridge (1632) and Oxford (1636), the former also relates the perhaps not so well-known story of the attempt to set up a London School of Oriental Languages (1647). To refer to these scholars as 'Arabists' is deliberate. It is in order to distinguish them from the Orientalists about whom Said writes, and thereby to insist that the objective of these early modern scholars is not that of 'a Western style for dominating, restructuring, and having authority over the Orient'. Instead, their interest in the region and its peoples signals the animation of a new spirit of scholarship,[15] of humanism that will, later in the century, transform itself into that of the contest between one missionary religion (Christianity) in confrontation with another missionary religion (Islam). And that story has a further familiar inflexion: the contestation between Protestant and Catholic (often symmetrical with England versus Rome) in Christianity is written up as having its counterpart in Islam in the contestation between Sunni and Shia (often symmetrical with Turks versus Persians). It was that symmetry which became (in part) a basis upon which Turkey and Persia, as well as England, Spain and the Holy Roman Empire, decided upon political and diplomatic alliances which cut across the oversimplified binaries of 'East' and 'West'. It is essential to draw particular attention to the constantly shifting nature of these encounters throughout this period. For instance, the Ottoman rulers were probably never as motivated by the desire to see their conquered peoples turn to Islam as was, at that time, held to be the case by Christian divines and rulers. Their primary objectives were economic aggrandisement and political power: one reason for Ottoman toleration of other religions.

Elizabeth exploited such differences to great advantage. For instance, in one of her letters transmitted to the Turkish monarch via her ambassador, William Harborne, she refers to herself as 'the most invincible and most mighty defender of the Christian faith against all kinds of idolatries of all that live among the Christians and profess the name of Christ'.[16] Her objective, as Arthur Leon Horniker states, is quite clear: 'She tried to depict the Protestants as a group akin to the followers of the Prophet, who were not to be included in the Turkish mind among the Christian idol-worshippers'.[17] And her overtures to the Turkish monarch were matched by the endeavours of the chief opponent of the Turk, the Persian monarch, when he enlisted the services of two Englishmen, the Sherley brothers, to seek support from Christian rulers for his proposed campaigns against the Turks. What is clear is the manner in which national self-interest is wrapped in the trappings of religious faith. The secular argument is couched in the rhetoric of a confessional mode, of biblical language, that relies upon deep awareness of antecedent histories of the Orient that was Muslim as well as Christian, Jewish and classical. And so, too, in popular culture. One of the first books printed in England, William Caxton's *The Dicts and Sayings of the Philosophers* (1477), was a translation of a compilation that relied as much upon Arabic as upon Greek sources and authorities. That the practice continued is evident from the popularity of the translation of Antoine Galland's *The remarkable sayings, apothegms and maxims of the Eastern nations, abstracted and translated out of their books written in the Arabian, Persian and Turkish tongue* (1695), as well as philosophical texts such as those translated by George Ashwell, George Keith and Richard Russell.[18]

And that was not unusual. Moritz Steinschneider pointed out some time ago that a significant proportion of Europe's knowledge of the Greek classics came via translations from the Arabic.[19] Furthermore, G. A. Russell, having shown how Arabic was used in the service of Protestant theology as well as of secular interests in England, comes to the conclusion that the seventeenth century was the 'Age of Arabic'. In so doing, Russell echoes William Bedwell,[20] the first translator of elements of the Qur'ān into English (1615), who had asserted that Arabic was the only language of religion as well as the chief language of diplomacy from the Fortunate Isles to the China Seas. And with some justification. After all, Arabic was arguably the chief language carried by missionaries and traders from Morocco to Zanzibar, from Syria to Java, Turkish the most widely spoken throughout the Ottoman Empire, and Persian not only the language spoken at the Mughal Court in India, but also the medium of polite contact. Not that praise of the language prevented Bedwell from producing a sustained invective against Islam, and Muhammad in particular: *Mohammedis Imposturae; that is, a discovery of the manifold forgeries, falsehoods, and horrible impieties of the blasphemous seducer Mohammed, with a demonstration of the insufficiency of his law*... (1615).

Thomas Coryate, the son of a West Country rector, who travelled widely in the Orient and in Mughal India simply because it seemed to him to be a good idea to do so, provides an excellent example of the importance of the need for Europeans to learn the languages of the countries through which they travelled. He recounts that:

> At this time I have many irons in the fire; for I learn the Persian, Turkish & Arabian tongues, having already gotten the Italian, I thank God. I have been to the Mogul's Court three months already, and am to tarry here (by God's holy permission) five months longer, till I have gotten the aforesaid three tongues, and then depart here hence to the Ganges, and after that, directly to the Persian Court.[21]

And why? In order to be able to fulfil his desire to deliver an oration to the Mughal Emperor Jehangir in Persian – which, he tells his readers, he eventually accomplished, standing in the street outside while the monarch apparently listened to him from an upper window.

While Coryate's story provides some sort of evidence that learning these languages was not limited to those engaged in scholarly activities, it is also perhaps important to note that the interest declines quite sharply after 1700. By that time two major changes would have taken place. The first of these, according to Toomer, was that by the end of the seventeenth century the Arabists had completed their principal task – that of establishing the texts of the Scriptures and of unlocking the wisdom of Arab sciences, especially of medicine. Having completed that task, Toomer suggests that the scholars thereafter became more interested in ethics and in reason. This is a reiteration, in a slightly different way, of the case argued by McKeon of a process of secularization allied to epistemological crisis then at work in England (McKeon, ch. 2).

The second major change was political rather than scholarly. When the genre of the travel tale began to emerge in the 1580s, England was an offshore island – one of no great significance. Apart from a precarious foothold in the plantation of Ireland, it did not have a single colony, and trade with the rest of the world was modest.[22] A hundred years later, it is a very different world, and a very different story. The effects of the experience of civil war, restoration and 'glorious revolution' at home, allied to increasing foreign trade and the foundation of the colonial enterprise, began to show.[23] Added thereto, humanist ideas that were a marked feature of the Renaissance in England were beginning to be supplanted by Enlightenment ideas. It is in this latter moment that we begin to see the formulation of those ideas about Others that, at the beginning of the eighteenth century, manifest themselves as 'Orientalism' in the terms in which Said defines them. Several of those formulations had their origins in, and can be traced back to, the radical politics of the mid-century. N. I. Matar has pointed out references to Islam and to the example of Turkey:

> many of the sectaries demanded freedom of worship on the ground that their coreligionists were allowed to do so in Muslim Constantinople. Edward Bagshaw, one of the first apologists for nonconformity after the Restoration, used the Turkish model in his appeal for the toleration of his community. John Locke, who wrote against Bagshaw's treatise, accepted the principle that Muslims and Jews should be tolerated in England, but not nonconformists; later in his career Locke changed his position and echoed Bagshaw in defending nonconformists by analogy with the toleration under Islam. George Fox bitterly wrote to the Quaker captives in North Africa that they had more freedom of worship under the Muslims than the Friends in England under the Anglicans. While the former were captives but could worship, the latter were free but could not worship. So extensive was the appeal of nonconformists to the toleration of Islam that they were castigated by an Anglican writer as 'Protestant Mahometans' who 'according to the law of the Alchoran (which for propagating Religion was in the late times translated into English) [are] so zealous of Toleration of all Jews, pagans, Turks, and Infidels; if they have but a Conscience, it is no matter of what colour or size it is, it must have Liberty'. For many nonconformists, the Koran provided a model of religious toleration absent in England, and many of them suggested that they would be better treated under Islam than under Catholicism or Anglican Protestantism.[24]

Contexts: translations, collections, cosmographies/geographies

While the overwhelming majority of the texts cited thus far are not travellers' tales, they nevertheless provide corroboration for the view that, in England, in the early modern period, interest in foreign spaces and peoples was enormous. That claim can be substantiated by drawing attention to the upsurge of books that have to do specifically with other places that were published between the 1580s and 1680s: translations, cosmographies and collections.

Translations from the classical texts (Pliny, Solinus, Pomponius Mela)[25] may have had more to do with the general desire of making such texts available in the English language than with an interest in travel. No such doubts arise with regard to the evidence from translation of contemporary travel tales from other European languages. What is noteworthy about these are two features: (a) the speed with which some accounts were translated into English: the merchant of Venice, Cesare Federici (1588); the Dutchman Jan Huyghen van Linschoten (1598);[26] and (b) how speedily these were incorporated into collections compiled in England: Hakluyt (1589, 1598), Purchas (1625) and Hacke (1699).[27] Pertinent here are texts with specific reference to the Orient: Haga (1613);

Olearius (1662); Grelot (1683); Struys and Tavernier (1684); Thevenot (1687); de Busbecq (1696); Du Mont (1696); Dandini (1698).[28]

Publication of these tales took place at more or less the same time as that of the emergence of a major interest in geography, in mapping of foreign lands and in descriptions of peoples. Here again, translations from other European languages – Botero (1601), Boemus (1611), Sanson (1670)[29] – vie with English contributions which were, in their own times, classics of their kind: Nathaniel Carpenter (1625); John Bulwer (1654); Thomas Porter (1659)[30] – perhaps above all, Peter Heylyn (1652)[31] and George Meriton (1671)[32]. One feature of these new geographies/cosmographies is the extent to which they rely upon the evidence of travellers' tales, though often still holding on to fixed prejudices. John Bulwer, for instance, can cite Hakluyt and Biddulph (among others) and yet, at the same time, carry illustrations that depict peoples in other places with physical features of the most inventive designs.

Publication of these geographies and cosmographies coincided with yet another new kind of writing: books which claimed that they provided accurate information for the prospective traveller. Even though there were instances of objection to what was seen as a new fad,[33] it is evident that, well before the Grand Tour of the eighteenth century, there was a place in the market for texts purporting to offer practical advice for travellers. That there had been a widespread custom on the part of Elizabethan and Jacobean gentlemen to complete their education by travel, particularly on the Continent, was charted by Claire Howard some time ago.[34] Writers range from as early as Jerome Turler [Hieronymus Turlerius] (1575) and William Bourne (1578) to Samuel Lewkenor (1600), Baptist Goodall (1630), James Howell (1642), Sir Thomas Neale (1643) and William Carr (1695).[35] Indeed, as early as 1577 Richard Eden had provided a justification for travel at the beginning of the new century:

> All studies have their special times....Learning may be right well compared unto the floods and fruits of the earth, and the special time of learning unto their singular seasons...there was a time when the art of grammar was so much esteemed that grammarians proceeded masters thereof as worshipfully as other professors now do in any other faculty. Then was it honourable to be a poet....There was a time when logic and astrology only so wearied the heads of young scholars (yea; and busied old age also) that true philosophy indeed was almost forgotten, eloquence defaced, the languages exiled. That time is past....Geography, having laid hidden many hundred years in darkness and oblivion, without regard and price, of late who takes it not upon himself to discourse of the whole world, and each province thereof particularly, even by hearsay, although in the first principles of that art he has been altogether ignorant and unskilful? This time is now.[36]

Contexts: trade, commerce, fashioning the nation

That time, and that interest in geography and in cartography, was increasingly related to one important context: that of the development of trade and commerce. Nineteenth- and twentieth-century commentators (notably those who edited the texts for Hakluyt Society editions, produced during more or less the century of British imperial hegemony) often manifest, in their 'Notes' to those editions, their immersion in the discourses of British imperial ideology. The effect is to obliterate one key feature that was different at the start of the early modern period: that England was not yet a colonial power. While it laid claim to Barbados (1605), and settled it (1611), that island was not formally annexed until 1625. Montserrat, the island to where Cromwell would send revolting Irishmen, was not colonized until 1632, and Jamaica not until 1655. And sometimes the attempt to settle English people was scuppered by Carib resistance – as was the case in Tobago in 1616. While the Portuguese had installed settlements in Africa and in India since the 1590s, and the Dutch in the East Indies from more or less the same time, there was no English interest in doing the same in those places. And the colonial outposts in North America were precariously held at first. Civil war followed by the Cromwellian interlude and the unsettled Restoration, as well as Ireland, all probably contributed to government unwillingness in foreign trade and commerce. And that despite the publication of books and pamphlets urging such action: Tobias Gentleman, *England's Way to Win Wealth* (1614, 1660); Sir Dudley Digges, *The Defence of Trade* (1615); Sir Thomas Mun, *A Discourse of Trade from England to the East Indies* (1621) and *England's Treasure by Forraign Trade* (1664, 1700), to name but a few. Those, in their turn, were followed, later in the century, by publication of sermons preached to the merchants by a variety of divines: for example, Charles Hickman, Bishop of Derry (1681); William Hayley, Dean of Christchurch (1687); Henry Maundrell (1696); Edmund Chilsull (1698).

One telling example of English reluctance to engage in commercial enterprises is the story of John Rastell, brother-in-law to Sir Thomas More, who had fitted out two ships for a trading voyage to the New World only to find that the master and purser were of the view that piracy was more profitable than either exploration or trade, and refused to set sail. For Rastell such behaviour was not only evidence of lack of commercial foresight; it was also proof of a reluctance to further national self-interest. His famous *A New Interlude and a Merry of the Nature of the Four Elements, declarynge many proper poynts of phylosphy naturall, and of dvyers straunge landys* (1530?) laments:

> O what a thynge had be than
> Yf that they be englyshe men
> Might have ben the first of all
> That there shude have take possessyon
> And made first buylding & habitacion
> And memory perpetuall.

That 'Memory perpetuall' was supplied by books. Richard Helgerson not only has shown how 'by the new cartographic and chorographic representations, "natural affection" for one's country...was pushing all other affections to the side', he also goes on to point to the influential role played by publication of the stories of the voyages of that emerging nation.[37] John Parker not only draws attention to the extent to which nationalism had been an ingredient in travel literature from the start, he also characterizes Richard Eden (mentioned earlier) as 'England's first literary imperialist'.[38] One conclusion follows: that it was not the forging of a colonial empire that led to the writing of travellers' tales; rather, that it was the tales that provided much of the impetus for the colonial venture.

Scholars in the period between the 1930s and 1960s briefly revived interest in early modern travel and in travel writing as a genre. Because their interest was mainly in the movement of ideas and in the impact of early modern travellers' tales on later English fiction in particular, these scholars, such as R. W. Frantz, Boies Penrose and Percy G. Adams, often include material from travellers to the Orient. Contrast that with the present. Some of the best critics (Eric J. Leed, Douglas Chambers, Eric R. Wolf, Urs Bitterli, J. M. Blaut) make no reference to the Ottoman Orient. Others (Dennis Porter, Caren Kaplan, Simon Gikandi)[39] proceed to construct their otherwise valuable general theses without reference to the early modern. To draw attention to the omission of the Orient in the early modern period in the work of present-day critics is not because of the wish to accuse them of neglect. Rather, it is to suggest that stories of European travellers in the Orient in the early modern period are left out because such stories resist being fitted neatly into a model of cultural encounter that conforms to a colonizer/colonized model of the world, one in which Europeans can impose upon the peoples whom they encounter. The Orient does not fit into the category of 'people without history'.

Indeed, the opposite was the case. At the time when European travellers went to those parts, the imperial power was not European but Ottoman, and a fixed European presence was precarious. The Portuguese had captured the strategically important port of Hormoz in 1574, but their hold was short-lived. Furthermore, when the Shah of Persia, Abbas I, recaptured it in 1622, he did so with English assistance. That support was to stand the traders of the nation in good stead when they later went there. They needed goodwill since they went to the Orient, not as dispossessors or settlers, but as supplicants for permission to ply their trade. And they did so to rulers whose power and authority they acknowledged. While they may not at all times have found the cultures they encountered congenial, on the whole, they showed respect. They did, of course, carry with them a sense of their own cultural superiority. But that was not because they saw themselves as 'European'. For the English that notion was then (as perhaps still) a long way off. No, what the most cursory reading of the travellers' tales will reveal is that the English inscribed themselves not simply as Christian, but very specifically as Protestant. The clash between religions (Christianity versus Islam) is conducted not only in the familiar terms of Protestant versus Catholic binary (Spanish; Portuguese; French) but now also refracted through English Protestant animosity against non-Catholic orthodox groups, notably Armenians and Greek Orthodox.

To emphasize such distinctions paid dividends for the English, especially for those who slowly began to test the prospects for trade. One example: after Elizabeth's excommunication by the Pope (1570), English merchants could operate outside the bounds of papal edicts that forbade trade with Muslims. Hakluyt (1598) has an account of the journey of Elizabeth's ambassador, William Harborne, to Constantinople, where he lived for some five years, and his reception there. That collection also includes a letter from Harborne to Richard Foster in which the former instructs the latter about how to conduct himself in his new role as English consul in Tripoli in Syria:

> Touching your demeanour after your placing, you are to proceed wisely, considering [that] both French and Venetians will have an envious eye on you. Whom, if they perceive wise and well advised, they will fear to offer you any injury. But if they shall perceive any insufficiency in you, they will not omit any occasion to harm you. They are subtle, malicious, and dissembling people, where you must always have their doings suspected, and walk warily in all your actions.

Such warning was not without foundation. Perhaps the most celebrated instance was that of the arrest in Hormoz by the Portuguese of Ralph Fitch, John Newberry, William Leeds and James Storey on the trumped-up charge that they were English spies. Hakluyt[40] published accounts of their ordeal, by Fitch as well as by the Dutchman, Jan Huyghen van Linschoten, who was in Goa at the time of their imprisonment and trial. Other Europeans were not the only problem. Harborne also advises Foster about how to deal with Englishmen who attempted to engage in trade without having obtained formal permission to do so:

> Touching any outlopers of our nation, who may happen to come here to traffic [trade], you are not to suffer, but [to] imprison the chief officer, and suffer the rest not to traffic at any time; and together enter into such bonds as you think meet, that both they shall not deal in the Grand Seignior's dominion, and also not harm, during their voyage, any his subjects' ships, vessels, or whatever other, but quietly depart out of the same country without any harm done.

Stories of diplomatic intrigue as well as economic dispossession of English traders were widely published at home. While such stories were often about French complots,[41] there was the (in)famous episode of the accusation by the merchants that they had been summarily robbed by their own ambassador, Sir Sackville Crow. The 'Epistle to the Reader' states that they had been forced to

> fly for assistance to the Agent there residing [in Constantinople] for the High and Mighty States of Holland, by whose meanes the cry of the people in these parts, the vast expense of the company's money, and by Turkish justice, they obtained the liberty of their persons, and releasement of their goods, with promise of the Grand Vizier that their business should be heard and determined according to justice.[42]

Palmira Brummett[43] has brilliantly tracked some of these relations. Her study is especially useful because of the manner in which she teases out the connections between Ottoman commercial and foreign policy in order to show that it had its own logic, its own imperial ambitions, and that it was one to which outsiders had to adapt. It is therefore an oversimplification to suggest that the habits and modes of cultural encounter developed by English travellers were motivated simply by the wish to be allowed to participate in commercial activities. That this collection starts with selections having to do with such relations is largely because such accounts were published near the beginning of the time-scale covered in the collection. But even those early accounts are not straightforwardly and simply accounts of trading relations.

Telling tales

Over time there slowly begins to be defined a range of general practices, forms of behaviour, ways of seeing, which eventually become codified into a set of precepts which themselves depend upon that new sense of national identity in the process of being formed. Noteworthy about the tales is that, in virtually every case, there seems to be a need to justify publication. The compiler of William Biddulph's *Travels* (1609), in his 'Preface to the Reader', explains that when Englishmen travelled abroad in order to acquire learning and culture they were engaging in a practice that had impeccable classical antecedents. Pythagoras, he says, had travelled to Memphis in Egypt to listen to the poets there; Plato had travelled to Italy; and Appolonius, who had 'passed and journeyed to the furthest parts of India to the philosophers there', had then returned via Babylonia and Chaldea to Egypt, a journey that had also been made by Solon. All these, as well as St Jerome and Jacob, the compiler asserts, 'travelled [there] to get wisdom and learning'.[44]

The unknown compiler also acknowledged that he had arranged for publication despite a direct plea by Biddulph that he should not do so. His justification was that, in reading such stories:

> all men may see how God has blessed our country above all others, and be stirred up to thankfulness. / Hereby subjects may learn to love, honour, and obey their good and gracious King [James I], when they shall read of the tyrannous government of other countries, and of the merciful government of theirs. / Hereby readers may learn to love and reverence their pastors, and to thank God for the inestimable benefit of the preaching of the Word amongst them, when they shall read in what blindness and palpable ignorance other nations live, not knowing the right hand from the left in matters that concern the kingdom of Heaven, and yet reverence and honour their blind guides and superstitious churchmen like angels, and provide for their maintenance royally. / Here wives may learn to love their husbands, when they shall read in what slavery women live in other countries, and in what awe and subjection to their husbands, and what liberty and freedom they themselves enjoy. / Hereby servants may be taught to be faithful to their masters, when they shall read of the brutish and barbarous immanity [monstrous cruelty] in other countries of masters towards their servants.../ Here rich men may learn to be thankful to God, not only for their liberty and freedom of their conscience and persons; but of their goods also, when they shall read how, in other countries, no man is master of his own, but as the fattest ox is nearest unto the slaughter, so the richest man is nearest unto death. / Here poor men may learn to be thankful to god for their benefactors, and not to be repining and impatient beggars (as many are) when they shall read how, in other countries, the poor live brute beasts.[45]

George Meriton, who acknowledged his debt to travellers' tales, was in no doubt that the English male is (on) top. Having comprehensively damned the peoples 'Of the land of Negros, Nigrarum Terra', of 'Ethiopia Superior, or the Empire of Prester John', of 'Ethiopia Exterior', of 'Caffraria' as well as of 'America', he says of the English that:

> The people are for the most part tall of stature, fair of complexion, and of their disposition courteous, and free, and too credulous and apt to believe the fair speeches and pretences of their enemies, whereby it hath often fallen out that they have lost more by treaties than they got by their strength and valour. The women are most amiable and beautiful, and attired in most comely fashion, and have the greatest respect and kindness of their husbands of any women in the world, sitting at meat with their husbands at the chief end of the table; and when walking in the streets their husbands give them the wall, and in other places the right hand, as countest greatest honour. They are also permitted to recreate themselves at plays, balls, masquerades, etc. and do often walk the fields, or go to

the tavern with an acquaintance or friend: which is imputed no blot or stain to their chastity or virtue. By reason of which kindness and freedom the women of England are less lascivious and vicious than those in other countries, who are under the restraints and slavery of their husbands.[46]

While Biddulph had lived in Aleppo for several years because he was the minister of religion for the company of English merchants resident there, the Lincolnshire-born Fynes Moryson (1566–1630) travelled widely in the Orient between 1591 and 1597 because his objective was to undertake a close study of the lands and peoples. His famous *Itinerary*[47] was, however, not published until 1617 because between 1598 and 1606 he was in Ireland as an aide to Mountjoy, commander of the English forces engaged in suppressing the Tyrone resistance. To draw attention to Moryson's role in the maintenance of English hegemony in Ireland is not a digression. The selections from the tale he tells are remarkable, not simply about what he has to say about Turks and Persians, but especially about Jews and gypsies. What stands out is that, invariably, his yardstick for measurement is that of the 'wild Irish' against whom he had fought at the siege of Kinsale.

Moryson also included a quite extensive chunk of advice about how English travellers should prepare themselves before going abroad, and what they should do (and not do) while away from home: in particular, the need to learn foreign languages, and to preserve personal health, notably by avoidance of the heat of the sun. For Moryson, 'the visiting of forraigne Countries is good and profitable', though not for everyone. The first category he excludes are English women, who (unlike 'the masculine women' of the Low Countries who trade all over the Continent) 'for suspition of chastity are most unfit for this course'. Others in this category are not only obvious examples such as old people and very young children, but also (for instance) 'they shall do well to keep themselves at home who have a scrupulous conscience, and think themselves so wise as they will not follow the advice of experienced men'.

Even then, not all who are, in principle, fit to travel can be relied upon for their judgements, especially

> grave university men, and (as they say) sharp-sighted in the Schools are often reputed idiots in the practice of worldly affairs, as on the contrary blockish men and...very asses, by continual practice in grave employments, gain the wisdom of them whose affairs they manage.

For Moryson, 'the fruit of travel is travel itself', provided that travellers follow what he describes as 'a large and intricate precept' whose practice he summarizes as 'Being in Rome, the Roman manners use / And everywhere each place's customs choose'. Except, it would appear, from his own practice, when in Ireland!

William Lithgow, who also travelled extensively on three continents largely because it seemed a good idea at the time, in his 'Prologue to the Reader', drew attention to yet another (and often the primary) justification for the travel tale: that the tale tells the truth because the writer was witness.

> Judicious lector, if good books may be termed wise guides, then certainly true histories may be termed perfect oracles, secret counsellors, private schoolmasters, familiar friends to cherish knowledge, and the best intelligencers for all intend-

ments, being duly pondered and rightly used. This laborious work then of mine, depending upon this preamble, is only composed of my own eyesight, and ocular experience...being the perfect mirror and lively portraiture of true understanding, excelling far all inventions whatsoever, poetic, or theoretic.[48]

The last example is chosen partly because of the general thesis it offers, and partly because the terrain upon which the test of that thesis takes place is Turkey. Henry Blount, whose *A Voyage into the Levant* [49] saw no less than six editions between first publication in 1636 and 1671, opens his 'Argument' as follows:

Intellectual complexions have no desire so strong as that of knowledge; nor is any knowledge unto man so certain and pertinent as that of human affairs. This experience advances best in observing of peoples whose institutions much differ from ours. For customs conformable to our own, or to such wherewith we are already acquainted, do but repeat our old observations, with very little acquist of new.

For Blount, the reason for his going to Turkey is that because

those parts being now possessed by the Turks, who are the only modern people, great in action, and whose Empire so suddenly invaded the modern world, and fixed itself such firm foundation as no other did, I was of the opinion that he who would behold those times in greatest glory, could not find a better scene than Turkey.

Later on, he will also give as reason for his willingness to serve the Turkish monarch was because Charles I spoke of his Turkish counterpart as 'the greatest monarch in the world'. Even more noteworthy is the formulation of the 'four cares' Blount tells his readers which need to be exercised – of which the first is:

to observe the religion, manners, and policy of the Turks. Not perfectly (which were a task for an inhabitant rather than a passenger) but so far forth as might satisfy this scruple: to whit – whether, to an impartial conceit, the Turkish way appears absolutely barbarous, as we are given to understand, or rather as other kind of civility, different from ours, but no less pretending.

Blount's view is clearly a minority one. But that an argument articulated along the lines quoted above is encountered at all deserves recognition, since what it points to is a further discernible difference with the popular construction of post-Enlightenment stories. Whereas the Orient fabricated by the writers encountered in Said's excavation is a largely undifferentiated geographical space, populated by cultural and political inferiors, for the travellers of the preceding century and a half there are several different Orients: Turkey; Persia; Egypt; the Holy Land. These, in their turn, are to be differentiated from the India of the Mughals, which is not part of the Orient. Compare, for instance, the tales of two sets of ambassadors, Harborne and Barton to the Turkish monarch, with that of the Sherley brothers to his Persian counterpart. Despite differences between them, the comparison is not so asymmetrical as to render the exercise invalid.

To lie abroad[50]

While Elizabeth sought to secure the support of the Turkish monarch for her political objectives, her merchants were motivated more by profit. That difference is evident in the manner of the appointment of William Harborne. He went there in a double capacity: as the first ambassador sent to intercede with Murad III as well as agent for the Turkey Company. It was the latter which paid his salary – the least amount that they could get away with, and even then only intermittently. That such parsimony did not help his status at a Court in which public display of lavish lifestyle was a source of approving as well as envious comment is evident from his letters. The nature of the appointment was, of course, in part, an attempt to fool Elizabeth's European adversaries. They, however, were not fooled. The subterfuge of Harborne's attachment to the merchants in order to delay the French and Spanish becoming aware of Elizabeth's diplomatic intentions did not last long. When Harborne was forced to go on a second visit in order to seek reinstatement of the agreements made with Murad on his first visit, but which had been abrogated soon after his departure as a consequence of intervention on the part of the French ambassador, the Spanish tried to lure him to leave his ship in order to capture him when it put into Majorca for supplies. And when that failed, they tried to prevent his departure by military means. What they sought to prevent was the conclusion of an Anglo-Turkish alliance against those whom the English queen regarded as the upholders of 'idolatries' – chiefly the Spanish. Above all, they wanted to prevent the possibility of limited Turkish naval support for the English against those 'idolaters'.

While Elizabeth could not express her wish publicly and Murad could plead the more immediate and pressing contestation with Persia as cause for delay, there was certainly a real English hope of having the support of the Ottoman fleet (rebuilt after the disaster at Lepanto) against Spain in the Mediterranean. Still, active Ottoman support had its own dangers. As Orhan Burian, one of the first generation of Kemalist scholars to come to Britain, but who died tragically early, neatly observed:

> Elizabeth must have undoubtedly felt relieved and thankful that the proposition had not been taken up by the Grand Signior and his government. Otherwise she could never have cleared herself of the blemish of having defeated a fellow Christian nation with the help of an infidel power.[51]

There was also a more immediate objective. Elizabeth set out to abrogate agreements with the Turks under which all Europeans had to conduct their business under the diplomatic protection of the French. Her objective was straightforward: the English should conduct their business under the colours of their nation.

Diplomatic missions required that lavish gifts be offered. The first extract from Harborne indicates that he took a variety of goods including a clock valued at £500 as well as an assortment of dogs, the whole paid for by the merchants at a cost of £1,082.6s.7d – by any standards a considerable sum for those times. Some members of the Company were sceptical about the whole business, but that probably had as much to do with the view that having to foot their monarch's diplomatic bills was at the expense of their profits. Return on the investment, when successful, could, however, be handsome. John Sanderson, who was on board the *Hercules* which left Tripoli in Syria in November 1587 and arrived in London at the end of March 1588, having been held up by 'an extreame storme, fowle wether, and contrary winds', recounts that while the cargo was officially valued at £37,683.2s.8d, two London alderman 'offered...£70,000 as an adventure, but suer [sure] the goods came to much more when they made the devision'.

Harborne perhaps unintentionally offers an insight into the real economic and political differences between the two states:

> All the time that we stayed at the Council Chamber door they were counting or weighing money to send into Persia for soldiers' pay. There were carried out 130 bags; and in every bag, as it was told us, 1000 ducats, which amounted...in sterling to fourscore and 19,000 pounds.

Whether or not the decision to perform that act of counting in front of the English diplomatic party was a deliberate device on the part of the Turkish monarch to impress upon his visitors the relative differences in power between them and thereby the even more modest nature of the gift sent by the English queen is speculation. What is clear, however, is that the English got the message.

Harborne's account also reveals the unqualified admiration on the part of those visitors for the manner in which they were received – and their clear willingness to participate on the terms offered by their hosts. There is a matter-of-factness that is not always present in similar instances later on: 'The gentlemen and we sat down on the ground, for it is their manner so to feed', followed by favourable comments about 'rosewater and sugar and spices brewed together'. A similar matter-of-factness, free of anti-Islamic sentiment that will invariably be present in later accounts, marks his brief comment on the visit to Saint Sophia

> which was the chief church when it was the Christians', and now is the chief see and church of primacy of this Turk present. Before I entered I was willed to put off my shoes, to the end [that] I should not profane their church, I being a Christian.

Wragge's account of Edward Barton's embassy reinforces stories of the nature of cultural encounter. Of interest in the extract from his tale are two details. Firstly, the letter to Elizabeth, sent by Murad's Empress. The obvious question has to be why the letter should be from her. Was it because the Emperor felt that his interests might be best served by having one female writing to another? Or, indeed, one Occidental to another, since the Empress was a member of the Venetian aristocracy who had been captured by corsairs and taken to Constantinople, where she was eventually singled out – selected, more precisely – for her role? Secondly, there is the account of the quarrel between Barton and the Turkish Vizier, especially for the manner by which that quarrel was resolved. Briefly, it is the story of political prisoners who had escaped from their cells in one of the many towers on the wall near the port, for which dereliction of duty the governor of the prison was executed. The English ambassador became involved because a certain John Field was arrested and threatened with death for his part in the escape. He was accused of being the letter-carrier on behalf of the escapees. When Barton went to see the Vizier (a stand-in while the usual one was on his way to the war being waged against Hungary) he was himself threatened with arrest. The extract offers a splendid and vivid account of Barton's actions as well as the process and manner by which the Sultan resolved the dilemma. Also important is

Wragge's account of the distinction Barton made between the Turkish Vizier as being the Sultan's slave, and himself: that the affront to him was an affront to his monarch in his (Barton's) person. There was also the neat touch (audacity?) to say that until the issue was resolved there could be no handover of the second present.[52] But then, Barton, like Harborne before him, had attained a position of great respect. Furthermore, he was not at all unwilling to be of assistance to the Turkish Sultan. John Sanderson (who was appointed as Barton's deputy during the ambassador's absence) recounts the story of how Barton had accompanied the new Sultan Muhammad to the wars against the Hungarians:

> This new king, Sultan Mahomet, went to the wars in Hungary against the Christian Emperor. The first year of his reign our ambassador, worthy Edward Barton, attended him (with also an ancient Galatean called Signior Matteo, who had [for] many years been servant and chief interpreter for the Emperor's ambassadors) to whom the Great Turk had, before his going, presented 22 Christians who had lain in prison in Constantinople [for] 3 years. They were the late ambassador's household, who had been resident there for the Christian Emperor when the peace was broken. The Great Turk also gave commandment that throughout his country their charges should be defrayed, and alike allowed 4 coaches and a chouse to conduct them to the Emperor's Court. / The chiefest cause of our ambassador accompanying the Great Turk was to have concluded a peace between the two great potentates, as formerly he had done between the Poles and the Great Turk deceased [Murad]. Which had been most easily performed had it pleased Her Most Excellent Majesty so to have commanded. The ambassador's absence was 6 months.[53]

That Elizabeth chose not 'so to have commanded' is almost certainly a well-chosen understatement. Fynes Moryson's view was probably nearer the mark when he suggested that the queen was probably not amused by her ambassador's action: 'for he had borne the English armes uppon his Tent, wherof the French Ambasador accused him to the Emperor, and the French King, who expostulated with the Queene that her Armes should be borne in the Turkes Campe against Christians'. But it is clear that at least one other English merchant was sufficiently impressed by the splendour of the Emperor's cavalcade that he not only wrote a letter about the event to a friend in London, but that document was soon published and brought into the public domain.[54] The contrast with the tales told by the Sherley brothers could not be sharper. That some of these tales were adapted, probably with either their participation in that venture, or their consent to it, by others is a further complication. All three brothers were involved in the Mediterranean and in the Levant. Thomas was a less than successful pirate. His predations on Turkish shipping, enacted with the connivance of the Grand Duke of Tuscany, were naval disasters of such magnitude that he was eventually imprisoned in the Tower for his interference with the Levant trade. Antony was a buccaneer who passed himself off to the Persian monarch Abbas I as an English diplomat. While it is not clear whether Abbas was convinced about such claims, or simply used the Englishman knowing that doing so could not be successful but would prove to be of considerable annoyance to his enemies, he was certainly sent on diplomatic missions to Moscow, Prague and Rome, later to Venice, Morocco and Spain – to which last-named place he eventually retired, and where he wrote his travel narrative. Lastly, Robert, who was made Persian ambassador to the European states of Spain, Poland,

Russia, Venice and England, as part of the diplomatic efforts against the Ottomans. Robert Sherley married one of the nieces of the Persian monarch, Teresia, reputedly the first Persian woman to visit England, where their first child was born, and at whose baptism Queen Anne (wife of James I) was one of the godmothers.

The outcome of these activities was a spate of publications, with Sherley's own narrative (1613) appearing in print some years after those about him and his brothers had been told by others.[55] One of the most important features of these writings is what they reveal about anti-Turkish sentiment in English writing of those times. To make a simple comparison: whereas the Persian monarch Abbas comes close to repudiating his English-born emissary Sherley, the Ottoman ruler Murad III writes to Elizabeth in the most glowing terms about her 'Orator' Harborne:

> Your Embassador, after he had with all care and diligence dispatched his Embassage, and here left in his place one Edward Bardon his deputy and Agent, now by our leave maketh his returne towards your kingdome, being for the good and faithfull service he there did, worthy to be of you esteemed, honoured and before others promoted: who when he hath obtained of you all those his deserved honours and preferments, let him or some other principall Embassador without delay be appointed to our Imperiall Court, to continue this office of legation.[56]

'The Terrible Turk'

The feature that most marks the accounts attributed to Robert Sherley is not simply the strength of the animosity against the Turk, but how that is rooted in religious sentiment. That the account of that journey, written by Anthony Nixon, is unreliable is less important than the possibility that readers at the time would have been likely to have accepted the sentiments as being in tune with their own. Instance here Nixon's assertion (attributed to Sherley) that:

> The Turks are beyond all measure a most insolent, superbous, and insulting people; ever pressed to offer outrage to any Christian if he be not well guarded by janissaries. They sit at meat, as tailors upon their stalls, cross-legged, and their meat served upon the ground, passing the day, for the most part, in banqueting and carousing. They will not permit a Christian to come within their churches, for they hold their profane and irreligious sanctuaries defiled thereby. They have no use of bells, but some priest three times a day mounts to the top of their church and with a loud voice cries out and invocates Mahomet to come in haste; for they have long expected his second coming.

Thomas Middleton, in another account of the story of the two brothers (1609), sings the praises of Robert Sherley who, in his view, 'comes laden with the trophies of war, and the honours of peace. The Turk has felt the sharpness of his sword, and against the Turk he is now whetting the sword of Christian princes'. That the diplomatic effort did not – indeed, perhaps, could not – lead to military alliances of the kind Middleton had in mind does not prevent him from going on to identify the nature of the threat:

That common enemy of Christ and Christians, the Turk, lifting up his sword continually (for the most part) not only against the Polack, the Hungarian, Bohemian, and other princes of Christendom, but also thirsting after the rich empire of Persia, and showing a mortal hatred to that kingdom by being ever up in arms against it.

Two years later (1611) John Cartwright, another commentator on the Sherley embassy, will, however, offer an alternative explanation – one that lays the blame squarely on the failure of the Christian rulers: 'And to say the truth, the discords of Christian Princes have laid more countries to the enrichment of the Great Turk than ever his bow or shield could have purchased'.

From the many purportedly eye-witness accounts of what took place at the first meeting between the Englishman and the Persian monarch, John Cartwright's is the most interesting – not because it is the most accurate (because that is impossible to ascertain) but because it probably captured, for English readers, the spirit and nature of the ideological connections in the process of being forged. According to the Preacher, Sherley

Declared first with what perfidious dealing, and with what greediness and pride the Turkish Emperors have always set upon the Christians; and that, being discharged of the war with them, he would of all likelihood set upon the Persians, having the selfsame quarrel unto the Persians that he had unto the Christians, viz. An ardent and insatiable desire of sovereignty – a sufficient motive for the greedy Turk to repute any king, the richer he is, the more his enemy. / After that he set forth to the full the prowess of the Christians, the wonderful preparation that they could make both at sea and land, persuading the king, with all his power, to invade the Turk, then altogether busied in the wars of Hungary, and to recover again such parts of his kingdom as his predecessors had lost. Wars, he said, were more happily managed abroad than at home [and] that since His Majesty alone is able to withstand the Turk's whole force and power, he needed not now to doubt of the most prosperous success.

Assuming the above to be a reasonably accurate account of what Sherley had said, the first question that arises is about the extent to which – if at all – Abbas believed it. A second might be about the motives for Abbas employing the brothers on the expeditions to the Christian monarchs. One thing is clear, however: that for English people these stories reinforced a pre-existing stereotype of the Turk, as 'a cruel, rigorous, or tyrannical man; any one behaving as a barbarian or savage; one who treats his wife hardly; a bad-tempered or unmanageable man. Often with alliterative appellation, *terrible Turk*' (*OED*). One contemporary account that might have been a source for that *OED* description might have been the following:

The Turks are justly branded with the character of a barbarous nation; which censure does not relate either to their cruelty and severity of their punishments… or to want of discipline…or to want of cruel behaviour among themselves, for none can outwardly be more respectful and submissive, especially to their superiors, in whose power it is to do them mischief, the fear of which makes them guilty of most base compliances; but to the intolerable pride and scorn whenever they treat all the world besides.[57]

And that image of the 'Terrible Turk' is to be found in plays as well as in popular literature. Indeed, *The Travels of the Three English Brothers* by John Day, William Rowley and George Wilkins, performed at Her Majesty's theatre (1607) and recently splendidly edited by Anthony Parr,[58] is based on the travel accounts written by and about the brothers. The central image is that of the qualities of the Englishman. He is the envy of the Persian monarch:

> What powers do wrap me in amazement thus?
> Methinks this Christian's more than mortal.
> Sure he conceals himself with my thoughts.
> Never was man so deeply registered.
> But God or Christian, or what else he be
> I wish to be no other but as he!

And a few lines later, an alliance having been swiftly concluded between Englishman and Persian against the Turk, the latter shifts effortlessly to construct the former as the embodiment of Christian virtues:

> It is for thy sake doe I love all Christians.
> We give thee liberty of conscience.
> Walk in our hand, thou hast possesst our heart.

If this tiny fragment offers more than adequate justification for the view that the play has deservedly not become as well known as other plays which date from that same year (Cyril Torneur's *The Revenger's Tragedy*, Thomas Heywood's *A Woman Killed with Kindness*, Shakespeare's *Coriolanus*, to name but three), the sentiments expressed amply elucidate the relationship between the national and confessional components. The play also reinforces ruling anti-Semitic sentiments in the form of a money-lending Jew. He gets his come-uppance not simply because he demands repayment of a loan but also because he insists that the Englishman should be imprisoned for not being able to pay. Finally, there is included a love story of a Persian princess who has to persuade her uncle not only to release the Englishman but also, instead of condemning his niece to death for her love of an infidel, to offer publicly his blessing for their future.[59]

The stories of the Sherley brothers, reconstructed by Anthony Parr in the context of Jacobean diplomacy,[60] tell of cultural encounter in official places. Those have their counterparts in popular culture in tales of English Christians captured and enslaved on Turkish galleys. One of the earliest of these is by Edward Webbe (1590).[61] Webbe's claim to fame is that, after many years working as a slave in Turkish galleys, he had risen from within the ranks to the elevated position of master gunner in the wars against the Persians, the Spanish, the Portuguese and Prester John. If the claim about the lands associated with the last-named monarch now calls into question the veracity of the whole story,[62] for the readers of his own time it would have been a familiar one: that of how the Turks ill-treated captured Christians. Webbe recounts that, having been captured and sent to Constantinople:

We were shaven head and face, and then a shirt of cotton, and breeches of the same, were put upon us; our legs and feet left naked. And by one of the feet is each slave chained with a great chain to the galley, and our hands fastened with a pair of manacles. The food which I and others did eat was very black, far worse than horse bread; and our drink was stinking water, unless it was when we came to the places where we took fresh water, at which time we supposed our diet to be very dainty.

Imprisoned for participating in a revolt against their enslavement, he tells that he and some twenty other Englishmen who were in the same prison were eventually released because of the English monarch's intercession on their behalf to his Turkish counterpart, as well as ransom money collected from City of London merchants. The Christian moral is couched in familiar rhetoric; the politics of a sense of English national identity is clear:

Here may the bountiful citizens of London see (as in a glass) the fruits of their liberality and charitable devotion, given at several times in the year toward the releasement of poor captives, such as are constrained to abide most wild and grievous tortures, especially the torture and torment of conscience, which grieved me and all true Christians to the very soul. For the Turk by all means possible would still persuade me and other my fellow Christians, while I was there the time of 13 years, to forsake Christ, to deny Him, and to believe in their god Mahomet. Which, if I would have done, I might have had wonderful preferment of the Turk, and have lived in as great felicity as any lord in the country. But I utterly denied their request, though by them grievously beaten, naked, for my labour, and reviled in a most detestable sort, calling me dog, hell-hound, and such-like names. But I give God thanks. He gave me strength to abide with patience these crosses. And though I were but a simple man, void of any learning, yet still I had remembrance that Christ died for me, as appears in holy Scriptures.

Turks vs Persians

The contrast drawn between Turks and other nations with regard to liberty of conscience, referred to in the play as well as in the popular tale, can be traced back to some of the earliest of the travel tales. It is a persistent theme in the travel tale throughout the early modern period. Invariably these tell of Persian and Syrian toleration and Turk suppression of Christian faith and observance. The merchant John Eldred, later a key figure in the formation of the English East India Company, in his account of his 1583 travels in Syria, sings the praises of Aleppo:

This is the greatest place of traffick [trade] in dry town [town without a harbour] in these parts. For hither resort Jews, Tartars, Persians, Armenians, Egyptians, Indians, and many other sorts of Christians, and enjoy freedom of their consciences, and bring thither many kinds of rich merchandise.[63]

William Parry (1601), having passed through the lands of the Kurds (whom he describes as a 'pilfering people'), goes on to say that they then happily entered the King of Persia's country where, upon our first entrance, we thought we had been imparadised, finding our entertainment there to be so good, and the manner of the people to be so kind and courteous (far differing from the Turks...).

Corroboration for English travellers' celebration of Persia is found in Biddulph (1609) as well as in John Cartwright (1611). The latter recounts that, as soon as he had crossed into Persia, he found

every man at his labour, and neighbour with neighbour going from one town to another, which bred much contentment, and made us wonder at the great peace and tranquillity which the common people in Persia live in above the commons of Turkey.

Later on, writing about 'the miserable thraldom that the poor Christians do endure under the Turkish tyranny', he thanks God that

in these northern parts[64] we may behold with safety, but not without pity, when we rightly consider, how that the people among whom Our Saviour himself conversed, at what his beautiful steps honoured the world...are now become a cage of unclean birds. Filthy spirits do possess them.

For which view Anthony Parr offers the following explanation:

To Western eyes in the early modern period, and long after, the Persian court was an exotic symbol like those of India, China and Japan. It was Spenser's 'nurse of pompous pride', reputed to be a place of fantastic luxury and wealth. Such locations fell into the category neither of the primitive (the unlettered, semi-nomadic societies of the New World and Africa) nor of the 'enemy within' the Old World, usually represented by the infidel Turks, or by Jews or Jesuits. In this sense, Persia was not so much Europe's Other as its opposite or foil; and while the fascination with the glamorous East was later to become a disabling Orientalism, arguably it was during the early modern period a positive alternative to views of Asia either as the home of barbarian hordes or of the hellish doctrine of Islam.[65]

Indeed, Parr goes on to quote Sherley's observation, later on, about 'the fashion of [the Shah's] government differing so much from that which we call barbarousnesse...it may justly serve for as great an *Idea* for a principality as Platoes Common-wealth did for a government'. Not that Persians are to be preferred to Turks. In Persia,

The difference between the gentleman and the slave is that the slave never rides, and the gentleman never goes on foot. Besides, the nature of this people is arrogant, seditious, deceitful, and very unquiet. But the fierceness of their nature is much restrained by the king's severe government. / They are much inclined to sensuality, having three sorts of women, as they term them, viz: honest women, half honest women, and courtesans...last of all, they are full of crafty stratagems, and are breakers of their promises (a vice that is very inbred in all barbarians).

21

Islam, and Muhammad in particular

John Cartwright is in no doubt that the root cause of everything with which he finds fault can be traced back to Islam. In that he is not alone. Parry calls believers in that religion 'damned infidels and sodomitical Muhammads', which, he explains, 'do answer the hate we Christians do hold them in'. Biddulph and Lithgow both offer lengthy accounts of the laws of Islam. One feature common to their accounts is that a relatively straightforward statement of the broad details of the religion is either followed by, or interspersed with, a vigorous and inflexible animosity against all things Islamic.[66] Without question, the most vicious of the commentators is Sir Thomas Herbert (1606–82).[67] In reading Herbert's accounts of his Persian visit[68] what should be borne in mind is not only the number of times that his account was published (1634, 1638, 1665, 1667, 1677, followed by inclusions in collections in 1704, 1744, 1764). Of even greater importance is that in every new edition he took the liberty to add and embellish upon his previous accounts with (often unacknowledged) bits and pieces gleaned from the tales told by travellers who had gone to those parts after he had been there. As is the case with the stories he told of the people of the Cape, so here too, his stories of Persia are, far and away, the most obnoxiously biased, with a rhetoric of intemperance and vituperation unmatched by that of any other traveller – even by those who felt as firmly opposed to Islam as Sherley clearly does:

> Now concerning their religion (if such I may term it, being as one says a confused hotch-potch or mass of superstition) at this day it varies not from the Turks' in any particle of the Alcoran; yet according to their heretics, being no less divided in their profession than we and the Papalins.

For him the source is obvious: Muhammad, 'son of Abdar, a Pagan, and Emma, a Jew' whose

> Alcoran or Sunna, i.e., the Book of Truth or a Legend for the Faithful is stuffed with philosophy moral and natural, and mixed with so many fantasies and inventions as readers renders the whole full of absurdities and contradictions; and farced with such trash as may powerfully provoke a student to a height of laughter.

That virulence of the rhetoric against Islam was not simply doctrinal. One consequence of the failure of the Crusaders was a continuing anxiety about Ottoman control over Christian holy lands. 'The Preacher', John Cartwright, sums up, with no little passion:

> And is it now not a wonder that the people of the Turks and Persians, being both warlike and politic, magnificent and stately (and, to say in a word) the very hammer of the world, as it was said of Babylon, should be thus led away with these vile enchantments of their wicked prophet Muhammad? I will say no more! But since the darkness of Turkey and Persia is so great that it may be felt, and that it is a wonder in our eyes to see such mists in those places, then let us in this land rejoice, who are not only endued with nature as they are, but with special inspiration from above besides, having the celestial doctrine of the everlasting Son of God, to guide us into true happiness. For certainly, the time will come when both the Great Turk and his Pashas, and the Persian king with his Chans,

shall bitterly rue the time and wish, with the loss of both their eyes, that they had but heard and seen as much as we have done.

Let us therefore persuade my loving countrymen who either shall hereafter serve in the wars of Hungary against the Turk, or trade in those places, utterly to detest the Turkish religion as the only way that treads to death and destruction. May we conclude with Ludovicus Vives, who compares heathenism with Mohametism, to glass: 'touch not glass. For though it be bright, yet it is brittle; it cannot endure the hammer'. And Christianism to gold: 'Do you melt it, or do you rub it, or do you beat it, it shine still more orient'.

It is a brilliant image, the (perhaps intentional?) pun on shining in the Orient. Albert Hourani has skilfully located the place of Islam in European thought,[69] and Edward Said (1978; 1995) has quite rightly remarked that:

Not for nothing did Islam come to symbolize terror, devastation, the demonic, hordes of hated barbarians. For Europe, Islam was a lasting trauma. Until the end of the seventeenth century the 'Ottoman peril' lurked alongside Europe to represent for the whole of Christian civilization a constant danger, and in time European civilization incorporated that peril and its lore, its great events, figures, virtues, and vices, as something woven into the fabric of life.

(pp. 59–60)

Other Others

English travellers were generally as dismissive of minorities they encountered in their travels. Recall the characterization, quoted earlier on, by Parry (1601) of the Kurds as a 'a thievish people'. William Biddulph (1609) goes further, and offers as explanation that it was because Kurds were descended from

the race of ancient Parthians, who worship the devil, and allege for their reason for doing so that God is a good man and will do no man harm; but that the Devil is bad, and must be pleased, lest he hurts them.

Cartwright (1611) repeats these assertions and then goes on to add that because 'very evil they are to all sorts of Christians', their land was called 'Terra Daibloi, the land of evil'. Lastly, Lithgow (1632) writes about them as people 'who in holes, caves and bushes lie obscured, waiting for the advantage upon travellers – not unlike the lawless woodkerns in Ireland', an echo of Parry, who offers his readers the following comparison: 'not much unlike the wild Irish'. It is a comparison that will also be regularly used by English travellers about the Khoikhoin peoples at the Cape of Good Hope, pejoratively referred to by them as 'Hottentots'.[70]

Travellers' references to particular peoples can often be traced to antecedent prejudices which they took with them. That contention is best illustrated by brief references made by the travellers about other Christians and to Jews. Biddulph differentiates between Armenians, Maronites, Jacobites, Georgians, Chelsalines, Greeks and Druzes. Sandys (1615) does the same with regard to Greeks and Franks. About Jews, about whom readers in England had no direct knowledge since their expulsion from the country by Edward I (1290), William Biddulph remarks that

> in every place where they come, they are contemptible and of base account, according to the cry of those crucifiers: 'His blood be upon us and our children'. Which is fulfilled this day in our eyes and ears. They are of more vile account in the sight of the Turks than Christians, insomuch that if a Jew would turn Turk, he must first turn Christian, before they will admit him to be a Turk.

That view, the writer insists, is based upon what Jews themselves told him:

> Sundry times had conference with many of them. And some of them, yea, the greatest part of them, are blasphemous wretches who, when they are pressed with an argument which they cannot answer, break out into opprobious speeches, and say Christ was a false prophet and His disciples stole Him out of the grave while the soldiers who watched Him slept; and that their forefathers did deservedly crucify Him, and that if He were now living, they would use him worse than His forefathers ever did.

The blatant and obvious racism finds expression in yet another popular genre, that of the conversion narrative – with respect not only to Jews, but also to those who worship Islam, and Turks in particular. With reference to Jews the titles *A Vindication of the Christians Messiah...Written by Paul Isaiah, a Jew born, but now converted and baptized a Christian* (1654) and *A Letter written to the Jewes, by Rabbi Moses Scialitti, a Jew of Florence, baptized June 14, 1663...declaring the reasons for his conversion, and exhorting them to embrace the Christian faith* (1663) are two instances of a long history of fabrication.[71]

That such prejudice went in parallel with a long-held and, it would seem, ineradicable view of the Ottoman Empire as oppressor of Jews is not simply an additional element to the story, but integral to it. It is one that, despite the evidence to the contrary, still continues embedded in the present. Thus, for instance, the distinguished and deservedly feted William Dalrymple, reviewing Philip Mansel's magnificent *Constantinople: City of the World's Desire, 1453–1924* (1995),[72] observes, it seems with some surprise, that 'Yet perhaps the single most surprising revelation contained in Mansel's book is the extent to which the achievements of Ottoman Constantinople were built on the foundations of religious and ethnic tolerance, not qualities one immediately associates with the Turks'.[73]

Who are the 'we' whom Dalrymple has in mind who do not immediately make such associations? And particularly since the documentation has not been that difficult to access: witness writings such as Stanford J. Shaw's general history[74] or as specialized as Ariel Heyd's[75] specialist reconstruction of the story of Moses Hamon, the Jew who was the physician-in-chief to Suleyman the Magnificent. According to Heyd, 'The Ottoman Sultans not only allowed the Jewish and Marrano immigrants to profess their religion openly but, unlike many Christian rulers in Europe, also permitted the physicians among them to treat non-Jewish patients'. Fascinatingly, Heyd points out that criticism of these Jewish physicians was couched in the contexts of religious and cultural difference:

> Muslim physicians, courtiers and officials who objected to the growing influence of these infidels. Contemporary Western diplomats and travellers also looked with

disfavour upon the eminent role played by the Jewish physicians at the Sultan's Court. Several of these Europeans criticised them for their imperfect knowledge of Latin and Greek and their ignorance of the fast developing medical science in the West.

(p. 153)

– equivalent, in the present, of the (still strong) dismissal of what is being said because it is not spoken in the appropriate accent.

Finally, James Shapiro is quite right in reminding us that

> The extent to which Elizabethan merchants and their agents worked through Jewish intermediaries tends to be underplayed in twentieth-century accounts of Elizabethan expansionism. Both the first English ambassador, William Harborne... and his successor, Edward Barton...had extensive dealings with Turkish Jews, some of whom they employed. Barton even wrote home to Francis Walsingham describing how indebted he was to Jews in Constantinople during the time of the Spanish Armada for their support 'against the false information of our adversaries'.[76]

Trans-formations: 'Learn of a Turke'

Examples cited earlier show what purports to be instances of converted Jews apparently telling their own tales. These have their counterparts where the converted are Turks.[77] But with this difference: the latter do not (are not allowed to?) tell their own tales. It is done on their behalf, and about them, by English divines – often in the form of sermons. Meredith Hamner does so as early as 1586(?) in his *The baptizing of a Turke*, which, he says, he based upon Matthew 5: 16 ('Let your light so shine before men, that they may see your good works, and glorify your Father which is in heaven'), while Jean d'Espargne's *The Joyful Convert: represented in a short but elegant sermon preached at the baptizing of a Turke who...was baptized in the French church May 2 1658* (1658) is another example of the speed of translation into English. The ideological project might be illustrated by two publications which appeared in that same year: (a) *The Baptized Turk, or a narrative of the happy conversion of Rigep Dandulo, the onely son of a Silk merchant in the isle of Tzio, from the delusions of that great imposter, Mahomet, into the Christian relgion...*, by the Dean of Worcester Cathedral, Thomas Warmstry; and (b) the anonymous *A Fine Relation of the Conversion and Baptism of Isuf the Turkish Chaous*.

Travellers' tales tell a different story, that of how English merchants were letting the (Christian) side down. Moryson says that of the seventeen merchants he found living in three houses in Aleppo, some had taken Jewish mistresses. Sanderson goes as far as naming names: 'Memorandum: that many Englishmen, old and young, have in my remembrance turned Turkes, as Benjamin Bishop, George Butler, John Ambrose, and others'. There is at least one play, Robert Daborn's *A Christian turn'd Turk...* (1612),[78] reputedly based upon the actions of two real-life pirates, that takes up this theme of going over to the other side.

The theme of Christian martyrdom is prominent in some of these stories, of which one example is *A true narrative of a wonderful accident, which occur'd upon the execution of a Christian slave at Aleppo in Turkey. Being a remarkable instance of Divine Providence, attesting the acceptableness of the Christian religion and the virtue of chastity to Almighty God. Written at first for the satisfaction of a friend only, and since made publick for the strengthening of virtue*, (1676). Though brief, the tale – as well as the telling of it – is typical. It is the story of a French slave who resisted being sodomized by his master's steward 'being much addicted to that horrid and unnatural sin (too frequent with Mahumetans…)' while the master was, with others, on the way to meet a Pasha and escort him into Aleppo. The slave resists, and eventually kills the steward with a scimitar, and then escapes, taking a horse to flee to Iskanderun, the nearest port, in the hope of finding an English ship on which he would be able to flee to safety – itself an interesting point: that of an English ship as guarantor of safety. But, uncertain of the route, he encounters his master and the others coming back. Confronted, he tells a lie: that the house had been burgled, the steward killed, and he was riding out to tell his master. Though the evidence flies in the face of his story, the Pasha first exonerates the slave. But, under pressure from other masters that if the slave escapes punishment then their lives might be at risk, the Pasha changes his mind and sentences the slave to death – but with the proviso that, instead of being tortured to death, the slave should simply have his head chopped off! Before that, the slave asks God for a sign of his innocence and chastity. Which sign is that, despite the beheaded body lying unburied in the fields for about ten days, it is the only one that is untouched by ravenous dogs bred specially for the purpose of consuming the remains of the executed. The upshot is that the writer concludes that though he 'will not stiffly confirm all this is miraculous…upon this occasion here was a considerable motive for God to exert His power to illustrate the innocence and virtue of a devout and chaste Christian', of which the proof was that 'the sign was so convincive and operative on the Turks that, to bury their shame, they were necessitated at last to dig a grave and intomb this chaste martyr'. Having started his tale by asserting that he is not 'one of those men of easy faith which…are apt to credit all reports', he is aware that some of his readers might wish for stronger proof. He advises such to go to

> Elfor's coffee-house in George Yard in Lombard Street, where he may meet with several eminent and worthy gentlemen, Turkey-merchants, that can confirm the truth of the thing, they having been at this place where this was acted, and at the same time when it was done.

That several of the examples date from after the period of the Civil War and the Restoration is no accident. Three examples will suffice to show that these kinds of conversion narratives are also written with one eye on events at home. One key element here is that of taking great care against the possibility of being duped. *The Devil's Last Legacy. Or a Round-head ironmonger made executor to Pluto. Wherein is shewed, the discent of round-heads. As also the Roundheads great desire of a Crowne…composed by W. K., first a Turke, and now turned Roundhead* appears in 1642, the year of the outbreak of the Civil War, while a text under the names of T. Welde, S. Hammond, G. Sidenham and W. Durant provides proof of the mendacity on the part of those who come from within the ranks of England's 'domestic foreigners': *A False Jew. Or a wonderfull discovery of a Scot, baptized at London for a Christian, circumcized at Rome to act a Jew; rebaptized at Hexham for a believer, but found at Newcastle to be a cheat. Being a true relation of the cheating of one T. Ramsey…who landed at Newcastle under the name of T. Horsley, but gave himself out for a Jew, by the name of Rabbi Joseph ben Israel…* (Newcastle 1653, 1654).

Lastly, and wonderfully clever, the tract *Learne of a Turk*[79] (1660) that claimed to have been written and sent by one of the attendants to the English Agent at Constantinople. In it, the readers are first told that

> thou mayest out of this discourse pick some knowledge of our miseries past; of our miseries present, with the root and spring of them, and of the most probable means of redeeming them for the future. God make our grandees in the Army, and out of the Army, wise to the harms of others (they that build much upon the confidence of an army, build upon quicksand) and God make them honest the example of others, or else the men of Nineveh shall rise up in judgement against this government.
>
> (Matthew 12: 41)[80]

The real reason emerges eventually. Having provided several examples of the unfortunate consequences that followed upon Ottoman rulers disbanding their armies, there emerges a warning to the English:

> First, how dangerous a thing it is for any supreme power to stand in need of a constant standing army. They do but bestride an unruly camel, which they cannot manage;...Second, what a dangerous thing it is for the civil power to permit the soldiers and officers of the army to hold their counsels and conventicles. These were the root of all the troubles in the Turkish Empire. Thirdly, how much better it is to be under the worst of monarchies than at the courtesy of a mutinied army, appears by this story. Fourthly, that the common soldier, having been debauched by their own officers, may at last prove honest and, delivering their misleaders to justice. May return them to their duty and obedience. Amen.

Staging Englishness and Otherness

It is highly unlikely that English readers would have been taken in sufficiently to believe that they were here reading a contribution from a Turkish soldier to the debate on whether or not there should be a standing army,[81] especially from an infidel capable of invoking chapter and verse from the Bible. One possible reason why they would have been able to dismiss advice coming from such a quarter was because of representations of Turks on the English stage. Once again, however, the most popular image offered was not always straightforward. It is true that that image of 'the terrible Turk' is there from the earliest examples: *The first part of the tragicall raigne of Selimus, sometime Emperour of the Turkes...wherein is showne how hee...raised warres against his own father Bazajet, and prevailing therein, in the end caused him to be poysoned. Also with the murthering of his two brethren, Corcus and Acomat* (1594, 1638);[82] William Alexander's *The Tragedy of Darius* (1603);[83] Fulke Greville's *Mustapha* (1608); Philip Massinger's *Emperor of the East* (1631); Robert Baron's *Mirza. A tragedie really acted in Persia, in the last age. Illustrated with historicall annotations* (1647); and Robert Boyle's *The Tragedy of Mustapha* (1694). But other plays, such as Lodowick Carlell's *Osmond, the Great Turk; or the Noble Servant* (1657), Thomas Southerne's *The Loyal Brother; or, the Persian Prince* (1682) – with Prologue and Epilogue by John Dryden – and two plays by Thomas Goffe, *The Couragious Turke* and *The Raging Turke*, both acted in the University of Oxford in 1632,[84] undermine that dominant model.

That image of 'the terrible Turk' is of course present in Shakespeare as well. Rosalind, disguised as Ganymede, tells Silvius that she is being defied 'Like Turk to Christian'. She then goes on to say that 'women's gentle brain / Could not drop forth such giant-rude invention / Such Ehiop's words, blacker in their effect / than in their countenance' (*As You Like It* 4.3.33–6). In *Richard II* 4.1.833ff., the Bishop of Carlisle reminds Bolingbroke about how the Duke of Norfolk, banished from England, had 'fought / For Jesu Christ in glorious Christian field / Streaming the ensign of the Christian cross / Against black Pagans, Turks, and Saracens'; and at the end of *2 Henry IV* (5.2.44–9), the Prince, entering for the first time as the new monarch, and being greeted as such by the Lord Chief Justice, retorts that

> This new and gorgeous garment, majesty
> Sits not so easy on me as you think.
> Brothers, you mix your sadness with some fear.
> This is the English, not the Turkish Court;
> Not Amurath an Amurath succeeds,
> But Harry Harry.

Conclusion

This has been a highly selective signposting of what to expect when looking at the selections which follow, as seen through the eyes of English travellers. Perhaps the most important aspect not mentioned thus far is that of the actual places to which they went – not now as merchants or diplomats, but simply as tourists. And not simply to the obvious places such as Constantinople and Baghdad but also others, chiefly those which were the cause for wonder, Espahan with its gardens being perhaps the most prominent example. The point was made, near the beginning, that early modern travellers took with some prior sense, derived from the Bible and from the Greek and Roman histories, of what to expect, and that these coloured their ways of seeing. It must therefore have been galling to them that Elizabethan and Jacobean London simply could not match the architectural and cultural riches of these cities of the Orient.

But that is a side issue. The fundamental point to stress is that cultural encounter was, in these Oriental spaces and under the circumstances of the English going there, a disorienting experience. Whether as merchant, as diplomat, as tourist, or as scholar, these travellers went there as supplicants. Their status, as well as the reasons for their travels, were wholly different from encounters in the New World and in Africa. Not only did they go to the New World and to Africa as dispossessors, but they also found themselves in places about which neither the Bible nor the Classics could offer reliable information. On the occasions on which those texts did so, that information was suffused with what subsequently became defined as racialized discourse, of which, as was shown above, the chief exemplar was invariably the Jew. The upshot was that whatever early modern travellers and their readers might have thought about the kingdoms and peoples of the Near East, their perceptions and attitudes had, perforce, to be modulated by the awareness that the peoples who inhabited those spaces had long histories of enviably high prestige. Some of it, they had to concede, was worthy of their emulation, not only in philosophy, science and medicine, but also to the most practical, such as the practice of training pigeons to carry messages to merchants giving details about the size and nature of the cargoes in transit by caravan.

The spaces to which these travellers went were ruled by monarchs who accepted Islam. Christian Europe was not only in fear of Ottoman power but, until the turn of the new century, that fear was also aggravated by a sense of being, if not irrelevant, then certainly marginal to the contest between Turks and Persians that was, in part, between competing versions of the common religion founded by Muhammad. Even if they had wanted to do so, there was no significant way in which Christians could influence either the course or the outcomes. It was to be their post-Enlightenment successors who would, in their turn, make use of the accounts of these travellers prior to their own departure to those places in the centuries of colonization and aggrandisement. It is that story that Edward Said, quite correctly, says dates from the late eighteenth century. But the foundations for that project, as several of the selections will show, are already beginning to be laid (in England anyway) in the half-century after the Restoration.

The Harry who succeeded Harry could be made to shape the story of his succession to suit the needs of English audiences who looked to that stage to see their national identities and aspirations expressed on it. Othello, abused at the beginning because of his colour, but deemed to be crucial to the success of the Venetian military enterprise, near the end of the play tells Lodovico that 'Like a base Indian' he had thrown away a pearl 'richer than all his tribe' and then goes on to tell him, further, in the few moments before he will commit suicide, to write down the story of how

> in Aleppo once,
> Where a malignant and turbaned Turk
> Beat a Venetian and traduced the state
> I took by th' throat the circumcisèd dog
> And smote him thus.
> (*Othello*: 5.2.362–5)

The politics of that account is even further complicated by a textual crux. The term 'Indian' in the quarto is matched, in the folio, with the term 'Judean', which makes the Moor's last words perhaps the most poignant of interrogations of the complexities of cultural encounter in a physical space, the Eastern Mediterranean, over which Ottoman sea power dominates.

My guess is that the predominant English hope was that what they saw as the inhumane scourge of Christianity that Milton several times calls 'the Turkish tyranny' would soon be defeated. Until that time, they hedged their bets. The early modern Orient they constructed out of a combination of precedent biblical and classical knowledge, allied to the diversity of travellers' tales that they claimed as accurate as well as up to date, they repudiated at the same time as they studied it. The inhabitants of a not very influential island offshore from the mainland of the continent of Europe, in the throes of all kinds of internal dissensions, were simultaneously fascinated by the wealth and power of the Ottomans and fearful of it. That is, until the late 1680s, the moment of the beginning of the end of Ottoman dominance in the aftermath of events such as the defeat of the Turkish Army under Suleyman and the deposition of Muhammad IV (1687). It was both the space that was created, in that moment, by that event itself, and the sense of European supremacy that began to fill that void, that mark the moment of the fabrication of the 'Orient' and of 'Orientalism' in the senses and meanings that we have inherited from Edward Said. But not before, and not until then.

NOTES

1 Anthony Ashley Cooper, *Characteristics of Men, Morals, Opinions, and Times*, ed. J. M. Robertson, London, 1900: 220.
2 Terry Eagleton, *The Ideology of the Aesthetic*, Cambridge: Basil Blackwell, 1990: 31–69.
3 Michael McKeon, *The Origins of the English Novel, 1600–1740*, Baltimore and London: Johns Hopkins University Press, 1987: 100–4.
4 Percy G. Adams, *Travellers and Travel Liars, 1600–1800*, Berkeley, CA: University of California Press, 1962; R. R. Cawley, *The Voyagers and Elizabethan Drama*, London: Oxford University Press, 1938; *Milton and the Literature of Travel*, Princeton, NJ: Princeton University Press, 1951; *Unpathed Waters. Studies in the influence of the voyagers on English literature*, London: Frank Cass, 1967 (originally published by Princeton University Press, 1940); R. W. Frantz, *The English Traveller and the Movement of Ideas, 1660–1732*, Lincoln, NE: Nebraska University Press, 1934; Boies Penrose, *Travel and Discovery in the Renaissance, 1420–1620*, Cambridge, MA: Harvard University Press, 1952.
5 Edward Said, *Orientalism. Western conceptions of the Orient*, London: Routledge, 1978, 1995.
6 See, for instance, Dennis Porter, 'Orientalism and its Problems', in *The Politics of Theory. Proceedings of the Essex Sociology of Literature Conference*, ed. Peter Hulme, Margaret Iversen and Diane Loxley, Colchester: University of Essex, 1983: 179–93; James Clifford, 'On *Orientalism*', in *The Predicament of Culture. Twentieth-century ethnography, literature and art*, Cambridge, MA: Harvard University Press, 1988: 255–76; Aijaz Ahmad, *In Theory. Classes, nations, literatures*, London: Verso, 1992.
7 *Europe and its Others*, ed. Frances Barker, Peter Hulme, Margaret Iversen and Diane Loxley, Colchester: University of Essex, 1985: 14–27.
8 Edward Said, *The World, the Text, and the Critic*, Cambridge, MA: Harvard University Press, 1983: 35.
9 Christine Woodhead, '"The Present Terrour of the World"? Contemporary views of the Ottoman Empire c.1600', *History* 72: 20–37, 1987.
10 Jerry Brotton, *Trading Territories. Mapping the Early Modern World*, London: Reaktion, 1997: ch. 3, 'Disorienting the Orient. The geography of the Ottoman Empire'.
11 Pococke, who had learnt his Arabic from Matthias Pastor (a German from Heidelberg who had given lectures on the language in Oxford in 1625), and later from William Bedwell, had been sent to Aleppo (where he arrived in October 1630) as a replacement as chaplain for the Levant Company for Charles Robson, who had been the first chaplain sent there. While the date of his return to England is uncertain (probably late 1635), he was back in the Orient in 1638, in the company of the Gresham Professor of Geometry, John Greaves. It was during the next two years that he set about acquiring Arabic texts to take back with him to Oxford, where his patron was Archbishop Laud. See Hans Daiber, 'The reception of Islamic philosophy at Oxford in the 17thC. The Pocockes' (father and son) contribution to the understanding of Islamic philosophy in Europe', in *Introduction of Arabic Philosophy*, ed. Charles E. Butterworth and Blake Andrée Kessell, London: Brill, 1994; P. M. Holt, 'An Oxford Arabist. Edward Pococke (1604–1691)', in *Studies in the History of the Near East*, ed. P.M. Holt, London: Frank Cass, 1973: 3–26.
12 A. J. Arberry, *British Orientalists*, London: William Collins, 1943.
13 G. J. Toomer, *Eastern Wisedome and Learning. The Study of Arabic in Seventeenth-Century England*, Oxford: Clarendon, 1996; G. A. Russell (ed.), *The 'Arabick' Interest of the Natural Philosophers in Seventeenth-Century England*, Leiden: Brill, 1994.
14 See especially P. M. Holt, 'Background to Arabic Studies in Seventeenth-Century England', Vivian Salmon, 'Arabists and Linguists in Seventeenth-Century England', Mordechai Feingold, 'Patrons and Professors. The origins and motives for the endowment of university chairs – in particular the Laudian professorship of Arabic'.
15 See e.g. Hans Daiber, 'The reception of Islamic philosophy at Oxford in the 17thC: the Pocockes' (father and son) contribution to Islamic philosophy in Europe', in *The Introduction of Arabic Philosophy in Europe*, ed. Charles E. Butterworth and Blake Kessel, Leiden: Brill, 1994: 65–82; Karl H. Dannenfeldt, 'The Renaissance Humanists and the knowledge of Arabic', in *Studies in the Renaissance* 2: 96–117, 1955; Mordechai Feingold, 'Decline and Fall. Arabic

Science in Seventeenth-Century England', in *Transition, Transmission, Transfiguration*, ed. F. Jamil Ragep, Sally P. Rageb and Steven Livesey, Leiden: Brill, 1996: 441–69.

16 Some of Elizabeth's replies were from the Sultana, rather than the monarch himself. Whether that was because the monarch was unwilling to enter into direct correspondence with a female (and a Christian at that) or whether he held the view that it might be advantageous because the Sultana was herself an Italian aristocrat who had been caught by pirates and sent to Constantinople, where he had selected her, is not clear. See Susan Skilliter, 'Three letters from the Ottoman "Sultana" Safiye to Queen Elizabeth', in *Documents from Islamic Chanceries*, ed. S. M. Stern, Cambridge, MA: Harvard University Press, 1965: 129–57.

17 H. G. Rawlinson, 'The Embassy of William Harborne to Constantinople, 1583–8', *Transactions of the Royal Historical Society* 4th Series: 1–27, 1922; Arthur Leon Horniker, 'William Harborne and the beginning of Anglo-Turkish diplomatic and commercial relations', *The Journal of Modern History* XIV(3): 289–316, 1942. Susan Skilliter, *William Harborne and the trade with Turkey, 1578–1582. A documentary study of Anglo-Ottoman relations*, Oxford: Oxford University Press for the British Academy, 1977.

18 George Ashwell, *The history of Hai Eb'n Yockdan, an indian prince; or, the self-taught philosopher. Written originally in the Arabick tongue by Abi Jaafar Eb'n Tophail [Abu Bakr Ibn Al-Tufail], a philosopher by profession, and a Mahometan by religion. Set forth in the Latin version by E. Pocock...and now translated into English by G. Ashwell*, Richard Chiswell, 1686; George Keith, *An account of the Oriental philosophy showing...particularly the profound wisdom of Hai Ebn Yockdan....Out of the Arabick translated into latine by E. Pocock and now out of his Latine translated into English*, 1674; Richard Russell, *The works of Geber...the most famous Arabian prince and philosopher, faithfully Englished by R. Russell, a lover of antiquity*, 1678.

19 Moritz Steinschneider, *Al Farabi (Alpharabius) des arabischen Philosophen Leben und Scriften, mit besonderen Rücksicht auf die Geschicte der griechishen Wissenschaft under den Arabaen*, 1859; *Die europäischen Uberstzungen aus den arabischen bis mitte des 17. Jahrhunderts*, Vienna, 1905.

20 Alistair Hamilton, *William Bedwell the Arabist, 1563-1632*, Leiden: Brill, 1985.

21 Thomas Coryate, *Thomas Coriate Traueller for the English Wits. Greeting. From the Court of the Great Mogul, Resident at the towne of Asmere [Ajmer], in Easterne India*, printed by W. Jaggard and Henry Fetherston, London, 1616: 30.

22 For a quite magnificent reappraisal of the theoretical and historiographical issues, as well as quite splendid attention to particular spaces, see Nicholas Canny (ed.), *The Oxford History of the British Empire*, Vol. 1, *The origins of Empire. British overseas enterprise to the close of the 17thC*, Oxford: Oxford University Press, 1998.

23 The most impressive narrative of that colonizing history is Angus Calder, *Revolutionary Empire. The rise of the English-speaking empires from the fifteenth century to the 1780s*, New York: Dutton, 1981; Penguin, 1998.

24 N. I. Matar, 'Islam in Interregnum and Restoration England', *The Seventeenth Century* 6.1(Spring): 57–71, 1991. The extract quoted is at p. 63. Nabil Matar, *Islam in Britain 1558-1685*, Cambridge: Cambridge University Press, 1998, esp. 'Introduction: Islam in early modern Britain' and 'Conclusion: Islam and Britain: centripetal to centrifugal'.

25 *The Historie of the World, commonly called The natural History of C. Plinius Secundus*, London, 1601; *The excellent and pleasant work of Julius Solinus, Polyhistor. Contayning the noble actions of humaine creatures, the secretes & providence of nature, the description of countries...*, translated out of the Latin by Arthur Golding, Gent., London: J. Chatterwoode for T. Hooker, 1587; *The Works of Pomponius Mela concerninge the situation of the world...*, translated out of Latin by A. Golding, London: T. Hacket, 1585.

26 Cesare Federici, *The voyage and travel of M[aster] Caesar Frederick, merchant of Venice, into the East India, the Indies, and beyond the Indies...for the profitable instruction of merchants and all other travellers, for their better direction and knowledge of those countries*. Out of the Italian by T. H[icock], London: R. Jones & E. White, 1588; Jan Huyghen van Linschoten, *His discours of voyages into the East and West Indies*. Translated by W[illiam] P[hillip], London, 1598.

27 Richard Hakluyt, *The Principall Navigations, Voiages and Discoveries of the English Nation*, 1589; *The Principal Navigations, Voiages, Traffiques and Discoveries...* 2 vols, 1598; Samuel Purchas, *Hakluytus Posthumous or Purchas his Pilgrimes*, 1625; *A Collection of Original Voyages*, 1699.

28 Cornelius Haga, *A true declaration of the arrival of Cornelius Haga, Ambassador for the General Sates of the United Netherlands at Constantinople*, 1613; *The voyages and travels of the Ambassadors sent by Frederic Duke of Holstein to the Great Duke of Muscovy and the king of Persia, begun in the year 1633, and finished 1639...whereto are added the travels of J. A. Mandelso, from Persia into the East Indies. Written originally by A. Olearius*, 1662; William Joseph Grelot, *A late voyage to Constantinople...published by permission of the French King*, 1683; Jan Struys, *The voyages and travels of J[an] S[truys] through Greece, Muscovy, Tartary, Media, Persia, India, Japan....Together with an account of the author's...dangers by shipwreck...slavery...torture*, 1684; Jean Baptiste Tavernier, *Collections of Travels through Turkey into Persia and the East Indies. Giving an account of the present state of those countries...*, 1684; *The Travels of Monsieur de Thevenot into the Levant. In three parts....Newly done out of French*, 1687; Ogier Ghiselin de Busbecq, *Travels into Turkey*, 1696; Sieur Jean Du Mont, *A New Voyage into the Levant*, 1696; Girolano Dandini, *A Voyage to Mount Libanus...*, 1698.

29 Botero, *The Travellers Breviat, or a historical description of the most famous kingdomes in the world*, 1601: [as] *An historicall description of the most famous kingdomes and commonweales in the world...*, 1603; [as] *Relations of the most famous kingdoms and commonweales...*, 1608, 1616; Boemus, *The manners, lawes, and customs of all nations. Collected out of the best writers by Johannes Boemus Aubanus, a Dutchman*, translated by Ed[ward] Astor, London: George Eld, 1611; [Blome], *A Geographical Description of the Four Parts of the World, taken from the notes and works of the famous Monsieur Sanson...and other eminent travellers and authors...also, a treatise of travel, and another of traffick...the work illustrated with...maps and figures*, London: T.N. for R. Blome, 1670.

30 Nathaniel Carpenter, *Geography, delineated...in two books*, Oxford: John Litchfield & William Turner for Henry Cripps, 1625; John Bulwer, *A View of the People of the Whole World; or, a...survey of their policies, dispositions...complexions, ancient & moderne customes, etc*, 1654, originally issued as *Anthropometamorphosis. Man transform'd; or, the Artificial Changeling*, 1653; reissued 1650, 1659; Thomas Porter, *A compendious view or cosmological and geographical description of the whole world. Also, a chronology...since the Creation*, 1659.

31 Peter Heylyn, *Cosmographie...containing the chorographie and history of the world*, 1652. Further editions 1657, 1666, 1669, 1670.

32 George Meriton, *A Geographical description of the World. With a brief account of the several empires, dominions, and parts thereof. As also the natures of the people, the customs, manners and commodities of the several countreys. With a description of the principal cities in each dominion*, 1671 (2nd edition). Further editions 1674, 1679.

33 Joseph Hall, *Quo Vadis? A Just censure of Travell as it is commonly undertaken by the gentlemen of our Nation*, 1617.

34 Clare Howard, *English Travellers of the Renaissance*, London: John Lane, The Bodley Head, 1914.

35 Jerome Turler, *The Traveiler of Jerome Turler, devided into two bookes, the first conteining a notable discourse of the maner and order of traveling oversea, or into strange and forrein countreyes...*, 1575; William Bourne, *A Booke called the Treasure for Traueillers*, 1578; Samuel Lewkenor, *A Discourse of Forraine Cities...*, 1600; Baptist Goodall, *The Tryall of Travell*, 1630; James Howell, *Forreine Travell*, 1642, 1650; Sir Thomas Neale, *Treatise of Direction how to Travell safely and profitably into Forraigne Countries. Written first in Latin*, 1643, 1664; William Carr, *Travellour's Guide and Historian's Faithful Companion*, 1695.

36 'Epistle' to *The History of trauayle in the West and East Indies....Gathered in parte, and done into Englyshe by Richard Eden....* Imprinted by Richard Iugge, 1577.

37 Richard Helgerson, *Forms of Nationhood. The Elizabethan writing of England*, Chicago: University of Chicago Press, 1992; esp. chs 3, 4. The quotation is at p. 128.

38 John Parker, *Books to Build an Empire. A bibliographical history of English overseas interests to 1620*, Amsterdam: N. Israel, 1965.

39 Eric J. Leed, *The Mind of the Traveller. From Gilgamesh to Global Tourism*, New York: Basic Books, 1991; Douglas Chambers, *The Reinvention of the World. English Writing 1650–1750*, London: Arnold, 1996; Eric R. Wolf, *Europe and the People without History*, Berkeley, CA: University of California Press, 1982; Urs Bitterli (transl. Ritchie Robertson), *Cultures in Conflict. Encounters between European and Non-European Cultures, 1492–1800*, Cambridge:

Polity, 1989; J. M. Blaut, *The Colonizer's Model of the World. Geographical diffusionism and Eurocentric history*, New York: Guilford Press, 1993; Dennis Porter, *Haunted Journeys. Desire and transgression in European travel writing*, Princeton, NJ: Princeton University Press, 1991; Caren Kaplan, *Questions of Travel. Postmodern discourses of displacement*, Durham, NC and London: Duke University Press, 1996; Simon Gikandi, *Maps of Englishness. Writing identity in the culture of colonialism*, New York: Columbia University Press, 1996.

40 Hakluyt *Voyages*, 1598, Vol. 2: 250–68. The story was also told in Linschoten's *Discours of Voyages into ye Easte and Weste Indies*, published in England in the same year and in Purchas (1625: 1730–44).

41 *The intreigues of the French king at Constantinople, to embroil Christendom. Discovered in several dispatches past [passed] betwixt him and the late Grand Signior, Grand Vizier, and Count Teckily. All of them found among that Count's papers seiz'd in December last. None of them being hitherto seen in English. With some reflections upon them. Published by authority*, London. Printed for Donovan Newman, at the King's Arms, Poultry, 1689.

42 *Subtilty and cruelty. Or a relation of the horrible and unparalleled abuses and intolerable oppressions exercised by Sir Sackville Crow, His Majesty's Ambassador at Constantinople, and his agents, in seizing upon the persons and estates of the English nation resident there, and at Smyrna. Together with the barbarous and tyrannical intent to do the like upon the persons and estates in all parts of the Grand Signior's dominions. Directly contrary to the trust reposed in him by His Majesty, and his owne agreement with the Company of Merchants of England trading into the Levant seas, at whose charge he is there maintained*, London, R. Cotes, 1646.

43 Palmira Brummett, *Ottoman Seapower and Levantine Diplomacy in the Age of Discovery*, Albany, NY: State University of New York, 1994.

44 For recent, and continuing, debates concerning Egypt as source of classical learning, see especially Martin Bernal, *Black Athena. The Afroasiatic roots of classical civilization*, London: Vintage (Vol. 1, 1987; Vol. 2, 1991); Mary Lefkowitz, *Not Out of Africa. How Afrocentrism became an excuse to teach myth as history*, New York: Basic Books, 1996; Mary Lefkowitz and Guy MacLean Rogers (eds), *Black Athena Revisited*, Chapel Hill, NC: University of North Carolina Press, 1996.

45 William Biddulph, *The Travels of certain Englishmen into Africa, Asia, Troy, Bythinia, Thracia, and to the Black Sea. And into Syria, Cilicia, Pisidia, Mesopotamia, Damascus, Canaan, Galilee, Samaria, Judea, Palestine, Jerusalem, Jericho, and to the Red Sea and to sundry other places....Very profitable for the help of travellers, and no less delightful to all persons who take pleasure to hear of the manners, government, religion, and customs of foreign and heathen countries*, London. Printed by Th. Haueland for W. Apsley, and are to be sold at his shop in Paul's Church-Yard, at the signe of the parrot, 1609.

46 Meriton, op. cit., pp. 374–5. Compare, for instance, his definition of the Scots: 'The people are much given to venery. Those that inhabit the south are the best and civilest, and speak the English language, but those in the northern part are savage and uncivil, termed sylvesters' [probably in the sense of being spirits of the woods].

47 Fynes Moryson, *An Itinerary containing his ten years' travel through the twelve dominions of Germany, Bohmerland, Switzerland, Netherland, Denmark, Poland, Italy, Turkey, France, England, Scotland and Ireland...*, London. Printed by John Beale, dwelling in Aldersgate Street, 1617.

48 William Lithgow, *The totall discourse of the rare adventures and painefull peregrinations...*, London, 1632.

49 Henry Blount, *A Voyage into the Levant...with particular observations concerning the modern condition of the Turkes, and other people under that empire*, London: I. L [John Leggatt], 1636. Further editions 1638, 1650, 1664, 1669, 1671.

50 The diplomat and poet Sir Henry Wotton (1568–1639) is credited with providing the following definition of an ambassador (written in a friend's album): 'An ambassador is an honest man sent to lie abroad for the good of his country'.

51 Orhan Burian, 'Interest of the English in Turkey as reflected in English literature of the Renaissance', *Oriens. Journal of the International Society for Oriental Research* 5(2): 209–29, 1952.

52 There is a wonderful story, unfortunately not published in its own time, of the sending of a gift of an organ to Mehmet and a carriage for his Sultana. There is, however, a splendid reconstruction of that event, based upon the original documents: Stanley Mayes, *An Organ for the Sultan*, London: Putnam, 1956. See also Samuel Chew, *The Crescent and the Rose. Islam and England during the Renaissance*, New York: Oxford University Press, 1937: 162–72.

53 John Sanderson, 'Sundry the personal voyages performed by John Sanderson of London, merchant, begun in October 1584, ended in October 1602; with an historical description of Constantinople', in Samuel Purchas, *Purchas his Pilgrimes*, (2): 1614–40, 1625.

54 *A letter from an eminent merchant in Constantinople, to a friend in London: giving an exact relation of the great and glorious cavalcade of Sultan Mahomet the fourth, present Emperour of the Turks, as he marched out of Constantinople, for the invasion of Christendome, and the siege of Vienna*, London: A. Jones, 1683.

55 For details, see section below devoted to Sherley extract.

56 Quoted from Horniker, op. cit., p. 314.

57 *Remarks upon the manners, religion and government of the Turks.... By Tho. Smith, B.D. and Fellow of St. Mary Magdalen College, Oxon. London: Moses & Pitt, 1678.

58 Anthony Parr (ed.), *Three Renaissance Travel Plays*, Revels Plays Companion Library, Manchester and New York: Manchester University Press, 1995.

59 Jacob Lopes Cardoso, *The Contemporary Jew in the Elizabethan Drama*, New York: Burt Franklin, 1958; originally published Paris, 1925.

60 Anthony Parr, 'Foreign relations in Jacobean England. The Sherley brothers and the "voyage to Persia"', in *Travel and Drama in Shakespeare's Time*, ed. Jean-Pierre Maquerlot and Michèle Willems, Cambridge: Cambridge University Press, 1995: 14–31

61 Edward Webbe, *The rare and most wonderful things which Edward Webbe, an Englishman born, hath seen and passed in his tiresome travels, in the cities of Jerusalem, Damascus, Bethlehem and Galilee, and in the lands of Jewry, Egypt, Greece, Russia and Prester John*, London: William Wright, 1590, 1600, 1610.

62 Some stories on this theme are of doubtful authenticity. It is likely that some are fabricated out of readings from earlier tales. One example of that sort of pastiche is 'Mr Roberts' adventures among the corsairs of the Levant', in *A Collection of Original Voyages*. Published by Capt. William Hacke, London. Printed for James Knapton, at the Crown in St Paul's Church-Yard, 1699.

63 John Eldred, 'The voyage of M[aster] John Eldred to Tripoli in Syria by sea, and from then by land and river to Babylon [Baghdad] and Balsora [Basra]', in Hakluyt, 1589: 268–80. See also Christopheros Angelos, *Christopher Angell, a Grecian, who tasted of many stripes and torments inflicted by the Turkes for the faith which he had in christ Jesus. (An epistle in commendations of England and the inhabitants thereof)*, Oxford, 1617.

64 Northern parts of Europe, presumably; and thereby also excluding those in southern Europe – mostly Catholics.

65 Anthony Parr, 'Foreign relations...', op. cit., p. 20.

66 Jean Andrés, *The comparison of Muhamet's sect; or, a confutation of the Turkish Alcoran, translated by I. N. [Joshua Notstock]*, H. Blunden, 1652; Lancelot Addison [Dean of Lichfield], *The first state of Muhamedism; or, an account of the author and doctrines of that imposture*, J. C. for W. Crooke, 1679; Alexander Ross, *The Alcoran of Mahomet, translated out of the Arabique into French by the Sieur Du Ryer and now Englished for the satisfaction of all that desire to look into the Turkish vanities. (The life and death of Mahomet, etc. – a needful caveat or admonition for them who desire to know what use may be made of, or if there be danger in reading the Alcoran)*, 1649.

67 Herbert had managed, by means of patronage, to be included in the embassy under the leadership of Sir Dodmore Cotton that was sent to the Persian monarch Abbas and his Mughal counterpart Akbar. That embassy was in response to Robert Sherley's visit to England and his dispute there with the Persian ambassador, Nakd Ali Beg, when the latter questioned the Englishman's credentials. Herbert's greatest claim to fame is that, appointed by Charles I as one of his Grooms of the Bedchamber, he was in attendance on his monarch on the day of the latter's execution, as well as at his subsequent burial. For biographical and critical commentary, see the notes to the extract from Herbert.

68 Sir Thomas Herbert, *Some yeares travel into divers parts of Africa and Asia the Great. Describing more particularly the empires of Persia and Hindustan, interwoven with such remarkable occurrences as happened in those parts during later times. As also many other rich and famous kingdoms in Oriental India, with the isles adjacent. Severally relating their religion, language, customs, and habits; as also proper observations concerning them*, London: R. Everingham for R. Scott, 1677.

69 Albert Hourani, *Islam in European Thought*, Cambridge: Cambridge University Press, 1991; esp. ch. 1.

70 Kenneth Parker, 'Telling Tales. Early Modern English voyagers at the Cape of Good Hope', *The Seventeenth Century* X: 1(Spring): 121–49, 1995.

71 James Shapiro, op. cit., esp. ch. 2: 'Myths, histories, and consequences'; ch. 5: 'The Hebrew will turn Christian'.

72 Philip Mansel, *Constantinople: City of the World's Desire, 1453–1924*, London: John Murray, 1995.

73 *The Independent* 4 November 1995: 7.

74 Stanford J. Shaw, *The Jews of the Ottoman Empire and the Turkish Republic*, Basingstoke: Macmillan, 1991.

75 Ariel Heyd, 'Moses Hamon, chief Jewish physician to Sultan Suleyman the Magnificent', *Oriens. Journal of the International Society for Oriental Research* 16, 1963.

76 Shapiro, p. 147.

77 Nabil Matar, op. cit., ch. 1: '"Turning Turke": conversion to Islam in English writings'; ch. 4: 'Baptizing the Turk. Conversion to Christianity in English writings'.

78 Robert Daborn, *A Christian turn'd Turk: Or, the Tragicall lives and deaths of two famous pyrates, Ward and Dansiker. As it hath beene publickly acted*, London: William Barrenger, 1612. The story of the exploits and eventual retribution for the crimes of these two pirates was told by (*inter alia*) Andrew Barker, *A true and certaine report of the beginning, proceedings, overthrowes and now present estate of Captaine Ward and Danseker, the two late famous pirates, from their first setting foorth to this present time*. Printed by William Hall; sold by John Holme, 1609; *Newes from the Sea, of two notorious pyrats Ward the Englishman and Danseker the Dutchman. With a true relation of all or the most piracies by them committed until the sixth of Aprill 1609*. N. Butter, 1609. See also Samuel Chew, op. cit., pp. 340–61.

79 *Learne of a Turk, or Instructions and Advise sent from the Turkish Army at Constantinople, to the English Army at London. Faithfully and impartially communicated by M. B. one of the attendants of the English Agent there...*, 1660.

80 Matthew 12: 41: 'The men of Nineveh shall rise in judgement with this generation, and shall condemn it: because they repented at the preaching of Jonas; and, behold, a greater than Jonas *is* here'. (Nineveh, on the eastern bank of the Tigris river, was not only the capital of Assyria, but reputedly the most powerful city in the world. Zephaniah 2: 13–15 and Nahum 3:1 anticipated its destruction.)

81 One of the most celebrated texts on the subject was *An argument, shewing that a standing army is inconsistent with a free government, and absolutely destructive of the constitution of the English monarchy*, London, 1697. The tract is usually attributed to John Trenchard (1662–1723) and Walter Moyle (1672–1721).

82 The 1638 edition gives the name 'T. Goff' (see note 84, below) on the title page, but is mistaken. If the same person, he would, in 1594, have been 4 years of age.

83 Reprinted 1604, together with 'Croesus', as *The Monarchick Tragedies*, in the 'enlarged' version (by the addition of other plays) 1606, 1616, 1637. Note that Alexander was also the author of *An Encouragement to Colonies* 1624, 1625 – about New England.

84 Thomas Goffe, *The Couragious Turk*, 1632; *Three Excellent Tragedies, viz. The Raging Turk, or Bajazet the Second; The couragious turk, or Amurath the First; and the tragoedie of Orestes (each in five acts and in verse)*, London, 1656.

1

EDWARD WEBBE

*The rare and most wonderfull things which Edward Webbe an English-
man borne, hath seen and passed in his troublesome travailes, in the cities
of Ierusalem, Damasko, Bethlem and Gagely: and in the lands of Iewrie,
Egypt, Grecia, Russia, and Prester Iohn. Vvherein is set forth his extreame
slauerie sustained many yeares together in the gallies and vvares of the
great Turke, against the lands of Persia, Tartaria, Spaine, and Portugale,
vvith the manner of his releasement and comming into England in May
last.*

London, William Wright, 1590.

BIOGRAPHY

From the text, we are informed that Webbe was born in St Katherine's, near the Tower of
London. His father, he tells us, was a master gunner in the English Navy. He does not
give his date of birth, but from the internal evidence (see note 1) it is possible to conjec-
ture that he was probably born in 1554.

* * *

[Dedication]

To the Most Mighty My Gracious and Renowned Sovereign, Elizabeth by the grace of
God Queen of England, France, and Ireland, Defender of the Faith, etc. Your Highness'
most humble subject Edward Webbe, heartily prays for the continuance of Your Majesty's
health and prosperous reign to the world's end.

Considering (most Gracious and dread Sovereign) the most wonderful providence of
Almighty God showed towards Your Highness since the time of your most happy and
prosperous reign, as well in the preservation of Your Majesty's person from the hands of
Your Highness' enemies, as also in defending this small angle or Realm of England from
the force of foreign foes, and the continual blessings of peace and plenty, with which ever
since he hath in bountiful sort maintained it: I could not therefore but (according to my
duty) render humble thanks to Almighty God for the same, when to my great comfort,
even in the midst of my grievous thraldom in Turkey, I heard it most truly reported by a
Christian captive, and your Highness' clemency by him highly commended. The report of

whose fame truly described, as well in the administration of justice, and in supporting the Christian religion, as also in relieving and encouraging the poor distressed members of this land, gave me just cause to pray heartily for my delivery, and to long inwardly until I came to see Your Highness (my dread Sovereign) and this my native country. And now having obtained my long expected wish, I do in all humbleness prostrate myself, and this plain discourse of my travels to your most excellent Majesty. Wherein may be seen, that if in Turkey I would have denied my Christ, or in my travail I would have forsaken my Prince to have served in Spain, thereby to have become a traitor to Your Majesty and my native country, I needed not to have lived in want, but in great prosperity. But forasmuch as Almighty God hath set me free from thraldom and delivered me from many dangers and sent me into England, my desire is that may be employed in such service and affairs as may be pleasing to God and found profitable to my prince and country. And thus trusting your Highness will accept in good worth this true discourse though rudely penned I humbly take my leave, praying for the prosperous health and continual reign of your most excellent Majesty.

Your Higness' humble servant, Edward Webbe.

The Epistle to the Reader

Courteous Reader, I have undertaken, in this short discourse, to utter the most part of such things as I saw and passed in the time of my troublesome travel and slavish life sustained in the galleys, and wars of the Great Turk. And this is to protest that in this book there is nothing mentioned or expressed but that which is of truth, and what mine own eyes have perfectly seen. Some foolish persons perhaps will cavil and say, that these are lies and feigned fables, and that it contains nothing else. But to those I answer that whatsoever is herein mentioned, he whosoever he be, that shall so find fault, and doubt of the truth hereof, let him but make inquiry of the best and greatest travellers and merchants about all this land: and they doubtless will resolve them that it is true which is here expressed, with a great deal more which now I cannot call to remembrance, for that my memory fails me, by means of my great and grievous troubles. And whereas in the first edition of this book a great fault in number did negligently escape in folio 3, in these words 30. thousand for 300. thousand: and 50. thousand for 500. thousand: that fault is truly amended in this edition.

From my lodging at Black-wall, this nineteenth day of May 1590.

Your loving countryman, Edward Webbe.

[Russia]

My father, having some natural affection for me, when I was but 14 years old, preferred me to the service of Captain Jenkinson, at such time as he was sent ambassador into Russia,[1] with whom I went by sea and upon whom I was daily attendant. In which my journey, I was conversant among the people of that country, who were apparelled like to the Turks and Tatarians, with furred caps and long garments down to their shins: much like to carbines, or Norsemen ready to the war. There I made my abode some space in the head city of Russia called Moscow, in which their building is all of fir, except the Emperor's Court, which is of lime and stone. They execute very sharp laws among them, and are a kind of tyrannous people as appears by their customs, of which among many other, these

I specially noted, viz. that if any man be indebted one to another, and doth not make payment at his day and time appointed the officers may enter upon the debtors and forcibly break down their houses, and imprison them in grievous sort; where judgement shall presently pass against him: which is [that] with a mallet of wood he shall have so many blows on the shins or on the forehead as the judge shall award. And this punishment shall be inflicted sundry days upon him.

The Turks also beat debtors with a mallet, but not in that sort. For in Turkey they are beaten for debt upon the soles of the feet with a cane or cudgel if payment is not made by a day. I also noted, that if any nobleman offends the Emperor of Russia, the said noble man is taken and imprisoned with all his children and kinfolks. And the first great frost that comes (for the country is wonderfully cold and subject to frosts) there is a great hole made in the ice over some great river, and then the party principal is first put in, and after him his wife, his children, and other his kinfolks, and to leave none of his posterity to possess his lands or goods but the same are bestowed upon others at the Emperor's pleasure. There I stayed three years attendant on my Master. In which time the Crim-Tatarians, otherwise named the 'New Christians', made war upon the said city of Moscow. Which soon after was betrayed and speedily burned, the people in great abundance massacred, and the Tatarian soldiers had wonderfully rich spoils in the same.[2] There was I at that time with 7 other Englishmen taken prisoners, and for slaves were all together conveyed to Cassan, where the king of the Tatarians abides and keeps a stately Court.

Being conveyed there, we were set to wipe the feet of the king's horses, and to become ordinary slaves in the said Court, to fetch water, cleave wood, and to do such other drudgery. There were we beaten three times a week with a bull's pissle, or a horse's tail. And in this sort and miserable servitude we stayed there five years. Then were we ransomed from thence by our friends, where we paid every man 300 crowns, which is seven shillings [and] six pence a piece of current English money.

Among that people called the Tatarians, I noted specially this one thing: the children being new born, do never open their eyes until they be nine days and nine nights old. Thus being ransomed as is aforesaid, I returned home into England, where having stayed some small time, I went again into Russia..., with 30 sail of ships more in our company, at which time Her Majesty's ship called the *Willoughby* was our Admiral, and the *Harry*, pertaining to the Company of the Merchants was our Vice Admiral, Master William Barrow then being our Captain and Master.

In which our voyage we met with 5 rovers or men of war, whom we set upon, & burnt their Admiral [lead ship] and brought those ships into Mar.[3] And there the men were massacred in this manner by the Russians: First, great stakes [were] struck into the ground. And [then] they [were] spitted upon poles, as a man would put a pig upon the spit. And so seven score were handled in that manner in a very tyrannous sort. We unloaded our burden at Mar, and took in other lading for our commodities. But the ship wherein the goods were laden [which] was called the *Hart*, having sailed but 12 miles from thence, struck upon a rock, whereby the ship and goods were lost. The residue of the fleet had no harm, and all the men in our ship saved their lives by taking them into the boat of the said ship.

By means of which ship so cast away, I left all that I had, and then came again to England, and gathered a new stock, and in the *Henry* of London I went to Lewanta alias Leghorn. This ship called the *Henry*, had been sold before to Doctor Hector and other Italian merchants, which was unknown unto us. So that, at our coming to Leghorn, the ship was seized on by the factors of those who were the owners thereof; and by them laden with merchandise to Alexandria. In which ship myself was master gunner.

[Captured, and enslaved, by Turks]

But here Fortune began to lower on me again, and turn her wheel in such sort against me, as that I was soon after brought to live in greater slavery, than ever I did before. For we, having safely arrived at Alexandria, discharged our burden and freighted our ship with great store of that country's commodities. And returning back to Leghorn, suddenly, in the way, we met with 50 sail of the Turk's galleys. Which galleys we fought two days and nights and made great slaughter amongst their men; we being, in all, but threescore men very weak for such multitude. And having lost 50 of our 60 men, faintness constrained us to yield unto them, by reason we wanted wind to help our selves, and the calm was so great a help unto them, as there was no way for us to escape. Thus did the Turks take the ship and goods, and in the same found 10 of us living, whom they took prisoners and presently stripped us naked, and gave us 100 blows apiece with an ore pissle, for presuming to fight against them.

Then were we sent to Constantinople, and committed unto the galleys, where we continued the space of 5 years. The manner of our usage there was thus. First, we were shaven head and face, and then a shirt of cotton and breeches of the same were put upon us, our legs and feet left naked. And by one of the feet is each slave chained with a great chain to the galley, and our hands fastened with a pair of manacles. The food which I and others ate, was very black, far worse than horse bread. And our drink was stinking water, unless it was when we come to the places where we took in fresh sweet water. At which time we supposed our diet to be very dainty. Thus, as I said before, I remained 5 years in this miserable estate, wonderfully beaten and misused every day. There have I seen of my fellows when they have been so weak as they could not row by reason of sickness and faintness; where the Turks laid upon them as on horses, and beat them in such sort, as oft times they died. And then [they] threw them into the sea.

[Master gunner in the Turkish forces]

Thus, seeing myself still to continue in this miserable state, I was constrained, for want of victuals, to discover myself, and to show them that I had good skills in [the] gunner's art; which I thought would have been greatly esteemed at the Turk's hand. But then, for the same I was more narrowly looked unto; yet somehow better esteemed of them than I was before. Nor long after, the Turk made wars against the Persians, and gathered 700,000 men together; and these were conducted by his Chief Pashas into Persia. At which time (because I had skill in artillery) I was chosen forth of the galleys to go with the army into Persia, and there to do the Turk's service in the field: with whom I travelled on foot. But in our going thither, there died so many of our army (by means of great sickness, disdiet, and want of victuals: about the number of 300,000), so that when we came into Persia we were 400,000 strong in the field. There we rested ourselves one month. By which time, we having hardened ourselves, gave a fierce assault upon the Persians: where the Turk's side got the worst, and lost 60,000 men. Then the general over the Turk's army...sent us as many soldiers more as made 500,000 strong. There we stayed a long time, making wars against the Persians, and the great city of Damascus; where the Turk little prevailed. For, if the Turk were as politic as he is strong of power, the Persians were not [would not be] able to resist him.

[Egypt, Goa]

Thus, leaving the Turk's army in Persia, we came through Damascus to our city, called the Great Cairo: which city is miles in compass, and is the greatest city in the world. It stands upon the river Nile. And in the said city there are 12,000 churches, which they term 'mosques'. This city at all times keeps 40,000 men continually in soldier's pay; and are ready, at one hour's warning, to serve under the Great Turk. There we stayed to see the cutting or parting of the river Nile, which is done once every year, upon the 25th August. This city stands in the land of Egypt, and is under the government of the Great Turk. And there is a king over the said city, who is called the king of Great Cairo, and is the Viceroy or Lieutenant to the Great Turk. And he is then present at the cutting of this river of Nile. At which time there is great triumph, and every town and country round about, to the value of a 1000 miles send gifts and presents to the king of the Great Cairo, in consideration of the water which comes to them from that river of Nile, by means of the cutting of it, which is but once every year.

It is therefore to be known, that in the land of Egypt it rains not at all, and all the ground throughout the land of Egypt is constantly watered by the water which, upon the 25th day of August is turned into the countries round about, by means of the wonderful growing and swelling of the water upright, without any stay at all: on the one side thereof to a height of a huge mountain, which begins to increase [by] the 15th day of August, and by the 25th is at its highest. On which day it is cut by the dividing of two pillars of a strange sort, near to the city of Cairo, and so turned off as from a great mountain unto the land of Egypt in subjection to himself, and might, if he would, dismiss them clean from having any water at all.

From thence I went with the Turk's power, and under his conduction, to the land of Jewry; and from thence to the city of Jerusalem, where part of the Old Temple is yet standing, and many monuments of great antiquity, as herein shall be showed. In the land of Syria, there is a river that no Jew can get or catch any fish in at all. And yet, in the same river there is great store of fish like unto salmon trout. But let a Christian or a Turk come thither, and fish for them, and either of them shall catch them in great abundance, if they do but put their hand into the water with a little bread, and an hundred will be about his hand.

Thus having seen a number of rare and most wonderful things, we went to the city of Goa, which is the head and chief city in all the East Indies. There we gave battle against the Christians that keep the said city, who are Portuguese, because the town appertains to the King of Portugal. There we gave battle and lost three score thousand of the Great Turk's men; and yet could not obtain it. Nevertheless the Great Turk's Lieutenant or General, with his power, took a place called Hormoz, where they had great store of treasure...

Thus, being chief master gunner in these Turkish wars, I was sent for again, by commandment of the Turk to Damascus, where I stayed all that winter with 20,000 men, and from thence made provision to make wars against the land of Prester John, who is, by profession, a Christian. In this land of Prester John, when it does rain, it continues, at the least, one whole month. And in Cairo, there is a plague once in every seventh year, which comes with such a fierceness, that the most part of all the people there do die of the said plague; and people in great numbers lose their eyesight with the vapours and great heat which comes from the ground.

I remember one battle which the Admiral of the Great Turk, named Ali Pasha, made with three score galleys, and seized upon a town where the said Ali Pasha was himself born named Trybusas, which is in the confines of Calabria, and under the government of the King of Spain. At which town he landed his army an hour before day, thinking to have taken it by treason; and thereupon, in great fury, scaled the walls with Ladders. But the watch betrayed us and on a sudden cried 'Arm!', 'Arm!' Which was soon done; for every man took him to his tools and weapons of defence. But it is worthy of memory to see how the women of that town did ply themselves with their weapons, making a great massacre upon our men, and murdered 500. of them in such speedy and furious sort as is wonderful. We needed not to have feared their men at all, had not the women been our greatest overthrow. At which time I myself was master gunner of the Admiral's galley. Yet chained grievously, and beaten naked with a Turkish sword flatling for not shooting where they would have me, and where I could not shoot.

It is but a few years since that, in the city of Constantinople, there happened a great plague, where there died in five months' space, 700,000 persons; at which time Master Harborne[4] Ambassador to the Turkey company was there, and lost sundry of his servants.

[The land of 'Prester John']

From Damascus we went into the land of Prester John who is a Christian and is called Chretien de Ceinture: that is, the Christian of the Girdle. Against this Prester John I went with the Turk's power, and was then their master gunner in the field. The number of Turkish soldiers sent thither, was 500,000 men; who went thither by land, and pitched themselves in battle array at Saran, near to the place where the son of Prester John keeps his Court. There Prester John, with his power, slew of the Turks to the number of 50,000: only by policy of draw-bridges to let forth water, made as secret sluices for that purpose, in which water so many Turks perished. The next day following, the Turk's power did encompass Prester John's son and take him prisoner, and sent him for a present to the Great Turk's Court, then being at Constantinople. But soon after, Prester John himself made an agreement between the Great Turk and his son that the one should not demand tribute of the other; and so his son was released and sent home again. It is to be understood that the Great Turk paid tribute unto Prester John before the time of these wars, and the Turk demanded a tribute of Prester John's son; which had been paid unto him many years before. Whereupon Prester John, when his son was taken prisoner, gave consent to forgive the one tribute for the other, and thereby they were set at liberty, the one from the other.

This Prester John of whom I spoke before, is a king of great power, and keeps a very bountiful Court, after the fashion of that country; and has every day, to serve him at his table, 60 kings, wearing leaden crowns on their heads. And these serve in the meat unto Prester John's table. And continually the first dish of meat set upon his table is a dead man's skull, clean picked and laid in black earth, putting him in mind that he is but earth and must die. These 60 kings are all his viceroys in several places, and they have their deputies to supply their rooms. And these kings live continually in Prester John's Court, and go no further than [that] they may be still attendant upon him without leave from their Emperor, Prester John.

In the Court of Prester John, there is a wild man; and another in the high street of Constantinople, whose allowance is every day a quarter of raw mutton. And when any man dies for some notorious offence, then are they allowed every day a quarter of men's flesh. These wild men are chained fast to a post every day: the one in Prester John's Court, and the other in the high street of Constantinople, each of them having a mantle cast about their shoulders. And all over their bodies they have wonderfully long hair. They are chained fast by the neck, and will speedily devour any man who comes in their reach.

There is a beast in the Court of Prester John, called 'Arians', having four heads. They are in shape like a wild cat, and are of the height of a mastiff cur. In his Court also there is owls called Pharaoh's Fowls whose feathers are very beautiful to be worn. These fowls are as big as a turkey; their flesh is very sweet, and their feathers are of all manner of colours. There are swans in that place, which are as large again as the swans of England; and their feathers are as blew as any blew cloth. I have seen in a place like a park adjoining unto Prester John's Court, three score and seventeen unicorns and elephants, all alive at one time. And they were so tame that I have played with them as one would play with young lambs.

The elephants, together with many other wild and tame beasts, will not drink of any water until the unicorns do begin thereof. These unicorns, when they come to drink of any river, they put in their horn, which is blackish and but short. And forth of that water will rise a great scum, and thereby cleanse all the filth and corruption that is within the same. And this horn, grated to powder in drink, is a present remedy against any manner of poison. When Prester John is served at his table, there is no salt at all set on in any saltcellar as in other places, but a loaf of bread is cut across, and then two knives are laid across upon the loaf, and some salt put upon the blades of the knives. And no more.

Being thus in the land of Prester John, I travelled within 18 degrees of the sun, every degree being in distance three score miles. I was at the Red Sea at the place where Moses made passage, with his wand, for the Children of Israel,[5] where I saw a ship called the *Grand Maria*....And against this ship three score galleys and ships have fought at one time and can not conquer her. And this ship is under the government of the Great Turk.[6] This ship is built almost flat, and is of such burden that she will carry in her 10,000 fighting men, with their furniture.

I have been in the Courts of the great Patriarchs, the first whereof is kept at Jerusalem, the second at Cairo, and the third is at Constantinople. These have their Courts in very stately sort, and attended on by none but priests. When I was at Jerusalem I saw the Sepulchre wherein it is said that Christ was buried. It is, as it were, in a vault, and has seven doors and seven rows of marble steps or stairs to go down into the same. And then, at the bottom of the stairs there is a fair chapel, with an altar, and a lamp burning continually day and night before it. And the grave is full of white earth, as white as chalk, and a tomb of the same earth made and laid upon stone; whereon are sundry letters written. But I could not read them. Upon the left hand of which chapel is a rack of stone, of a blackish colour, being all of that stone that we commonly call the lodestone, which is of this nature: that it will draw unto it: this stone is the principal instrument which mariners and sailors do use for directing of their compass at the sea.[7]

The Great Turk has some profit coming by the keeping of this monument, and has therefore built, at his own charge, a hospital within Jerusalem, which his janisarries keep.

And this hospital is to receive all Pilgrims and travellers to lodge in whensoever they come. And all who come to see the Sepulchre pay ten crowns apiece; whereof the Turk has but one, and the rest goes to the Church. And so they may stay there for as long as they list to lodge in that new Hospital, and have lodging, bread, victuals and water so long as they will remain there. But no wine. Such as come there as pilgrims have no beds at all, but lie upon the ground on Turkey carpets. And before the Sepulchre of Christ Mass is said every day. And none may say the Mass there, but a man who is a pure virgin. There was one who died when I was there, who daily said and sung the Mass before the Sepulchre. And he was a 130 years of age before his death. And now another is in his room. But whether the old man who is dead, or this [one] who is now in his place to sing and say the said Mass, were pure Virgins I know not. But sure I dare not swear for them, for they are men, and flesh and blood as other [men] are.

[Imprisoned in Constantinople; attempt at escape]

After that I had thus long travelled and spent my time in the wars and affairs of the Great Turk, I was returned again to Constantinople, where, at my arrival, a penny loaf of English sterling money was worth a crown of gold. Such was the sickness, misery, and dearth then upon that city. And happy was he who could so get bread to eat. Nevertheless, because I was a Christian, and because the Turk had no cause presently to use me in my office of gunnership, I was there imprisoned, where I found 2000 Christians pinned up in stone walls locked fast in iron chains, grievously pinched with extreme penury, and such that wished death rather then in such misery to live. Amongst these was I placed, and took part with them accordingly, grieving at my hard hap that the wars had not ended me before I came thither. Thus I remained there with the rest, guarded and daily watched, that we could stir no manner of way. There we were suffered to work upon any manner of trade or occupation wherein we were any way expert. And what we did or made, we sold to the Turks. And they gave us money for the same. And thus were we suffered to work until it was time to go and gather snow, which is there used yearly, of custom, to be gathered. For the Turk has great sums of money paid him for the said snow, which is gathered and sold to his subjects for a penny the pound, which pound, is two pound and a half English. And this snow they use only to cool their drink in the summer season. And no man may sell any snow until the Turk hath sold all his.

Thus, living in this slavish life as is before said, a long time, several of us complotted and hammered in our heads how we might procure our releasement. Whereupon I attempted, with the consent of 500 Christians, fellow slaves with myself, to break a wall of 14 foot broad, made of earth, lime, and sand, which we greatly moistened with strong vinegar, so that the wall being made moist therewith through the help of a spike of iron. [The] 500 of us had almost escaped out of prison, but look: what shall be, shall be! And what God will have, shall come to pass, and no more. As appeared by us. For we, having made means for our speedy flight, as we were issuing forth, we were betrayed by the barking of a dog, which caused the Turks to arise. And they, taking us with the manner, stopped us from flying away and gave us, in recompense of our pains taking therein, 700 blows apiece with a bull's pissle upon the naked skin, viz. 300 on the belly, and 400 on the back.

[Release; and journey back to England]

Thus lying still prisoner in the Turk's dungeons, it pleased God to send thither for the releasement of me and others, a worthy gentleman of this land, named Master Harborne Ambassador there for the Company of Merchants; who, to the great honour of England did behave himself wonderfully wisely, and was a special means for the releasement of me and sundry other English captives, who were set at liberty soon after the death of the Great Pasha. Thus, by the means of the said Master Harborne, I was set free from thraldom, and by him sent into England, where I arrived on the first of May 1589.

Whilst I was remaining prisoner in Turkey, and kept in such slavish manner as is before rehearsed, the Great Turk had his son circumcised, which was the fore-skin of his privy members was taken off. At which time there was great triumphs and fee liberty proclaimed for a 100 days' space, that any nobleman, gentleman, traveller, Christian, or other, might freely (without being molested) come and see the triumphs there used, which were wonderful. I myself was then constrained to make a cunning piece of firework, framed in form like to the Ark of Noah, being 24 yards high, and 8 yards broad, wherein were placed 40 men drawn on firewheels. Yet no man seen, but seemed to go along, as though it were newly drawn by two fiery Dragons: in which show or Ark there was 12,000 several pieces of fireworks.

At the same time that I was released, there were set at liberty about 20 Englishmen, whereof I was one of the last. Some of them are, at this present, in England. Myself and others were released by means of Her Majesty's favourable letters sent to Great Turk, brought by the aforesaid Master Harborne, some by the ransom money gathered at sundry times by the merchants in the City of London, for that Godly purpose; of which, some of their names that were released were these: Hammond Pan; John Beere; John Band; Andrew Pullins; Edward Buggin; and others.

Here may the bountiful citizens of London see (as in a glass) the fruits of their liberality and charitable devotion given at several times in the year towards the releasement of poor captives, such as are constrained to abide most wild and grievous tortures; especially the torture and torment of conscience which grieved me and all true Christians to the very soul. For the Turk, by all means possible, would still persuade me and other my fellow Christians while I was there the time of 13 years, to forsake Christ, to deny him, and to believe in their God Muhammad. Which, if I would have done, I might have had wonderful preferment of the Turk, and have lived in as great felicity as any lord in the country. But I utterly denied their request, though by them grievously beaten naked for my labour, and reviled in most detestable sort, calling me dog, devil, hellhound, and such like names. But I give God thanks, [that] He gave me strength to abide with patience these crosses. And though I were but a simple man, void of all learning, yet still I had in remembrance that Christ died for me, as appears in the Holy Scriptures, and that Christ therein said: 'he that denies me before men, I will deny him before my Father which is in heaven'. And again he said: 'whosoever believes in me shall be saved and have life everlasting'. This comfort made me resolute [resolve] that I would rather suffer all the torments of death in the world, than to deny my Saviour and Redeemer Christ Jesus.

After my free liberty granted in Turkey, I, intending my journey towards England, came by land to Venice, where I met at Padua 30 Englishmen students. I met also with an Englishman who lived in the state of a friar. He brought me before the High Bishop, where I was accused for an heretic, and he brought in two false witnesses to be sworn against me (having before known me in Turkey). Nevertheless, I disproved his witnesses, and they were found forsworn men. Then was I set at liberty, and constrained to give 15 crowns towards the finishing of Our Lady's shrine at Padua, and my accuser and his witnesses were punished. From thence I came to the Duke of Ferrara, where I was well entertained and liberally rewarded with a horse and 25 crowns for the sake of the Queen's Majesty of England.

From then, with my passport, I came to Bologna in Italy, where I met with a popish Bishop, being an Englishman who showed me great friendship. He is called Doctor Poole. From thence to Florence. There I met with an English gentleman named Master John Stanley. And from there I went to Rome. There I was [for] 19 days in trouble with the Pope and the English Cardinal, Doctor Allen, a notable arch Papist, where I was often examined. But finding nothing by me, they let me pass. And understanding that I had been a captive a long time in Turkey, the Pope gave me his blessing, and 25 crowns. And before I went out of Rome, I was again taken by the English College, and put there in the holy house three days, with a fool's coat on my back, half blue, half yellow, and a cockscomb with three bells on my head. From where I was helped, by means of an Englishman I found there and presented my petition and cause to the Pope. Who again set me at liberty. From thence I departed to Naples, where I met with a Genovese, who apprehended me and brought me there before the Viceroy, saying [that] I was a man of great knowledge and an English spy. Then I was committed to a dark dungeon [for] 15 days, [during] which time they secretly made enquiry where I had been before, what my words and behaviour had been while I was there. But they could find nothing by me.

Thrice had I the strappado, hoisted up backward with my hands bound behind me; which struck all the joints in my arms out of joint, where a physician was ready to set my arms in joint again. Presently, I was also constrained to drink salt water and quicklime, and then a fine lawn or calico thrust down my throat and plucked up again, ready to pluck my heart out of my belly: all to make me confess that I was an English spy. After this there were four bare horses prepared to quarter me, and I was still threatened to die, except I would confess some thing to my harm.

Thus, seven months I endured in this misery. And yet they could find no cause against me. Then I wrote to the Viceroy to do me justice. He wrote to the King of Spain, to know what should be done with me. Whereupon the King of Spain wrote that I should be employed in a gunner's room. Then was I entertained, and had 35 crowns a month, and had the King's patent sealed for the same. And then, understanding that 3 ships were coming towards England, I departed and fled from thence with them to my native country, in the *Grace*, of London, by the help of one Nicholas Nottingham Master thereof. Thus came I into England with great joy and heart's delight, both to myself and all my acquaintances.

The report in Rome, Naples, and all over Italy, in my travel which was at such time as the Spaniards came to invade England.[8] After I had been released from my imprisonment, as I passed through the streets, the people of those parts asked me how I durst acknowledge myself to be an Englishman, and thereupon, to taunt me, said, that England was taken by the Spaniards, and that the Queen of England (whom God long preserve) was taken prisoner, and was coming towards Rome to do penance and that Her Highness was brought thither, through deserts, moist, hilly and foul places; and [that] where plain ground was, [there] holes and hollow trenches had been dug in the way of Her Majesty's passage, to the intent that she might have gone up to the mid leg in ooze or mire. With

45

these speeches they checked me, and I said that I trusted [that] God doubtless would defend my Prince better, then to deliver her into the hands of her enemies.[9] Wherefore they did greatly revile me....

Thus have you heard the manner of my tedious and grievous travel, my misery, slavery, and captivity, which I suffered therein; the manner of some old monuments; and the customs of such as dwell in foreign nations far off, and in places where Our Saviour and His Apostles were resident, and preached upon the earth; my services done under the Great Turk in Persia, Tataria, Greece, and places of service. I omit herein my service at the taking of Tunis, and what I did in the *Royal* under Don John de Austurias;[10] and many other things which I could here discover unto you, only let this suffice, that I shall be glad, and do daily desire that I may be employed in some such service as may be profitable to my Prince and country.

NOTES

1   Captain Anthony Jenkinson made three trips to Russia. The first (1557–60) took in a visit to Bokhara (see Hakluyt, 1589: 310–38); the second (1561–4) included a visit to Persia (see Hakluyt 338–52); for the third (1566–8), see Hakluyt 372 for 'A very briefe remembrance of a voyage made by M[aster] Anthony Jenkinson from London to Moscovia, sent from the Queenes Maiestie to the Emperour, in the yeere 1566'. Little is known about Jenkinson. See E. Delmar Morgan and C. D. Coote, *Early English Voyages and Travels in Russia and Persia*, London: Hakluyt Society, 1886.
2   The Tatars, who had first burnt Moscow in 1381, did so again in May 1571. Hakluyt prints two contemporary accounts of the event: (a) a letter from Richard Uscombe to Henry Lane; (b) by Giles Fletcher, Elizabeth's Ambassador to the Russian Emperor, under the title 'Of the Russe Common Wealth'.
3   Not known.
4   Harborne: see Chapter 2.
5   Exodus 14: 21–31.
6   It is important to bear in mind the contribution made by the Turkish Navy. See, especially, Palmira Brummett, *Ottoman Seapower and Levantine Diplomacy in the Age of Discovery*, New York, 1994.
7   Lodestone: stone that has magnetic properties.
8   Spaniards came to invade England: Spanish Armada, 1588.
9   'defend my *Prince*...deliver *her*' is a fascinating rendition as well as corroboration of the construction of the notion of English monarchy as male. See e.g. Louis Adrian Montrose, ' "Shaping Fantasies": Figurations of Gender and Power in Elizabethan culture', *Representations* 2: Spring, 1983; Carole Levin, *The Heart and Stomach of a King: Elizabeth I and the Politics of Sex and Power*, Philadelphia: University of Pennsylvania Press, 1994; Allison Heisch, 'Queen Elizabeth and the Persistence of Patriarchy', *Feminist Review* 4: 47–53, 1980; Marie Axton, *The Queen's Two Bodies. Drama and the Elizabethan Succession*, London: Royal Historical Society, 1977.
10   Having already managed to wrest the Citadel from the Turks, the Spanish (under Don John) retook the town of Tunis from the Turks in October 1572.

OTHER EDITIONS

The popularity of the text might be measured by the appearance of three separate editions, all apparently in the same year. The first, 'Printed by Ralph Blower, for Thomas Pavier, & are to be sold at his shop in Corn-hill, at the signe of the Cat and Parrats, over against Popeshead alley, near the Royal Exchange', is dated 1590; another, 'Printed by A.J. for William Barely', is undated; finally, the one used here, 'Newly Enlarged and Corrected', printed for William Wright, also bears the date 1590. The 'Corrected' here presumably refers to the substitution of 300,000 for 30,000 and 500,000 for 50,000 in the section 'Master Gunner in the Turkish forces'. The only other edition is by Edward Arber in the 'English Reprints' series he edited (London: Alex Murray & Son, 1868).

2

WILLIAM HARBORNE

'The voyage of the *Susan* of London to Constantinople, wherein the Worshipfull Master William Harborne was sent Ambassador unto Sultan Murad Khan, the Great Turk; with whom he continued as Her Majesty's Ligier [resident Ambassador] almost six years.'
In Richard Hakluyt, *The Principall Navigations, Voiages and Discoveries of the English Nation*, 1598, Vol. 2, 168–71.

BIOGRAPHY

William Harborne (d. 1617) is best known as being the very first English Ambassador to Turkey (1582–8), though that was not the first time he had visited there. Because of Harborne's close connections to Principal Secretary Thomas Wilson and to Lord Burghley, as well as a record of an earlier visit to Turkey (1577), Susan Skilliter is of the opinion that Harborne was (before he became ambassador) a secret agent. Certainly, the documentary material (especially from Turkish sources) concerning the negotiations that led up to the granting of trading privileges which resulted in the formation of the Turkey Company (1579) owed a great deal to Harborne's participation. Clearly, one letter from Thomas Wilson to Harborne (see Introduction, note 17) might be read as corroboration. Much more importantly, two letters from Elizabeth (see Introduction, note 17) offer fascinating insights into the ideological codes that underpinned the processes of the establishment of Anglo-Turkish relations in the moment of their inception.

After various adventures en route the party left London on 14 November 1582, bound for Constantinople. Contrary winds kept them off the Isle of Wight for two months. Harborne came aboard on 14 January 1583.

* * *

...when the ship came against the Great Turk's palace, we shot off all our ordnance to the number of four and thirty pieces. Then our Ambassador landed. And then we discharged four and twenty pieces; which was received by more than fifty or threescore men on horseback. The 9th April he presented the Great Pasha with 6 cloths, 4 cans of silver doubly gilt, and one piece of fine Holland.[1] And to 3 other Pashas (that is to say, the second Pasha, who is a gelded man, and his name is Muhammad Pasha; to the third, who married the Great Turk's sister; and to the fourth, whom they called Abraham Pasha) to every one of these he gave 4 cloths.

48

Now, before the Great Pasha, and Abraham Pasha, at their return from the Court (and, we think, at other times; but at that time, for certain) there came a man in manner of a Fool, who gave a great shout 3 or 4 times, crying very hollowly. The place rebounded with the sound. And this man, they say, is a Prophet of Muhammad: his arms and legs naked, on his feet he wore wooden pattens of two sorts; in his hand a flag or streamer set on a short spear painted. He carried a mat, and bottles and other trumpery, at his back, and sometimes under his arm. On his head he had a cap of white camel's hair; flat, like a helmet; written about with letters. And above his head, a linen roll. There were other serving-men with the said Pashas, with red attire on their heads: much like French hoods, but the long flap somewhat smaller towards the end; with scuffs, or plates of metal like unto the shape of an ancient arming sword, standing on their foreheads like other janisarries.

These Pashas entertained us as follows. First, they brought us into a hall; there to stand on one side, and our Ambassador and gentlemen on the other side, who sat down on a bench covered with carpets, the Ambassador in the middle. On his left sat our gentlemen; and on his right, the Turks, next to the door where their master went in and out. The common sort of Turks stayed in the courtyard, not suffered to come near us. When our Ambassador had sat half an hour, the Pashas (who sat by themselves in an inner small room) sent for him; to whom the Ambassador and his gentlemen went. They all kissed his hand, and presently returned (the Ambassador only excepted, who stayed there, and a Turk chaus² with him). With the Ambassador and his men went in also many of our men as there were presents to carry in; but these neither kissed his hand, nor tarried.

After this I went to visit the Church of Santa Sophia, which was the chief church when it was the Christians', and now is the chief see and church of primacy of this Turk present. Before I entered I was willed to put off my shoes, to the end [that] I should not profane their church, I being a Christian. The pillars on both sides of the church are very costly and rich; their pulpits seemly and handsome: two are common to preach in, the third reserved only for their Paschal. The ground is covered with mats, and the walls hung with tapestries. They also have lamps in their churches: one, in the middle of the church, of excessive greatness; and another, in another part of the church, of clean gold, or double gilded, fully as big as a barrel. Round about the church there is a galley built upon rich and stately pillars.

That day I was in both the chapels, in one of which lies the Turk's father and five of his sons, right costly, with their turbans very white and clean: shifted (as they say) every Friday: They are not on their heads, but stand on moulds made for that purpose. At the ends, over and above their tombs, are belts, like girdles, beset with jewels. In the other chapel are four others of his sons, and one daughter, in like order. In the first chapel is a thing four foot high, covered with green, beset with mother of pearl very richly. This is a relic of Muhammad, and stands on the left side of the head of the Great Turk's tomb.

These chapels have their floors covered, and their walls hung with tapestry of great price. I could value the coverings and hangings in one of the chapels at no less than £500 (besides their lamps, hanging richly gilded). These chapels have their roofs curiously wrought with rich stone, and gilded. And there lie the books of their laws for every man to read.

The 11ᵗʰ day of April the ship came to the key of the custom-house. The 16ᵗʰ the Ambassador and we, his men, went to the Captain Pasha, who is Admiral of the Seas.... He would not receive us into his house, but into his galley, to deliver our present; which was as follows: 4 pieces of cloth; and 2 silver pots, gilt and engraved. The poop or stern of his galley was gilded within and without, and under his feet. And where he sat was all covered with rich tapestry. Our Ambassador and his gentlemen kissed his hand; and then the gentlemen were commanded out, and our Ambassador sat down by him on his left hand, and the chaus stood before him. Our men might walk in the galley, fore and aft. Some of us tarried; and some went out again. The galley had 7 pieces of brass in her prow, small and great. She had 30 banks or oars on either side; and at every bank or oar sat 7 men to row.

The 18th day the ship went from the Key. The 21st the Admiral took his leave of the Great Turk, being bound to the sea with 36 galleys, very fairly beautified with gilding and painting, and beset with streamers; all the which galleys discharged their ordnance. And we, for his farewell, gave him 20 pieces. Then we went to his house with his galleys; and the 22nd he went to sea, and the castle that stands in the water gave him 14 or 16 pieces. And when he came [over] against the Turk's Seraglio, he shot off all his calivers[3] and his great pieces; and so he went his way. The 24th our Ambassador went to the Court, whose entertainment with the order thereof, follows.

When we came first on land there was way made for us by 2 or 3 pashas and several chauses on horseback, with their men on foot, to accompany our Ambassador to the Court. Also they brought horses for him and his gentlemen to ride; which were very richly furnished. And on the way there met with us other chauses to accompany us to the Court. When we came there, we passed through two gates. At the second gate there stood very many men with horses attending on their masters. When we came within that gate we were within a very fair courtyard, in compass twice as big as St. Paul's churchyard.[4] On the right of the said court was a fair gallery like an alley; and within it were placed rails and such other provision. On the left side was the like. Half the court over, it was divided into two parts; the innermost fairer than the other. The other part of that side is the place where the Council usually sits. And at the inner end there is a fair place to sit in, much like unto that place in St. Paul's churchyard where the Saint and his brethren used to sit. Thither was our Ambassador brought, and sat in place. Within the said place is another like open room, where he ate.

As soon as we came in, we were placed in the innermost alley of the second room, on the left side of the Court, which was spread with carpets on the ground fourscore or fourscore and ten foot long, with a 150 several dishes set thereon: that is to say, mutton boiled and roasted; rice diversely dressed; fritters of the finest fashion; and dishes daintily dight[5] with pretty pap; with infinite others. I know not how to express them. We had also roasted hens, with sundry sorts of fowls, to me unknown. The gentlemen and we sat down on the ground, for it is their manner so to feed. There were also Greeks and others set to furnish out the room. Our drink was made with rosewater and sugar and spices brewed together. Those who served us with it had a great bag tied over their shoulders, with a broad belt like an arming belt, full of plates of copper and gilt, with part of the said bag under his arm, and the mouth in his hand. Then, he had a device to let it out when he would into cups, when we called for a drink.

The Ambassador, when he had eaten, passed by us, with the chauses aforesaid, and sat himself down in an inner room. This place where he sat was against the gate where we came in, and hard by the Council Chamber end, somewhat on the left side of the Court. This was the east end of the Court, for we came in at the west. All this time our presents stood by us until we had dined; and dinner, once ended, this was their order of taking up the dishes. Certain were called in, like those of the Black Guard in the Court of England.

The Turks call them 'Moglans'. These came in like rude and ravening mastiffs, without order or fashion, and made clean riddance. For he whose hungry eye one dish could not fill turned two, one into the other. And thus, even on the sudden, was made a clear riddance of all.

Then came certain chauses and brought our gentlemen to sit with the Ambassador. Immediately came officers and appointed janisarries to bear from us our presents; who carried them on the right side of the Court, and set them hard by the door of the Privy Chamber, as we call it. There all things stood for the space of an hour. Thus the Ambassador and his gentlemen sat still. And to the southward of them was a door whereas the Great Turk himself went in and out at. And on the south side of that door sat, on a bench, all his chief lords and gentlemen. And on the north of the west gate stood his guard, in number (as I guess them) a 1000 men. These men have on their heads round caps of metal like scusses, but sharp in the top. In this they have a bunch of ostrich feathers, as big as a brush, with the corner or edge forward. At the lower end of these feathers there was a smaller feather, like those that are commonly worn here.

Some of his guard had small staves, and most of them were weaponed with bows and arrows. Here they waited, during our abode at the Court, to guard their Lord. After the Ambassador, with his gentlemen, had sat for an hour and more, there came 3 or 4 chauses and brought them into the Great Turk's presence. At the Privy Chamber door, two noblemen took the Ambassador by each arm one, and put their fingers within his sleeves, and so brought him to the Great Turk, where he sumptuously sat alone. He kissed his hand and stood by until all the gentlemen were brought before him in like manner, one by one; and led backwards again, his face towards the Turk. For they might neither tarry nor turn their backs. And in like manner returned the Ambassador. The salutation that the noblemen did, was taking them by the hands.

All this time they trod on cloth of gold. Most of the noblemen who sat at the south side of the Privy Chamber sat, likewise, on cloth of gold. Many officers or janissaries there were with staves, who kept very good order; for no Turk whatsoever might go any further than they willed him. At our Ambassador's entering, they followed [those] who bore his presents, viz: 12 fine broadcloths; 2 pieces of fine holland; 10 pieces of plate, fine gilt; one case of candlesticks, the case whereof was very large, and 3 foot high and more; two very great cans of pots, and one lesser, one basin and ewer; two popinjays[6] of silver, the one with two heads: they were to drink in; 2 bottles with chains; 3 fair mastiffs in coats of red cloth; 3 spaniels; 2 bloodhounds; 1 common hunting hound; 2 greyhounds; 2 little dogs in coats of silk; 1 clock, valued at 500 pounds sterling. Over it was a forest of trees of silver, amongst the which were deer [being] chased by dogs, and men on horseback following; men drawing of water, others carrying mine-ore on barrows. On the top of the clock stood a castle; and on the castle, a mill. All these were of silver. And the clock was round beset with jewels.

All the time that we stayed at the Council Chamber door they were counting or weighing of money to send into Persia for his soldiers' pay. There were carried out 130 bags; and in every bag, as it was told to us, 1000 ducats, which amounted...in sterling money to fourscore and 19,000 pounds. The captain of the guard, in the meantime, went to the Great Turk; and returned again. Then they set off. The Court made obeisance to him, bowing down their heads, and their hands on their breasts. And he, in like manner, re-saluted them. He was in cloth of silver. He went and came with two or three with him, and no more. Then we went out at the first gate. And there we were commanded to stay until the captain of the guard had passed by, and all his guard with him – part before him, and part behind him; some on horseback, and some on foot, but the most part on foot, carrying on their shoulders the money before mentioned. And so we passed home.

There was in the Court, during our abode there, for the most part a fool resembling the first; but not naked as was the other at the Pasha's. But he turned himself continually, and cried; though very hollowly. The 3rd day of May I saw the Turk go to church. He had more than 250 horses before and behind him; but most before him. There were many empty horses that came in no order. Many of his nobility were in cloth of gold; but himself in white satin. There rode behind him 6 or 7 youths, 1 or 2 whereof carried water for him to drink, as they said. There were many of his guard running before him and behind him, and when he alighted, they cried (though very hollowly, as the aforesaid fools).

A letter of directions of the English Ambassador to Mr Richard Forster, appointed the first English Consul at Tripoli, in Syria

...these few words are for your remembrance when it shall please the Almighty to send you safe arrival in Tripoli in Syria. When it shall please God to send you there, you are to certify our nation at Tripoli of the certain day of your landing, to the end [that] they both may have their house in a readiness, and also meet you personally at your entrance, to accompany you, being yourself apparelled in the best manner.

The next, second, or third day after your coming, give it out that you are crazed and not well-disposed, by means of your travel at sea; during which time, you and those there are most wisely to determine in what manner you are to present yourself to the Beglerbi, Cadi,[7] and other officers; who, every one of them, are to be presented according to the order accustomed of others formerly in like office. Which, from the note of John Blanke [Jean Blanc?], formerly vice-consul in Tripoli for the French, delivered to you herewith, is very much. And therefore, if you can save anything, I pray you do it; as I doubt not but you will. They are to give you there also another janissary, according as the French have; whose outward proceedings you are to imitate and follow in such sort as you are not his inferior, according as those of our nation heretofore with him resident can inform you.

Touching your demeanour after your placing, you are to proceed wisely, considering [that] both French and Venetians will have an envious eye on you; whom, if they perceive wise and well advised, they will fear to offer you any injury. But if they shall perceive any insufficiency in you, they will not omit any occasion to harm you. They are subtle, malicious, and dissembling people; where you must always have their doings suspected, and warily walk in all your actions. Wherein, if you call for God's divine assistance, as both become every faithful Christian, the same shall in such sort direct you as He shall be glorified, yourself preserved, and both blessed; and your enemies confounded. Which, if contrary-wise you omit and forget, your enemies' malice shall be satisfied with your confusion. Which God defend, and for His mercy's sake, keep you.

Touching any outlopers[8] of our nation, who may happen to come there to traffick, you are not to suffer, but to imprison the chief officer, and suffer the rest not to traffick at any time; and together enter in such bonds as you think meet, that both they shall not deal in the Grand Seignior's dominion, and also not harm, during their voyage, any of his subjects' ships, vessels, or whatever other, but quietly depart out of the same country without any harm doing. And touching those who are there for the [Turkey] Company, you are to defend them according to your privilege and such commandments as you have had hence, in the best order as you may.

In all and every [one of] your actions, at any hand, beware of rashness and anger; after both which, repentance follows. Touching of your dealings in their affairs of merchandise, you are not to deal otherwise than in secret and council. You are carefully to foresee the change of the house, that the same may be in all honest measure to the Company's profit. And your own health, through moderation in diet, and at the best hand, and in due time to provide things needful, to save what may be. For he who buys everything, when he needs it, harms his own house, and helps the retailer. So, as it is, in my opinion, wisdom to foresee the buying of all things in their native soil, in due time, and at the first hand every year, as you are to send the Company the particular accounts of the same examples.

Touching yourself, you are to cause to be employed 50 or threescore ducats, *videlicet*: 20 in soap, and the rest in spices, whereof the most art to be pepper, whereof we spend very much. The spices are to be provided by our friend William Barratt, and the soap you [should] buy at your first arrival, because the ship lading the same commodity will cause it to mount in price. From our mansion 'Rapamat', 5th September, 1583.

NOTES

1 Fine Holland: a linen fabric.
2 Chaus: chouse; Chiaus – Turkish official messenger (*OED*).
3 Calivers: apparently (in weight) the lightest kind of portable firearm, excepting for the pistol, capable of being fired without the need to make use of a 'rest'; introduced in the sixteenth century.
4 St Paul's Cathedral referred to here was the building that had been struck by fire (1561), for which rebuilding did not begin until 1628, when Inigo Jones was placed in charge of the restoration. Severely damaged once again in the Great Fire (1666), the present-day cathedral, in the form of a Greek cross associated with the name of Christopher Wren, was not begun until 1675, and completed thirty-five years later.
5 Dight: arranged.
6 Popinjay: an early name for a parrot; here, an ornament in the shape of a parrot.
7 Beglerbi: Beglerbeg: governor of a province of the Ottoman Empire; Cadi: civil judge; usually of a town or of a village.
8 Outlopers: one who makes a run out (excursion) on a voyage.

FURTHER READING

A. L. Horniker, 'William Harborne and the beginning of Anglo-Turkish diplomatic and commercial relations', *Journal of Modern History* XIV(3): 289–316, 1942.
H. G. Rawlinson, 'The Embassy of William Harborne to Constantinople, 1583–8', *Transactions of The Royal Historical Society* IV(5): 1–27, 1922.
S. A. Skilliter, *William Harborne and the Trade with Turkey 1578–1582. A documentary study of Anglo-Ottoman relations*, Oxford: Oxford University Press for The British Academy, 1977.

3

RICHARD WRAGGE

'A description of a voiage to Constantinople and Syria, begun the 21 of
March 1593 [n.s.1594], and ended the 9 of August 1595, wherein is
shewed the order of deliuering the second present by Master Edward
Barton, Her Maiesties Ambassador, which was sent from Her Maiestie to
Sultan Murad Can, Emperour of Turkie.'
from Richard Hakluyt, *The Principall Navigations, Voyages, Traffiques and
Discoveries of the English Nation*, 1598, Vol. 2, 303–7.

The 1st September [1593] we arrived at the famous port of the Grand Seignior, where we
were not a little welcome to Master Edward Barton, until then Her Majesty's Agent, who
(with many other persons) had for many days expected the present. 5 or 6 days after the ship
arrived near the 7 Towers (which is a very strong stronghold, and so called because of so
many turrets, which it has) standing near the seaside, being the first part that we came unto.

Here the Agent appointed the Master of the *Ascension* to stay with the ship until a fit
wind and opportunity served to bring her about the Seraglio to salute the Grand Seignior
in his mosque, or church. For you shall understand that he had built one near the wall of
his Seraglio (or Palace) adjoining to the seaside; whereunto twice or thrice a week he
resorts to perform such religious rites as their law requires. Where he being within a few
days after, our ship set out in their best manner, with flags, firearms, and pennants of a
variety of coloured silks, with all the mariners, together with most of the Ambassador's
men, having the wind fair, and came within 2 cables[1] of this, his mosque, where he (to his
great content, beholding the ship, in such bravery) they discharged first 2 volleys of small
shot; and then all the great ordnance twice over, there being 27 or 28 pieces in the ship.

Which performed, he appointed the Bustangi-Pasha (or captain of the great and
spacious garden, or park) to give our men thanks; with request that [on] some other day
they would show him the like sport, where he would have the Sultana or Empress a
beholder thereof; which, few days after, as the ships were going to the Custom House,
they performed. The Grand Seignior's salutation thus ended, the Master brought the ship
to an anchor at Rapamat, near the Ambassador's house; where he, likewise, saluted him
with all his great ordnance, once over, and where he landed the Present, the delivery
whereof a time was stayed – the cause of which stay it shall neither be dishonourable to
our nation, or that worthy man, the Ambassador, to show you.

At the departure of Sinan Pasha, the Chief Vizier[2] (and our Ambassador's great friend)
towards the wars with Hungary, there was another Pasha appointed in his place; a churlish
and hard-natured man, who upon occasion of certain Genovese, escaping out of the castle

standing out towards the Euxine Sea (now called the Black Sea) there imprisoned, apprehended, and threatened to execute one of our Englishmen, called John Field, because he was taken [apprehended] thereabouts, and known, not many days before, to have brought a letter to one of them. Upon the soliciting of whose liberty there fell a jar between the Pasha (being now Chief Vizier) and our Ambassador. And in choler, he gave Her Majesty's Ambassador such words as, without sustaining some great indignity, he could not put up. Whereupon, after the arrival of the Present, he made an Arz (that is, a complaint) to the Grand Seignior against him, the manner in exhibiting thereof is thus performed.

The plaintiffs expected the Grand Seignior, going abroad from his palace, either to Saint Sophia, or his church by the seaside, whither, with a Perma (that is, one of their usual whirries[3]) they approach within some two- or threescore yards, where the plaintiff stands up, and holds his petition over his forehead, in sight of the Grand Seignior (for his church is open to the seaside) the rest sitting still in the boat; who appoints one of his dwarfs to receive them, and to bring them to him.

A dwarf, one of the Ambassador's favourites, so soon as he was discerned, beckoned him to the shore's side, took his Arz and, with speed, carried it to the Grand Seignior. Now, the effect of it was this: that unless His Highness would redress this so great an indignity which the Vizier, his slave, had offered him and Her Majesty in his person, he was purposed to detain the Present until such time as he might by letters overland from Her Majesty be certified whether she would put up [with] so great an injury as it was. Whereupon he [the Grand Seignior] presently returned answer, requesting the Ambassador, within an hour after, to go to the Diwan[4] of the Vizier, unto whom himself, of his [own] charge, [he] would send a gown of cloth of gold; and commanded him publicly to put it upon him [the Ambassador], and with kind entertainment to embrace him, in sign of reconciliation.

Whereupon, our Ambassador, returning home, took his horse, accompanied with his men, and came to the Vizier's Court, where, according to the Grand Seignior's command he, with all show of kindness, embraced the Ambassador, and with courteous speeches reconicle himself; and with his own hands put the gown of cloth of gold upon his back. Which done, he, with his attendants, returned home – to the no small admiration of all Christians who had heard of it; especially of the French and the Venetian Ambassadors, who never in the like case against the second person in the Turkish Empire durst have attempted so bold an enterprise with hope of so friendly audience, and with so speedy redress. This reconciliation with the Grand Vizier thus made, the Ambassador prepared himself for the delivery of the Present; which was the 7th of October, 1592, in this manner performed.

The *Ascension*, with her flags and streamers as aforesaid, repaired near unto the place where the Ambassador should land to go up to the Seraglio. For you must understand that all Christian Ambassadors have their dwelling in Pera, where most Christians live; from which place, unless you would go 4 or 5 miles about, you cannot by land go to Constantinople; whereas by sea it is a little broader than the Thames. Our Ambassador, likewise apparelled in a suit of cloth of silver, with an upper gown of cloth of gold, accompanied by 7 gentlemen in costly suits of satin, with 30 other of his men, very wel apparelled, and all in one livery of French russet cloth gowns, at his house took boat. At whose landing, the ship discharged all her ordnance. Where, likewise, attended 2 Pasha's, with 40 or 50 chauses, to accompany the Ambassador to the Court. And also horses for the Ambassador and his gentlemen, very richly furnished, with Turkish servants attendant, to take the horses when they should alight.

The Ambassador, thus honourably accompanied: the chauses foremost; next, his men on foot, all going by two and two; himself last, with his chaus and dragoman (or interpreter), and 4 janisarries (whom he usually entertains in his house to accompany him continuously) came to the Seraglio about an English mile from the water's side. Where first he passed a great gate into a large court (much like the space in front of Whitehall Gate[5]) where he, with his gentlemen, alighted, and left their horses. From there they passed into another stately court, being about 6 score in breadth, and some 10 score yards long, with many trees in it, where all the Court was, with great pomp, set in order to entertain our Ambassador.

Upon the right hand, all the length of the Court, was a gallery, arched over, and borne up with stone pillars; much like the Royal Exchange,[6] where stood most of his [the Grand Seignior's] guard, in ranks, from the one end to the other, in costly array; with round headpieces on their heads, of metal, and gilt over, with a great plume of feathers somewhat like a log brush, standing up before. On the left hand stood the cappagies, or porters, and the chauses.

All these courtiers being about the number 2000 (as I might well guess), most of them apparelled in cloth of gold, silver, velvet, satin, and scarlet, did together with bowing of their bodies, laying their hands upon their breasts in courteous manner of salutation, entertain the Ambassador who, likewise, passing between them, and turning himself sometimes to the right hand, and sometimes to the left, answered them with the like. As he thus passed along, certain chauses conducted him to the Divan, which is the seat of Justice; where certain days of the week the Grand Vizier, with the other Viziers, the Cadi (or Lord Chief Justice) and the Mufti (or the High Priest) sit to determine upon such causes as are brought before them; which place is upon the left side of this Great Court, whither the Ambassador, with his gentlemen, came; where he found the Vizier, thus accompanied as aforesaid; who, with great show of kindness received him.

And, after receipt of Her Majesty's letters, and conference had of the Present, of Her Majesty's health, of the state of England, and such other matters as concerned our peaceable traffick [trade] in those parts, dinner being prepared, was by many of the courtiers brought into another inner room next adjoining; which consisted of 100 dishes, or thereabouts, mostly boiled and roasted, where the Ambassador, accompanied by the Vizier, went to dinner; his gentlemen, likewise, with the rest of his men, having dinner, with the like variety prepared upon the same side of the Court, by themselves sat down to their meat, 40 or 50 chauses standing at the upper end attending on the gentlemen, to see them served in good order. Their drink was water mingled with rosewater and sugar, brought in a luthro (that is, a goatskin) which a man carries at his back; and under his arm lets it run out at a spout into cups, as men will call for it. The dinner thus, with good order brought in, and for half an hour with great sobriety and silence performed, was not so orderly taken up; for certain Moglans officers of the kitchen (like Her Majesty's Black Guard) came in disordered manner and took away the dishes. And he whose hungry eye one dish could not satisfy, turned two or three one into the other. And thus, of a sudden, was a clean riddance made of all.

The Ambassador, after dinner with his gentlemen, by certain officers were placed at the upper end upon the left side of the Court, near unto a great gate which gave entrance to a third Court, being but little, paved with stone, in the midst whereof was a little house, built of marble, as I take it, within which sat the Grand Seignior. According to whose command given, there were gowns of cloth of gold brought out of the wardrobe, and put upon the Ambassador and 7 of his Gentlemen; the Ambassador himself having two: one of gold, the other of crimson velvet; all the rest apiece. Then certain cappagies had the Present, which was in trunks there ready, delivered them by the Ambassador's men: it being 12 goodly pieces of gilt plate, 36 garments of fine English cloth of all colours, 20 garments of cloth of gold, 10 garments of satin, 6 pieces of fine holland, and certain other things of good value: all which were carried round about the Court, each man taking a piece; being, in number, very near 100 parcels; and so, 2 and 2 going round that all might see it, to the greater glory of the Present, and of him to whom it was given. They went into the innermost Court, passing by the window of that room where the Grand Seignior sat; who, as it went by to be laid up in certain rooms adjoining, took view of all. Presently, after the present, followed the Ambassador, with his gentlemen. At the gate of which stood 20 or 30 Agaus,[7] who are eunuchs.

Within the Courtyard were the Turk's dwarfs and dumbmen; being most of them youths. At the door of his room stood the Bustangi-Pasha, with another Pasha to lead the Ambassador and his followers to the Grand Seignior, who sat in a Chair of State, apparelled in a gown of cloth of silver. The floor under his feet (which part was a foot higher than the rest) was covered with a carpet of green satin, embroidered with silver, orient pearls, and great turquoises. The other part of the house was covered with a carpet of carnation satin, embroidered with gold. None were in the room with him, but a Pasha who stood next to the wall over against him, hanging down his head, and looking submissively upon the ground, as all his subjects do in his presence.

The Ambassador thus, betwixt 2 who stood at the door, being led in, either of them taking an arm, kissed his hand; and so, backward, with his face to the Turk, they brought him near unto the door again; where he stood until they had likewise done with all his Gentlemen. Which ended, the Ambassador, according as is the custom when any Present is delivered, made his 3 demands, such as he thought most expedient for Her Majesty's honour, and the peaceable trade of our nation into his dominions. Whereupon he answered, in one word: *Nolo*; which is, in Turkish, as much as It shall be done! For it is not the manner of the Turkish Emperor familiarly to confer with any Christian Ambassador, but he appoints his Vizier, in his person, to grant their demands, if they are to his liking. As to our Ambassador, he granted all his demands; and gave order that his daily allowance for his house, of money, flesh, wood, and hay, should be augmented with half as much more as it had been before.

Hereupon the Ambassador, taking his leave, departed with his Gentlemen the same he came, the whole Court saluting him, as they did at his coming in. And, coming to the second Court to take our horses, after we were mounted we stayed half an hour until the Captain of the Guard, with 2000 horsemen (at the least) passed before [us]; after whom followed 40 or 50 chauses next before the Ambassador, to accompany him to his house. And, as before at his landing, so now at his taking boat, the ship discharged all her great ordnance. Where arriving, he likewise had a great banquet prepared to entertain those who came to bring him home. The pomp and solemnity of the Present, with the day thus ended, he shortly after presented the Sultana or Empress (who, by reason that she is the mother to him who was heir to the crown imperial) is had in far greater reverence than any other of his queens or concubines. The Present sent her, in Her Majesty's name, was a jewel of Her Majesty's picture, set with some rubies and diamonds; 3 great pieces of gilt plate; 10 garments of cloth of gold; a very fine case of glass bottles, silver and gilt; with 2 pieces of fine holland. Which so gracefully she accepted, as that she sent to know of the

Ambassador what Present he thought she might return that might delight Her Majesty; who sent word that a suit of princely attire being after the Turkish fashion would, for the rareness thereof, be acceptable in England. Whereupon she sent an upper gown of cloth of gold, very rich; an under gown of cloth of silver; and a girdle of Turkey work, rich and fair, with a letter of gratification, which, for the rareness of the style (because you may be acquainted with it) I have at the end of this discourse, hereto annexed [see below]. He [the Ambassador] likewise presented…the Admiral of the Seas, with Abraham Pasha (who married the Great Turk's daughter) and all the other Viziers, with divers pieces of plate, fine English cloth, and other costly things, the particulars whereof, to avoid tediousness, I omit.

All the presents thus ended, the ship shooting 10 pieces of ordnance at the Seraglio Point, as a last farewell, departed for England [on] the 1st of November; myself continuing in Constantinople until the last day of July after.

This year, in the Spring, there was great preparation for the Hungarian Wars; and the Great Turk threatened to go himself, in person. But, like Heliogabalus[8] his affections being more serviceable unto Venus than to Mars, he stayed at home. Yet a great army was dispatched this year. Who, as they came out of Asia to go to Hungary, did so pester the streets of Constantinople for the space of 2 months in the Spring time as scarce either Christian or Jew could, without danger of losing his money, pass up and down the city. What insolencies, murders and robberies were committed (not only upon Christians, but also upon Turks) I omit to write; and I pray God in England the like may never be seen. And yet I could wish that such amongst us as have enjoyed the Gospel with such great and admirable peace and prosperity under Her Majesty's government these 40 years, and have not all this time brought forth better fruits of obedience to God, and thankfulness to Her Majesty, were there but a short time to behold the miserable condition (both of Christians and others living under such an infidel Prince) who not only are wrapped up in most palpable and gross ignorance of mind, but are clean without the means of the true knowledge of God. I doubt not but [that] the sight hereof (if they are not clean void of grace) would stir them up to more thankfulness to God, that ever they were born in so happy a time, and under so wise and goodly a Prince, professing the true religion of Christ.

A letter written by the Most High and Mighty Empress, the wife of the Grand Seignior Sultan Murad Khan, to the Queen's Majesty of England, in the year of Our Lord 1594[9]

Let the beginning of our discourse be a perfect writing in the 4 parts of the world, in the name of Him who had indifferently created such infinite numbers of creatures which has neither soul nor body; and of Him who moves the 9 Heavens, and established the earth seven times, one above another; who is Lord and King without any deputy; who has no comparison to his creation and work; and is one inestimable, worshipped without all comparison, the Most High God, the Creator, who has nothing like unto Him, according as he is described by the Prophets, to whose power no man can attain, and whose absolute perfection no man may control; and that omnipotent Creator and fellow-worker, to whose majesty all the Prophets submit themselves, among whom the greatest, and who had obtained greatest favour, the Garden of Paradise, the beam of the sun, the beloved of the Most High God is Muhammad Mustapha, to whom and to his adherents and followers be perpetual peace, to whose fragrant sepulchre all honour is performed. He who is Emperor of the 7 climates and of the 4 parts of the world, the invincible king of Greece, Hungary, Tatary, Wallachia, Russia, Turkey, Arabia, Baghdad, Caramania, Abyssinia...and always most happy, and possessor of the Crown from 12 of his ancestors, and the seed of Adam, at this present, Emperor, preserved by the Divine Providence, a king worthy of all glory and honour, Sultan Murad, whose forces the Lord God always increase, and father of him to whom the imperial crown is to descend, the paradise and wonderful tall cypress, worthy of the royal throne, and true heir of the imperial authority, most worthy Mehmet Khan, the son of Sultan Murad Khan, whose enterprises God vouchsave to accomplish, and to prolong his happy days: the behalf of whose mother this present letter is written to the Most Gracious and Most Glorious, the wisest among women, and chosen among those who triumph under the standard of Jesus Christ, the most mighty and most rich governor, and most rare among womankind in the world, the most gracious Queen of England, who follows [in] the steps of the Virgin Mary, whose end be prosperous and perfect, according to your heart's desire, I send Your Majesty so honourable and sweet a salutation of peace that all the flock of nightingales with their melody cannot attain to the like; much less this simple letter of mine. The singular love which we have conceived one toward the other is like to a garden of pleasant birds; and the Lord God vouchsave to save and keep you, and send Your Majesty an happy end, both in this world and in the world to come.

After the arrival of your honourable presents from the Court of Your Majesty, Your Highness shall understand that they came in such a season that every minute ministered occasion of long consolation by reason of the coming of Your Majesty's Ambassador to the triumphant Court of the Emperor, to our so great contentment as we could possibly wish; who brought a letter from Your Majesty which, with great honour, was presented unto us by our eunuchs: the paper whereof did smell most fragrantly of camphor and ambergris; and the ink of perfect musk; the contents whereof we have heard, very attentively, from point to point.

I think it therefore expedient that, according to our mutual satisfaction in any thing [that] may concern the countries which are subject to Your Majesty I never fail, having information given unto me, in whatsoever occasion shall be ministered, to gratify Your Majesty to my power in any reasonable and convenient matter, that all your subjects' business and affairs may have a wished and happy end. For I will always be a solicitor to the most mighty Emperor for Your Majesty's affairs, that Your Majesty at all times may be fully satisfied. Peace be to Your Majesty, and to all such as follow rightly the way of God.

NOTES

1 Cable's length: a cable is approximately 200 yards in length.
2 Vizier: in Ottoman Turkey, a high state official or minister.
3 Whirry: a rapid or sudden movement (OED); thus, probably petition being waved about, in order to attract attention.
4 Diwan: Dewan – senior Treasury official.
5 Whitehall Gate: Whitehall, now associated with government business as well as state ceremonials, but then with the palace first built by Hubert de Burgh in the thirteenth century, and rebuilt by Cardinal Wolsey in the sixteenth. Henry VIII acquired it from the cardinal and made it a royal residence. With the notable exception of the Banqueting House, it virtually all burnt down. Most of present-day Whitehall buildings are nineteenth century.

6 Royal Exchange: first built, in classical style, with a quadrangle in which merchants transacted their business, by Sir Thomas Gresham (1519?–79), during reign of Elizabeth I. Destroyed in the Great Fire and rebuilt again by Edward Jarman, it was again destroyed by fire (1838) but once again rebuilt (1842), again in Renaissance style, with an open quadrangle – though that was roofed over in 1842.

7 Agaus. Perhaps 'Aga': in the Ottoman Empire, a field officer in the army. It is to be doubted that a qualification was to be a eunuch.

8 Heliogabalus: Elagabalus (c. 205–22; Emperor of Rome under the name Marcus Aurelius Antoninus 218–22); chosen by troops in Syria, in opposition to legitimate heir, Macrinus. Associated with the cult of a local sun god, whose priest he became. That apparently shocked the Roman patricians almost as much as his decision to appoint to high office the likes of an actor, a charioteer and a butcher. Together with his mother (who made all sorts of fabricated claims for her son's high birth) he was eventually murdered by the Praetorian Guard.

9 Original in Latin, as well as the translation into English, in Hakluyt 311–12.

4

ANTHONY SHERLEY

Sir Antony Sherley His Relation of his Travels into Persia. The dangers, and distresses, which befell him in his passage, both by sea and land and his strange and unexpected deliuerances. His magnificent entertainement in Persia, his honourable employment there hence, as Embassadour to the Princes of Christendome, the cause of his disappointment therein, with his aduice to his brother, Sir Robert Sherley. Also, a true relation of the great magnificence, valour, prudence, iustice, temperance, and other manifold vertues of ABAS, now King of Persia, with his great conquests, whereby he hath inlarged his Dominions. Penned by Sir Antony Sherley, and recommended to his brother, Sir Robert Sherley, being now in prosecution of the like honourable imployment.

London. Printed for Nathaniell Butter, and Ioseph Bagfet. 1613.
Reprinted in facsimile Amsterdam: Theatrum Orbis Terrarum/
Norwood, NJ: Walter J. Johnson, Inc., Da Capo Press, 1974.

BIOGRAPHY

While biographical information about the Sherley brothers, Thomas (b. *c.* 1564), Anthony (b. *c.* 1565) and Robert (b. *c.* 1581), tends to vary either about the detail, or because details are not available, there would appear to be general agreement about the following: that they were the sons of Sir Thomas Sherley, sometime an officeholder under Elizabeth. According to one account,[1] both Thomas and Anthony were present at the Battle of Zutphen (1586) at which Sir Philip Sidney was killed. While biographers (notably those from within collateral branches of the family) refer to each of the three brothers as 'Sir', that accolade is not applicable in all cases. In that of Anthony the 'knighthood' was almost certainly a relatively minor honour awarded by Henry IV of France (1593) who had become his patron following his service there under Essex. It would appear that Elizabeth I not only instructed Anthony Sherley to return the insignia, but also to forswear all allegiance to the foreign monarch.

Anthony's account of a buccaneering expedition to the West Indies which he organized in 1595 is published in Hakluyt (1598). In that same year he commenced his journey to Persia, where he (quite evidently falsely) passed himself off as an English diplomat. Having gained some commercial privileges from the Persian monarch (though arguably not as sweeping as is claimed in his account, near the end of this section), his main claim – that he became the Persian monarch's envoy to several Christian princes in order to lobby their support for a war with Turkey – has considerable substance. Even though these efforts on behalf of Abbas were largely unsuccessful, in 1605 the Holy Roman Emperor Rudolf sent Sherley on a diplomatic mission to Morocco. His reputation went into decline after the failure of a Spanish expedition he led against the Turks in the Mediterranean (1609), after which he lived out the rest of his life, in severely reduced circumstances, in Madrid. That did not prevent at least one nineteenth-century commentator from claiming Anthony Sherley as the writer of the plays of Shakespeare.[2]

Thomas, his elder brother, having left Oxford without taking a degree, was knighted while serving in Ireland under Sir William Fitzgerald (1589) but was later imprisoned in the Marshalsea by Elizabeth because, as a courtier, instead of seeking her permission so to do, he married secretly (1591). He returned to the Netherlands (1593) as a mercenary, accompanied by 300 men – partly in order to attempt to restore the family fortune lost by his father. When that did not work, he set out with four ships (two of which were his own) on 'a voyage of mercantile adventure' for Portugal. But that, as well as a subsequent piratical adventure, with three ships and 500 soldiers, against the Turks (for which he had apparently been given permission by the Grand Duke of Tuscany), ended in disaster. Penrose (1938, pp. 35ff.) offers an excellent account, citing Venetian state documents, about the annoyance his activities created. Caught and imprisoned by the Turks, first on an island in the Mediterranean, later transferred to Istanbul, where he suffered great hardship until released after intercession on his part by the English monarch,[3] he returned to England in 1607, the date when he is heard of as arrested and placed in the Tower for interfering in the Levant trade. Released soon after, and now in dire poverty, in 1612 he is once again in gaol – this time for debt. Penrose says that this time he tried to commit suicide by taking poison. Penrose also later has him as elected as Member of Parliament for Hastings (1613) and as writing (1615) a letter to the king, pleading to be released from a debt of £7,000 (an enormous amount, in those days) he owed the Crown. Thomas died on the Isle of Wight, where he was Keeper of the Royal Park (1628), having fathered eighteen children: seven by his first wife; eleven by the second.

Robert, who had accompanied Anthony on the Persian voyage, apparently stayed on there until 1608, when he was sent by Abbas on a diplomatic mission to Spain. He returned to England in 1611, accompanied by his wife, Teresia, the daughter of a Circassian noble Christian[4] (and, reputedly, one of the first Persian women to visit England) about whom Fuller comments as follows: 'She had more of *ebony* than *ivory* in her complexion; yet amiable enough, and very valiant, a quality considerable in that sex in those countries'.[5] Following the birth of their first child in London (with Henry, Prince of Wales, as sponsor, and Queen Anne as godmother) they returned to Persia (1613), via the Cape of Good Hope. Because of difficulties with the Portuguese, they could not travel direct to Esfahan, but made a much longer journey via India (where, at Agra, they were received by Jehangir). None of the party of English and Dutch who had left Gravesend lived long enough to get to Persia, and one other Persian woman, married to an Englishman from Herefordshire, Captain Powell, died in childbirth. Robert and Teresia eventually reached Persia, travelling via Lahore and Kandahar, arriving in March 1615 and having met Thomas Coryate going in the other direction.[6]

In 1617 Robert was once again in Spain, where he stayed for almost five years, in an unsuccessful attempt to interest the Spanish king, Philip IV, in his Persian counterpart's adventures. Leaving there, with lavish presents bestowed upon husband and wife by the Spanish king, they were next heard of in Rome, where Teresia had her portrait painted by

Van Dyck, then on his first visit to Italy. In 1623 they were back in England, now living near Newmarket, and with a house in London (Fleet Street). Sherley's attempts to interest James in introducing silkworms into England foundered with the death of the king. His successor, Charles, had no interest in projects of that kind, and Sherley's relations with the English monarch were not helped by an encounter between himself and a Persian nobleman, Nakd Ali Beg, who had been sent to Charles at the instigation of the English East India Company (and who committed suicide soon after the party arrived in India). Called an impostor by the Persian, Charles decided to send Robert back to Persia, accompanied by Sir Dodmore Cotton, in order to ascertain the truth between the contending versions. On arrival at Dover, they found that the fleet had already sailed, so Robert was forced to live for another ten months in Deptford. When he finally arrived in Quasvin, it was to find that he had been totally rejected by the Persian monarch. Sherley died in 1628, and Cotton soon after him. Teresia, in the aftermath, was stripped of virtually all her possessions (except a jewel chest that had belonged to Robert). Having converted to Catholicism (1608), she managed to travel to Esfahan, where she was given refuge by the Carmelites, until she could escape, via Constantinople, to Rome (1634), where she lived until her death (1668). Robert's remains were disinterred and brought to Rome, where they were reinterred (1658) in the Church of Santa Maria della Scala.

(From the variety of texts available at that time, I have chosen extracts from Parry (1600) and Anthony Sherley (1613) – from the former because it is the first eye-witness account; from the second because it is written by the key protagonist. I might add that one reason for devoting so much space to the Sherley story is precisely because (if we are to judge by the number and variety of editions) that it would appear to have had a considerable appeal; so that, reliable or not, there is a strong suspicion that the stories told, and the positions adopted, might well have had some sort of effect upon the making of attitudes towards Turks and Persians.)

* * *

The true history of Sir Anthony Sherleys trauels into Persia, penned by himselfe

[Government]

It will not be amiss…to discourse of the Turk's whole government of those parts; which I did not behold with the eyes of a common pilgrim or merchant, who (passing only by goodly cities and territories) make their judgement upon the superficial appearance of what they see, but as a Gentleman bred up in such experience, which hath made me somewhat to penetrate into the perfection and imperfection of the form of the State, and into the good and ill orders by which it is governed. And though it be true that my weakness in judging may rather do harm than good to such as will favour me with too much belief, yet will it ever be a help of some feeling to those which know less: Our duties being to further all, and chiefly those who have most need.

The origin of the Turks many have written well of. The maintaining of their State hath been their subjects' true, and devoted adherence to their religion, without schism or faction[7] and obedience to their Princes. They increase the same religion also, which continually instigates them to the propagation of it, and the reason of their beginning, which was arms.

They, induced by a confidence in them, have ever desired to use them. And, to detain such a stirring disposition from civil dissensions, their Princes have ever, with foreign enterprises, led them to the exercise of them.

The means of the preservation of their States so great, and so many acquisted, have been the securest of any other, the Princes personally inhabiting of the most dangerous; and ruinating, and possessing by colonies actually (though in another name) the rest. So that where the dominion joins with the power of the Christian Princes; his presence keeps those parts from danger of innovation. Where he is further separated, his *Tymarri*,[8] (who are certain to whom he distributes so much land for their desert in virtue, which was their first institution; and by that tenure are bound to find him their persons, and so many horses in his wars): they, I say, having their estates solely depending upon his government, assuring him from all peril of alteration. And besides, to strengthen himself the more, he hath no only destroyed the noble blood of the countries; but in most places the cities, towns and houses, to remove from the very memory of men, by the renewing of those spectacles the apprehension of their former condition of living.

And since the government of those states were so far separated, least the mind of him to whom he gave such an administration might lift itself up to higher thoughts, he changes them continually from time to time, without any prefixed order; and gives them by the ancient form, which the virtuouser Princes enacted, but [only] to men of great merit. Besides, so dissolves all strength from their supreme authority in case of absoluteness, that without a special commission to some special cause, the Pasha had nothing to do with the soldiery; but those are ordered in their functions, by either one Agam or Sarda, the Pasha's ends directing themselves to the civil government. From the just administering of which they were learned heretofore by terrible examples not to decline; their faults being brought speedily to the Court, the emulation of which as speedily presented them to the Prince; the main point of whose estate drove him to execute rigorous remedies to confirm his awfulness and obedience, by which he did subsist among his subjects.

[Persian monarch]

And now that I am in Persia, and speak of the King's absence; since he is both one of the mightiest Princes there are, and one of the excellentest for the true virtues of a Prince, that is, or has been. And, having come to this greatness, though by right; yet through the circumstances of the time and the occasions, which then were, solely his own worthiness and virtue, made way to his right. Besides, the fashion of his government differing so much from that which we call barbarousness that it must justly serve for as great an *Idea* for a Principality as *Plato's* Commonwealth did for a government of that sort. I hold it not amiss to speak amply first of his person, the nature of his people, the distribution of his government, the administration of his justice, the condition of the bordering princes and the causes of those wars in which he was then occupied; that by the true expression of those, this discourse may pass with a more lively, and more sensible feeling.

His person then is such as a well-understanding Nature would fit for the end proposed for his being, excellently well shaped, of a most well proportioned stature, strong, and active. His colour somewhat inclined to a man-like blackness, is also more black by the sun's burning; his furniture of his mind infinitely royal, wise, valiant, liberal, temperate, merciful, and an exceeding lover of justice, embracing royally all other virtues, as far from pride and vanity as from all unprincely signs or acts; knowing his power justly what it is. And the like acknowledgement will also have from others, without any gentilious adoration; but with those respects, which are fit for the majesty of a Prince; which founded itself upon the power of his state: general love, and awful terror. His fortunes determining to make proof of his virtue, drew him (in his first years) into many dangerous extremities; which he; overcoming by his virtue, had made great use of, both in the excellent increase of his particular understanding, and general tranquillity, strength of his country and propagation of his Empire. For the laws, and customs, or both, of that kingdom, being such that, though the king has a large increase of issue, the firstborn only rules. And to avoid all kind of cause of civil dissension, the rest are not inhumanly murdered, according to the use of the Turkish government, but made blind with burning basins: and have otherwise all sort of contentment and regard fit for princes children. Shah Tamasp, king of Persia dying without issue...his brother was called blind to the kingdom; who had issue Sultan Hamzire Mirza, the eldest, who succeeded him, and this present King called Abbas.

[Sir Anthony Sherley's first salutation and speech to the King]

When we came to the King, we alighted, and kissed his stirrup. My speech was short unto him; the time being fit for no other: That the fame of his royal virtues had brought me from a far country, to be a present spectator of them; as I had been a wonderer at the report of them afar off. If there were any thing of worth in me, I presented it with myself, to His Majesty's service. Of what I was, I submitted the consideration of His Majesty's judgement; which he should make upon the length, the danger, and the experience of my voyage, only to see him, of whom I had received such magnificent and glorious relations.

[The King's answer]

The King's answer was infinitely affable: That his country, whilst I should stay there, should be freely commanded by me, as [a] gentleman who had done him infinite honour, to make such a journey for his sake. Only, [he] bade me beware that I were not deceived by rumours which had, peradventure, made him other than I should find him. It was true that God had given him both power and mind to answer to the largest reports which might be made good of him, which, if he erred in the use of, he would ask counsel of me, who must needs have much virtue in myself, that could move me to undergo so many perils and to know that of another. And that he spoke smiling, willing me to get on horseback. Which when I had done, he called...his Vizier and...his General and commanded them to take my brother and me betwixt them. And my company was disposed...amongst the rest of the King's Gentlemen of his Court.

And in that order the King entered Quasvin....He alighted with the chief of his Princes and Officers...and went into a kind of banqueting house, in which there were stairs to ascend by into a terrace, where the King sat down: and the greatest of those Princes. And we among them....While we sat there, the King called me again unto him. And when I had confirmed more words, the very same I had said before unto him, then, said he: 'You must have the proof of time to show you, either the errors, or the truth of these rumours, since you can make no judgement of what you have seen, which is but the person of a man. And the eminence which God hath given me, for any thing you know, may be more through my fortune, than my virtue. But since your pains and travel has no other aspect but to know me, we must have a more intrinsic acquaintance to perfect that knowledge. And how you will endure the fashions of my country, you can judge best your self, who is master of your own humour. This I will assure you of [that] you shall want no respect from my people, nor honour from myself.' And therewith bade me farewell, for that present, committing me and my company to...be conducted to my lodging.

[Sir Anthony Sherley's present to the King of Persia]

Next morning I sent the King a present, of six pairs of pendants of exceedingly fair emeralds, and marvellously artificially cut; and two other jewels of topazes, excellent well cut also; one cup of three pieces, set together with gold enamelled;...and a very fair ewer of crystal, covered with a kind of cutwork of silver and gilt, the shape of a dragon; (all which, I had of that noble Florentine) which His Majesty accepted very graciously. And that night I was, with my brother, invited by him to a banquet...there he had several discourses with me. Not of our apparel, [our] building, [the] beauty of our women, or such vanities; but of our proceeding in our wars, of our usual arms, of the commodity and discommodity of fortresses, of the use of artillery, and of the orders of our government. In which, though my unskilfulness was such that I knew my errors were greater than my judgement; yet I had that felicity of a good time that I gave him good satisfaction, as it seemed.

For, in my discourse, having mentioned the having of certain models of fortification in some books at my lodging, which were only left me in the spoil which was made me at Babylon [Baghdad], next day, after dinner, he came thither, with all the principallest of the Court, where he spent at least, three hours in perusing them, and not unproperly speaking of the reasons of those things himself. Next day he sent for me again, into a place which they call [a] Bazaar, like our Bourse,[9] the shops and the roof of which were so full of lights that it seemed all of a fire...in which time he took me aside, with my interpreter, and asked me, very sadly, whether I would content myself to stay with him. Not forever, for that were too great a wrong to my friends, who should lose me from their comfort, being divided so far from them. For my own fortune he would not speak of, but only this much: since I had told him I was a subject of a Prince he knew that then my fortune must also depend upon the will and favour of that Prince. And he assured himself that he was as able, and more desirous, to do me good than any. Therefore [if] I would resolve to give him that little satisfaction; he should persuade himself the more confidently that the cause of my coming was such as I [had] told him: the love of his person and nothing else.

I answered him [that] I could not say no more to His Majesty than I had already done; that a report only of his excellent virtues had brought me thither; that a better experience had bound me so fast to him and them that as he was master of my mind, so he should be of my person and time, which were both subject to his command. For those things of fortune, they were the least things that I regarded, as His Majesty well saw by my great expense thither, only to satisfy my sight. But as I knew myself infinitely honoured by His Majesty vouchsafing to serve himself of me so that was to me above all other fortunes and satisfactions. His Majesty seemed wonderfully well content with my answer; and that night began to show me extraordinary public favour, and so continued all the time of his being in Quasvin, daily increasing by some or other great demonstration.

A memorable punishment of extortion

Six weeks he [the King] stayed there [in Quasvin], giving his accustomed audience to the people; in which time I saw the noblest example of true impartial royal justice, that I think any prince in the world could produce. The Governor of Quasvin had been appointed to that administration, in the main service of the King's state when the rebels were first suppressed. A man exceedingly and particularly favoured by the King, he, taking advantage of the time, which being troubled, gave him lively colour to make great profit upon the people, and, confident in the King's favour, [he] abused both the one and the other by extreme extortions, thinking (because of his own greatness, and the country's offence against the king, the memory of which every man would fear to receive) that what he did by violence and force should by as great power of terror remain unknown.

But some, to whom he had offered so much that they thought no extremity could happen them of a worse condition, made desperate through that hazard to put up lamentable supplications to the King; who, having read them (as his fashion is), commanded the parties to speak freely: with this caution, that they should beware that they charged nothing falsely; for as he would not that any minister of his should abuse his authority by any unjust burden upon the woes of the people; so he would also provide, by severe example, that none should presume to impose false accusations upon any whom he had thought worthy to carry authority under him. Notwithstanding, those poor men did not only maintain these accusations, but brought forth several witnesses. And others, perceiving so just a course held by His Majesty, emboldened by it, laid before him also, in their humble sort, their own oppressions, suffered by the like violence. Upon which he commanded...the Master of his house in Quasvin [to be sent for], demanding of him whether he had heard of those things. He answered 'no'; being private acts of the Governor: (public causes, which were brought before the president, judges, advocates, and His Majesty's Council, appointed for the good of the Province, having ever taken those direct ways which were fit for His Majesty, and benefit of the Province). If the Governor, in his particular acts, had taken counsels with his particular appetites, and executed them according to the same, neither he, nor any of the council were blameable; never having heard a voice only to that effect: which those men also, (who were a great number) falling down upon their faces, confessed to the kin; and that their long silence had given the governor the more boldness to use the uttermost extortion, and tyrannous exaction upon them.

The Governor denied some, maintained others to be done upon just causes. But all so confusedly, and with so unstable fashion of proceeding, as he betrayed his own guiltiness. Notwithstanding, the King stayed his judgement: either of him, or the causes, until another day of hearing. In the meantime he appointed one Margan Beg, [the] Bastan-Aga, and one Maxaus Beg; (who was, as it were, Treasurer of his house) to take secret ways to find the true carriage of the governor, during the whole time of his function; Which they did with great uprightness and dexterity. And, having related what they approvedly found, there were so many, and so great causes brought against him, I mean of wresting of money, bribery, monopolising, and such things, as more could not be imagined. Which had been small matters in a Prince's state, whose favours and graces are privileged above the common good of the people; and who change by their own connivance their royal estate to a tyranny of favourites. And a few counsellors who, concurring in the spoil of the people, concur also in so cruel a suppression of their just cries that their lifting up their voices for justice, is as great a sin as almost a perfect rebellion. And the same justice, which should protect them against unique oppression, inflicts severe chastisement, only for presuming to palesate[10] such oppressions: a miserable calamity for the poor flock where the shepherd shears the wool and the brambles rent the flesh.

But this King (whom we call barbarous, though from his example we may learn many great and good things), knowing that the true care of a prince must be ever the public good and the capableness of his ruling, would be adjudged by his true justice, and election of his Ministers, and distribution of his favour upon the worthiest (who also should make a worthy use of it). The next day that he sat in judgement, he called the governor. Then, having told him that he who had lived with him in the time of his greatest calamity, must needs be so well acquainted with the inwardness of his disposition that all the world would imagine [that], as Princes ever are examples of good or evil to their subjects; so they are most to those which are the nearliest conversant with them. And according to that opinion, he had given him his authority, for the great favour and confidence he reposed in him, that he knew well the error which they had both committed: the one not making a true judgement of the other's disposition That the transgression of laws and orders in any State was the first natural corruption which grew in it: to provide for which, good princes did both watchfully industriate themselves, and dispersed part of the care, which grew too great for themselves, to the trust they had in the virtue of their Ministers, who should ever, as the very greatest and truest causes, beware of those courses of justice which should be of least terror, and procure themselves and their Princes most hatred, which was still the subject's good: a thing of no example, but to evil, and of infinite odiousness, especially when there was no just cause why any sort of punishment should be inflicted.

And because these acts of so great a Minister, as he was, both for the place he held of authority, and favour with him; might give the world cause to suspect his own inclination; the which since no former example could make him know, he would now show the world and teach him, that the wickedness of princes, and [of] great men are worse in the example than in the fault; since, by the evil custom of the world to follow them, they generate great corruptions by the imitations of others. And because in a man of his place, there could be no more wicked acts than he had committed; nor in a Prince nothing more proportionable with his place, nor fitter for his security, than the chastisement of such wicked acts. And if he should pardon so great extortions, and scelerate[11] wrongs as he had inflicted upon people committed to his charge, besides, that he should verify the worst suspicions men might have of him, he should, by so ill a precedent, trouble the minds of his whole state, cast many good men and their goods into ruin; multiply the like, or worse, scandals, oppressing the causes of justice; and so draw into the world, without shame or fear, all sort of excesses. This should be his judgement: That all his goods, and lands should be sold, for the satisfaction of those men, whom he had spoiled: And if any thing wanted, since the King, by giving him that authority, was partly the cause of those excesses, he condemned himself to pay the residue out of the Treasury. That if any thing advanced, it should be given to his children, with a grievous edict, that no succour should be ministered unto himself. For that [because] since death was a concluder to his offence, shame, and the memory of it, he should not die; but go, during his life, with a yoke, like a hog's yoke, about his neck; have his nose and ears cut off, and have no charitable relief from any but what he gained by his own hands, that he might feel in himself the misery which poor men have to get, and what a sin it is to rent from them by violent extortion, the birth of their sweat and labour.

This judgement struck a mighty amazement into all the great men present, and gave infinite joy and comfort to the people. The Turkish Ambassador, who was there, after he had stood silent for a great while, as a man half distracted, swore publicly that he saw before his eyes, his master's ruin, being impossible that such fortune and virtue as the King was accompanied with, could receive any obstacle.

[Religion]

[Sherley recounts that the King decided to call him Mirza – 'by that great example of his duty: Constantino, a brave young gentleman, being a Christian of Georgia, [whom] he called Mirza, and gave him the government of Espahan'.]

Yet for all this, that I meant to make Oliver di-Can, his General, and...Tamasp Kuli Beg, both of whom were Georgians [aware of my views]...though they were made Mahometans by the father of the King, to whom they had been brought [when] young, yet they had ever Christians hearts, and [were] infinitely well-inclined to those things which might promote the Christian enterprise, publicly wishing well to their proceedings, and taking all offered occasions, to give them honour and reputation. Those, the main helpers of my design, I left no sort of fashion forgotten which might procure me favour from all the other: though I soon found their appearances answered not their minds, which were only contained from ill demonstrations against me by the King's favour to me, and their fear of offending him; not only through the ordinary envy which follows all Courts, but by the great hatred which they had to the very name of a Christian, being in their souls Turks; though not daring to palesate it for their own certain danger.

For the King, knowing how potent a uniter of men's minds the self-same religion is for the tranquillity of an Estate and the like dis-uniter several religions are for the disturbance of the peace of an Estate, he is exceeding curious and vigilant to suppress, through all his dominions, that religion of Muhammad, which follows the interpretation of Husayn and Omar, and to make his people cleave to that of Ali: Not (as I judge) through any conscience, which carries him more to the one than [to] the other; but first to extirpate intrinsic factions; then to secure himself the more firmly against the Turk, who being head of that part which follows Omar and Husayn, should have too powerful a way into his country, if his people's hearts were inclined unto him by the force of religion. Therefore he does not only strive to root it out, but to defile it, and make it odious; having in use, once a year, with great solemnity, to burn publicly, as main heretics, the images of Husayn and Omar. Then does he cause his great men publicly (in scorn of their institution) to go with a flagon of wine, carried by a footman and, at every village, or where they see any assembly, to drink. Which himself also uses. Not for the love of the wine, but to scandalise so much more the contrary religion that by such a kind of profaning it, they may wear the respect of it out of the people's hearts. Which, when it failed with reverence in religion, the pillars thereof are utterly broken. Yet (as I say) there are the very greatest, exceedingly precise, Turks if they durst do other for their own fortune's sake than cover, with all artifice, that infection.

[Persuasion to make war against the Turk]

Sherley reports that, in an earlier conversation, Oliver di-Can had volunteered that:... 'if I [Sherley] had intended it to move him [the King] in the war in so fit a time against the Turk, I had done well; and assured me that both he, and Tamasp Kuli Beg would, with all their powers concur with me to bring it to an essential deliberation. Though, said he, there are three dogs, Halden Beg, Bastan-Aga, and Courthcy Pasha, who will mainly oppose themselves against it: Yet in the conscience of my duty, which I owe to His Majesty, I assure myself that there is no secure way, either for the preservation of his person, or state, but that. Therefore since you have begun in so happy an hour, to break the ice of so great and so good an enterprise, follow it without fear, since God will prosper your good intention in it, and we will second you, with all the strength and industry that we have.' This was all I desired: to be assured of some friend; especially such a one, as might have both opinion and credit of wisdom and favour with the King.

Now...taking the opportunity of the King's being alone with me and my brother in a garden, with my interpreter only and Tamasp Kuli Beg I spoke unto him to this effect...being emboldened by his royal gracious answer unto me upon the way, (which I took as a kind of commandment) I would presume to say some-thing more largely than I had done then, of that which I took to concern His Majesty as much as any thing else could. Neither would I speak any thing of other condition than such as he, in his great judgement, should find so well grounded that nothing could be added – either to the just cause, honour, utility, or facility of the enterprise, which I would propose. And because I would clear all clouds which might hang about it, myself, who propounded it, was such that I was only a shadow which, by the urging of my own nature, and delight, should follow the body of his victories, rather than have, or hope, for any other particular interest in them myself.

For the first points. There could no deliberation be grounded upon a greater founda-tion of equity than that which had his end: only directed to the recovery of that which had been, by force and violence, usurped from his State; nor nothing more honourable for a Prince than to be able, without hazard, not only to revenge private and public wrongs; but [also] to recover their members again to his feats by his wisdom and virtue, which have been separate – either by the defect, or fortune, of his predecessors. All this, both public and private profit, followed so great an increase of State (increasing in all points the force of his State) and his poor subjects, who were thrown out of their possessions, (either through their true devotion to His Majesty, which could give them no peace under another government,) or through the extreme tyranny of the Turk, should be recovered again to their own, with his infinite glory and utility.

The facility showed itself in several ways. Principally in his own fortune, wisdom, and virtue; against which there was no likely resistance. Especially when there was no equal obstance [opposition] than the reputation of his late victories, joined with the other, would find, or make a way through all difficulties than his militia, which was fresh and uncorrupted. Then the incapacity of the Turk, his corruptions of government, want of obedience, sundry rebellions, and distractions from any possibility of being able to make any potent resistance against His Majesty's proceedings, by his wars in Hungary, which His Majesty might assure the continuance of; if it pleased him to invite the princes Christian to his amity. Which he should offer upon that condition by which also, he should receive one other worthy benefit fit for such excelling parts, as he was most richly abundant in: not to conclude the true knowledge of them, in that one corner of the world: but with making these great princes known unto himself, he should make his own worthiness, like-wise, known unto them.

Neither (as I said at the first to His Majesty) though these were great points to move so high a spirit, intending to glory and great things as his were, that they were so important as others were. For these might either be deferred, or not at all acted, being bound unto them by no greater necessity than his own will, that he must resolve, both for the security of his estate and person, to make or endure a war.

Halden Beg (the Vizier's) response in presence of Bastan-Aga Di Can

Your Majesty may now perceive that true which some of your servants [advisors] have been bold to tell you, at the first coming of these Christians, and many times since: that they were sent to disquiet Your Majesty's tranquillity of your state; and to embark you in dangerous enterprises for other interests. For what likelihood was there, that a gentleman of quality, without some great disaster fallen him, should take such a voyage, so full of dangers and expenses, upon a fame of a Prince, spread by ordinary merchants, since I know [that] he could never have spoken with men of better quality in those parts who could have known Your Majesty.

And if it were true that such a motion only had brought him why should he not give time to the growing of his better fortunes by Your Majesty's munificencies and favours; without drawing himself into the danger, to be a persuader of a perilous enterprise than which he cannot be so ignorant as to understand no way to be so precipitous for himself. But because it is enjoyed him, he must do it; without regard to Your Majesty, to whom he is only newly bound for present benefits; which he cares but to enjoy, until he hath entangled you in his designs. And then will he rely upon those to whom he owes greater obedience, for more permanent benefits, and greater through so great a merit. God keep Your Majesty from giving ear to his persuasions, which carry nothing with them but extreme peril. The Turk, having been a heavy neighbour to Your Majesty's state, when it was found through a long peace, and when your predecessors were abundant in money; which is the heart of the wars and the sinews which bind together an estate.

Your Majesty has now a certain peace with him, and that the more certain through his necessity, which assures you of time to gather treasure, and all kind of strength against him. If he [the Turk] should break the faith of his truce, or move against you hereafter that it is just, honourable, and profitable for Your Majesty, perhaps I may agree; though it be a question, whether it be just, or honourable, to break a peace without a just occasion given. But howsoever, it is more wisdom for Your Majesty to find a better, and more fit time which shall furnish you with all the necessary provisions for so great an enterprise. And further, I say [that] if the Turk's government be corrupted, give it more time, and the sickness will increase....How dangerous a thing it is to embrace several and continual action, Your Majesty's greatest wisdom can better tell than I....Moreover, for you to send, and beg an amity of the Christian Princes, what a persuasion is it [that] for Your Majesty's greatness? Which notwithstanding, if you were compelled by necessity, somewhat from your self, yet necessity would make it tolerable: But for you to seek them which have need of you, there is so little reason, that he has sinned against your power, person, and state, who has propounded it.

[King's conclusion to his deliberations]

To conclude as many deliberations in their many points, must be grounded upon the example of the past, the experience of the present, and the judgement of the future. And the Turk has been ever heavy to my State: in long past, and late past times; and is now, by some accidents partly proceeding from himself, partly from others (in all likelihood) easy to be perpetually assured. Which point of time that gives so good an occasion if it be let pass, may give him power (for a mind he can nor will never want) to be intolerable again hereafter. Or, if not intolerable, at the least dangerous.

We have two great powers of our minds: the one, a wise power of understanding, by which we penetrate into the knowledge of things; the other a strong power of resolving it, by which we execute things well understood. And now that we have judged of all, we must resolve of somewhat; and of that which is probabliest best. Therefore our necessity, our honour, and our justice calling us against the Turk, and since with all these concurs so good an opportunity, he must be the main end of which we will determine. And because to prepare us to that end amongst many other circumstances, the sending to [other nations of emissaries] has been intimated as one of the most necessary, we shall do well in the general good use which we must make of this interposition of time to do also that. For though it be true that their interests will ever make such a proposition acceptable yet where there is a proffer of such a condition, as bears with it a kind of obligation, as it is of more honourable fashion for us, so it adds grace and reputation and more strength to it, or any such like purpose.

[The King of Persia agrees to the persuasion of Sir Anthony Sherley]

The next morning the King came unto me and, after some other discourses, he told me [that] he had well considered of my proposition which, though otherwise he had no great inclination unto, both because of the great separation by distance, and difficult means of correspondence which could be made between the princes Christian and himself besides the small necessity he had of them, (God having given him so ample, so rich, and so warlike a dominion). And if he had, their own disunion against themselves gave him small hope of any great good effect in what he should propoind[12] unto them; besides, the derogation from his own greatness to be a demander of their amity, whose predecessors had fought it of his by several means, and upon great conditions. Yet, to show me how dear an estimation he held of me, he was contented not to see what belonged to himself, but only to regard my satisfaction: which he willed me to determine of, and assured me of the effecting of it whatever it was.

[Sir Anthony Sherley confirms the King in his purpose of sending an embassy to the Princes of Christendom]

And after I had given His Majesty [the] thanks which was convenient for so high a favour, I told him that I propounded nothing but that which the future experience, and present reason of things would prove not only infinitely available, but also necessary for his honour, profit and security. To which counsel I was ready and desirous to add my own peril, which could by no other means bring an answerable benefit to the greatness of itself, but only in the true estimation which I made of the merit of His Majesty's virtue, and my infinite affection to his service.

The necessity of his state, I knew, either counselled him to provide for a war, or to make a war; private cogitations having their progress of such a condition, that they may take (as themselves will) either more or less of fortune. But those which had raised their thoughts to the sublimity of dominion are no more in their own power – having no mean to step upon between the highest of all, and precipitation. For His Majesty to sleep longer, called upon by so main reasons which did evidently demonstrate unto him the inevitable danger, (if not ruin) of his state, and contrariwise, the certain addition which His Majesty might make to his glory and state, would seem to those that did not rightly understand the excellency of His Majesty's heart: such a weakness in him, as is incident to those which have not power to temper felicity from glutting themselves with the abundant fruits of present prosperity, though they have a patient forced vigour to withstand adversity.

That the Turk was to be vanquished, his own rebels had shown, who overcame with small forces his great power in sundry encounters. If his militia had heretofore more vigour and valour; it is now changed through pleasure, ease, and surfeitings by (their Prince's example) with great corruptions; which a more virtuous Prince may reduce to their soundness. His Majesty's wisdom should work immediately upon the present general defect and error. Neither should he make a proportionable concurrence between his facts and wisdom, if he did loose time in doubtful deliberations, in such a case which evidently shows him that if he might securely continue in peace. Yet that peace was more pernicious unto him than war, leesing[13] so many fair occasions of propagating his empire, and making his estate eternally invincible, and too dangerous to be attempted again by the Turk, which then should be so equal a balance of potency as would be between them, but by the recovery of his own, if his desire and fortune and virtue disposed no more unto him than that which [was] justly his own, and was unjustly detained from him.

For those rebellions of the Turks, they were likely rather to increase than diminish: such manner of people evermore easily consenting in unity in war, than in peace to be commanded, or yield obedience: And the greatest powers which are have been, or may be, which united bear all before them, the violence of their strength, once divided either by time, by patience, or by diversity of fortune, (which cannot be at all times, and in all places alike) may be, and are subverted. The war itself will open and disclose many hidden and swelling wounds, which are now only covered by ignorance; and others, detracting of their determination.

And though it be true that the Princes Christian be far divided; and some of them encumbered with particular designs amongst themselves, through the passions of their private interests; yet the Emperor (who is the greatest in title, and by alliance of the most power) is already engaged against the Turk. Which war he will more or less prosecute according as he shall have more or less hopes. And what greater almost assurance of prosperous success can he have than the conjunction with Your Majesty, whose power and virtues he shall know? And the moving of both your ends, being the same, can loose no property in their working, by the large separation or distinction of places. The Pope also (who carries a supreme authority among the princes to move them to those things which shall best preserve or augment the limits of his Church) animated by Your Majesty's great name and offer; will assuredly use the uttermost of the strength of his authority and industry to reconcile all particular enmities, and to combine all hearts to that general war, in which every particular is truly much interested; if they consider their conscience to their profession, and the danger wherewith they all have been threatened by that great enemy's potency, several princes having already by it suffered the uttermost of ruin.

Neither shall Your Majesty despair, but that all may be persuaded to so honourable and pious an action being a property in man's nature to follow that which hath been contrary to their disposition to begin. And if they all should not; yet the Emperor, Pope, and King of Spain absolutely will embrace the amity, honour the name of Your Majesty, and unite themselves in any terms of princely alliance. And Your Majesty shall have an eternal glory amongst all; for inviting them all to so noble, generous and royal an action; and, at the least, draw great intercourse of merchants of all those parts: which will give an entrance to a kind of sociableness and that will proceed to a common respect, and so to a mutual friendship, which will give the communication and knowledge of many things hidden (both in the knowledge, use and profit of them) for want of such an intercourse.

Your Majesty also wisely desires to take away all reputation from the Turkish religion, through your Dominions, both by scandalising it publicly, and punishing it in particular persons: Since heresy in all religion caused division, and the corrupted part becomes a pernicious enemy to the prince who supports the contrary, from it arises, as from a main turbulent spring, treasons, conspiracies, secret conventicles, and seditions. Besides the greatest and largest way, which the Turk has in your dominions, is the faction of his sect; as Ishmael your predecessor had, of that which Your Majesty sees so divides your state from his. He is an absolute and tyrannous enemy to the Christians; Your Majesty's religion has a charitable opinion of them. And if drinking of wine, burning of their Prophet's images, and such less appearances be in Your Majesty's opinion effectual things to estrange the peoples' hearts from that religion, by a contrary use, with those opporbies to the other, a greater means Your Majesty may work by [it] in giving liberty of Christian religion, so much abhorred of their part, and security of trade, goods and person to Christians: by which you shall bind their princes, express the charity of Your law, serve yourself in several things of them which have been hidden unto you, both for your utility, strength and pleasure,: and more inveigh Your people to despise the other religion, by so contrary, so apparent, and so great effect.

Neither can they ever be dangerous to Your Majesty, their increase being always to be limited by your will. This also will give Your Majesty great fame, since by their means you shall recover available instruments both to preserve and augment your estate by – as founders of ordnance, makers of all sorts of arms and munitions. So that though it may seem a strange act of Your Majesty to be contented in large to Christians [to?] so new and so great a favour. Yet since all great examples ever have them in some thing of an extraordinary quality, those are to be made use of that repair by public profit, those particular disgusts which private men may receive of them. I know that it is for the most part a fallacious ambition which embraces greedily new and dangerous things. But to determine and execute fit and convenient things is the proper effect of wisdom and courage. Your Majesty knows your present estate, remembers the courses of the times past; and the excellency of your judgement weighs that which may succeed hereafter. No man receives harm, but from himself; nor Your Majesty can suffer none but from that which yourself will determine of yourself. You are invited to no act depending upon Fortune, but such a one as shall have his foundation upon counsel, reason, and judgement. My satisfaction shall be, above all other greatest, if Your Majesty resolves of that which will be most secure, honourable and commodious for your person, state, and particular subjects.

[The coming of two friars to insinuate with Sir Anthony Sherley]

In this time came unto me a Portuguese friar, named Alphonso Cordero, of the Order of the Franciscans Secular, and another Armenian friar of Jerusalem, with a message from another friar of better estimation, called Nicola Di Meto; the effect of which was this: that he told me [that] he had been Inquisitor-General of the Indies and, his time being finished, as also having received commandment from the Pope and the King of Spain to return (and for some other causes) to the Christianity of these parts, not being willing to attend [endure] the tedious voyage of the Portuguese fleet by sea, chose rather to hazard to go overland – to which he was the more animated, having heard of the favour and esti-mation which certain Christians held in that Court, whom he did not doubt would, Christian-like, honour him, being so great an instrument of the Church, and of so great a potentate as the king of Spain. For though we were English and he Portuguese, and by the private interests of our princes, their names were made enemy in the ordinary sort of our nation, yet religious men were ever privileged from common malice, and that placer which was opposite of itself to the possession of Christ would be a persuading argument enough for any noble or pious mind to honour, in all persons of our oppressed faith, without regarding the title or country of the profession thereof.

But when he came (through this insinuation of his were like a good mean, and showed to proceed from the best condition of spirits), yet he did so much [de]generate from the name of a Christian, much more of a religious man, of a true subject of his prince, and of a pious wisher of those things which tended to the general good of the whole common-wealth of Christendom, that he forgot not only the honour which I had freely, and with good hear, done him (waking again the name of those enemies which he desired to have suppressed: at the first secretly, at the last openly) setting forth many pretences against me; which, if it had proceeded from the ordinary imperfections of Nature (which runs more headlongly to the revenge of injuries even in opinion than to the recordation of essential and civil benefits: gracious acts being a burden; revenge esteemed a gain by us) though the cause of it had proceeded from that imperfection had been ill, yet, being natural to it, had been somewhat tolerable. And if he had not also added to that fault another inexcus-able one, not only to neglect, but even to despise all those other great duties which, if they bound him not in affection, yet they must have bound in awfulness and fear any crea-ture who had not been utterly given to power over to the worst of temptations of the wicked spirit and enemy of mankind and substantial subverter of all goodly causes.

For I (though likewise unobliged) willing, in the beginning, of the foundation which the king permitted me to lay, of God his true knowledge in those parts, to show all devout respects to God and all his ministers (and knowing that the name of division amongst ourselves would but scandalise all) used him with all those duties and reverences which I could possibly devise, or any ambitious heart could desire: which gave (as it fell out) but a freer passage of the iniquity of his soul – to my great grief, prejudice of the estimation in those parts, of religious men; and to the most infinite affliction of the other Franciscan, that can be expressed; he being certainly a good man and, as far as understanding guided him, zealous to persuade others to be so, helping to express, by a sincere and holy example of life, what he wanted in discourse. But *ubi Dei numen prætenditur sceleribus, subit animum timor, ne fraudibus humanis vindicandis, divini juris aliquid immixtum violemus* [when God's authority is cited as justification, one is always afraid that, instead of exposing a human wrong one may be violating a divine right].[14] For which reason I will say only this: that to free myself from the crosses which daily rose against my business, I pressed the king as hotly (as civilly I could) for my despatch.

* * *

[William Parry's story of the encounter with the Portuguese friar: from *A new and large discourse of the travels of Sir Anthony Sherley Knight, by sea, and over land, to the Persian Empire. Wherein are related many strange and wonderful accidents and also the description and conditions of those countries and peoples he passed by, with his returne into Christendom.* Written by William Parry Gentleman, who accompanied Sir Anthony in his travels. London. Printed by Valentine Simmes for Felix Norton. 1601. Reprinted in *Illustrations of Early English Popular Literature,* edited by J. Payne Collier, London: Privately Printed, Vol. 1. 1863.]

...we were ready to depart from the King's Court, lying then at Espahan, when suddenly there came news of a Portuguese friar, who was coming there, accompanied with two other friars, and four servants. This friar stayed some 3 miles off the town, and sent the other two with letters for Sir Anthony, whereby he signified unto him that he was the last King of Portugal's brother, and that he was sent by the King of Spain as Procurator-General of the East Indies. Sir Anthony, believing it, went himself, accompanied with as many Christians as he could get, to the frigot [friar]. And after mutual greetings, he told Sir Anthony that, hearing of his great and weighty businesses, and so godly a work (he being a great bishop of the King of Spain's) came posting night and day to assist him therein; which Sir Anthony was right glad of. And to manifest the same the better, he brought him along to his own house, and there dislodged his brother to lodge him.

This being done, he told Sir Anthony [that] that he greatly desired to see the King because he had a present to bestow on him. Which Sir Anthony soon procured. But now, by the way, this present was delivered him in trust, to be delivered to the King. Howbeit, he presented it in his own name, in requital whereof the King gave him a crucifix worth (by estimation) a hundred pounds and better: which villainy, and many others, Sir Anthony afterwards discovered, though the meanwhile he held him for a holy man. Before we departed from the King, he [the friar] would fain (by the King's commission) have been an agent in the present action, wherein Sir Anthony was principally employed. And likely he was to have bin one, with universal consent, but that the writings and all other things thereunto incident were before perfected and finished.

And seeing [that] he could not be an actor (as he desired) by reason thereof, he entreated Sir Anthony to procure the King's favourable letters, in his behalf, to the Pope and the King of Spain: which Sir Anthony did accordingly. In requital whereof he began (under-hand) to deal with those of the King's council who had bin backwards in the beginning of these businesses; who assured them that Sir Anthony was not able to perform so great a negotiation. Which Sir Anthony perceiving, he made all the haste he possibly could to be gone, the rather, because he had waded somewhat too far with this execrable friar who, the first night he lodged in Sir Anthony's house, found the means to have a Persian courtesan to lie with him. And so had night by night during his continuance there; which if he wanted, he would hire a boy sodomitically to use.

And that he was a sodomitical wretch, it appears hereby: Sir Anthony, at his first coming, bought two Christian boys in the market; which afterwards he bestowed on this Friar, whose name was Nicolao de Melo. He no sooner had them, but he was in hand with them concerning his sodomitical villainy. The boys, finding whereto he was inclined (being incessantly importuned by him to yield to his beastly desire), complained to him that sold them; he likewise, to the officer; the officer to the King – by means whereof the King espied his villainy. Whereupon the King sent for the boys from him, and sent him word, that were it not for Sir Anthony's sake, he should loose his head.

Soon after we departed, taking the friar and one of his fellows with us, having 18 days' journey from the Persian Court...in which time, the friar confessed [that] he was but an ordinary Augustinian friar. And in a gamesome vein he further confessed how he would bring men's wives, after he had shriven them, to his bent: as taking advantage of their confessed faults. And to close up this and such like good talk in the day, we should be sure to take him with a whore at night. And I will tell you a test concerning him, which I had almost forgotten. One day, at Quasvin he sent his man to a whore, seeing her with two chickens, (which is two rials) to come unto him at night, taking upon him the name of the Ambassador. The kind wench, being true of promise, came unto Sir Anthony who, demanding the cause of her coming, she told him all, etc. So the wench went away, *gratis*, with the money, the friar not daring to demand it.[15] Thus having merrily passed the time with this sorry friar, and being come to the place where we should be embarked, we stayed there one month for the Persian peer, [Husayn Ali Beg] who was to go along with us, as before was mentioned.

Leaving here a while, I will turn again to the friar, who was by this time grown into mortal hatred with his fellow friar...whose name was Alfonso, a friar of the order of Saint Francis. Which friar had acquainted Sir Anthony that friar Nicolao has spent his life most lewdly in the Indies, the particularities whereof he at large related. Moreover, he told him, that by reason of his licentious life, the King of Spain had sent for him, because he did much more hurt than good in those parts, but never would come until now that he was going thitherward. He also told Sir Anthony, that that present which he delivered the King of Persia in his own name was sent by a friend of the King's from Hormoz, by another, who had withal, a letter to the King. Which bearer (being of his acquaintance) he inveigled and enticed, by the gift of 50 crowns, and fair words, to deliver him the present, together with the letter to carry to the King, who finally prevailed with him. And when he came to Persia, he suppressed the letter, but delivered the present in his own name, as before is declared; upon discovery of which villanies, Sir Anthony took him prisoner, and carried him along with him, as one deprived of former liberty.[16]

[The true copy of Sir Anthony Sherley's oration to the Great Sophy,[17] as follows][18]

I am so assuredly free from any just imputation that I will not draw into suspicion so noble a cause as this of my coming with circumstances which (though they bear the name) yet are, in substance, nothing but uncertain excuses that betoken a fault, whereas truth seeks no starting-holes but, as a pilgrim who follows the notion of his affections, is come from far to yield and to pay unto virtue his zeal his seal and devotion, and to no other end.

If it may please Your Majesty to accept the consecration of his poor carcass unto you, which my mind has carried hither to be made an offering or hanging vow in the temple of your most singular virtues, being brought to this point by the extremity of my desires, with expenses of much time, and not without great peril; which, though it is not present in any degree of worth estimable to such a Prince, it may please Your Majesty to remember that the pitch of an eagle's flight far surmounts the fluttering of a fly, and that common, base minds are not capable of such noble thoughts as might raise themselves with the true seeking of these, your most rare and worthy parts, which have drawn me to your presence, whereof I have heard men speak with wonder, and now give me cause to think myself most happy.

And therefore I humbly beseech Your Majesty, when you have read the history of the inward thoughts of my mind, you will vouchsafe to judge hereof, not as of conceits hanging on the threads of flattering terms, but that you will be pleased to understand, through the conscience of your own virtues, that words of never so great magnificence are but the least part of so high and excellent desert; and that the less I am to display their dignity with my speeches, the more will I, with my blood, make proof of my zeal towards them, if I may be made worthy to be commanded by Your Majesty.

I am a soldier, whose profession is clean contrary to words; which shall soon fail me, than my courage to greater effect. If the present be acceptable to Your Majesty, I shall esteem it as a most singular good hap unto me; but much more, if it shall be employed. For it would be but a very idle end and conclusion of so long a travel, full of so many perils, if it were knit up with words only; and a very poor and slender harvest of so fervent affection, if it should bring forth only buds or blossoms, and no fruit; and finally too meek a subject for Your Majesty's most excellent virtues, if my devotion and observances were not so sealed with my blood, the which I do humbly and freely offer at Your Majesty's feet, to be shed and spent at the least sign and token of Your Majesty's pleasure.

[The copy of Sir Anthony Sherley's Letters of Credence from the Great Sophy, to the Christian princes]

There is come unto me, in this good time, a principal gentleman, Sir Anthony Sherley, of his own free will out of Europe into these parts. And all you Princes who believe in Jesus Christ, know you that he has made friendship between you and me; which desire we have also heretofore granted; but there were none who came to me [in] this way. And, to remove the veil that was between us and you, but only this gentlemen who, as he came of his own free will, so also upon his desire I have sent with him a chief man of mine. The entertainment which that principal gentleman has with me is that daily, while he has been in these parts, we have eaten together of one dish, and drunk of one cup, like two brothers.

Therefore, when this gentleman comes unto you Christian Princes, you shall credit him in whatsoever you shall demand, or he shall say, as my one person. And when this gentleman shall have passed the sea, and is entirely in the country of the great King of Muscovy (with whom we are in friendship, as brothers) all his governors, both great and small, shall accompany him, and use him with all favour, unto Moscow. And because there is great love between you, the king of Moscow, and me, that we are like brothers, I have sent this gentleman through your country, and desire you to favour his passage without any hindrance.

[The copy of the free privileges obtained by Sir Anthony Sherley, of the Great Sophy, for all Christians to trade and traffick into Persia]

Our absolute commandment, will, and pleasure is that our countries and dominions shall be, from this day, open to all Christian people, and to their religion; and in such sort that none of ours, of any condition, shall presume to give them any evil word.

And because of the amity now joined with the Princes who profess Christ, I give this Patent for all Christian merchants, to repair and traffic in and through our dominions without disturbances or molestations of any duke, prince, governor, or captain, or any of whatsoever office or quality of ours; but that all merchandise that they shall bring shall be so privileged that none of any dignity or authority shall have the power to look unto it – neither to make inquisition after, or stay for any use or person, the value of one asper.[19] Neither shall our religious men, of whatever sort they are, dare disturb them or speak in matters of their faith. Neither shall any of our justices have power over their persons or goods, for any cause or act whatsoever.

If, by chance, a merchants shall die, none shall touch any thing that belongs unto him; but if the merchants has a companion, he shall have power to take possession of those goods. But if (by any occasion) he is alone, only with his servants, the governor, or whomsoever shall be required by him in his sickness, shall be answerable unto any of his nation, who shall come to desire them. But if he dies suddenly, and have neither companion nor servant, nor time to recommend to any what he would have done, then the governor of that place shall send the goods to the next merchant of his nation; which shall be abiding in any parts of our dominions.

And those within our kingdoms and provinces, having power over our tolls and customs, shall receive nothing, nor dare to speak for any receipt, from any Christian merchant. And if any such Christian merchant shall give credit to any of our to require, any Cadi or governor to do him justice; and thereupon, at the instant of his demand, shall cause him to be satisfied. Neither shall any governor or justice of whatsoever quality he be, dare take any reward from him, which shall be to his expense. For our will and pleasure is that they shall be used in all our dominions to their own full content, and that our kingdoms and countries shall be free unto them, that none shall presume to ask them for what occasion they are here.

And although it has been a continual and unchangeable use in our dominions, every year, to renew all patents, this patent notwithstanding shall be of full effect and force for ever, without any renewing, for me and my successors, not to be changed.[20]

NOTES

1 E. Denison Ross (ed.), *Discours of the Turkes, by Sir Thomas Sherley the Younger*, Camden Miscellany, 1936.

2 Scott Frederick Surtees, *William Shakespeare of Stratford. His epitaph unearthed, and the author of the plays run to ground (with a supplement, alleging that Sir Anthony Sherley was the author of Shakespeare's plays)*, Hertford: Privately Printed, 1888; London: Henry Gray, 1888.

3 Anthony D. Alderson, 'Sir Thomas Sherley's piratical expedition to the Aegean and his imprisonment in Constantinople', *Oriens* 5: 1–38, 1956.

4 According to Anthony Parr (1995b: note 10, p. 57), the story of Teresia being a niece of the Persian monarch had originated in the play *The Travailes of the Three English Brothers*. Parr also

quotes Nixon as describing Teresia as 'cousin germaine to the king of Persia (being now the widow of a Duke in that country)'.

5 Thomas Fuller, *History of the Worthies of England* (1662), edited, with an introduction, by John Freeman, London: George Allen & Unwin, 1952: 571.

6 The Somerset-born Thomas Coryate (*c.* 1577), who travelled widely in Europe and later in India, offers the following account of the chance meeting with the Sherleys in *Thomas Coriate Traueller for the English Wits. Greeting. From the Court of the Great Mogul, resident at the town of Ajmere in Eastern India.* Printed by W. Jaggard and Henry Fetherston, London, 1616:

> About the middle of the way, between Esfahan and Lahore, just about the frontiers of Persia and India, I met Sir Robert Sherley and his Lady, travelling from the Court of the Mogul (where they had been very graciously received, and enriched with presents of great value) to the King of Persia's court; so gallantly furnished with all necessaries for their travels that it was a great comfort unto me to see them in such a flourishing estate. There he showed me, to my singular contentment, both my books, neatly kept; and had promised me to show them, especially my *Itinerary*, to the Persian King, and to interpret unto him some of the principal matters in the Turkish tongue, to the end [that] I may have the most gracious access unto him after my return there. / For through Persia I have determined (by God's help) to return to Aleppo. Besides other rarities that they carried with them out of India, they had 2 elephants and 8 antelopes; which were the first that I ever saw. But afterwards, when I came to the Mogul's Court, I saw great store of them. These they meant to present to the Persian King. Both he and his Lady used me with singular respect; especially his Lady, who bestowed 40 shillings upon me in Persian money. And they seemed to exult for joy to see me, having promised me to bring me in good grace with the Persian King, and that they will induce him to bestow some princely benefit upon me. This I hope will be partly occasioned by my book; for he is such a jocund Prince that he will not be meanly delighted with divers of my facetious hieroglyphics, if they are truly and genuinely expounded unto him.

7 While Sherley might have in mind here the Great Schism, or Schism of the West (the separation between the Roman Catholic and the Orthodox Eastern Churches, 1378–1417), it is perhaps more likely that his reference is to the Reformation in England, begun in the reign of Henry VII, notably for legislation enacted by Thomas Cromwell (1532–6) carried on more radically after Henry's death by Thomas Cranmer, marked especially by the printing of two Books of Common Prayer (1549, 1552) and the forty-two Articles of Religion (1553) which not only replaced Henry's ten articles (1536), but which became the basis for the thirty-nine articles (1563) enacted under Elizabeth and still in place at this day within the Church of England.

8 Formerly, in the feudal system of Turkey, a fief held by military service (*OED*).

9 The Royal Exchange, in the City of London, built (1566–71) by Sir Thomas Gresham (1519?–79) and modelled on Antwerp, as a place where merchants and bankers could meet. Destroyed in the Great Fire (1666), it was rebuilt (1667–9), then destroyed once again by fire (1838), and again rebuilt (1842–4).

10 Palesate: to reveal, manifest. OED cites Sherley as evidence of usage.

11 Scelerate: atrociously wicked (*OED*).

12 Propoind: propose; offer.

13 Leese: to loosen; open; unfasten (*OED*).

14 *ubi Dei numen.*...Almost for the only time in his text Sherley omits citing his source. And while I have to admit failure to establish the name of the author of a fascinating observation, I am delighted (as on previous occasions in the past) to acknowledge my gratitude to Maurice Pope for providing not only a precise, but also a characteristically elegant, translation.

15 Ross leaves out this story. He offers no explanation for doing so.

16 Parry recounts that, not only were they imprisoned for some ten days when they arrived in Moscow, but that the emperor, in conjunction with the Persian ambassador, attempted to downgrade Sherley from being the leader to the delegation to being third. When Sherley refused to accept that, the emperor retaliated by releasing the friar. According to Parry, it was only after

Sherley had given 'the fat friar such a sound box on the face (his double cause of choler redoubling his might, desire for revenge withal augmenting the same, that down falls the friar as if he had been struck with a thunderbolt)' that the English were treated with greater consideration. Parry's last words on the friar are that while they were in the port of Saint Nicholas [Archangel], waiting for a ship to take them back to England,

> one Master Megrick [according to Penrose, probably Sir John Meyrick, governor of, and agent for, the London Muscovy Company in Moscow and late Ambassador to Russia], a merchant, came from Moscow, and brought the friar's two letters with him, reporting that the Lord Chancellor, in satisfaction of the wrong and ill usage he [had] extended Sir Anthony, sent after the friar to the borders [of Russia]; who took both his letters and all his substance that he had deceitfully and lewdly gotten in many years before in the Indies, from him, leaving him not so much as his friar's weeds. And whether he caused his throat to be cut, it was uncertain; but not unlike;

from which Parry goes on to conclude that the story was

> A good caveat for all those that, under God Almighty's coat, will play all devilish pranks, whereof there are but too many, in these last days (and therefore the worst days) crept into His Holy Church, in all quarters of Christendom, making the same sacred house of prayer (which ought with all prayer an holy endeavour to be preserved from all pollution and polluted persons) a very den of thieves, as it is in the Gospel, that walk continually in sheep's clothing, but inwardly, ravening wolves. They are known by their works.

17 Great Sophy: the name by which the Safavid rulers of Persia (1499–1736) were known in Europe. 'Sophi' is probably a corruption of the dynastic name of 'Safavi', itself derived from Safi-ud-Din. The 'Sophy' here is Shah Abbas the Great.

18 Extracted from the abridged version of Parry, in *Purchas his Pilgrims*, 1625.

19 It is interesting to note the minor detail that the unit of money referred to, the asper (a coin of low value), in a document purportedly from Persia, is Turkish.

20 It would be of considerable interest to be able to ascertain if the original Persian document has been preserved, in order to compare that with the translation.

OTHER EDITIONS

[William Parry] *A true report of Sir Anthony Shierlies journey overland to Venice, from thence by sea to Antioch, Aleppo and Babilon, and so to Casbine in Persia: his entertainment there by the great Sophie: his oration: his Letters of Credence to the Christian Princes: and the privilege obtained of the great Sophie, for the quiet passage and trafique of all Christian merchants, throughout his whole dominions (Reported by two gentlemen who have followed him in the same the whole of his travaille, and are lately sent by him with letters into England).* London. Printed by R. B. by J. J. (1601). Parry is also reprinted in Vol. 2 of J. Payne Collier, *Illustrations of Early English Popular Literature*, 1863.

John Day, William Rowley, George Wilkins, *The Travailes of the Three English Brothers, Sir Thomas, Sir Anthony, Sir Robert Sherley, as it is now play'd by Her Maiesties Seruants.* Printed by George Eld(?) at London for Iohn Wright, and are to be sold at his shoppe neere Christ-Church gate, 1607. [See also Anthony Parr, *Further Reading*, below].

[Nixon] *The Three English Brothers. Sir Thomas Sherely his travels, with his three yeares imprisonment in Turkie: his inlargement by his Maiesties Letters to the great Turke: and lastly, his safe returne into England this present year, 1607: Master Robert Sherley his wars against the Turkes, with his marriage to the Emperor of Persia his Neece.* London. Printed, and are to be sold by John Hodgets in Paules Churchyard, 1607.

[Middleton] *Sir Robert Sherley sent Ambassadour in the name of the King of Persia, to Sigismund the Third, king of Poland and Svvecia, and to other Princes of Europe. His Royall entertainement in Cracovia, the chiefe citie of Poland, with his pretended coming into England. Also, the Honourable praises of the same Sir Robert Sherley, given vnto him in that kingdome, his here likewise inserted.* London. Printed for J. Windet for John Budge, and are to bee sold at his, shop at the Great south doore of Pauls. 1609 [see also *Harleian Miscellany*, 1744, 1808, below].

Vera relatione della solenne entrata, fatta in Roma da Don Roberto Scerlei, Ambasciatore di Xa Abbas Rè di Persia, della Santità di Nostro Signor Papa Paolo Quinto, Bologna: B. Cocchi, 1609.

John Cartwright, *The Preachers Travels*, 1611 [see next entry], includes a section in which he tells of Sherley's arrival in Persia. While Cartwright gives the impression that his was an eye-witness account, he was not there at the time that Sherley was there. By Cartwright's own account, accompanied by John Mildenhall, he had left Aleppo in July 1600 and by the time of his arrival in Persia, Sherley had already set out on his mission. Not only is his presence not mentioned by either Sherley or Parry, but Cartwright's 1611 version is very close (in detail, as well as in description) to that in Parry (1607), on whose version, it would appear, it relies to a considerable extent.

Sir Anthony Sherley His Relation of his Travels in Persia...Printed for Nathaniell Butter and Joseph Bagfet, 1613. Reprinted, Farnborough: Gregg International, 1972; Reprinted, in facsimile, Amsterdam: Theatrum Orbis Terrarum/Norwood, NJ: Walter J. Johnson Inc., Da Capo Press, 1974.

Thomas Herbert, *A Relation of Some Yeares Travaile, Beginninge Anno 1626, into Afrique and the Greater Asia, especially the Territories of the Persian Monarchie*, London, 1634. Reprinted 1638, 1665, 1667; also in Harris, *Navigantium atque Itinerarium Bibliotheca. Or, a Compleat Collection of Voyages and Travels*, 2 vols, 1705; reprinted 1744–8, 1764 [see subsequent entry].

Opmerkelyke Reystogten van...A. Sherley gedaan in den Jare 1599 naar Persien...uit het Engels vertaald, in *Nauukeurige Versameling der...Zee-en-Land Reysen*, Vol. 79, 1707.

'Sir Robert Sherley...Ambassadour...of the King of Persia to Sigismond the Third...and to other Princes of Europe. His Royal entertainment into Cracara [*sic*], the chiefe citie of Polnd, with his pretended coming into England, 1609', in *Harleian Miscellany*, Vol. 5, 1744; Vol. 5, 1808.

The Three English Brothers; or, The Travels and Adventures of Sir Anthony, Sir Robert, & Sir Thomas Sherley, in Persia, Russia, Turkey, Spaine, etc. With portraits. London. Printed for Hurst, Robinson & Co., 90 Cheapside, & 8 Pall Mall & A. Constable & Co., Edinburgh, 1825.

FURTHER READING

F. Babinger, *Sherleiana. I. Sir Anthony Sherleys persische botschaftsreise, 1599–1601; 2. Sir Anthony Sherleys marokkanische Sendung, 1605–6*, Berlin, 1932.

Samuel Chew, *The Crescent and the Rose. Islam and England during the Renaissance*, New York: Oxford University Press, 1937: 239–339.

D. W. Davies, *Elizabethans Errant. The strange fortunes of Sir Thomas S herley and his three sons...as well in the Dutch wars as in Muscovy, Morocco, Persia, Spain, & the Indies*, Ithaca, NY: Cornell University Press, 1967.

Sir E. Denison Ross, *Sir Anthony Sherley and his Persian Adventure. Including some contemporary narratives relating thereto*. London. George Routledge & Son, Broadway House, Carter Lane, 1933 ['The Broadway Travellers series'].

Anthony Parr, 'Foreign relations in Jacobean England. The Sherley brothers and the "the voyage of Persia"', in Jean-Pierre Maquerlot and Michèle Willems (eds) *Travel and Drama in Shakespeare's Time*, Cambridge: Cambridge University Press, 1995: 14–31.

Anthony Parr (ed.), *Three Renaissance Travel Plays*, Manchester: Manchester University Press, 1995.

Boies Penrose, *The Sherleian Odyssey. Being a record of the travels and adventures of three famous brothers during the reigns of Elizabeth, James 1, and Charles 1.* Taunton: Barnicotts, Ltd, The Wessex Press; London: Simpkin Marshall, 1938.

E. P. Sherley, *The Sherley Brothers. An historical memoir of the lives of Sir Thomas Sherley, Sir Anthony Sherley & Sir Robert Sherley. By one of the same house.* Chiswick: Roxburghe Club, 1848.

5

WILLIAM BIDDULPH

The travels of certaine Englishmen into Africa, Asia, Troy, Bythinia, Thracia, and to the Blacke Sea. And into Syria, Cilicia, Pisidia, Mesopotamia, Damascus, Canaan, Galilee, Samaria, Judea, Palestina, Ierusalem, Iericho, and to the Red Sea; and to sundry other places. Begunne in the yeere of Iubilee 1600 and by some of them finished this yeere 1608. The others not yet returned. / Very profitable for the helpe of trauellers, and no lesse delightfull to all persons who take pleasure to heare of the manners, gouernement, religion, and customes of forraine and heathen countries.

London. Printed by Th. Haueland, for W. Apsley, and are to bee sold at his shop in Paules Chuch-yard, at the signe of the Parrot, 1609.

BIOGRAPHY

William Biddulph was preacher to the English merchants resident in Aleppo.

* * *

The Preface to the Reader

I find (gentle reader) in histories commended unto us, the painful travels of some (both by land and sea) which visited far countries, that they might be made more wise and learned. For this Pythagoras travelled into Egypt to hear the Memphitical Poets purpose.[1] Plato, leaving Athens where he taught with great commendation, went into Italy to Architas of Tarentum, that he might learn somewhat of that philosopher and disciple of Pythagoras. Appolonius (with no less labour than danger and cost) passed and journeyed to the furthest parts of India to the philosophers there, that he might hear Hierarcha, sitting in a throne of gold, and drinking of the Well of Tantalus,[2] disputing amongst a few scholars, of Nature, of manners, of the course of days and stars. From thence, returning by the Elamites, Baylonians, Chaldeans, Medes, Assyrians, Palestines, he came to Alexandria:[3] and from thence to Ethiopia, that he might see the philosophers in India, who went always naked, and the table of the sun, which was famous throughout the world. Solon went from Greece to Egypt for a like purpose. All these travelled to get wisdom and learning.[4]...

It is written of Jerome that he went from Dalmatia to Rome, from thence to Germany; then to Constantinople; then to Alexandria; then to Jerusalem – only to see and hear famous men, that he might always go forward in wisdom. Jacob, in his old age, travelled into Egypt, partly constrained by necessity, and partly by love of Joseph. The Queen of the South,[5] a woman (whom Aristotle called imperfect creatures) travelled far to hear the wisdom of Solomon.

Amongst us there have been (and are still) sundry travellers of great name, who have enterprised and taken in hand great voyages, and dangerous journeys; some to Venice, some to Rome, some to Constantinople; some to Jerusalem, some to Syria, some to Persia; some to the Turk, some to the Barbarians. And these have travelled upon diverse respects: some for pleasure, some for profit, some to see their manners, some to learn their languages, some to get experience, some to get wisdom and knowledge; not sparing any cost, fearing any danger, nor refusing any pains. Others would travel, but are loath to be at any charges. Others would be at the cost, but fear to expose themselves to dangers by sea and by land. It is good (say they) to sleep in a whole skin. They cannot abide to be tossed and tumbled like tennis-balls on the turbulent and tempestuous seas, as Ovid, in his exile, complained he was, when he said…'What boisterous billows now (O wretch!) / Amidst the waves we spy / And so forthwith should have been heaved / To touch the azure sky? / What vacant valleys be there set / In swallowing seas so wrought, / As presently thou lookst I should / to dreary Hell be brought?'…

Wherefore (albeit I am no great traveller myself) yet to be set forth the praise of one who has been at the cost, hazarded the danger, and returned with credit; and to help the pusillanimity of others who fear to undertake the travel in regard of the danger; and to relieve the misery of others who are loath to be at the cost, though they delight to hear and see strange countries, peoples, and manners; I have thought good to publish the travels of others, which latterly (by good chance) is come into my hands, after the death of Master Bezaliel Biddulph, a learned and religious gentleman, to whom they were first written, in whose study (amongst his letters and loose papers) was found first of all a copy of a voyage to Jerusalem by land, from Aleppo in Syria Comagena (not long since under-taken and performed by five Englishmen there sojourning, viz. Master William Biddulph, Preacher to the Company of English Merchants resident in Aleppo; Master Jeffrey Kirby, merchant; Master Edward Abbott, merchant; Master John Elkin, gentleman; and Jasper Tyon, jeweller.

The voyage was well penned, and generally liked of all who saw it, who craved copy thereof, by which means at length it came to my hands; which I, thoroughly perusing, and finding therein mention made of former letters concerning other voyages by one of these five travellers formerly performed…I could not satisfy myself until (by the means of friends) I came to the sight of the rest also, which were many in number, at least twenty letters…all directed unto one man: some by the preacher above named, master William Biddulph; and some by his brother Peter Biddulph, lapidaire[6] and diamond cutter in those countries. Out of which letters I have gathered the matter therein contained (leaving out only some salutations and private matters) and have thought good (for the help of trav-ellers, and the delight of others) to make one body of them, and (without the consent of either of them) to put them in print. For one of these two brethren is yet beyond the seas. The other (after 10 years' travel) is lately arrived into England, and has many times been requested, by many of his good friends, to publish his travels, but could never be persuaded so to do, but answered that he knew how to spend his time better, and that he was not ignorant of the incredulity of others in such cases, who will hardly believe anything but that which they themselves have seen. And when they hear anything that seems strange unto them, they reply that travellers may lie by authority.[7] But they are liars themselves, who say so; for travellers have no more authority to lie than others, neither will they arrogate unto themselves more liberty to lie than others, especially being men who fear God, as they (of all others) should be, who go down to the sea in ships, and see the works of the Lord, both by sea and by land, and his wonders in the deep.

In regard whereof he has been so far from printing his travels that he, being a very modest man, takes no delight to speak thereof, except it be to some familiar friend. But, for that old acquaintance I have had with him (having been his scholar) and that mutual love betwixt us of long continuance, I was so bold as to make known unto him that I had seen all the letters which both he and his brother Peter Biddulph had written to their friend Bezaliel Biddulph (wherein they discoursed all their travels) and what pains I had taken to gather them together for my own delight, and direction of my travels, which I purposed shortly to undertake. Whereupon he requested me to keep them secretly to myself, which I told him that I had done, forasmuch as I had read in one of his letters to Mr. Bezaliel Biddulph the like request, which he made unto him in these words: 'I pray you, keep my letters to yourself, leastwhiles to give content unto you in writing what you would, I receive discontent myself in hearing what I would not'.

Hereby I found him very affable, and willing to confer with me of his travels, and to give me direction for mine, and to resolve me in anything I desired, concealing my purpose of imprinting them when (by conference with him and other travellers into those parts) I had perfected them. Yet, forasmuch as a public good is to be preferred before a private one, I could not but impart unto others that which I myself had learned of others: for that which Persius speaks interrogatively in this case I understand positively:... 'It is nothing for thee a good thing to know, / Unless thou impart it to others also'. And who knows what good may redound unto others by reading of this discourse of other countries.

For hereby all men may see how God has blessed our country above others; and be stirred up to thankfulness. Hereby subjects may learn to love, honour, and obey their good and gracious king,[8] when they shall read of the tyrannous government of other countries, and of the merciful government of theirs. Hereby readers may learn to love and reverence their pastors, and to thank God for the inestimable benefit of the preaching of the Word amongst them, when they shall read in what blindness and palpable ignorance other nations live, not knowing the right hand from the left in matters that concern the kingdom of Heaven, and yet reverence and honour their blind guides and superstitious churchmen like angels, and provide for their maintenance royally.

Here wives my learn to love their husbands, when they shall read in what slavery women live in other countries, and in what awe and subjection to their husbands, and what liberty and freedom they themselves enjoy. Hereby servants may be taught to be faithful and dutiful to their masters, when they shall read of the brutish and barbarous immanity[9] in other countries of masters towards their servants; who not only beat them like dogs, but sell them at their pleasure, and sometimes kill them for small offences.

Here rich men may learn to be thankful to God, not only for their liberty and freedom of their conscience and persons; but of their goods also, when they shall read how, in other countries, no man is master of his own, but as the fattest ox is nearest unto the slaughter, so the richest men are nearest unto death. Here poor men may learn to be thankful to God for their benefactors, and not to be repining and impatient beggars (as many of them are) when they shall read how, in other countries, the poor live brute beasts, on grass and water, the rich having no more mercy on them than the rich glutton had of Lazarus.

Here men who travel in England may learn what a benefit it is to have the refuge of inns in their travel, and be content to pay well for it, where they are well fed; whereas, in other countries, they lodge without doors all night; and carry their provision with them. And the publishing here without the author's consent may perhaps be an inducement to him to enlarge this discourse, by adding thereunto the diversities of religions in those countries, and what conference and disputation he had with Jews, Jesuits, and people of sundry other countries; and by perfecting anything which herein shall be thought imperfect.

A description of the famous city of Constantinople, as it is now under Sultan Ahmed I, 15th Grand Cham of the line of Ottoman

[Starts with geographical situation; continues with the information that it had formerly been called Byzantium; how Byzantium had been ruined by the Emperor Severus; the reasons why Constantine had left Rome and his rebuilding of the city; his death during the Turkish invasion under Muhammad II; and then continues that]...afterwards Muhammad, not contenting himself with the violating and deflowering of the Emperor's wife, daughters, and other ladies of honour, by a savage cruelty forced them in his presence to be dismembered and cut in pieces. During the time of the sacking (which continued three days) there was no kind of fornication, sodometry, sacrilege, nor cruelty by them left unexecuted. They spoiled the incomparable Temple of Saint Sophia (which had been built by the Emperor Justinian) of all ornaments and hallowed vessels, and made thereof a stable and a brothel for buggerers and whores.

This lamentable loss of Constantinople, being chief of the Oriental Empire, and likewise of the city of Perah (by the Turks called Galata, being the seat of trade of the Genovese) laying hard by Constantinople, upon the other side of the channel, was in the year of Our Saviour 1453, March 29th (some do say of April, and others of May) after it had remained under the dominion of the Christians [for] 1198 years.

But this is a marvellous thing, and worthy to be noted, that Constantinople being re-edified and new set up by Constantine the son of Saint Helen (whom some report to have been an Englishwoman born at Colchester) after the proportion and likeness of Rome, was by a Constantine, son of another son of Helen, sacked, and brought into the hands of the Turks; which forever is like to be (in the judgement of man) an irreparable damage unto all Christendom. Yet the Turks have a prophecy that as the Empire was got by Muhammad, so by yet another of that name Muhammad shall it be lost again.

Muhammad, after he had thus taken the city, resolving to keep there the seat of his Empire, caused (with diligence) the walls to be new made, and certain other ruinated places to be repaired. And instead of the great number of the people that were there slain and carried away as prisoners he caused to be brought thither, out of all the provinces and cities by him conquered, a certain number of men, women and children, with their faculties and riches, whom he permitted there to live according to the institutions and precepts of such religion as it pleased them to observe, and to exercise with all safety their handicrafts and merchandises; which ministered an occasion unto an infinite number of Jews and

Maranes,[10] driven out of Spain, to come and dwell there; by means whereof, in very short time the city began to increase in traffic, riches, and abundance of people.

This Muhammad was the first founder of the Great Seraglio (where the Great Turk now usually dwells) which he built at the entry of the channel, about one of the corners of the city, upon the promontory Christoferas; which afterwards, by the Great Turks who successively dwelt there, have been greatly beautified and augmented.

He founded likewise, upon one of the mounts of the same city, a sumptuous mosque or church, with an amarath and college, endowing them all with great yearly revenues; which is not to be marvelled at, for Fortune was so favourable unto him that after he had ruinated the Empire of Constantinople and Trebizond he took from the Christians 12 kingdoms and 200 cities; so that, by reason of his great prowesses and conquests the name and title of 'Great' was given unto him, and to this day remains unto the house of the Ottomans; as the Turk who died about four years since was called Sultan Muhammad, the Grand Cham of Turkey, and the 14th of the line of Ottoman.[11] And his son, who now reigns (being not above 20 years of age) is called Sultan Ahmed [Ahmed I], the 15th Grand Cham of the line of Ottoman, and invested himself also (as his predecessors have done) King of the Black and White Seas, and of the Holy Cities of Mecca and Jerusalem.

Christians in Syria

...Tripoli [is]...a city on the mainland of Syria, near unto Mount Lybanus, which is a mountain of 3 days' journey in length, reaching from Tripoli near to Damascus. While our ship stayed in the road[12] at Tripoli, I and some others rode up to Mount Lybanus to see the cedar trees there, and lodged the first night at the Bishop's house of Eden, who used us very kindly. It is but a little village, named Anchora by the Turks; but mostly by the Christians dwelling there it is called Eden – not the Garden of Eden (which place is unknown to this day), but because it is a pleasant place, resembling in some sort the Garden of Eden (as the simple inhabitants thereof suppose); therefore it is called Eden.

This Bishop was born in the same parish, but brought up at Rome; his name was Francis Amyra. From him I understood that the Pope of Rome many years since sent unto the Christians inhabiting Mount Lybanus to persuade them to embrace the Romish religion, and yield themselves to the Church of Rome; making large promises unto them if they would so do. Whereof they deliberated long, but in the end yielded, upon condition [that] they might have liberty to use their own liturgy and ceremonies and Lents (for they strictly observe 4 Lents in the year), and other customs; ever since which time the Pope has and does maintain some of their children at Rome. These Christians who dwell upon Mount Lybanus are called Maronites.[13] They are very simple and ignorant people; yet civil, kind, and courteous to strangers. There are also many Turks dwelling in the same mountains, and an Emir or great lord called Emir Ysuf, who governs all the rest, both Christians and Turks, being himself a Mahometan; yet one who holds the government of Mount Lybanus in despite of the Great Turk; and has done for a long time.

From Eden we rode 10 miles further up the mountain, to see certain cedar trees; where we saw 24 tall cedar trees growing together, as big as the greatest oaks, with several rows of branches one over another, stretching straight out, as though they were kept by Art.... From these cedars we returned towards Tripoli [by] another way, descending by the side of the Mount towards a village of the Maronitical Christians...where (as we were descending down the side of the mountain) all the men, women and children came out of their houses to behold us. And when we were yet far off riding towards them, they gave a joyful shout all together jointly, to express their joy for our coming. And when we came near, their women, with chafing dishes of coals, burnt incense in our way, and their Cassises, that is, their churchmen (with blue sashes about their heads) made crosses with their fingers towards us (as their manner it is a sign of welcome) and blessed us, giving God thanks that He had brought Christian Franks (that is, freemen) of such far countries as they understood we were of, to come to visit them.

So soon as we were dismounted from our horses, the Chief Sheh,[14] with all the rest of their ancientest men, came and brought us to the chief house of the parish, called the Townhouse or Church-house, and there spread carpet and tablecloths on the ground (as their manner is) and made us all sit down. And everyone who was able, brought baskets of such good cheer as they had, to welcome us, which was many bottles or ingesters of exceeding good wine, with olives, salads, eggs, and such like things as on the sudden they had ready, and set them before us. And both by the cheerfulness of their countenance, gestures of their bodies, and presents of such present things as they had, expressed their gladness for our coming; and would also have prepared hens, kids, and other good cheer, but we would not suffer them [to do so]. This was about 11 or 12 o'clock. They would have had us continue with them all night; and with great importunity craved it.

But we, understanding that the Patriarch was but 3 miles off...we went to salute him; who, hearing of our coming (albeit he were at a feast amongst all his neighbours) came to meet us, and saluted us, and brought us all in amongst his neighbours into a room foursquare, and round about set with carpets and tablecloths on the ground, and such cheer as the season of the year did afford, set thereon, and made us sit down, and conferred with us of our country, and many other matters – saving matters of religion. For the poor man had no Latin, and little learning in any other language; only he had the Syriac (which was his natural language) with the Turkish and the Arabian tongue. After we had spent one hour with him, we left him with his neighbours...where we [had] found him; for he could not conveniently come from them, for their manner is, that when they feast, to sit from midday until midnight, and sometimes all night; never altogether rising from their good cheer, but now and then one by intercourses, as occasion required, returning again speedily....

At this monastery of Saint Mary that is the Patriarch's house, we lodged all night. And both on Saturday at evening prayer, and on Sunday at morning prayer, we both heard and saw the manner of their service in the Syriac tongue, both read and sung very reverently, with confessions, prayers, thanksgivings; the Psalms of David sung, and chapters both out of the Old and the New Testament distinctly read. It rejoiced me greatly to see their Order, and I observed in these ancient Christians called Nazarites the antiquity of using set forms of prayers in churches, and also the necessity thereof that the people might have something to say 'Amen' unto, being read in their mother tongue, that they may learn to pray privately by those prayers which they daily hear read publicly. This is too much neglected in England. God grant reformation thereof....

There are dwelling on one side of Mount Lybanus, towards the foot of the mountain (and in some other places in that country) a kind of Christians called Druzes,[15] who had come into the country with King Baldwin and Godfrey of Boulogne. When they conquered that country (whose predecessors or ancestors are thought to have been Frenchmen) and afterwards, when the Saracens recovered it again, these men (whom they now call Druzes) fled into the mountains to save themselves, and there dwelling long, in the end their posterity forgot Christianity, yet used still baptism, and retained still the names of Christians, whom the Turcomans call 'Rasties', that is, Infidels, because they eat swine's flesh, which is forbidden by the Turk's laws.

These Turcommani are kind and simple people, dwelling always in the fields, following their flocks; born, and brought up, living and dying in tents. And when their flock and herds remove, then all their men, women, and children remove with their household stuff; and houses too, which are but tents made to remove, after the manner of the ancient Israelites. And where they find good pasture, there they pitch their tents – the men following their locks of sheep and herds of cattle; the women keep their tents, and spend their time spinning, or carding,[16] or knitting, or some household housewifery, not spending their time in gossiping and gadding abroad from place to place, and from house to house, from ale-house to wine-tavern, as many idle housewives in England do. Yet sometimes are these simple souls abused by janissaries who, in travelling by them, take from them perforce victuals for themselves and for their horses, and give them nothing but sore stripes if they but murmur against them. But when Christian merchants pass by them, they will (of their own accord) kindly present them!

Scanderone [Eskunderun];[17] Tarsus; Aleppo [Halab]; Baghdad

Scanderone is the port for Aleppo, where our merchants land their goods and send them up to Aleppo on camels. The caravans usually make 3 days journey between Scanderone and Aleppo. While our camels were preparing, we took boat and went to an ancient town by the seaside, called...of old Tarsus, a city in Cilicia where Saint Paul was born, mentioned *Acts* 22:3. Which town is arched about (as many of their cities are) to keep away the heat of the sun, with arches which they called 'bazaars'. At the gardens near Tarsus (and likewise at other gardens within 3 miles of Scanderone) we saw great store of silkworms, which at the first are but little grains like unto mustardseed; but by the bearing of them in women's bosoms, they do gather a heat whereby they come into life, and so prove worms. They keep them in tents made of reeds, with one loft over another full of them, and feed them with leaves of mulberry trees. These worms (by natural instinct) do fast often; as some report, every third day...

About 8 miles from Scanderone we came to a town called Bylan [Belen?] where lies buried an English gentleman named Henry Moryson, who died there, coming down from Aleppo in company with his brother, Master Fines Moryson;[18] who left his arms in that country with these verses underwritten: 'To thee dear Henry Moryson, / Thy brother Fynes here left alone / Has left this fading memory; / For monuments, and all, must die'.

...we came to the plain of Antioch, and went over the river Orontes by boat; which river parts Antioch and Syria....We lodged the first night at Antioch in Pisidia, an ancient town about 25 miles from Scanderone, mentioned *Acts* 11:26, where the disciples were first called Christians. Here we lodged in a house; but on the bare ground, having nothing to sleep on, or to cover us, but what we brought with us, viz. a pillow, and a quilt at the most; and that was lodging for a lord....The inhabitants at this day are Greeks; but under the government of the Turk, but for matters of religion, ordered and ruled by their Patriarchs. For the Greeks have 4 Patriarchs to this present day, viz. the Patriarch of Antioch; the Patriarch of Jerusalem; the Patriarch of Alexandria; the Patriarch of Constantinople, who rules all the rest. Yet, as the Jews, so also the Greeks to this day are without a king, and both they and their Patriarchs are but slaves to the Great Turk.

And although their Patriarch of Constantinople is counted their chief Patriarch, yet I have known one Milesius (a learned man indeed) who was first Patriarch of Constantinople, preferred to the place by Master Edward Barton,[19] an English gentleman and Lord Ambassador for Queen Elizabeth of famous memory[20] (and the mirror of all ambassadors who ever came to Constantinople) who, for his wisdom, good government, policy and Christian carriage had left an immortal fame behind him in those countries to this present day; and lies buried at an island of the Greeks, within 12 miles of Constantinople, called Barton's Island to this day. After whose death this good man Milesius was by the Greeks displaced from being Patriarch of Constantinople, which they durst not do while Master Barton was living; because, being a man of knowledge, he laboured to reform the Greeks from many of their superstitious customs. Whereupon presently (after the death of Master Barton) they said [that] their Patriarch was an Englishman, and no Greek, and therefore mazulled him; that is, displaced him; yet, bearing some reverence towards him for his learning, made him Patriarch of Alexandria. And being there Patriarch, he excommunicated the Patriarch of Antioch because he accepted relief at the Pope's hand; and made him come to Alexandria to humble himself unto him, and acknowledge his fault before he would suffer him to execute his Patriarch's office.

In the mountains betwixt Scanderone and Aleppo there are dwelling a certain kind of people called the Kurds,[21] coming of the race of the ancient Parthians; who worship the Devil, and allege for their reason for so doing, that God is a good man, and will do no man harm, but that the Devil is bad, and must be pleased lest he hurt them...

The second night in our travel from Scanderone we lodged at a place called The Gardens, in the open fields, having the ground to our bed, a stone to our pillow (as Jacob in his travels had) and the sky for our covering. And many poor travellers in these parts (who come unprovided) have nothing else but the air for their supper, except [that] they can meet with the fruits of trees, or herbs of the fields....Their bread is made all in cakes, after the ancient manner, as Abraham entertained Angels with hearth cakes.[22] At one place we had also presented to us very good sweet goat's milk, and also good our milk, turned by art, which is the most common dish in those hot countries.

The following day we came about noon to a village called Hanadan [Amadan?], 8 miles on this side of Aleppo, over against which village, on the right hand, on the top of the hill, there is (as the Jews report) the sepulchre of the Prophet Jeremiah....At this village we dined on muskmelons, samboules,[23] and a mucklebite.[24] And after dinner we slept an hour or two (as the custom of the country is) and then rode forwards towards Aleppo; whither we came by 5 o'clock, and there were kindly entertained...by the worshipful Richard Colthurst Esq., Consul to the English nation there....

Pigeons as carriers of messages[25]

Between Aleppo and Babylon, merchants travel often over the desert of Arabia, and every quarter of the year, caravans come from there with many hundred camels laden with merchandise. And their custom has been, and is still sometimes, when they have occasion to send some sudden news from Babylon to fasten some brief writing to one of the wings of a Baghdad or Baylonian pigeon, or about her neck in such sort that it may not hinder her flying, and to send her therewith to bring news to Aleppo; which is at the least 10 days' journey off: which, when I heard at the first, it seemed to me wonderful strange, and almost incredible.

But after I understood how they train them to it, the strangeness thereof was diminished. For when the hen dove sits [on her eggs], or has young ones, they take the cock pigeon and put him in a cage; and when the carriers go with their camels, they set the pigeon in an open cage on the camel's back, set her at liberty; who, presently mounted up aloft and beholding her way, never ceases to fly until she comes to her mate. Which, any of the house perceiving, look for some paper fastened about her, and so in post haste understand speedy news. And so, by degrees, they train them further and further to the places of their traffick [trade]. This I have known put in practice and performed by an English merchant of Aleppo, who in such sort sent a Baghdad pigeon to Scanderone, 3 days from Aleppo, and by her return understood when ships arrived thither, and departed from there.

Which seems unto me not so strange as that which we read of, performed by a cobbler of Rome, who taught a [jack]daw to speak, and to salute the Emperor, as he passed by, with these words: 'Salve Caesar'; which the Emperor hearing, gave unto the cobbler a good reward, and bought his daw. Which, another poor man in Rome perceiving, hoping to get the like reward, took upon him to teach another daw the same lesson. And day and night, as he sat at his work, used still to prattle unto his daw, and bid him say 'Salve Caesar'. And when he perceived that he could not make his daw once frame himself to pronounce those words he, chafing, rapped him on the bill and said '*Operam & oleum perdidi*', that is, 'I have lost my labour in vain'; yet still continued his diligent endeavour, and by repeating often both 'Salve Caesar' and '*Operam & oleum perdidi*' in the end his daw had learned both the one and the other; and when the Emperor passed by, said 'Salve Caesar'. The Emperor answered '*Tales habeo domi salutores*', that is, 'I have saluters enough at home'; whereupon the daw replied '*Operam & oleum perdidi*'. Which the Emperor hearing, bought his daw also, because he had one lesson more than the other, and rewarded the poor man well for his labour....

Muhammad

I promised you in my last letters to write unto you by the next of the religion, government, manners and customs of the Turks, and other nations there dwelling or sojourning. Wherefore, that I may the better make known unto you their religion, I will begin with the first author thereof, who was (no doubt) the Devil, who used that false prophet Muhammad as his instrument to broach it abroad. Many prophets have foretold of the wickedness and tyranny of the Turks; but I will only recite the prophecy of Daniel 7:7 which is very notable, and agrees especially unto the time when his impiety and tyranny did begin. After this (says Daniel) 'I saw in the visions by night, and behold, the fourth beast was fearful, and terrible, and very strong. It had great iron teeth; it devoured and broke in pieces, and stamped the residue under its feet. And it was unlike to the beasts that were before it, for it had 10 horns'. Hitherto spake Daniel of the fourth, that is, the Roman Empire and of the cruelty of the same, and of the 10 Kings in subjection thereunto.

Now follows the prophecy of the Turkish Kingdom, in these words: Daniel 7:8 'As I considered the horses, behold, there came up among them another little horn, before whom there were 3 of the first horns plucked away. And behold, in this horn were eyes like the eyes of a man, and a mouth speaking presumptuous things'. And afterwards, verse 23: 'The fourth beast shall be the fourth kingdom in the earth; which shall be unlike to all the kingdoms, and shall devour the whole earth, and shall tread it down, and break it in pieces. And the 10 horns of this kingdom are 10 kings who shall rise. And another shall rise after them, and he shall be unlike to the first; and he shall subdue 3 kings, and shall speak words against the most high, and think that he may change times and laws'.[26]

Hitherto Daniel, whose prophecy the event had proved to be true; for *Anno Dom.* 591 (Mauritius then the Emperor of the Romans, and reigning in Constantinople) was Muhammad born in Arabia, in a base village called Itraipia. His parents were of different nations, and different in religion. His father, Abdallah, was an Arabian; his mother, Hadidja, a Jew both by birth and by profession. His parentage (according to most histories) was so mean and base that both his birth and infancy remained obscure and of no reckoning till that his riper years (bewraying in him a most subtle and crafty nature and disposition) did argue some likelihood that the sharpness and dexterity of his wit would in time abolish the baseness and obscurity of his birth.

And soon did he make show and proof thereof. For, being trained up of a boy in the service of a rich and wealthy merchant, by his great industry and diligence, he so insinuated and wrought himself into the good favour and liking both of his master and mistress, that when his master died and had left all his wealth and riches unto his wife, she made choice of her servant Muhammad for her husband, making him lord and master of her person, and of her substance. The man, being thus raised from base and low degree, to great wealth and possessions, and having a working and aspiring head, did from thenceforth plot and imagine how he might raise himself in honour and reputation; presuming that the greatness of his wealth would be a fit means to work his higher fortunes. Neither was he deceived in the expectation of his hope. For, consorting himself with one Sergius, a fugitive monk [and] a notable heretic of the Arian sect[27] (whom he had made bounden unto him by his great liberality) there grew so strict a league of amity and secret familiarity between them, that they had many times private conference [about] how, and by which means, Muhammad might make himself ways to rise in honour and estimation.

After much consulting and debating of the matter, the best course which they conceived to effect their purpose was to coin[28] a new kind of doctrine and religion, under colour whereof (the times then being troublesome, the people full of simplicity and ignorance, religion also waxing cold, and neglected) they thought it an easy matter to draw many followers unto them, and by that means to grow great in the eye and opinion of the world. Whereupon these two hellhounds (one of them being an arch-enemy unto Christ and the truth of His religion, and the other seeming a mere atheist or profane person; neither perfect Jew, nor perfect Christian) patched up a particular doctrine unto themselves out of the Old and New Testament[s], depraving the sense of both of them. And, framing their opinions according to their own corrupt and wicked affections, they brought forth a monstrous and most devilish religion, savouring partly of Judaism, partly of Christianity, and partly of Arianism, as I will show you more particularly in what follows. But first (I pray you) how Daniel's prophecy (before set down) is proved true.

Anno Dom. 623, Hirachius being Emperor, Muhammad moved sedition. And forthwith the Saracens or Arabians joined together these 3 dominions: Egypt; Syria; and Africa – which are the 3 horns plucked from those 10 horns of the fourth beast. And Daniel ascribes to this little house (that is, to the Turkish Empire) three notes whereby it may be known. The first whereof is a new law contrary to the Law of God; for the eyes do signify a law subtly invented. The second mark is blasphemy against the Most High, who is Christ. For the mouth speaking words against the true God signifies blasphemies against the Son of God. The third note is cruelty towards the Church: 'And he shall consume' (said he) 'the saints of the Most High'. The fourth is an endeavour to abolish the Gospel and the Church. 'He shall think' (said he) 'that he may change times and laws'.

God would have this prophecy to be extant for a strengthening of the godly against the cruelty of Turks, that when they should see the event, to answer to the prophecy, [that] they might not be offended at the stumbling block of so great persecution, and of such revolting from the true Church. And therefore, being thus forewarned by the Prophet, let us take heart to our selves against this Turkish tyranny and wickedness, especially seeing how the event has answered the prophecy. For there have four monarchies been one after another. And now reigns a people who are the enemies of God, who openly abolishes the prophetical and apostolical Scriptures. Thus you may see how fully Daniel's prophecy is fulfilled. I will now proceed to show more plainly how the Turks began, multiplied, and increased.

Muhammad, in his youth, by reason of his poverty, lived by theft and robbery. Afterwards, having heaped much riches together, he was a soldier among his countrymen, the Arabians, under Heraclitus. In the war he found occasion of principality and power. For when the Arabians (being offended with Heraclitus for denying them their pay, and because his religion had severed themselves from him) Muhmmad joined himself to the angry soldiers and stirred up their minds against their Emperor, and encouraged them in their defection. Whereupon, by a certain company of soldiers, he was chosen to be their captain (as they commonly are extolled in every commotion which favour the wicked enterprise of the rebellious people, and set upon the mighty, and governors).

In this new captain many could not abide the baseness of his birth, nor the odiousness of his former life. Especially they loathed him for a disease he had; which was the falling sickness. He therefore, to redeem himself from this contempt (which is an easy matter among the foolish common people) pretended a divinity in his doings, feigning himself to enter communication with God, and so when he talked with him, to be ravished out of himself, and seemed like unto one afflicted with the falling sickness. And therefore, he said plainly (but untruly) how he was no more a captain and prince elected through the favour of soldiers, but a prophet and messenger of Almighty God who, under the show of divinity, he might have all men the more obedient unto his words.

But, for as much as he was rude altogether and unlearned, he adjoined unto himself two masters and counsellors who were Christians, the one whereof was Sergius, an Arian, and the other, John Nestorius; to whom there came a third, who was a Jew, a Talmudist: of which three, every one of them defended his several sect. Whereupon Muhammad, supposing that he should not only gratify his companions, but also the more easily allure all nations unto himself, received all; that is: the pertinacity of Arius, the error of Nestorius, and the vain inventions of the Talmudist. And therefore he received from the Jew circumcision; from the Christians sundry washings, as it were, baptisms. And, with Sergius, he denied the divinity of Christ. Now, some worshipped fools; others were baptised and somewhat instructed in Christianity, who, as soon as they had left the Roman Emperor for the hatred they bore against him, renounced forthwith the religion which he defended, even after the example of those 10 Tribes of Israel, which (revolting from the house of David unto Jeroboam) despised the laws of their fathers, and went from the service of the only true God unto the invocation of devils.

Muhammad's manner to enlarge and establish his kingdom was this (which also his master taught him). He said how God, at the first, to mankind sent Moses; after him, Jesus Christ, who was indued with the power to work miracles. But men gave small heed to them. therefore he determined to send Muhammad, a warrior without miracles, that [those] whom miracles had not moved, weapons might compel. He said how he was the last messenger, and that after him none should come; how Christ, in the Gospel, had prophesied of him, and how tidings was of him through a wonderful light, which passed from Eva by succession of kind through all women, even to his very mother.

See the subtlety of this dissembler and deceiver, Muhammad; who, knowing that he was destitute altogether of the heavenly gift to work miracles, he feigned that he was sent with the sword. But this armed man at the length was vanquished, and received a sore wound in his mouth, whereby he lost some of his cheek teeth; and was thrown into a ditch, and put into shameful soil; and that, the very day before he had (from the Oracle of God) promised victory to him and his. Yea; and while he was yet a common thief, he was often-times beaten sore of the Drianites, who camels he set upon returning from Mecca. And that city (which has him now in honour) sometimes adjudged him unto death, as a very hurtful thief; and appointed a reward if any could bring him unto them, either alive or dead.

This champion (first a thief, afterwards a seditious soldier, then a renegade, after that a captain of a rebellious host) persuaded lightheads, enemies of the true religion, how he is the Messenger of God; whereby we may gather how great the power of Satan is in them who embrace not the truth. Whereof it is that at this day that adversary of God defends his blasphemies against God, by Turkish and Mahometical force, according to the prophecy of Daniel.

Of Muhammad's laws and 8 Commandments

And for the better broaching of his devilish religion he has prescribed certain laws or Commandments, and fortified the same by policy. His laws are in number 8, which are partly political and partly ceremonial. The first concerns God, which is this: God is a great God, and the only God; and Muhammad is the Prophet of God....The second Commandment is concerning their duty towards their parents, in these words: Obey thy parents, and do nothing to displease them, either in word or deed. How badly this duty is performed among them, I know by experience: for I did never read or hear of more disobedient children to their parents, either in word or deed. The third is concerning their neighbours, which is this: do unto others as thou wouldst be done unto thyself. Some of them are just in their dealings one with another; but most of them [are] unjust and deceitful in their proceedings with strangers – some few shopkeepers only excepted.

The fourth is concerning prayer, wherein is required: that every man five times a day repair to their churches, to make public prayer unto Muhammad. The Turks have no bells; but very fair churches, and high steeples. And at the hours of their public prayer they are called to the church by the voice of criers, who go up into their steeples, and cry with a loud voice: 'Come now and worship the great God'....

Their fifth Commandment is concerning fasting, viz. that one moon in the year, everyone (of any reasonable age) spend the whole time fasting....Their sixth Commandment is concerning almsdeeds. Let every man, out of his store, give unto the poor liberally, freely, and voluntarily. Their alms are either public or private. Their public alms is a sacrifice or offering of some beast for sacrifice unto Muhammad once every year; which, being killed, is cut into small pieces, and given all to the poor.

Their private alms (notwithstanding their Law) is much neglected; for I have heard of many poor people who have died amongst them for want of relief: and in the way, as I have travelled, I have found some dead for hunger and cold. And though a man be never so poor, yet if he is not able to pay his head money to the king, yearly, they are beaten, and their women and child sold to pay it. If our murmuring and impatient poor were here but a short time, they would learn to be more thankful to God and man, and how to esteem of a benefit bestowed upon them, and not curse and revile (as many of them do) if any one that passes by them do not give unto them. The Turks are more merciful to birds, cats, and dogs, than to the poor.

Their seventh Commandment is concerning marriage: that every man must of necessity marry, to increase and multiply the sect and religion of Muhammad. Their custom is to buy their wives off their parents, and never to see them until they come to be married; and their marriage is nothing but enrolling in the Cadi's book. And it is lawful for them to take as many wives as they will, or as many as they are able to keep. And whenever he dislikes any one of them, it is their use to sell them or give them to any of their men-slaves. And although they love their women never so well, yet they never sit at table with men. No, not [even] with their husbands; but wait at table and serve him. And when he has dined, they dine in secret by themselves, admitting no man or mankind amongst them, if he is above 12 years of age. And they never go abroad without leave of their husbands; which is very seldom, except it is either to the bannio (or hot bath), or once a week to weep at the graves of the dead; which is usually on Thursday, being the eve before their Sabbath, which is Friday. And the Jews' Sabbath on Saturday; and the Christians' on Sunday – three Sabbath days together in one country.

If their husbands have been abroad,[29] at his entrance into the house, if any one of their women is sitting on a stool, she rises up, and bows herself to her husband, and kisses his hand, and sets the same stool for him whereon they sat, and stand so long as he is in presence. If the like order were in England, women would be more dutiful and faithful to their husbands than many of them are. And especially if there was the like punishment for whores, there would be less whoredom. For there, if a man has a 100 women, if any one prostitute herself to any man but her own husband, he has authority to bind her, hands and feet, and so cast her into the river with a stone about her neck, and drown her. And this is a common punishment amongst them; but it is usually done at night. And the man, if he be taken,[30] is dismembered.

But the daughters and sisters of the Great Turk are more free than all other men and women. For when their brethren die, they live; and when they come to years of marriage, their father (if he is living) or brother (if he is king) will give unto them, for their husbands, the greatest Pashas or Viziers whom they shall affect, and say unto them: 'Daughter, or sister, I give thee this man to be thy slave and bedfellow; and if he is not loving, dutiful, and obedient unto thee, here I give thee a canzhare (that is, a dagger) to cut off his head'. And always after, those daughters or sisters of the king wear a broad and sharp dagger. And whenever their husbands (who are given unto them by the King to be their slaves) displease them, they may and do cut off their heads....

Their eight Commandment is the same as our first: 'Thou shalt not kill'. In their Qur'ān it is written that God hates murder. And they say that it is the second sin which crept into the world after the Creation, being first committed by cursed Cain, who killed his brother Abel. And their belief is that this sin of wilful murder is impardonable....Often have I heard Turks brawl with one another, and in words most vilely revile one another.

But never did I see or hear of two Turks, in their private quarrels, strike one another; for, if they do so, they are presently brought before the magistrate, and severely punished. Yea; if one does but lift up his hand to strike another, he is cast in prison, and kept in irons, until he has paid some great fine, or received some other punishment. But they will strike Jews and Christians oftentimes; who dare not strike them again....

Yet their churchmen they have in great reverence. And not only theirs; but they reverence churchmen of all nations and call them 'holy men', 'saints', and 'men of God'. I myself have had great experience hereof, both in my place of abode at Aleppo, and in my journey towards Jerusalem; and in other places. In Aleppo, as I have walked in the streets, both Turks and Moors, and other nations, would very reverently salute me after the manner of their country; yea, they very soldiers, as I have walked in the fields with many others of our nation, without a janissary to guard us. Though they have been many hundreds together, yet have they not offered either me or any of my company wrong, for my sake, but have said one to another:...'This is a churchman; and therefore take heed what you do unto him, for he is a good man, etc'.

They also account fools, dumb men and madmen santones, that is, saints. And whatsoever such madmen say or do, though they take anything out of their house, or trick them and wound them, yet they take it in good part and say that they shall have good luck after it. And when such madmen die, they canonise them for saints, and erect stately monuments over their graves, as we have here many examples – especially of one who (being mad) went always naked, whose name was Sheikh Boubac; at whose death they bestowed great cost on his funeral, and erected a house over his grave where (to this day) there are lamps burning night and day, and many idle fellows (whom they call Dariuses) there maintained to look after the sepulchre, and to receive the offerings of such as come to offer to Sheikh Boubac; which they take to themselves. And there is no week but many come out of the city of Aleppo and other places, to offer. For this sepulchre is built on a hill, 3 miles from Aleppo, between the king's garden and the fountain of fishes. If any be sick, or in danger, they vow that if they recover or escape, they will offer so much money, or this or that good thing to Sheikh Boubac.

Language of the Arabians

The chief thing that I have observed in them, worth the praise, is this: that they retain the use of speaking their natural tongue to this day, speaking the Arabic naturally; which is a far more learned language than the Turkish. For, as the Turks' religion is a mixed religion compounded of many religions, so is their language also a medley language or (as I may say) a linsey woolsy[31] religion and language, compounded of many other languages, wherein nothing is written.

But the Arabian tongue is a learned language wherein ancient and many learned physicians have written much. And to this day the Turks' Qur'ān and all their law and religion is written in the Arabic tongue; which is one of those Oriental languages which depend upon the Hebrew tongue wherein (because you have some knowledge, and are studious in the tongues) – according to your request in your last letter – I will acquaint you what languages are here spoken, and which languages are most common and commendable to travellers to go furthest withal.

There are here spoken so many several languages as there are several nations here dwelling or sojourning; every nation (amongst themselves) speaking their own language.

And here are of most nations in the world some, who either come with their merchandise to sell or buy commodities, or sojourn here as strangers, or else have access and recess to this city as strangers. But, of all Christian languages, the Italian tongue is the most used; and therewithal a man may travel furthest. But, of all the Oriental tongues, these 4 are most spoken in these parts: Arabic; Turkish; Armenian; and Persian, or Agimesco.

Of the Jews

Besides all these Mohametans (which I have already named) there are many Jews in Constantinople, Aleppo, Damascus, Babylon, Grand Cairo, and every great city and place of merchandise throughout all the Turkish dominions; who are known by their hats: for they were accustomed to wear red hats without brims, at my first coming. But lately, [by] the Head Vizier (being their enemy), they are constrained to wear hats of blue cloth; because red was accounted too stately and princelike a colour for them to wear.

They are called by three names, which were given to them of old. First, they are called 'Hebrews' (as some suppose, of Heber, the fourth from Noah, in whom the Hebrew tongue remained at the confusion of tongues, whence he had his name).[32] But St. Augustine and other Fathers affirm that they were first called Hebrews of Abraham, with the alteration of a few letters, *Hebrai quasi Abrahai*, that is, Hebrews as it were Abrahites. Secondly, they were called 'Israelites', from Jacob surnamed Israel, whose grandfather Jacob was. Thirdly, they were called 'Jews', after that Judah and Benjamin (which for the unity of minds were, as it were, one tribe) following Rehoboam the son of Solomon of the tribe of Judah, made the kingdom of Judah. The other 10, betaking them to Jeroboam of the tribe of Ephraim, set up the kingdom of the Ephramites, or Israel.[33]

And what became of those 10 tribes the Jews acknowledge themselves to be ignorant. Only, some of their rabbis think them to be in Tarracia.[34] The only reason which I have heard them allege for their opinion is this: because they often understand by Tatarians, who came from thence to use merchandise in Aleppo or elsewhere, that there are many amongst them called by Hebrew names to this day. Of these three names whereby they are known, the most common name whereby they are called to this day is the name of Jews. One and the same people thrice changed their names, and often the place of their abode. And to this day they have neither king nor country proper to themselves; but are dispersed throughout the whole world. And in every place where they come, they are contemptible and of base account, according to the cry of those crucifiers: 'His blood be upon us and our children'.

Which is fulfilled this day in our eyes and ears. They are of more vile account in the sight of the Turks than Christians; insomuch that if a Jew would turn Turk, he must first turn Christian before they will admit him to be a Turk. Yea, it is a word of reproach amongst the Turks. And a usual protestation amongst them, when they are falsely accused of any crime, to clear themselves they protest in this manner: 'If this be true, then God grant that I may die a Jew'. And the Jews in like cases used to say: 'If this be not a false accusation, then God grant that I may die a Christian', praying better for themselves than they believe; and as all of them must be that shall be saved.

And the poor Christians sojourning and dwelling in these parts do hate them very uncharitably and irreligiously (in that we read Romans 11) many arguments proving that they shall be converted again. For, on Good Friday, in many places (especially in Zante)[35] they throw stones at them, insomuch that they dare not come out of their houses all that day, and yet are scarce in safety in their homes; for they used to throw stones at their windows and doors, and on the roofs of their houses. On Thursday, about noon, the Jews begin to keep within doors, and continue there, with their doors shut, until Saturday about noon; for if they come forth before that time, they are sure to be stoned. But after noon on Easter eve they come abroad; [then] they may pass as quietly as ever they did. These, in their blind zeal, think to be revenged on them for whom Christ prayed, saying 'Father, forgive them for they know not what they do'.[36]

And some ignorant Christians refuse to eat of their meat or bread. Their reason is because the Jews refuse to eat or drink with Christians to this day; or to eat any meat that Christians kill. But it is not unusual amongst Christians of better knowledge to eat of the Jews' meat; which ordinarily they buy of them. For the Jews to this day eat not of the hinder part of any beast, but only of the former parts, and sell the hinder quarters of their beef, mutton, kids, goats, etc. to Christians. They observe still their old ceremonies and feasts, sacrifices only excepted; which the Turks will not suffer them to do. For they ere wont amongst them to sacrifice children; but dare not now, for fear of the Turks. Yet some of them have confessed that their physicians kill some Christian patient or other, whom they have under their hands at that time, instead of a sacrifice.

If a man dies without children, the next brother takes his wife, and raises up seed unto his brother. And they still marry in their own kindred. Many of them are rich merchants; some of them dragomen;[37] and some, brokers. Most of them are very crafty and deceitful people. They have no beggars amongst them; but many thieves. And some who steal for necessity; for they dare not beg. They are also very great usurers; and therein the Turks excel them. For although there be usurers amongst them, yet they allow it not. For if a Christian or any man borrows money of a Turk (though he promises him interest) yet if he pays the principal, he dares not molest him for interest, nor complain of him; being against their law.

Their Jews' Sabbath is on Saturday; which they observe so strictly that they will not travel upon any occasion on that day, nor receive money, nor handle a pen to write: as I have known from experience in a Doctor of Physick; but on the morrow he would take double fees of his patient. They read their Law in the Hebrew tongue, written in phylacteries, or long rolls of parchment. And the Old Testament is also read in the Hebrew. But their Cakams and Cohens preach in the Spanish tongue. All matters of controversy between themselves are brought before their Cakam to decide; who is their chief churchman. Cakamin Hebrew is as much as 'sapiens' in Latin; that is, a man and a wife; and a Cohen, in Hebrew, is as much as 'sacerdos' in Latin; that is, a priest.

Most of the Jews can read Hebrew, but few of them speak it, except it be in two places in Turkey; and those are at Salonika (formerly called Thessalonika, a city in Macedonia...) and at Sasetta, in the Holy Land, near unto the Sea of Galilee. Which two places are, as it were, universities or schools of learning amongst them; and there...they speak Hebrew. I have sundry times had conference with many of them. And some of them; yea, the greatest part of them, are blasphemous wretches who, when they are pressed with an argument which they cannot answer, break out into opprobrious speeches, and say Christ was a false prophet and that His disciples stole Him out of His grave while the soldiers who had watched him, slept; and that their forefathers did deservedly crucify Him; and that if He were now living, they would use Him worse than ever His forefathers did.

Of Christians of sundry sorts, sojourning in Aleppo

Besides these Turks, Moors, and Arabians (who are all Mohametans) and Jews (who are Talmudists) there are also sundry sorts of Christians in this country; who are of two sorts: either such as were born, brought up, and dwelled in the country, or such as were born in Christendom, and only sojourn here for a time to exercise merchandises. The first sort who were born in this heathen country, and dwell there, are either Armenians, Maronites, Jacobites, Georgians, Chelsalines, or Greeks: who are all governed by their Patriarchs for ecclesiastical matters. But for civil government, both they and their Patriarchs are subject to Turkish laws; yea, they are all slaves unto the Great Turk, whom they call their Grand Seignior.

Of the Nostranes or Nazaritans

Among all these sorts of Christians, there is amongst the Maronites an ancient company of Christians, called Nostranes, *quasi* Nazaritans, of the sect of the Nazarites, more civil and harmless than any of the rest. Their country is Mount Lybanus (as I wrote to you heretofore) but many of them dwell at Aleppo, whereof some of them are Cassisses; that is, churchmen. Some of them are cooks and servants unto English merchants and others; some artificers. All of them live somewhat poorly; but they are more honest and true in their conversation than any of the rest, especially at their first coming from Mount Lybanus to dwell in Aleppo. And many, during their continuance here, if they are not corrupted by other wicked nations there dwelling: in whom I observed more by experience than I heard of them, or noted in them when I was amongst them on Mount Lybanus. And especially for the manner of their marriage, and how they honour the same.

They buy their wives off their fathers (as others there dwelling do), but never see them until they come to be married. No, then neither, until the marriage be solemnized betwixt them. For there is a partition in the place where they meet to be married; and the man and his friends stand on the one side, and the young woman and her friends on the other side, where they may hear, but not see, one another, until the Cassises [allows it] but the young man put his hand through a hole in the wall, and take his wife by the hand. And while they stand hand in hand, the mother of the maid comes with some sharp instrument made for the purpose, and all [in order to] prick the newly married man's hand, and make it bleed. And, if he lets her hand go when he feels his hand smart, they hold it for a sign that he will not love her. But if he holds fast (notwithstanding the smart) and wring her hard by the hand until she cries, rather than he will once think, then he is counted a loving man, and her friends are glad that they have bestowed her on him....

Of the Chelsalines

The Chelsalines are Christians dwelling upon the borders of Persia, between Mesopotamia and Persia, at a place called Chelsa. These bring silk to Aleppo to sell. They are plain-dealing people. If a man pays them money and, by over-reckoning himself, gives them more than their due, though there is but one piece over, so soon as they perceive it, though it is many days, they will bring it back again and restore it and think they shall never return safely into their country if they should not make retribution thereof. There people persuade themselves, and report unto others, that they dwell in that place which was called Eden, whereinto Adam was put to keep it and dress it. But some hold that this pleasant garden Eden did extend over all the earth. But by the second chapter of Genesis it appears manifestly that this garden wherein man was placed, which we call Paradise, was a certain place on earth; not spreading all over, but only a part thereof, containing a convenient portion of the country called Eden, bounding upon the river Euphrates. Which river is divided into 4 streams, and runs (or at leastwise did then flow) in manner as it is described in Genesis 2:10 ff. And Eden is the name of a country so-called for the pleasantness of it; for 'Hadan' in Hebrew is in English 'to delight'; from hence also the Greeks call 'pleasure'....

And these Chesalines are ignorant people, and have no reason to prove that they now dwell in the place which was called Eden, whereinto Adam was put to keep it and to dress it; but that the river Euphrates, and other rivers in Genesis 2:10–12 run by their country. Others of them say that they have received it by tradition, from their elders, from time to time. But that which God concealed, I will not search out. But, notwithstanding all that I have read, heard, or seen in my travels, I resolve myself that no man living can demonstrate the place which God (for the sins of Adam) cursed; and ever since the place is unknown.

Of the Greeks

The Greeks are a very superstitious, subtle, and deceitful people, insomuch that it is grown to a proverb amongst the Italians [that]...'He who trusts a Greek shall be intrigued, and still to seek'. They hate the Papists, and yet in many things agree with them, as in auricular confession,[38] transubstantiation,[39] and some other opinions. But their liturgy is read in the vulgar tongue. The Greeks in Aleppo are very poor, for they are there (for the most part) but brokers or bastages, that is, porters; and many of their women as light as water, maintaining their husbands, themselves, and their families by prostituting their bodies to others. And their own husbands are oftentimes their panders or procurers to bring them customers.

But the Greeks who live in Constantinople are many of them great merchants, and very rich; but exceedingly proud, and sumptuous in apparel. Even the basest of them – and especially their women, who (though they are but cobblers' wives, or poor artificers' wives) – yet they go on gowns of satin and taffeta; yea, of cloth of silver and gold, adorned with precious stones; and many gems and jewels about their necks and hands. They care not how they pinch their bellies so that they may have fine apparel on their backs. And at the time of their marriage, the women condition with their husbands to find them decent apparel, and convenient diet, and bring them before the Patriarch of Constantinople to confirm it. Which, if it be not performed accordingly, if they complain to their Patriarch, they are divided presently; and she takes another man to her husband, better able to maintain her. And he may marry another woman, if he pleases.

The only instance hereof I will give [is] in a matter notoriously known to all nations sojourning or dwelling in or about Constantinople. In Perah (or Galata, on the other side of the water) there is a most famous (or rather, infamous) Greek, whore called Charatza Sophia; that is Mistress Sophia – the daughter of a poor Greek widow, who lived by laundry – who, being married unto a Greek, because he kept her not fine enough, complained of him to the Patriarch, and was divorced from him; and presently thereupon took another man, who was a Christian in name, but no Greek, but one who was (as is reported of him) born in no land in the world, but by sea, and brought up in Poland until he was 13 or 14 years of age, and then came to Constantinople, and served many masters there; at the first, in the basest services, both in the stable and in the kitchen, and afterwards in better services than he deserved, being both unlearned and irreligious.

This man had many children by this infamous woman Sophia. Yet, after many years, arising to higher fortunes, turned her away and married another woman. And (to daub up the matter somewhat smoothly) procured a Greek tailor to marry with this Sophia; and gave many hundred dollars with her to her marriage. But this Charatza could not content herself with this Greek tailor, but admitted daily other men into her company. Whereupon the poor tailor ran away with his money, and left his light housewife to the mercy of her former lovers, having 3 husbands living, yet she herself living with none of them. This is common in every man's mouth thereabouts, and talked of many thousand miles off; to the disgrace of his country, and slander of Christianity.

And both at Constantinople, Aleppo, and other places in Turkey where there is trafficking and trading by merchants, it is no rare matter for Popish Christians of many other countries to 'cut cabin' (as they call it), that is: to take any woman of that country where they sojourn (Turkish women only excepted; for it is death for a Christian to meddle with them) and when they have bought them, and enrolled them in the Cadi's book, to use them as wives as long as they sojourn in that country; and maintain them gallantly, to the consuming of their wealth, diminishing of their health, and the endangering of their souls. And when they depart out of that country, they shake off these their sweethearts, and leave them to shift for themselves and their children. And this they account no sin; or at leastwise, such a sin as may be washed away with a little holy water.

And these are the virtues which many Christians learn by sojourning long in heathen countries. Which is not to be marvelled at; for, if Joseph (a good man) living in Pharaoh's court, had learned to swear by the life of Pharaoh, and Peter, a great Apostle, being in the High Priests' hall but once, denied Christ thrice,[40] we may well think that those who dwell long in wicked countries, and converse with wicked men, are somewhat tainted with their sins, if not altogether soured with the leaven of their ungodliness.

Of those whom they call 'Franks', or 'Free Men', sojourning in Aleppo

The other sorts of Christians living in Aleppo are such as are born in other parts of Christendom, and only sojourn there for a time to use traffick and trade in merchandise; and these are Englishmen, Italians, Frenchmen, Dutchmen, and others whom they call by a general name, 'Frangi', that is, Franks, or 'Free Men'. For all the rest, even from the greatest Pasha or Vizier unto the poorest peasant, are slaves unto the Grand Seignior; who only is free. And all the rest are born, brought up, live and die his slaves; for the Grand Seignior can command the head of any one of them at his pleasure. Yea, if some Vizier or Pasha to whom he had committed the government of some city or country, fall into his disfavour, if he sends but a cappagie, that is, a pursuivant to him with his writing, with a black seal in a black box, none of them all dare withstand him, but suffer this base cappagie to strangle him; though it be in the house before his wives, children and servants, yet none dare lift up their hands against him.

There was a Pasha of Aleppo, who governed the city and country adjoining, who was in the disfavour of the king. And the king sent a cappagie to strangle him; who, inquiring for the Pasha's house at Aleppo, and understanding he was at his garden 4 miles from the city, he rode and met him on the way, and opened his black box, and showed him his commission to strangle him. Whereat his countenance changed, and he only craved this favour: that he might have liberty to say his prayers before he died; which performed, he yielded his head, and was strangled, sitting on his horse, before his followers, which were (at the least) 100 men. And no man durst speak one word against it, much less offer to resist him; but said [that] it was God's will it should be so.

And [it is] not only the Great Turk doth thus tyrannise over his slaves; but every Pasha who has government over others in a city or country tyrannises over those who are under their regimen; and sometimes strangled, sometimes beheaded; and sometimes put into terrible tortures those who offend. Yea, oftentimes without offence. Only because they are rich and have fair houses the Pasha will lay to their charge such things as he himself knows to be untrue; and put them to death that he may seize upon his goods....And sometimes, for small offences, they will lay a man down on his back, and hoist up his feet, and with a cudgel give him 300 or 400 blows on the soles of their feet; whereby many are lamed. And some they set on a sharp stake, naked, which comes from his fundament up to his mouth, if he finds not favour to have his throat cut sooner. And some are ganched[41] in this manner: they are drawn up by a rope fastened about their arms to the top of a gazouke or gibbet full of hooks, and let downwards again; and on what part soever the hook takes hold, by that they hang until they die of hunger. And some, in like sort, are drawn over a gibbet, and they, being compassed about the naked waist with a final cord. The cord is drawn by 2 men to make them draw up their breath, and still pulled straighter and straighter, until they are so narrow in the waist that they may easily be cut off by the middle at one blow. And then the upper part is let down on a hot gridiron, and there seared up, to keep them in sense and feeling of pain for as long as is possible; and the nether part is thrown to the dogs. Unspeakable is this tyranny to those who fall into their hands; not unlike the tyranny of the Spaniards towards the poor Indians, who never offend them.

They, whom they call Franks or freemen, live in greater security amongst them than [do] their own people, by reason that they are governed by Consuls of their own nation; and those Consuls are backed by Ambassadors for the same nations, who are always leigers[42] at Constantinople. And when their Consuls abroad are offered wrong, they write unto the Ambassadors [about] how and why they are wronged. And then the Ambassador procures from the Great Turk commandments to the Pasha of Aleppo to redress such wrongs, and punish such as offend them. Otherwise there were no dwelling for Franks amongst them, but they should be used like slaves by every slave. And notwithstanding their Consuls, and Ambassadors too, yet they are oftentimes abused by Turks, both in words and deeds. In words, they revile them as the Egyptians did the Israelites, and call them 'Giaours', that is, 'Infidels'; and 'cupec', that is, 'dog'; and 'canzier' that is, 'hog': and by many other odious and reproachful names. And though they strike them, yet dare they not strike again lest they lose their hand, or be worse used. They also oftentimes make auvenias of them; that is, false accusations; and suborn false witnesses to confirm it to be true. And no Christian's word will be taken against a Turk; for they account us infidels, and call themselves Mussulman, that is 'True Believers'.

This misery abroad will make us love our own country the better when we come thither. And that is the best lesson that I have learned in my travels: *Mundi contemptum*, that is 'The contempt of the world'. And St. Paul's lesson, Philippians 4:11 'In whatever state I am, therewith to be content'.[43] Oh, how happy are you in England, if you know your own happiness. But, as the Prodigal Son until he was pinched into penury abroad,[44] never considered the plenty of his father's house, so: many in England know not their own felicity, because they do not know of the miseries of others. Now, if they were here in this heathen country, they would know what it is to live in a Christian Commonwealth, under the government of a godly King, who rules by law and not by lust; where there is plenty and peace; and preaching of the Gospel; and many other Godly blessings, which others miss. And God long continue His mercies to our noble King James, and his noble realms, and give us grace as far to excel other nations in thankfulness as we do in happiness.

NOTES

1 Pertaining to Memphis, capital of the Old Kingdom (*c.* 3100 to *c.* 2250 BCE), approximately twelve miles from present-day Cairo. Surpassed in status only by Alexandria under the rule of the Ptolemies, it declined with the founding of Fustat by the Arabs.

2 According to the myth, Tantalus (son of Zeus and father of Pelops and Niobe) was punished by the gods for a crime over which there is some disagreement (he had divulged some of the secrets of the gods; he had stolen food; he had killed his son) by being suspended upside down from the bough of a fruit tree overhanging water. Whenever he attempted to drink, the water would recede; when he tried to eat the fruit, the wind would blow it out of reach. Hence 'tantalize'.

3 Alexandria: founded 332 BCE by Alexander the Great, became capital of empire created by his successors, the Ptolemies (340–304 BCE). Became largest city in the Mediterranean basin, overtaking Carthage by 250 BCE. Important for contributions to both Hellenistic and Jewish cultures. For instance, the Septuagint (translation by Jews of Old Testament into Greek: according to legend, completed in seventy-two days by seventy-two translators, hence name). Also site of two famous libraries: one in Temple of Zeus, other in museum. Around latter there grew a famous university that drew many of most famous scholars of the ancient world (including the mathematician Euclid, the anatomist Herophilus, and the collator of the texts attributed to Homer, Aristarchus of Samothrace). Following defeat of Antony and suicide of Cleopatra, entry of Octavian (later Augustus Caesar) in 30 BCE, became part of Roman Empire. Under Roman (and later, under Ottoman) rule, continued to be centre of Christian learning that rivalled both Rome and Constantinople. But not always unchallenged. Successive invaders tended to seek to destroy libraries: not only after Julius Caesar's occupation (47 BCE), but especially AD 391, when Theodosius had temples razed. Arabs captured city after prolonged siege (641), transferred capital to Cairo (969). That, plus decline of shipping because of silting up of Nile canal (fourteenth century) and even more after the discovery of sea route to India.

4 For recent (and continuing) debate concerning Egypt as source of classical learning: see especially Martin Bernal, *Black Athena. The Afroasiatic roots of classical civilization*, London: Vintage, Vol. 1, 1987; Vol. 2, 1991; Mary Lefkowitz, *Not Out of Africa. How Afrocentricism became an excuse to teach myth as history*, New York: Basic Books, 1996; Mary Lefkowitz and Guy MacLean Rogers (eds), *Black Athena Revisited*, Chapel Hill, NC: University of North Carolina Press, 1996.

5 Queen of the South: Queen of Sheba.

6 Lapidaire: someone with knowledge of gems and precious stones; also skilled in cutting and polishing them.

7 'Travellers may lie by authority' strictly, 'Old men and travellers may lie by authority', usually attributed to William Camden (1614); to which might be added the even more telling definition by the diplomat Sir Henry Wotton (1568–1639), who wrote, in a friend's album, that 'An ambassador is an honest man sent to lie abroad for his country'.

8 James I, King of England (1566–1625), James VI of Scotland (1567–1625), of England and Ireland (1603–25).

9 Immanity: 'monstrous cruelty; atrocious savagery' (*OED*).

10 Maranes: from within the ranks of Sepharddic Jews (one of the two main divisions of the Jewish people, those who had settled in Spain and Portugal since the Middle Ages, as compared with

those who had settled in northern Europe and were known as Ashkenazi): marrano (pig), the pejorative name given by the Christians to Jews who were forced to convert to Christianity after massacres in Spain in 1391 and forced baptisms in Portugal a century later, who secretly maintained their faith and customs. Following the conquest of Granada (1492), Sephardi Jews settled not only in southern Europe but also in the Middle East.

11 Turk who died about four years since: Muhammad III (1567–1603), Ottoman Sultan, 1595–1603.

12 Road: in absence of a harbour, a protected place near a seashore: where ships may lie at anchor.

13 Maronites: a distinct community of Christians since the seventh century, who broke with the Church of Rome over the issue of monotheism. They returned to communion with the Catholic Church in the twelfth century. Their spiritual head, named Patriarch, lives in Lebanon. As is the case with most other eastern Christian rites, the priests tend to be married.

14 Sheh: marginal note in text 'Sheh, signifies ancient man'.

15 Small communities of tightly knit sect who generally inhabit hill country in Syria, Lebanon, Israel. Their religious tenets vary from Sunni as well as Shiite Islam. They carried on protracted guerrilla resistance against Ottoman Empire, whose control they refused to accept.

16 Carding: combing, disentangling of wool or cotton etc. fibres to prepare them to be suitable for spinning.

17 Founded by Alexander the Great to commemorate his victory over the Persians at Issus (333 BCE), it was conquered by the Ottomans under Selim (AD 1515).

18 Fynes Moryson: see Chapter 7.

19 Edward Barton: see Chapter 3.

20 Near the beginning of this letter, before he starts to recount the story of his travels, Biddulph observes:

> the doleful and lamentable beginning of your last letter made me exceeding sorrowful, for therein you acquainted me with the death of blessed Queen Elizabeth, of late and famous memory; at the hearing whereof not only I and our English nation mourned, but many other Christians who were never in Christendom, but born and brought up in heathen countries wept to hear of her death, and said she was the most famous Queen that ever they heard or read of since the world began.

21 Kurds: a non-Arab minority who inhabit extensive plateau and mountain regions of SW Asia, including parts of present-day Turkey, Iraq, Iran, and Syria. Conquered by (respectively) the Seljuk Turks (eleventh century), the Mongols (thirteenth to fifteenth centuries), and then by the Safavid and Ottoman Empires, they are predominantly Sunni Muslim by faith.

22 Abraham entertained Angels with hearth cakes: Genesis 18.

23 Samboules: note in margin of text 'Samboules are little pasties'.

24 Mucklebite: note in margin 'dish made of eggs and herbs'.

25 William Parry, in his account of his travels with Sherley, tells a similar story.

26 In the King James Authorized Version (1611, thus two years after the printing of the Biddulph text) the final sentence adds the following: 'and they [the laws] shall be given into his hand until a time and times and the dividing of time'.

27 Arian sect: Christian heresy, founded fourth century AD by Arius, priest in Alexandria, spread widely the notion that God's first creation was a Son who was not co-equal with his Creator, but a supernatural figure: neither completely human, nor wholly divine. Condemned at the Councils of Nicaea (325) and Constantinople (381). Retained strong hold in Western Europe until well into end of sixth century but continued, in early modern Europe, to be used as term of abuse against doctrinal enemies.

28 Coin: in the sense of 'counterfeit'.

29 Out of the house.

30 If he be taken: if he is caught.

31 Linsey woolsy: originally a textile material, woven from a mixture of wool and flax; now, a dress material of coarse inferior wool, woven upon cotton warp (*OED*).

32 Confusion of tongues: according to Genesis 11: 1–9 for story of Noah's descendants, who sought, at a place named Babel, to build a tower to reach the sky. For this presumption on the

part of people from whom God observes that 'nothing will be restrained from them, which they have imagined to do', and who hitherto had all spoken the same language, His punishment was to 'confound their language, that they may not understand one another's speech' as well as to 'scatter them abroad on the face of all the earth…'.

33 Ten tribes: strictly twelve (although the lists are not identical in each of the OT accounts) were named after the sons of Jacob (the eponymous ancestor of the Hebrews): Reuben, Simeon, Judah, Zebulon, Issachar, Dan, Gad, Asher, Napthali, Benjamin; Levi and the other two after two of the sons of Joseph: Ephraim; Manasseh (which therefore comes to thirteen names).

34 Tarracia: probably Thrace.

35 Zante: Zakinthos, one of the Ionian Islands.

36 Father forgive them…: Luke 23: 34.

37 Dragomen: an interpreter in countries where Turkish, Persian, and Arabic is spoken.

38 Auricular confession: by hearing. The 'illegitimate' Edmund, in seeking to usurp his 'legitimate' half-brother Edgar, tells their father, the Earl of Gloucester: 'If your honour judge it meet, I will place you where you shall hear us confer of this and by an auricular assurance have your satisfaction…' *King Lear* 1.2.88–90.

39 Transubstantiation: the changing of one substance into another; in Christian doctrine, the belief that the substances of bread and wine celebrated in Holy Communion are miraculously transformed into the substance of Christ himself; a repeat of the action at the Last Supper (Matthew 26: 26–8; Mark 14: 22–224; Luke 22: 17–20; 1 Corinthians 11: 24–6).

40 Joseph and Pharaoh: Genesis chs 39–41; Peter denies Christ thrice: John 18: 17–18; Matthew 27: 58; 69–75.

41 Ganched: to be impaled upon sharp hooks or stakes, as a mode of execution.

42 Leiger. Leaguer: resident in the capacity of an ambassador, commissioner, or agent (*OED*).

43 The verse starts 'Not that I speak of want, for I have learned…'. Verse 12 goes on: 'I know how to be abased, and I know how to abound: every where and in all things I am instructed both to be full and to be hungry, both to abound and to suffer need'.

44 Prodigal Son: a parable by Jesus, concerning heaven, and about the sinner who repents. A young man not only leaves home, but also (by the standards of the society) becomes a wastrel. On his return, he is, nevertheless, received with joy by his family – including by his older brother, who had initially objected to the decision by their father to slaughter a fatted calf in honour of his younger brother's return (Luke 15: 11–32).

OTHER EDITIONS

Reprinted 1612; included in Purchas, 1625: 1334–53; *A Collection of Voyage and Travels*, ed. Thomas Osborne, 1745. Reprinted in facsimile, Amsterdam: Theatrum Orbis Terrarum; New York: Da Capo Press, 1968.

6

JOHN CARTWRIGHT

The Preacher's Travels. Wherein is set downe a true Iournall to the confines of the East Indies, through the great countreyes of Syria, Mesopotamia, Armenia, Media, Hircania, and Parthia. With the author's returne by the way of Persia, Susiana, Assyria, Chaldea, and Arabia. Containing a full surdew of the Kingdom of Persia; and in what terms the Persian stands with the Great Turk at this day. Also a true relation of Sir Anthony Sherleys entertainment there; and the estate that his brother, M. Robert Sherley, lived in after his departure for Christendome. With the description of a port in the Persian Gulf, commodious for our East Indian merchants; and a briefe rehearsal of some gross absurdities in the Turkish Alcoran. Penned by J. C. sometimes student in Magdalen Colledge in Oxford.
London. Printed for Thomas Thorppe, and are to be sold by
Walter Burre. 1611. Reprinted in facsimile, Amsterdam:
Theatrum Orbis Terrarum/Norwood, NJ:
Da Capo Press, 1977.

BIOGRAPHY

John Cartwright is invariably recollected as 'The Preacher'. His name is often listed as being employed by the Levant Company in that capacity. Yet one of the oddest features of an otherwise fascinating travel tale is that Cartwright not once makes mention of preaching either in any of the places to which he went, or to any congregations. In the absence of any hard evidence in support of the conventional view of Cartwright as 'Preacher' it is likely that there might well be merit in the assertion made by the distinguished scholar Boies Penrose that this was not the case and that 'the sole reason for his presence in Aleppo was to satisfy his desire for sight-seeing' (*Urbane Travellers*, p. 40).

Cartwright probably left England in April 1600, and travelled to Aleppo via Sicily, Zante (Xakinthos) and Crete. At Aleppo, where he was welcomed by the consul, Richard Colthurst, he met John Mildenhall, then in the employ of Richard Staper, a member of the newly formed English East India Company, who was in Aleppo, on his way there. Having stayed in Aleppo for some two months, the two Englishmen travelled together for part of the way, members of a caravan of some 1,000 people.

Penrose has a somewhat jaundiced view of Cartwright. He describes him, on the evidence of the book, as 'neither a magnetic nor even particularly interesting person'. The critic does, however, pay generous tribute to the singular nature of the traveller's achievement, as undoubtedly being the first Englishman to have been to all four key sites of antiquity in the Near East: Babylon; Nineveh; Persepolis; Susa. For my part there is an even more interesting reason for including him: Cartwright's travels, like those by Coryate, especially the latter's journey to the Mughal Court in India, offers evidence in support of the view that the notion of travel simply out of personal interest, not tied to either commerce or diplomacy (or earlier, to pilgrimage), had been in existence (albeit fitfully and sporadically) some time before it became established in the eighteenth century.

* * *

The description of Aleppo

...which in ancient time was called Heliopolis, and was that ancient Haram mentioned so often in Scripture. The Moors call it Halep, which in our tongue signifies milk; for the famous Arabians say that it was so called for the abundance of milk which (in the time of the Patriarchs) was yielded by the herds and flocks of cattle which fed in those champaigns. This city stands in the province of Camogena, which runs up to Euphrates, and to the confines of Armenia, and is now become the third capital city of the Turkish Empire. And well it may be so accounted, since it is the greatest place of traffick for a dry town[1] in all those parts; for hither resort Jews, Tatarians, Persians, Armenians, Egyptians, Indians, and many sorts of Christians, all enjoying freedom of conscience, and bringing thither all kinds of rich merchandise: the trade and traffick of which place is, because it is so well known to most of our nation, I omit to write of.

The air of this city is much pleasing and delightful to a sound and healthy body, but very piercing and dangerous for such as have received any contagion at Scanderone; and therefore it is not good for any passenger to lie long at that road[stead], but to hasten, at his first arrival, so soon as he can, up further into the country. The city lies upon the river Singa which...has a channel underground which produces many fountains, both public and private, yielding no small pleasure and contentment to the inhabitants. It contains, in circuit, four hills, upon one of which is raised a goodly Castle, having a deep ditch entrenched about it, and a bridge ascending step by step, with 4 gates, before you can pass into the Castle itself, being guarded by a strong and sure garrison of 400 or 500 janissaries; both to curb the rebellion of the city, and to keep it from foreign invasion. The walls of this city are about 3 English miles in compass; and the suburbs almost as much more. And round about, for 4 miles' space, are goodly gardens, orchards, and vineyards, which bear abundance of delicate fruit, and the best wines (which are, notwithstanding [being] very dear, by reason of the quality thereof) that there is sold and eaten.

The number of people who resort to this city may easily be comprehended, since between the city and the suburbs in the year of grace 1555 there died of the plague more than 120,000 persons in 3 months. No building of importance is here to be seen, save the temples or mosques and cains,[2] all fabricated of hard quarry stone, arched and vaulted, with cisterns full of water in the middle of the courts. In a word; this city is one of the most famous marts of the East. The customs [duties] that are paid by our English nation, the French, the Venetians. The huge caravans which come from Basra, Persia [and] Mecca are exceeding great, and therefore [the city] may well obtain the third place of the Turkish Empire....

Having rested in Aleppo two months and better, Mr John Mildenhall and myself took our leave of the consul and merchants, with a full intent and purpose to travel unto the great city of Lahore, in the Great Mogul's country in the East Indies; lodging all that night on a thin Turkish carpet in woodscain, where the caravan[3] was assembled, to the end that we might be with the foremost; for delay in such travel produces great and inevitable danger. From Aleppo we spent 3 days journeying unto the banks of [the] Euphrates, passing by many villages not worth the naming, and fertile plains abounding with all sort of provision necessary for man's life....

Having arrived on the banks of the Euphrates, we found it as broad as the Thames at Lambeth; but in some places it is narrower, in some broader, running with a very swift stream and current, almost as fast as the river Trent....Here it is that merchants pass down by bark into Baghdad, thereby to avoid and shun the great charge and wearisomeness of travel through the desert of Arabia. Which passage they make sometimes in 15 days, sometimes in 20 days, and sometimes in 30 days; answerable to the rising and falling of the river. And the best time to pass there is either in April, or October, when the river swells with the abundance of rain. The boats are flat-bottomed, because the river is shallow in many places. So that when they travel in the months of July, August, and September, they find the river at so low an ebb that they are fain to carry with them a spare boat or two, to lighten their own, if they should chance to fall on the shoals. Every night, after sunset, they fasten these boats to a stake, the merchants lying aboard, and the mariners on the shore, as near as they can unto the same.

In this passage down the river you shall meet with several troops of Arabians, who will barter their provision of diet (for they care not for money) as hens, kids, lambs, butter, and sour milk, for glasses, combs, coral, amber, knives, bread and pomegranates, pills wherewith they may tan their goatskins in which they churn withal. All of them, women, children, as well as men, are very good swimmers, who oftentimes will swim to the bark's side with vessels full of milk upon their heads. These people are very thievish. And therefore, in your passage down, good watch must be kept.

But, to return where we left. We were constrained, by the deepness of the river, to ferry over our whole caravan, which consisted of 1000 persons, besides camels, horses, mules and asses. By reason of which multitude we spent a whole day in transporting over the said caravan, the gains of which transportation yielded the ferryman a shaugho, which is 5 pence English upon a beast. It was the manner of the Egyptian Sultans not to account themselves worthy of the name of Sultans, or generals, before they had encamped their army upon this side of the river, and in this place, and there with solemn pomp had, in the sight of the army, forced their horses into the river to drink; giving to understand, by that ceremony, the greatness of their empire, and that they were ready, by force of arms, to prove that all those countries were theirs, which lay along the river, from the mountain Taurus unto the desert of Arabia.

The description of the Kurds, a most thievish people

We were no sooner over, but forthwith we were encountered with a certain troop called the Kurds, which some think to be a remnant of the ancient Parthians, who so much annoyed the Romans with their bows and arrows...This rude people are of a goodly stature, and well-proportioned, and do never go abroad without their arms: as bows and arrows, scimitar and buckler. Yea, and at such time, when a man for age is ready to go down to his grave. They do adore and worship the Devil, to the end [that] he may not hurt them or their cattle. And very evil are they to all sorts of Christians. In which regard the country which they inhabit is, at this day, termed 'Terra Diabloi', the land of the evil. They participate much of the nature of the Arabians, and are as infamous in their ladrocinies[4] and robberies as the Arabians themselves. They live under the commandment of the Great Turk, but with much freedom and liberty. For Suleiman II, having a great multitude of them in his army against the Persians, they did him little service, performing no more than what well pleased themselves. This thievish company did sundry times arrest our caravan, affirming that their Prince had sent for a dollar on a sum of goods, without the payment whereof (being 5 several times demanded) we should not pass through their country.

One village of note is there in this country, wholly inhabited by the Kurds...called by the country people Manuscute. This town is seated in a most fertile and fruitful valley between two mountains, abounding with pasture and cattle. And about a mile from it is a hospital dedicated to St. John the Baptist; which is much visited, as well by Turks as Christians, who superstitiously affirm that whosoever will bestow either a sheep, kid, or some piece of money to relieve the poor of that place, shall not only prosper in his journey, but obtain forgiveness of all sins. To the governor of this village we paid for our custom a shaughee on a sum of goods, and so were dismissed. The next day following, we passed over many craggy and steep mountains, and at the last rested ourselves and [our] wearied beasts on the banks of Euphrates, being the outmost bounds on this side of Mesopotamia, and so entered the day following on the borders of Armenia the Great....

A description of the people of Armenia, as they are at this day

At our first entry into this country, we travelled through a goodly, large, and spacious plain, compassed about with a row of high mountains, where were many villages, wholly inhabited by Armenians, a people very industrious in all kinds of labour, their women very active in shooting, and managing any sort of weapon, like the fierce Amazons in antique times, and the women, at this day, who inhabit the mountain Xatach, in Persia. Their families are very great; for both sons, nephews, and nieces do dwell under one roof, having all their substance in common. And when the father dies, the eldest son governs the rest, all submitting themselves under his regiment. But when the eldest son dies, the governance does not pass to his sons, but to the eldest brother. And if it chance to fall out that all the brothers die, the government belongs to the eldest son of the eldest brother. And so, from one, to another. In their diet and clothing they are all fed and clad alike, living in all peace and tranquillity, grounded on true love and honest simplicity.

To discourse how populous this nation is at this day is needless, since they inhabit both in Armenia the Greater and Armenia the Less, as also in Cilicia, Bithinia, Syria, Mesopotamia, and Persia. Besides, the principal cities of the Turkish Empire be much populated with them....Some of this nation affirmed unto us that the chief cause of their liberty in the Ottoman kingdom is for that [because] certain of their kings bore great affection and love for Muhammad, their lewd Prophet. In regard whereof Muhammad did recommend them, as his kind friends, to his successors; who ever since have permitted the poor Armenians to live amongst them. But the true reason is for that [because] they are very laborious in transporting merchandise from one city to another. By which means, through the Customs which are paid in each city, the coffers of the Grand Seignior are wonderfully enriched. Unto which doth well agree that scoffing chant that Abbas, now king of Persia, threw upon an Armenian, who (being desirous to forsake his Christian faith, and to embrace the wicked and filthy superstition on the Persians) upon hope of reward and preferment, the king did not only rebuke his tepidity and coldness to his religion, but sent him away with this scornful reproof: that an Armenian now was good for nought, save as a camel to transport merchandise from one city to another: implying that howsoever in ancient times they had been warlike and outrageous, yet now they were become buffaloes and poltroons, altogether unfit for martial affairs....

The people of this nation have retained amongst them the Christian faith, as it is thought from the time of the Apostles. But at this day it is spotted with many absurdities.[5] They hold with the Church of Rome in the use of the Cross, affirming it to be meritorious if they make the same with two fingers, as the Papists use; but idle and vain if with one finger, as the Jacobites.[6] They adorn their churches in every place with the sign of the Cross; but for other images, they have none, being professed enemies against the use of them. In keeping ancient relics, they are very superstitious, and much devoted to the Blessed Virgin Mary, to whom they direct their prayers. They imitate the Dioscorians, in eating white meats on Saturday, which to do on Wednesday and Friday were a deadly sin. Nevertheless, they do not refrain from the eating of flesh on every Friday, between the Feast of the Passover and the Ascension. They abstain 5 Sabbaths in the year from eating flesh, in remembrance of that time in which the Gentiles sacrificed their children unto idols. They celebrate the Annunciation of the Virgin Mary on the 6th April, the Nativity of Blessed Saviour on 6th January, the Purification on 4th February, and the Transfiguration on 14th August.[7]

The ministration of their Liturgy or Service is performed in their native language, that all may understand. But in their service of the Mass for the dead they are most idolatrous, using, at the solemnising thereof, to sacrifice a lamb, which they lead round about the church. And after they have killed and roasted it, they spread it on a fair, white linen cloth, the priest giving to each of the Congregation a part and portion thereof. For which cause they are called by some 'Sabbathists' and 'Julianists', as too much addicted to the ceremonies of the Jews, and devoted to the errors of Julian. I have heard some Papists boast and brag much that Armenians, Jacobites and Greeks are united to the Church of Rome; but I could never hear either Armenian or Greek avouch any such matter. They are (unless so few families) so far from yielding obedience unto the See of Rome that they assume all antiquity unto themselves, as having retained the Christian faith from the time of the Apostles. Many Jesuits and priests have been sent from Rome to bring this oppressed nation under her government, but they have little prevailed; for neither will they yield obedience, nor be brought by any persuasion to forsake their ancient and inveterate errors, to become more erroneous with her.

Having well refreshed ourselves amongst these villages, we proceeded in our ordinary travel. But before we had passed 2 miles, certain troupes of Kurds encountered our caravan, with a purpose and intent to have robbed the same. But finding themselves too weak to contend with so great a company, they departed until the next day following, when again they met us in a very narrow passage between two mountain, where they made a stay of our whole caravan, exacting a shaughee on every person; which, to purchase our peace, we willingly paid, and so arrived that evening at Bithlis, an ancient city – but a city of much cruelty and oppression, where little justice and right is to be found to relieve distressed passengers.

The description of Bithlis

In Bithlis we stayed 2 days, and at our departure paid unto the governor of the said city a dollar on a sum of goods, and so set forwards towards the great city of Van, 3 days' journey further. In which travel we had a very wearisome and painful journey, over high mountains and craggy rocks, the way being exceedingly narrow [so] that a beast could hardly pass with his burden without much heaving and tumultuous shouldering. The which narrow passage, the Turks told us, was by the commandment of Murad III, the Great Turk, cut through by the main industry of labourers, for his army to pass: like that incredible work that Hannibal, with vinegar, brought upon the Alps.[8] In this place our travel was very dangerous, by reason of a brackish lake, or little sea, called the lake Arctamar, which was under the rock over which we passed; and we enforced to ride shoaling on the side of the said rock, that had not our mules been sure of footing, both they and we had perished with an insupportable downfall into that sea....

The description of Tauris

It is seated at the foot of the hill Orontes, 8 days' journey or thereabouts, from the Caspian Sea, and is subject to the winds, and full of snow; yet of a very wholesome air, abounding with all things necessary for the sustentation of man: wonderfully rich, as well by the perpetual concourse of merchandises that are brought thither from the countries of the East to be conveyed into Syria and into the countries of Europe, as also those that come thither out of the Western parts, to be distributed all over the East. It is very populous, so that it feeds almost 200,000 persons; but now open to the fury of every army: without strength of walls, and without bulwarks, saving a castle built of late by the Turks. The buildings are of burnt clay, and rather low than high. On the south side of this city is a most beautiful and flourishing garden, large and spacious, replenished with sundry kinds of trees and sweet-smelling plants; and a thousand fountains and brooks, derived from a pretty river, which with his pleasant stream, divides the garden from the city; and is of so great beauty that, for the delicacy thereof, it is by the country's inhabitants called...'the Eight Paradise'; and was, in times past, the standing house of the Persian kings while they kept their residence in this city. And after they withdrew their seat from there, by reason of the Turkish wars, to Quasvin, became the habitation and place of abode for the Persian governors.

Sundry mutations, even of late years, has this city endured, both by the Great Turk and the Persian. For, in the year 1514, it was yielded unto Selim, the Turkish tyrant who, contrary to his promise, exacted a great mass of money from the citizens, and carried away with him 3000 families, the best artificers in that city, especially such as were skilful in making of armour and weapons, only to enrich and appopulate the great city of Constantinople. Afterwards, in the year 1535, it was again spoiled by Suleyman, the Turkish Emperor, who gave the whole city for a prey unto his soldiers; who left neither house nor corner thereof unransacked, abusing the miserable citizens with all manner of insolency, every common soldier, without controlment. Fitting himself with whatsoever best pleased his greedy desire and filthy lust. Besides, the most stately and royal palace of king Tamasp, together with the most sumptuous and rich houses of the nobility, were by the Great Turk's commandment, all razed down to the ground, and the greatest part of the best citizens and beautiful personages of all sort and condition were carried away captives.

And, in the year 1585, it was miserably spoiled by Osman, Vizier unto Murad III; who commanded his soldiers to do the worst that they possibly could or might do to it. Here a man had need of a very learned and eloquent pen, to set forth the fierce and cruel execution of [by] the Turkish soldiers. For, in truth, who is able (either by writing, or by speech) sufficiently and lively to lay open the treachery, the covetousness, the cruelty, the impiety, the wickedness of these triumphing Turks? And, on the other side, who can express the crying of infants, the groanings of the wounded, the tears of parents, the prayers of old men, the fears, the griefs and (to be short) the misery of the Taurisians? There was nothing but slaughter, pillage, ravishings, spoiling and murdering; virgins deflowered; men children defiled with unspeakable and horrible sodomety; younglings snatched out of their mothers' arms; houses laid even with the ground and burnt; riches and money carried away; and (to be brief) all things wasted and ruinated. Neither were those outrages committed once only, but the second followed worse than the first, and the third upon that, worse than the second. So that it was a misery almost inexplicable to behold that city, which was once so populous and so rich, sometimes the Court and palace of the Crown, and the honour of the Persian Empire, now subject to the fury and cruelty of the Turk, plunged in calamity, and utterly destroyed. This is the uncertain fate of the world: sometimes up, and sometimes down; sometimes conquerors, and, within a while after, conquered.

For this city groaned not full 24 years under the Turkish slavery, but Abbas (now king of Persia), reposing no less confidence in his own good fortune than the valour of his soldiers, marched, in the year 1603, with his army directly to the city of Tauris; and that with such expedition that he was come before it before any such thing was feared, much less provided for: stirred up hereunto partly by the Great Turk's troubles at home and his wars with the Christians in Hungary,[9] as also with the disposition of the Taurisians, whose minds were then so alienated from the Turkish governor that, upon the approach of Abbas, they were all ready to forsake him. Nevertheless, the king was constrained to besiege the city, being then kept by a strong garrison of Turkish soldiers. In which siege he, for battery, used the help of the cannon, an engine not long time by the Persian scorned as not beseeming a valiant man, until that by their own harms taught, they are content to use it, being with the same, as also with skilful cannoniers furnished by the Portuguese from Hormoz. So, after 6 weeks' siege, the city was surrendered up into the Persians' hands, to the great rejoicing of all Persia, together with the whole country...except a fort or two which still stands out....

By this time we came to the full borders and outmost bounds of the Great Turk's dominion, as far as the Ottoman Empire on this side extends. And so entered into the territories of the Persian king....This night we rested at a Persian village called Darnah, much ruined, but seated in a very delightful place, both for springs of water, and plenty of all things....From Darnah we spent 3 days further to Sultania, a very ancient city; travelling by many Persian villages, and finding every man at his labour, and neighbour with neighbour going from one town to another. Which bred much contentment, and made us wonder at the great peace and tranquillity which the commons of Persia live in above the commons of Turkey. The ruins of many fair Christian churches we beheld, but not without pity, built all with great arches and high towers, lavorated [elaborated] with gold, and other rich paintings, to the beautifying of the same. And verily, I take them to be those churches which Cosroe, king of Persia, destroyed: who, being in battle discomfited, fought between himself and Heraclitus the Emperor, wreaked his teen and malice on the Christian churches throughout his dominions....

The description of Quasvin

...a city very wealthy by reason of the king's palace and the great concourse of merchants who resort thither. It was, in ancient time, called Arcasia (as in Strabo), but now termed Quasvin which, in the Persian language, signifies chastisement, or a place of punishment, because the kings were wont to banish or confine such persons as for their offences and misdemeanours had deserved such chastisement. This city is seated in a goodly, fertile plain, of 3 or 4 days' journey in length, furnished with 2000 villages to serve the necessary uses thereof. But evilly built; and, for the most part, all of bricks not hardened with fire, but only dried in the sun: as are most parts of the buildings of all Persia. It is now one of the seats of the Persian king's empire, which was translated by King Tamasp (this king's grandfather) from Tauris; who built one goodly Seraglio for himself, and another for his women, and has been ever since continued by his successors; though the king who now reigns makes most of his abode in Esfahan, 14 days' journey further towards the east.

There are three places in the city most of note: viz, the king's palace, the bazaars, and the At Maidan. The gate of the king's palace is built with stone of several colours, and very curiously[10] enamelled with gold. On the ceiling, within, is carved the wars of the Persian kings, and the several battles fought by them against the Turks and Tatars. The pavements of the rooms beneath, and chambers above, are spread with most fine carpets, woven and tissued with silk and gold: all ensigns of the Persian greatness. There are, likewise, in this city, sundry bazaars where in some you may buy sashes and turbans, and Indian cloth of wonderful fineness; in others, silks of all sorts: as velvets, damasks, cloth of gold and silver; in others, infinite furs: as sables and martin, out of Muscovy, and Agiam furs brought from Khorassan. In a word: every speech has a general science or trade, wherein is sold whatsoever is necessary for the use of man.

The At Maidan is the high space or chief marketplace of this city, and is foursquare, containing in a circuit very near a mile, and serves as the bourse for all sorts of merchants to meet in, and also for all others to sell whatsoever commodities they possess. So that, in one place, is selling of horses, mules, and camels; in another place, carpets, garments, and felts of all sorts; and in another, all kind of fruit: such as muskmelons, anguries [watermelons], pomegranates, pistachios, Adam's apples, dates, grapes, and raisins dried in the sun. In this place sits daily 12 Sheraffes,[11] that is, men to buy and sell pearls, diamonds, and other precious stones, and to exchange gold and silver, to turn Spanish dollars, to great advantage, into Persian coin; and to change the great pieces of the Persian coin, such as Abbasses, Larines and such, into certain brass monies for the poor. They will also lend upon any pawn, and that with as great interest as our devilish brokers and scriveners take in London. Finally, the strength of this city consists not in walls and bulwarks, but in the soldiers who are continually maintained in and about this city; for, out of Quasvin and the villages belonging unto the same are maintained 20,000 soldiers on horseback. Howsoever, in the king's father's time were levied but 12,000....

The description of Cassan

We arrived at Cassan, a principal city in Parthia, very famous and rich (howsoever Ortelius and others make no mention of it). This city is seated in a goodly plain; and because it has no mountains near it, but [so] within a day's journey the heat is very fastidious; as great, almost, as it is in Hormoz. The spring and harvest is sooner in this climate than in any other parts of the Persian dominions. It wants neither fountains, springs, nor gardens, but abounds with all necessaries whatsoever, consisting altogether in merchandise. And the best trade of all the land is there, being greatly frequented by all sorts of merchants; especially out of India. The people are very industrious and curious in all sciences, but especially in weaving girdles and sashes, in making velvets, satins, damasks, very good Hormozenes, and Persian carpets of wonderful fineness; in a word, it is the very magazine and warehouse of all the Persian cities for these stuffs.

Here may you buy all manner of drugs and spices, and turquoise, with store of pearls, diamonds, and rubies; as also all sorts of silks, as well wrought as raw. I am persuaded that in one year there is more silk brought into Cassan than is of broadcloth brought into the City of London. This city is much to be commended for the civil and good government which is there used. An idle person is not permitted to live among them. The child that is but 6 year's old is set to labour. No ill rule, disorder, or riot is there suffered. For they have a law among them…whereby every person is compelled to give his name to the magistrates, therewith declaring what kind of life he liked, how he lives, and what art [skill] he exercises. And if any do tell untruly, is either well beaten on the feet, or employed in public slavery. The greatest annoyance that this city is invested withal is the abundance and multitude of black scorpions, of an exceeding greatness, which many times do much harm, if a special care is not had of them. John Mildenhall and myself parted company; he travelling to Lahore in the East Indies [India], and myself setting towards the great city of Esfahan, 3 days travel distant from Cassan.

The description of Esfahan

This city, as some affirm, was built by Arsaces, the first King of Parthia, being then called Dara. But whether so or no, is not much material. Sure it is that, in times past, it was called Hecatombpolis, 'the city of a 100 gates'. And well it may keep that name still since the huge walls of the same containing circuit an easy day's journey on horseback, and is become the greatest city in all the Persian kingdoms. Which is so much the more magnified and made populous by reason of the King's residence therein. For there is the supreme place of justice. All matters of importance have recourse to this place. All ambassadors of princes, and agents of cities, make their repair hither. And such as aspire and thirst after offices and preferments run thither amain with emulation and disdain of others. And (in a word) thither are brought the revenues that appertain to the Crown; and there are they disposed out again. By all which means the city has wonderfully increased and appopulated itself within these 25 years.

Very strong is this city by situation, compassed about with a very great wall, and watered with deep channel of running springs, conveyed into it from a part of the Coronian Mountains which are, as a wall, inaccessible about it. On the north side is erected a strong fort or castle, being compassed about with a wall of 1700 yards. And in the midst thereof is built a tower (or rather, a strong keep), sundry chambers and lodgings therein; but stored with little ordnance. On the west side of this city stands 2 Seraglios; the one for the King, the other for his women: palaces of great state and magnificence, far exceeding all other proud buildings in this city. The walls glitter with red marble and pargetting of many colours. Yea, all the palace is paved with chequered and tesselled work; and on the same is spread carpets wrought with silk and gold, the windows of alabaster, white marble, and much other spotted marble, the posts and wickets of massy ivory checked with glittering black ebony, so curiously wrought in winding knots, as may easier stay than satisfy the eyes of the wondering beholder.

Near unto this palace is a garden, very spacious and large, all flourishing an beautiful, replenished with a thousand sundry kinds of grafts, trees, and sweet-smelling plants; among which the lily, the hyacinth, the gillyflower, the rose, the violet, the flower-gentle, and a thousand other odoriferous flowers do yield a most pleasant and delightful sight to all beholders. There are a thousand fountains, and a thousand brooks; among them all, as the father of them all, a pretty river which, with its mild course and delightsome noise, divides the garden from the King's palace. Neither is this garden so straightly looked unto, but that both the King's soldiers and citizens may (and do) at their pleasures oftentimes on horseback repair thither to recreate themselves in the shadows and walks of those greens.

And as a guard for this sumptuous palace the King keeps certain orders of soldiers, whereof the most noble and the greatest in number are called 'churchi', who are (as it were) the King's pensioners, being 8,000 in number, all of them divided under several captains; which captains do yield obedience to the general captain, called 'Church-Pasha', a man always of great authority. Next unto this order is another called 'Esahul', to the number of a thousand, distinguished also under particular captains. And the chief captain is called Esahul-Pasha. All these are maintained by certain towns and villages, which are feudatories to the Crown of Persia. And they receive, at certain times, of the King, armour, horses, apparel, and tents; every one as he is in place and degree. With this strong garrison is the King daily attended upon, and maintains the majesty of his court; especially where he rides in progress....

The nature of the Persians

Finally, the inhabitants of this city do much resemble the ancient Parthians in several things; but especially in their continual riding. They ride on horseback, for the most part. On horseback they fight with the enemy. They execute all affairs (as well public as private) on horseback. They go from place to place on horseback. They buy and sell on horseback, and on horseback they confer and talk with one another. And the difference between the gentleman and the slave is that the slave never rides, and the gentleman never goes on foot. Besides, the nature of this people is arrogant, seditious, deceitful, and very unquiet. But the fierceness of their nature is much restrained by the King's severe government.

They are much inclined to sensuality, having three sorts of women, as they term them, viz: honest women, half honest women, and courtesans. And yet they chastise no offence with like extremity as adultery. And that as well in the half honest woman as in the honest. Last of all, they are full of crafty stratagems, and are breakers of their promises (a vice that is very inbred in all barbarians); not content with any man's government long, and lovers of novelties. For testimony whereof we may avouch those ancient poisonings and wicked treacheries which were plotted not only by subjects against their sovereigns, but also by children against their natural parents. For the name of 'father' was in so small estimation with those 50 sons of Artaxerxes that, with one consent, they all conspired to murder him. The which monstrous impiety ever since has been practised in this nation: sometimes the father with the children, sometimes the children with the father; and sometimes the children with one another.

For instance we may take Abbas who now reigns; who, being the governor of Heri while his father reigned, did not only conspire to have his elder brother Emir Hameez (the hopefullest Prince that ever was in Persia) to be betrayed into the hands of the Turkish general in the year 1586, but also (by force of money and gifts) persuaded one of his own eunuchs to kill him. Who was no sooner corrupted [but] put his treason into practice; and, upon a sudden, in the night time, as he slept on his pallet, struck him through the body with a lance. And so the most resplendent and bright shining lamp that ever was in Persia was utterly extinguished. And [Abbas] not content with this impiety towards his brother, did shortly after condescend (as the full report goes) to have his aged father, Muhammad (surnamed Khudabanda) poisoned without either regard of his fatherly majesty, or reverence to age or natural piety, that so he might ascend into the kingdom. Infinite also are the calamities which he has brought, since he came to the throne, nobility on the houses of the ancient his Court (before mentioned) receive horses at his hands, as they are in place and degree. And these their horses are of a singular virtue, equal with those of the old time, which (as Strabo writes) were accustomed to be fed and brought up in Armenia for the King's use. They are wonderfully swift in course, fierce in battle, long breathed and very docile. When they are unloaded, they are gentle and mild, but when they are armed, they are warlike, hardy and manageable, even at the pleasure of the rider. And I have seen [some] of them sold for 1000, and sometimes 1500, ducats a piece.

After he has viewed his horses, he passes into his armoury; certain buildings near unto his palace, where are made very strong cuirasses (or corselets), headpieces and targets; most of them able to keep out the shot of an arquebusier; and much more to daunt the force of a dart. Here also the King furnishes his soldiers. Not only with cuirasses, headpieces, and targets, but with bows and arrows, pouldrons, and ganglets;[12] and of lances made out of good ash, armed at both ends; with scimitars and shirts of mail, most finely and soundly tempered, wherewith both themselves and their horses are defended in times of war.

By this time, having spent most of the forenoon, he returns again unto his palace, and remains there until 3 o'clock in the afternoon; at which time he makes his entry into the At Maidan, which is the great marketplace, or high street, of Esfahan. Round about this place are erected certain high scaffolds where the multitudes sit to behold the warlike exercises performed by the King and his courtiers: as running and leaping; their shooting with bows and arrows, at a mark above and beneath; their playing at tennis. All which they perform on horseback, with several more too long to write of. In this place, too, is to be seen, several times in the year, the pleasant sight of fireworks, of banquets, of music, of wrestling, and of whatsoever triumphs else there is to be shown, for the declaration of the joy of this people.

Besides, the King very often, in this place, in the presence of the peers of the realm, will give judgement in several causes. Much like unto the ancient kings of France, who used ordinarily to hear the complaints of their subjects; but, of late years the more the pity, they have committed this business unto the consciences of subordinate officers; hearing by other men's ears, and seeing by other men's eyes well nigh concerning all their affairs. Which course the Persian King holds neither good nor comfortable for the people, nor yet by any means to further justice. And certainly, where such carelessness does enter into the majesty of Kings, the Estate and the Realm cannot choose but be weakened, and the royal majesty imbased [debased]. So that, in the end, it might be showed that the people have not refused to rise against the person of the King, and sometimes to murder him.

To be brief. In the execution of justice, he is very severe: as well to the greatest, as to the meanest – not sparing (as might be showed) to hang his chief Cadi, or judges when he shall perceive how that, upon bribes and favours, they delay the suits of the subjects,

Figure 1 Abbas the Great (1557–1629), Shah of Persia from 1587 to 1628

Source: Herbert (1677) By permission of the British Library (ref. 215e12)

against the clear and manifest truth; imitating here Cambyses who commanded Sisamnes' skin,[13] for giving an unjust sentence, to be flayed off, and covered the judgement seat therewith; appointing also his son to judge in his space, to the end that by sight thereof, all other judges might be warned to be just and upright. And I have seen him many times alight from his horse, only to do justice to a poor body. Besides, he punishes theft and manslaughter so severely that in an age man shall not hear either of the one or of the other. Which kind of severity were very needful for some parts of Christendom. I will not say for England (though we have some fault therein); but for France especially, where within 10 years 6000 gentlemen have been slain (as it happens) by the King's pardons. So that since King Abbas came to the throne, full 20 years and upwards, the Persian Empire has flourished in sacred and redoubted laws, the people demeaning themselves after the best manner they can, abundance of collections coming plentifully in, the rents of his chamber were increased [more] than ever they were in his grandfather Tamasp, his time. Arms, arts, and sciences do wonderfully prosper, and are very highly esteemed.

The great power that the Persian King is able to make against the Turk

As to the first: the strength of the Persian consists now in three kinds of soldiers. The first are the soldiers of his Court, to the number of 9,000 (as we said before). The second kind are such who, by custom and duty, are bound to serve him in his wars. And these are his ancient gentlemen of his country, who hold lands and possessions descended unto them from their ancestors, or held by the gift of the King. These are sent for, in times of war, and are in duty bound to perform such like service as the gentry of Italy, France, and Spain do unto their sovereign. These amount (since Abbas came to the throne) very near to 40,000. Most of them come well armed; the rest content themselves with headpieces and jacks,[14] and use for their weapons either horsemen's staves or bows, which they can most cunningly handle; discharging their arrows also very near unto what they aim at, either forward or backward. The third sort are such as are sent unto him from the princes and neighbours, his confederates. And these are commonly sent from the princes of Iberia, Albania, and the countries bordering upon Media and Armenia; who, being half Christians, bear mortal hatred against the Turk....

And for his soldiers, they are for the most part, very valorous and noble. Which, being compared with the Turkish people (who, for the most part, are [a] a very rascal, or vile, race) are by good right very highly to be esteemed. For the naked Turkish horseman is not to be compared with the Persian man-at-arms, who comes into the field armed with a strong cuirass, a sure headpiece, and a good target; whereas the Turkish European horsemen, altogether naked, use only a square or crooked buckler, wherewith they do scarcely cover themselves. And the Asian horsemen [use] bucklers made of soft reeds, wound round and covered with some kind of silk.

Again, the Persian horseman wears his pouldrons and ganglets, and bears a staff of good ash, armed at both ends, fighting with them as occasion serves at the staff, after the manner of the Numidians. And, with doubling and redoubling their thrust from on high, doe easily wound or kill the unarmed Turks with their horses, whereas the Turkish horseman, after the manner of the Greeks, couch their staves in their rest; and so that the first course most commonly breaks the same, being made of light and brittle fire; and so, presently, come to their scimitars or horseman's mace, being, in all other things far inferior to the Persian man at arms. And [as] for the Turkish archers on horseback: they are in no respect to be compared with the Persians, who are well mounted and surely armed, using both greater and stronger bows, and shoot more deadly arrow, making small account of the Turks. So that all things well considered, the Persian is now able to deal in field with the Great Turk, having both numbers of soldiers, good store of shot and other warlike furniture, as also (which is the chief stay of a state) obedience of his subjects. And verily, when Persia was at the weakest, had not the Turkish Emperors Selim, Suleiman, and Murad, been allured either by treason, rebellion, or intestine discords, they would never have taken that war in hand. And so much for the Persian forces.

The miserable thraldom of the Christians under the Turkish tyranny

And as for the miserable thraldom that the poor Christians endure under the Turkish tyranny, we (thanks be given unto God) in these northern parts of the world may behold with safety, but not without pity, when we rightly consider how that the people among whom our Saviour himself conversed, at that time when his beautiful steps honoured the world, with those churches in Greece, which his Apostle so industriously planted, so carefully visited, so tenderly cherished, instructed, and confirmed by so many peculiar Epistles, and for whom they sent up so many fervent prayers, are now become a cage of unclean birds: filthy spirits do possess them. The Turk, with his Qur'ān, and Muhammad with his...are lords of these places, so that now the Greeks have lost their liberty; (which their ancestors had many times before, to their immortal praise, worthily defended against the greatest monarchies of the world) and are now so degenerate by the means of the Turkish oppression that in all Greece is hardly to be found any small remembrance of the ancient glory thereof. Insomuch that, whereas they were wont to account all other nations barbarous in comparison with themselves, they are now become no less barbarous than those rude nations whom they before scorned.

Infinite are the miseries which they, from time to time, have endured under the Turkish tyrants. And so great has been the fury of that barbarous nation, that no tongue is able to express, or pen describe. For what tongue is able to express the miseries that the poor Greeks endured when the imperial city of Constantinople was taken and spoiled by Muhammad the Great in the year 1453, when the cruel tyrant could not content himself with the spoil and riches of the fair city, but caused also as he sat feasting with his Pashas and great commanders, most of the chief Christian captives, both men and women (of whom many were of the Emperor's line and race) to be, in his presence, put to death: deeming his feast much more stately and magnificent by such effusion of Christian blood.

There might a man have seen the poor Christian captives driven up and down by the merciless soldiers, as if they had been droves of cattle, or flocks of sheep. It would have pitied any strong heart to have seen the noble gentlewomen and great ladies, with their beautiful children, who flowed in all worldly wealth and pleasure, to become the poor and miserable bondslaves of most base and contemptible rascals, who were so far from showing them any pity, as that they delighted in nothing more than to heap more and more misery upon them, making no more reckoning of them than of dogs. There might the parents see the woeful misery of their beloved children, and the children of the parents; the husband might see the shameful abuse of his wife, and the wife of her husband; and generally, one friend of another.

Yea, such was their malice to the Christian faith that they coveted the Temple of Sophia,[15] built for God to be honoured in, into a stable for their horses, making it a place for the execution of their abominable and unspeakable filthiness. Yea, the image of the crucifix they also took down, and put a Turk's cap upon the head thereof, and so set it up and shot at it with bows and arrows. And afterwards, in great derision, carried it about in their camp as it had been in procession, with drums playing before it, railing and spitting at it, and calling it the God of the Christians: which I note not so much done in contempt of the images as in despite of Christ and the Christian religion.

Neither have they committed these outrages and monstrous cruelties in Greece alone, but in other parts of Christendom also, as Italy has sundry times tasted of their cruel incursions and bloody invasions. Besides, Serbia, Bulgaria, Transylvania, Moldavia and Wallachia groan under the yoke of Turkish tyranny. What should I write of Hungary, that royal kingdom, since, in the reign of one Turkish Emperor (I mean Suleiman the Magnificent) the number of those who were slain, and carried into miserable captivity, were wellnigh 200,000 Hungarians? So spoiled and harried in this kingdom by the Turks that it may well breed an astonishment not only to the neighbour countries adjoining, but to others further remote. So that to wind up all in a word: there is now to be seen, in these Christian countries which the Great Turk possesses, nothing but triumphs over Christ, and scorners of his religion; insolencies and violences against the professors [of the Christian faith]; extortions and oppressions upon their goods; rapines and murderings upon the very souls of their children – a case to be wailed with tears of blood by all Christian hearts that know it; hearing the only anchor and stay of their souls (our blessed Saviour) daily derided and blasphemed by the pride of the Turks.

Indeed it were a small thing if the Turks' extortions were only on their goods and labours, or if the bodies and lives of those poor Christians were only wasted and worn out in his works and slaveries, it might be suffered: for goods are transitory, and death the end of all worldly miseries. But to be forced (as those poor countries are) to pay a tribute also of souls to wicked Muhammad, to have their dearest children (both sons and daughters) snatched out of their parents' bosoms to be brought up in his impious abominations, and to be employed (after they are so brought up) in murdering their fathers and mothers that begat them; and in rooting out that faith wherein they were born and baptised, and which only were able to bring their souls into happiness. This surely is a calamity insupportable, and which cries out unto God in the heavens for relief.

I will say no more touching this matter, but even wish, with the humble petition of a mind pierced with grief, to the just Judge of the World, redeemer of mankind, and Saviour of His people, to cast down his pitiful eyes upon those nations: to behold, on the one side, His triumphing, fierce enemies persecuting without measure; on the other, His poor servants trodden down and persecuted without help, hope, or comfort; and to dissolve the pride and power of the one, to comfort the astonished and wasting weakness of the other, with some hope of succour and small delivery; to inspire the hearts of Christian princes (their neighbours) compounding or laying aside their endless and fruitless contentions, to revenge their quarrel against their unjust oppressors. For certainly, if mean princes have encumbered the course of the Great Turk's conquest, what would not the united Christian forces do? If we might but once see the glorious beams of that bright, shining day appear!

Which union the Persian King has often and instantly sought of the Christian princes; and that within these few years. For first (as we said before) he sent Sir Anthony Sherley, a man very wise and valiant, if he had not been too prodigal. And after him, in the year of grace 1605, he sent three other several Ambassadors, one after another....The two first came directly to the Emperor at Prague; and the other two were sent unto the French King, whose embassy was for the common good also, though it wanted the wish to succeed. And, to show the great desire that the Persian still has to have the pride of the Great Turk abated, he has since employed Master Robert Sherley as his ambassador to the same purpose.

Never did Christendom miss times of more advantage to have prevailed against the Turk: not only to have held their own (which they do not in Hungary), but to have recovered some good part of their losses before received, also. And indeed, true it is that the time then well served for both, by reason that the Great Turk was (and is still) troubled with wars: both against his own rebels, and the Persian King in Asia; most part of his forces being turned that way. But what avails opportunity, without unity? For howsoever the Persian King did instantly request the Emperor to join with him in all friendship and brotherly love, and to continue his wars against the Great Turk, their common enemy;

and also promised that, for his part, he would never lay down arms until his enemy was brought to nought and destroyed, so that the Christian princes would, on the other side, likewise impugn him. And though the Emperor, for his part, did promise to continue his wars, and to raise greater forces, and also, by letters, to exhort and incite the greatest Christian princes and potentates to extend also their power against the common enemy, yet could he not effect it, neither perform any part of his promise to the Persian King.

For the next year following, seeing the Hungarians revolted from him, and taking part with the Turks, and the Turks with them, and finding himself not able, with his own power, to hold the field against them, much less to maintain a defensive war, and his friends and allies, his wonted and greatest stays, then at his greatest need, to fail him, was glad to leave the Persian in the field to his own strength, and to conclude a reasonable peace with Achmet, the Great Turk who now reigns; being no way able, without the great aid of other Christian princes, to withstand the huge and dreadful power of the Ottoman Emperor. Which (be it spoken without ominous presage) is to be feared, will too truly appear and manifest itself whensoever the wars of the Great Turk, and his troubles in the East with the Persian be ended, he shall then again turn his victorious and insulting forces this way, towards the West.

I conclude then, that those distressed parts of Christendom which are subject to the Turkish fury cannot but be much beholden, both to Sir Anthony Sherley, as also his brother, master Robert Sherley, for 20 years' peace which is concluded between the Emperor and the Great Turk, they being (I dare be bold to say, under God) the only means that stirred up the Persian King to take up arms against the Great Turk, and to draw, by degrees, the whole war upon his neck, thereby to free and give a time of breathing to the champions of Jesus Christ to refresh themselves. And increase their forces: a peace not only well pleasing to the Emperor, but to the Turk also: who, no sooner had he heard from the Pasha of Buda that it was concluded, but forthwith conceived so great joy that, with a number of janisarries and others, he went from his palace in Constantinople, in great magnificence, to the church, to give thanks therefore unto his Prophet, Muhammad; spending the next day in great sport and pleasure, purposing from thenceforth to turn all his force and power for the subduing of the Persian King. But, to leave these two great monarchs, the only enemies to the name of Christ, in field against the other, I come now to my return from those parts.

The return of the author by the way of Persia,...Assyria, and Arabia

Having taken my leave of Master Robert Sherley, and the rest of my countrymen, I left them to the mercy of the King (whose bounty and goodness by their return has plentifully showed itself) and betook myself to the protection of the Almighty, to bring me in safety again into my own country; being, in my return, accompanied by one Signor Belchior Dios di Croce, an Armenian Portuguese, or Portuguese Armenian, and one Christophero, a Greek, who had been sent with letters from the governor of Goa to the King of Spain; but lost afterwards their lives, and letters, by shipwreck in the Venetian Gulf.

From Esfahan we spent 10 days' travel to Shiraz, by persuasion of some Persian merchants who were bound for Aleppo with us, travelling through the very heart of Persia itself; paying, paying, now and then, a shaughee a piece to certain villages in the way. No matter of importance worth the relating, till we come to the city itself.

The description of Shiraz, ancient Persepolis[16]

This city is situated on the banks of Bindamir, a great and famous river that courses through Persia and the kingdom of Lar, and so empties itself into the Persian Gulf, and was once the metropolitical seat of all the kingdom until, of late years, Esfahan has gained that privilege from her. Notwithstanding, it is large and spacious, containing very near 10 miles in circuit, and lies just in the roadway which leads from Esfahan to Hormuz. Pliny called it 'Perciciregni'; for so it was during the monarchy, the head of the Persian kingdom, which continues famous, many years together, being stuffed with the spoils of the whole world. For Alexander, when he took it, found in the Treasury 40,000 talents[17] of gold; every talent being 600 crowns....And the same time, at the request of a drunken strumpet, he set this gallant city on fire; himself being the first president in that woeful misery, which in short time was burnt to the ground, as Diodorus Siculus relates....Such a miserable end befell to the regal city of all the East, whence so many nations derived their laws and customs; which had been the seat of so many kings; and, in times past, the only terror of Greece.

So that in and about this town are to be seen many ancient monuments: as two great gates that are distant, one from the other, the space of 12 miles. Which shows the circuit of this city, as it was in the times of the monarchy, to be both large and spacious. On the south side we viewed the ruins of a goodly palace built (as they say) by King Cyrus...and to the north side, the ruins of an old castle which seems was girt about with a threefold wall: the first wall being 24 foot high, adorned and beautified with many turrets and spires. The second was like unto the first, but twice as high; and the third was foursquare, being fourscore and ten foot high: all fabricated of free stone. On each side were 12 gates of brass, with brazen pales set before them, very curiously wrought: all which did show the magnificence of the founder.

On the east side of this ruined castle, some 4 acts of ground distant, is a mountain on which is erected a goodly chapel, in which most of the Persian kings in ancient times were entombed. And though this city has endured sundry mutations and changes, yet is it not to be esteemed one of the least cities of Persia; for out of it, in short time, is levied 20,000 horsemen, well armed. Besides, it is one of the greatest and most famous cities of the East, both for traffic of merchandise, as also for most excellent armour and furniture, which the armourers, with wonderful cunning, make [out] of iron and steel and the juice of certain herbs, of much more notable temper and beauty than those which are made with us in Europe: not only headpieces, cuirasses, and complete armours, but whole caparisons for horses, curiously made of thin plates of iron and steel.

Now, by the situation of this town on the river Bindamir, a very profitable trade for the [English][18] East India Company might be at Batan, a haven town in the Persian Gulf; which trends in the form of a half moon, having a little pretty island, as a most commodious shelter, in the mouth of the same whereby a ship of 500 tons and better may ride at pleasure. Very desirous is the Persian King that our shipping should come thither, or to any other port in his dominions; promising oftentimes (as may be justified very probably) that it should be lawful for us to build and fortify, and enjoy all privileges in as ample as his own subjects; and that if the Portuguese in Hormuz should offer violence to our shipping, that then he would become their professed enemy: whose league of friendship (I am assured) they dare not, in that island, break, standing so many ways beholden to the Persian King as they do. Besides, were we planted in Batan,[19] the King would quickly cut off the greatest trade of merchandise (either the raw silk or indigo from Tauris) from Constantinople, and turn it into that harbour. There we should have a speedy vent for our broadcloth, kerseys, tin, and lead; and have in barter for the same whatsoever either the kingdom of Persia or India, or both, affords. So that, in my opinion, to have Batan for a resting and refreshing harbour after our tedious sailing through the great ocean, were far better than Bantam, or Java, or Aden, or any other port in Arabia Felix: places altogether of wrong and oppression, where little justice is to be found, being so far from Constantinople; whereas Batan stands in such a country as is full of peace and tranquillity, having a most just and upright prince (the only true stay of traffic), Lord of the same, whose only care and endeavour is to maintain and uphold the trade of merchandise. But to leave these things to the merchants, we come now to the kingdom of Assyria.

The description of New Babylon, now called Baghdad

By this river [Euphrates] the city of Baghdad is very abundantly furnished with all kinds of provision of corn, fowl, fish, and venison of all sorts; besides great store of fruit: but especially dates – and that very cheap. This city, by some is called New Babylon; and may well be, because it rose out of the ruins of Old Babylon, not far distant; being nothing so great, nor so fair, for it contains, in circuit, but 3 English miles, and is built but of brick, dried in the sun; their houses also being flat-roofed, and low. They have no rain for 8 months together, nor almost any cloud in the sky, night nor day. Their winter is in November, December, January and February; which months are, nevertheless, as warm as our summer in England. In a word, this town was once a place of great trade and profit, by reason of the huge caravans which were wont to come from Persia and Basra. But since the Portuguese, Englishmen and Hollanders have, by their trade into the East Indies, cut off almost all the trade of merchandise into the Gulfs of Arabia and Persia, both Grand Cairo and Egypt, and Baghdad in Assyria, are now of that benefit, as they have been, either to the merchant, or Great Turk; his tributes, both in Egypt, and his customs in this place, being much hindered thereby.

Memorable, notwithstanding, is this town because it was the only place where, for the space of 600 years, the Muhammadan Caliphs were resident and kept their sumptuous Courts, until the Tatar prince and the king of Armenia (as before was declared) besieged it and, in the end, took it: with the Caliph also, together with an inestimable mass of treasure. Which treasure, when the two princes saw [it], they demanded of the Caliph why he would not, with the same, levy and wage soldiers for his won defence. Whereunto he answered that unto that time he thought his own subjects had been sufficient enough to have resisted any foreign enemy. Which they understanding, immediately caused all that treasure to be carried up into the castle, and the covetous wretch set in the midst of the same, forbidding that any man should give him either meat or drink; where he miserably died through famine, in the midst of his riches.

After[wards], it continued under the Tatar and Persian government until it was taken by Suleiman, the Turkish Emperor, from Tamasp, the Persian King who (after it was yielded unto him), according to an old superstitious manner, received, at the hands of a poor Caliph, the ensigns and ornaments of the kings of Assyria. So this city, with the great countries of Assyria and Mesopotamia (sometimes famous kingdoms of themselves, and lately part of the Persian kingdom) fell into the hands of the Great Turk, in the year 1534; and so have continued ever since, provinces of the Turkish Empire. It was reported unto

Emperor Rodolphus,[20] for a certain truth, that the King of Persia had won this city and these countries again from the Turk, in the year 1604. But that news was not true; for, in April 1611, it was then under the Turkish government.

Within 2 days' travel of Baghdad lies...a little village where the bodies of Ali (whom the Christians honour) and his sons Hassan and Husayn lie entombed by whose sepulchres it is in great credit, and is every year visited by the Persians in all respects, after the same sort that the Turks visit the sepulchres of the three first successors Aboubakir, Otman, and Omar. Yea, the very kings of Persia used to be crowned, and girt with the sword, in this place, where the caliph was wont to keep his residence, as being a man who represented Ali, and occupied the choice room of their filthy and abominable priesthood.

Having stayed 20 days in Baghdad, we put ourselves in the company of a chaus who was bound from the Pasha of Baghdad, for Constantinople: being in number 16 persons, and no more, to travel through a great part of Chaldea and the desert of Arabia....

[Muhammad]

...it shall not be amiss to insert a word or two of Muhammad and his superstition, who was born in this country, and has seduced the greatest part of the world with his abominable religion. Concerning Muhammad, the people of Mecca (where he lies intombed) do altogether condemn him, both for his robberies and murders. And himself, in his Qur'ān, confesses himself to be a sinner, an idolator, an adulterer, and inclined to women, above measure and that, in such uncivil terms that I am ashamed to repeat. And concerning his Qur'ān, wherein he has inserted the precepts of his invention, there is no truth in it. For, first, upon pain of death, it may not be disputed upon; whereas the truth loves trial, so that though the Arabians, Turks and Persians will not spare to say (and that, vauntingly) that the doctrine of Muhammad is divine, and conformable both to the Old and the New Testament; yet, as good as they make it, you may not examine it, or call it into question. As if a man should say: 'Behold, you are paid in good money. But you must not weigh it, neither look upon it by daylight'. 2. Besides, his Qur'ān is pestered with a number of fables and falsities, as 900 untruths; whereof two are most gross: that Abraham was the son of Lazarus; and Mary the sister of Aaron. 3. Again, it points out at things sensible and corporal; and not to things internal and spiritual. For Muhammad most blasphemously reports [that] in his progress up to the Throne of God, that he felt the hand of God threescore and ten times colder than any ice; yea, that he saw an angel that had a thousand heads; a diamond table of a thousand miles in length; and a cock of a wonderful bigness, which is kept until the Day of Doom, that then, by the shrillness of his crowing, the dead may be raised. And further, he sets it down that the Devil is circumcised: with this leasing also, that the stars are very candles, hung out every night from the firmament. 4. And for his promises to all such as call upon him faithfully [these] are mere carnal and earthly, such as I am ashamed to name; being fit for none but Heliogabalus, and Sardanapalus. 5. His precepts are indulgent to perjury, giving leave to have as many wives as a man will, to couple themselves not only with one of the same sex, but with brute beasts also; to spoil one another's goods, and none to be accused under four witnesses. 6. For his miracles: he wrought none at all; but he confesses that God sent Moses with miracles, and Christ (his forerunner) with miracles. But for himself, he was come with fire and sword to force men to obey his law: whereas the Truth draws men of their own accord.

Ridiculous also is that which he writes of himself; how, when he was a child, an angel was sent from God to open his heart, and to take out that lump of blood which is the cause of sin: as though the cause thereof were not spiritual. 7. The effect of his doctrine is perjury, as they need not to keep any oath made with a Christian, who is an infidel; and also murder, as the eldest brother, as soon as he comes to wear the crown, to strangle all the rest. For instance whereof Muhammad III (this King's father, who now sways the sceptre at Constantinople) did not only murder his brothers but (to rid himself of the fears of all competitors – the greatest torment of the mighty) at the very same time caused 10 of his fathers' wives and concubines (such as by whom any issue were to be feared) to be all drowned in the sea.

And is it now not a wonder that the people of the Turks and Persians, being both warlike and politic, magnificent and stately (and: to say in a word) the very hammer of the world, as it was said of Babylon, should be thus led away with these vile enchantments of their wicked prophet, Muhammad? I will say no more! But since the darkness of Turkey and Persia is so great that it may be felt, and that it is a wonder in our eyes to see such mists in those places, then let us in this land rejoice, who are not only endued with nature as they are, but with special inspiration from above besides; having the celestial doctrine of the everlasting Son of God, to guide us unto true happiness. For certainly, the time will come when both the Great Turk and his Pashas, and the Persian King with his Chans, shall bitterly rue the time and wish, with the loss of both their eyes, that they had but heard and seen as much as we have done.

Let us then persuade my loving countrymen who either shall hereafter serve in the wars of Hungary against the Turk, or trade in those places, utterly to detest the Turkish religion as the only way that treads to death and destruction. We may conclude, with Ludovicus Vives, who compares heathenism with Mohametism, to glass. 'Touch not glass. For though it be bright; yet it is brittle, it cannot endure the hammer'; and Christianism to gold: 'Do you melt it, or do you rub it, or do you beat it, it shine still more orient'.

NOTES

1 Dry town: a town not on the sea or on a navigable river.
2 Side note: 'cains are storehouses for [use by] foreign merchants'.
3 Side note: 'a caravan is a great many of camels laden, not much unlike our carriers here in England'.
4 From old French 'ladron': robber.
5 Side note: 'The religion of the Armenians is spotted with many absurdities'.
6 Supporters of the deposed James II (1633–1701), King of England, Scotland and Ireland (1685–8). They agitated for some sixty years that his heirs should succeed, but their movement died when, in 1714, the Hanoverian succession to the British throne eliminated all possible hope for the eventual victory for their cause.
7 The dates given in Cartwright are those as laid down in the Orthodox (Eastern) tradition. Their equivalents, in the Roman Catholic and Protestant traditions are, respectively: 25 March (Annunciation); 25 December (Nativity); 2 February (Purification – also sometimes known as Candlemas); 6 August (Transfiguration).
8 Livy, in his *The Roman History*, Book 21, ch. 35, recounts that, in their crossing of the Alps, Hannibal and his soldiers came

> to a place more difficult than they had yet met with. For the rock was so perpendicular that a light-armed soldier durst hardly attempt it, or let himself down by laying hold on the twigs and bushes that grew around it. The place had been of itself

extremely steep before, but of late, by the falling of the earth, had been so divided that it formed an abyss near a thousand feet deep. When Hannibal seemed surprised [at] what stopped them, he was told that the rock was impassable. The he went to view it, and saw for certain, that he must take a long compass through paths and untrodden ways. This was likewise unpracticable. For though he could easily march in the new snow which was of moderate depth and soft above the old which had never been touched, yet when it came to be melted by the treading of such numbers of men and beasts, they walked in streams of liquefied snow with bare ice underneath. They had a terrible struggling....At length, when both men and beasts were tired to no purpose, they encamped on the top of the rock. There was so much snow to be dug and carried away that with the greatest difficulty they got the place cleared. Then the soldiers were set to level the rock; by which alone they could find passage. In order to split it, huge trees were felled and laid around it. Thus they raised a great pile of wood, and when the wind blew favourably, set it on fire. When the rock was red hot they poured vinegar on it to calcine [to burn to ashes, to consume] and dissolve it.

9 Turkish hegemony over Hungary is generally dated as commencing with the defeat of Louis II by Suleiman the Magnificent at Mohacs in 1526. That led to some 150 years of Turkish rule, resistance to which was not helped by the division of the kingdom. Louis II's brother-in-law, Ferdinand of Austria (later Emperor Ferdinand I), claimed the Hungarian throne, and was elected to it by one fraction of the nobles, while another chose John Zapolyta (John I). Later still the country was split into three competing rivalries. The Turkish victory at Mohacs paved the way for victory at Buda (1541). It was, in part, this continuation of Turkish–Hungarian hostilities that prompted the Safavid Persian monarch Abbas I to pursue his policy of military, as well as diplomatic, alliances with European rulers against the Turks.
10 Skilfully; elaborately.
11 Sheraffes; Shroff: Anglo-Indian corruption of 'saraf', a banker or money-lender (OED).
12 Pouldron: a piece of armour covering the shoulder, a shoulder-plate; ganglet: probably 'janglets', objects with which to make a discordant or unmusical noise.
13 Cambyses, father of Darius the Great (ruled 529–522 BCE). Reputed for his great cruelty. He not only apparently arranged that his own brother be murdered, but was especially brutal in his treatment of the Egyptians, insulting their religion after he had conquered them. The incident referred to here is that he had a judge by the name of Sisamnes put to death for pronouncing what he deemed to be an unjust sentence. The King then had the skin of the judge splayed and then stretched over the seat the dead man used to occupy in court. He thereupon installed Otanes, the dead man's son, as a judge and required him to sit in that seat whenever he sat in judgement. That son, Otanes, was later a highly successful military commander: he took Byzantium, Chalcedon and Lemnos for the Persians, and some scholars believe him to be the same Otanes who became the son-in-law of Darius Histapis.
14 A kind of sleeveless tunic, usually worn by foot-soldiers and others; usually of leather quilted, and in later times often plated, with iron; sometimes applied to a coat of mail (OED).
15 Hagia Sophia, or Santa Sophia, Istanbul. Now a museum of Byzantine art, but originally a Christian church, later a mosque. Constantinus II had first built a church there some thirty years after the capital of the Roman Empire was transferred to Byzantium. Destroyed and rebuilt many times, but the present structure is reputedly largely the one that was commissioned by the Emperor Justinian and built 532–7 CE. With Turkish victory in 1453, the church became a mosque, with all the transformations associated with that change: the replacement of the cross with the crescent; the removal of the altar and pulpit; the painting over of mosaics depicting the Christian faith. Modern architectural historians consider Santa Sophia to be the pre-eminent masterpiece of Byzantine architecture and the model for several mosques that were subsequently erected in Istanbul and elsewhere.
16 The ruins of Persepolis, with remnants of the palaces of Darius I, Xerxes, and others, as well as the Treasury looted by Alexander, lie some 50 km from Shiraz.
17 Denomination of weight, used by Assyrians, Babylonians, Greeks, Romans, and other ancient nations. The value varied greatly with time, people and locality (OED).

18 Awareness of potential economic and financial benefits to be gained from trade in the East in the context of decline of Portuguese power, EEIC was granted royal charter in 1600. But, following upon the 'massacre at Amboina' (1623), when ten English merchants were first tortured, then murdered by the Dutch on Ambon in the Moluccas, the English withdrew to Bengal.
19 Batan: Bandar Abbas –'The port of Abbas'.
20 Presumably Rudolf II (1552–1612, Holy Roman Emperor 1576–1612), King of Bohemia (1575–1611), King of Hungary (1572–1608).

OTHER EDITIONS

Reprinted 1745; abridged edition, 1905.
'Mr Johan Cartwrights reyse van Aleppo in Hispahan; en van daar terug...', in P. van der Aa (ed.), *Naaukeurige versameling der gedenkwaardigste zee en land reysen naar Oost en West-India*, Amsterdam, 1707; in P. van der Aa (ed.), *Die aanmerkwaardigste zee- en landreizen der Portugeesen*, Amsterdam, 1727; *Exerpta Itinirario* Ioannis Cartwright, Antwerp, 1633, 1647.

7

FYNES MORYSON

An Itinerary written by Fynes Moryson Gent., First in the Latine Tongue, and then translated by him into English. Containing his Ten Yeeres Travell through the Twelve Dominions of Germany, Bohmerland, Sweitzerland, Netherland, Denmarke, Polnd, Italy, Turky, France, England, Scotland & Ireland...

London. Printed by John Beale, dwelling in Aldersgate Street, 1617.

BIOGRAPHY

Fynes Moryson (1566–1617?), born Lincolnshire, studied at Cambridge. Although elected a fellow of his college (1584?), his primary interest being in foreign travel, he apparently spent two years (as it were) preparing himself for what was to become some six years of travel in Europe and the Orient by visits to London and to other parts of England. Leaving from the small Essex port of Leigh (1591) he travelled to Prague (at which place, he tells, he dreamt of his father's death having taken place on a certain day: to have that confirmed when he arrived at Nürnberg). His modest inheritance enables him to travel (1593–5) in Denmark, Poland and Italy; after which (December 1595), accompanied by his brother Henry, he embarks on the journey to the Orient: via Germany and Italy (Venice) to Joppa (with two months in Jerusalem), Tripoli, Aleppo, Antioch (near which place his brother dies). Following a short visit to Constantinople, Moryson is back in England in 1597. Following a tour of Scotland (1598) and visits to the family (1599), he is persuaded by his brother Richard (then Governor of Dundalk) to resign his Cambridge fellowship and become part of the English administration there. Appointed secretary to Sir Charles Blount, the Lord Deputy then in the process of attempting to resolve the Tyrone resistance, Moryson participates in the siege of Kinsale. Eventually, retired with a small pension, he returns to England where he continues to serve Blount (now elevated to the peerage) until the latter's death (1606); after which he again returns to Ireland at the request of his brother (now Sir Richard, and vice-president of Munster). Between 1606 and 1610, Moryson writes an abstract of the history of the countries through which he had travelled. Finding it to be far too vast for publication, he apparently destroyed it and wrote a completely new version – the still incomplete text now in existence, consisting of three broad parts: the first on his travels; the second on the Tyrone story; the last part, with comments on the advantages of travel, and observations on the characteristics of peoples and places he had visited.

* * *

Our journey from Jerusalem, by land to Joppa, by Sea to Tripoli in Syria, by land to Haleppo and Scanderona, and of our passage by Sea to the Island Candia

On Friday the fourteenth of June, in the year 1596 we went out of Jerusalem, and by the same way, and in the same manner as we came, rode back to Ramma....Neither did any memorable thing happen to us by the way, save that when we came near to Ramma, and by chance rode over the place of burial for the Turks, where some women were then mourning for their dead friends they, thinking it a reproach that we should ride over their graves did, with enraged countenances, fling stones at us, till we appeased them by dismounting from our asses. The 15th June we came back to Joppa....Then, without delay, we went aboard our little Greek bark, which (according to our bargain at Cyprus) [had] stayed here for our return. For the Master thereof was further tied to transport us from hence to Tripoli in Syria. Neither had he yet received full payment for transporting us hither, the money being left in Cyprus with an Italian Merchant, who was to pay it [to] him at his return, if he brought a testimony under our hands that he had performed his bargain to us. This condition we made providently, and by advice of experienced men. For otherwise the Master of our bark, upon any profitable occasion, would have left this port before our return from Jerusalem, and we should hardly have found another bark here, in a place not much frequented with ships. Besides that, the restraint of the money not to be paid but upon a testimony brought under our hands, was a good caution, that he should not use us ill, nor any way betray us. The 16th June, upon Sunday by twilight of the morning, we set sail from Joppa and, coasting the shore of Asia, had the land so near us every day, as we might easily distinguish the situation of the cities and territories....

...and so upon Thursday the 17th June [1596] we landed at Tripoli of Syria, (so called for difference from Tripoli in Africa). The harbour is compassed with a wall, and lies upon the west-side of the city, wherein were many little barks, and some ships of Marseilles in France. The harbour is fortified with 7 towers, whereof the fourth is called the Tower of Love, because it was built by an Italian Merchant, who was found in bed with a Turkish woman: which offence is capital, as well to the Turk as Christian, if he had not thus redeemed his life. Upon the harbour are built many store-houses for merchants' goods, and shops wherein they are set to sail. The city of Tripoli is some half a mile distant from the harbour, to which the way is sandy, having many gardens on both sides. In this way they show a pillar fastened upon a hill of sand, by which they say the sand is enchanted, lest it should grow to overwhelm the City. Likewise, they show other pillars, under which they say great multitudes of scorpions were, in like sort, enchanted: which, of old, wasted all that territory. And they think that if these pillars were taken away, the city would be destroyed by the sand and the scorpions.

The length of the city somewhat passes the breadth, and lies from the South to the North, seated upon the side of a hill, so cut by nature that it conveys a brook into the streets. Upon the west side of the city, towards the south corner, is a castle upon a high hill, which the French built of old to keep the citizens in subjection. And therein the Great Turk, to the same end, keeps a garrison of soldiers, under his Aga (or Governor) of the City. Upon the east side are two bridges over the aforesaid brook, whence many pleasant fountains spring, which running from the south to the north, pass through the streets of the city, and then water the gardens. Beyond this brook are fruitful hills, and beyond the hills Mount Lybanus lies – so high that it hinders all further prospect: which mountain is very pleasant, abounding with fruitful trees, and with grapes yielding a rich wine. Upon the North side, outside the gates, are many most pleasant gardens, in which they keep great store of silkworms. For the Turks sell their raw silk to the Italians, and buy from them the stuffs woven thereof.

The building of Tripoli and of these parts is like to that of Cyprus and Jerusalem. The street that leads to the way to Aleppo is broad. The rest is narrow, and the air and waters are unhealthful. Mount Lybanus (as I formerly said) is incredibly fruitful, and the plain of Tripoli, reaching 10 miles, is more fruitful than can easily be expressed, bearing great store of pleasant fruits: whereof one among the rest is called 'Amazza-Franchi' that is 'Kill Franks (or French)' because the men of Europe died in great numbers by eating immoderately thereof.

The plain of Tripoli of old yielded 200,000 crowns yearly to the Count thereof, as historians write. And although the old trade of Tripoli is, for the most part, removed to Damascus and Aleppo, yet the city of Tripoli still yields 400,000 crowns yearly to the Great Turk. It may seem incredible, but it is most certain that here and throughout Syria, they have sheep of such bigness that the very tails of them, hanging in many wreaths to the ground, weigh 25 pounds, and many times 30 three pounds.

A Christian who used to entertain the French, treated us very well here. And when I saw a bed made for me and my brother, with clean sheets, I could scarcely contain myself from going to bed before supper, because I had never lain naked in a bed since I came from Venice to this day, having always slept by sea and land in my doublet, with linen breeches and upon a mattress, and between coverlets or with my breeches under my head. But after supper all this joy vanished by an event least expected. For in this part of Asia great store of cotton grows (as it were) upon stalks, like cabbage...and these sheets, being made thereof, so increased the perpetual heat of this country, now most unsupportable in the summer time, that I was forced to leap out of my bed, and sleep as I had formerly done.

My host told me a strange thing, namely that in Alexandria in Egypt, seated upon one of the mouths of the River Nile there was a dovecote and that also at Cairo (or Baghdad), far within the land of Egypt there was another dovecote. And because it much concerns the merchants to have speedy news of any commodity arriving, he assured me that they used to tie letters about the necks of the doves at Alexandria, and so to let them loose. Which doves, having formerly bred in the dovecote at Cairo flew there most swiftly, and the keeper of them there, taking the letters they brought, used to deliver them to the Merchants. This I did not believe until I came to Aleppo, and telling it for a fable to the English merchants there, they seriously affirmed the same to be true: Moreover the host of Tripoli told me news from Constantinople, namely, that the Greeks had burnt great part of the city, (which he thought to be false, and only invented to oppress them in other parts); and that the janissaries had raised a great tumult against the Sub Pasha of the City, who used great severity towards them, by restraining them from drinking wine, and from keeping harlots; and that some 100 of these seditious janissaries were drowned in the harbour, and the rest were daily sought out to be punished. Moreover that Khalil Pasha, the Admiral of Turkey, had left Constantinople with 60 galleys, having taken many Greek and Armenian Christians by force, to row in his galleys. Besides that, for want of mariners, he had left there 20 galleys, which were prepared to keep that narrow sea. Finally, that the Great Turk was presently to go with his army into Hungary, but was not yet departed from the city.

Now the Frenchmen, our consorts, went aboard a ship of Marseilles to return into France. But myself and my brother, being to go by land to Aleppo, agreed to give our muccaro[1] nine piastres[2] for two asses to ride upon, and their meat....Moreover we were forced to give a sugarloaf, to the value of a zechine,[3] to the Governor of the City, and a piastre to the Scribe or Clerk of the city, for the privilege to go without a janisarry to conduct us, (so they pretended, omitting no occasions to extort from Christians).

But we covenanted not to pay the nine piastres to our muccaro until our journey was ended; only giving one piastre into his hands for earnest, and pretending that we would pay the rest at Aleppo, where we were to receive money; lest they, thinking that we had store of crowns with us, should practise any treason or oppression against us. This piastre we gave him in hand, to buy meat for his beasts, and the eight we paid after at Aleppo. And besides gave him, of free gift a zechine for his faithful service to us by the way. We were to take our journey with the caravan going from Tripoli to Aleppo. The Turks call a Caravan the company of merchants, passengers, and drivers of loaded camels, keeping together, for safety against thieves, and using to lodge in the open field. For in Turkey they make journeys in great troops. Neither did I ever see anyone ride alone, but only a horseman of the Army. And that very rarely.

Omitted: details of journey to Aleppo: except for the story about how

...it happened that one of the women (whom the leaders of the caravan have for their attendance) lighting a fire to make ready for supper, by chance some spark or flame broke out of the stones wherewith it was compassed, and set the dry herbs of the field on fire. Which, being neglected at first, spread itself for a great compass. Whereupon the Governor of the province, dwelling upon the mountain and beholding the fields on fire, sent to us one janissary, armed only with a cudgel; who fell upon the men of our caravan (being some one hundred in number) beating them with his cudgel till they fell upon the fire with the upper long garments they are used to wear; and so extinguished it.

In the meantime, myself and my brother went aside, lying out of his sight by the advantage of a high ground between him and us; where we were astonished to see one man, armed only with a cudgel, beat a hundred men (and the very santones, or priests) armed with swords and many calivers.[4] The fire being put out, we thinking all safe, joined ourselves to the company again: but soon espied our error. For the janissary drove us all before him like so many calves, to appear before the Governor, and satisfy him for this damage. And if, at any time, we went slowly, he wielded his cudgel about his head...[and] presently struck those who were next [to] him. My brother and myself treated with him on the way, to give him a reward that he would dismiss us. But when he gave this warning, we were the first to run from him, with laughter to see our men thus driven like beasts, and commending to ourselves the honesty of the man, who first gave us warning, before he struck. Then presently, as soon as we saw the gentleman pacified, we returned again to him, with our muccaro to interpret our words, and told him that we were the servants of a Christian merchant, and had no goods in the caravan, nor anything to do with them; and offering a reward if he would let us return.

For we knew that the Turks would take any occasion to oppress us as Christians, and that the Governor would have dealt worse with the caravan, if he perceived that Christians were with them. Thus we often fled from him when he gave the said sign of anger. For howsoever we offered him a gift, yet we could not otherwise escape his blows. And often we returned to him being pacified, offering him a gift to dismiss us. Which, at last, we obtained, giving him a zechine. When we were dismissed, we were in no less fear of some violence while we returned, alone and unarmed, to the place where our baggage lay. But going forward between hope and fear, at last we came safe thither. And there hid ourselves until our consorts should return. Who, after an hour's space returning, told us, that the chief of the caravan, being the cause of the fire making, had paid ten piastres for the damage. And the Governor swore that if the fire had gone over the mountain into the plain field of corn, he would have hanged us all upon the highest trees on the top of the mountain. This tragedy ended, we refreshed our selves with meat and sleep...

Aleppo

...we came by noon...[on] the 29th June, (after the Pope's new style,[5] which I have followed hitherto, being in company of Italians and Friars) to the famous city of Aleppo, where the English merchants living in 3 houses (as it were, in colleges), entertained my brother and me very courteously. And George Dorington, the Consul of the English there, led us to the house wherein he lived with other merchants, and there most courteously entertained us, with plentiful diet, good lodging, and most friendly conversation, refusing to take any money for this our entertainment. And although we brought him only a Bill of Exchange[6] for 100 Crowns, yet when we complained to him that we now perceived the same would not serve our turns, he freely lent us as much more upon our own credit. Yea, when, after my brother's death I fell dangerously sick, and was forced to go from those parts before I could recover my health, so that all men doubted of my return into England, yet he lent me a far greater sum upon my bare word; which, however, I repaid after my coming into England. Yet I confess that I cannot sufficiently acknowledge his love to me and his noble consideration of poor and afflicted strangers....

The trade in this place is exceedingly great, because the goods of all Asia and the Eastern Islands are brought hither, or to Cairo in Egypt. And before the Portuguese found the way into East India, these commodities were all brought from these two Cities. And the Venetians and some free Cities of Italy solely enjoyed all this trade, of old. But after that time, the Portuguese, trading in East India, served all Europe with these commodities, selling them, yea and many adulterated drugs, at what price they listed, cutting off most part of this trade from the Italians. At last the French King, making league with the Great Turk, the merchants of Marseilles were made partners of this trade; and in our age the English, under the reign of Queen Elizabeth, obtained [a] like privilege, though great opposition was made against them by the Venetians and French merchants. And the Turkey Company[7] in London was, at this time, the richest of all other, silently enjoying the safety and profit of this trade. (Understand that when I wrote this, the trade into the East Indies was nothing at all or very little known to the English or Flemings.)

This City lies within land, the Port whereof (called Alexandretta by the Christians, and Scanderone by the Turks) I shall hereafter describe. The building of this city (as of all houses in Syria) is like to that of Jerusalem, only one roof high, with a plain top plastered to walk upon; and with arches before [in front of] the houses, under which they walk dry, and keep shops of wares. The city is nothing less than well fortified, but most pleasantly seated, having many sweet gardens. The air was so hot, as me thought I supped hot broth, when I drew it in; but it is very subtle; so that the Christians coming here from Scanderone, (a most unhealthful place, having the air choked with fens), continually fall sick, and often die. And this is the cause that the English Factors employed here seldom return into England, the 20th man scarcely living till his apprenticeship being out, he may trade here for himself.

The Christians here, and the Turks (at the Christians' cost), drink excellent wines, whereof the white wines grows in that territory, but the red wines are brought from Mount Lybanus. Moreover, all things for diet are sold at cheap rates. And indeed, the Turks want not good meat, but only good cooks to dress it. The English merchants can bear me witness that these parts yield sheep whereof the tail of one wreathed to the ground, weighs some 30 or more pounds in fat and wool. In one of the city gates they show the Sepulchre of Saint George, where the Turks maintain lamps continually burning. For among all the Christian Saints, they only reverence Saint George. In a garden of the suburbs I saw a serpent of wonderful bigness. And they report that a male serpent and young ones, being killed by certain boys, this she-serpent, observing the water where the boys used to drink, poisoned the same, so that many of the boys died thereof; and that the citizens thereupon came out to kill her. But, seeing her with her face upward, as complaining to the Heavens that her revenge was just, that they (touched with a superstitious conceit) let her alone. Finally, that this serpent had lived here many ages, and was of incredible years. Moreover they show a well near to the city, in which, they report that a chest of treasure was of old cast, so that it might be seen by passengers; and that some, attempting to take it out, were assaulted and affrighted with Devils.

In this city myself and my brother Henry lay sick some few days. But, by the help of a Jew physician, we soon recovered our health; and for fear of wanting money, and especially out of our desire to return home, we made too great haste to begin our journey for Constantinople. If we would have expected 8 days, the Cassenda, (so they call a troop of horsemen guarding the Great Turk's treasure) was in that time to go to Constantinople, in whose company we might safely and swiftly have performed this journey, namely in 16 days, whereas those who followed the slow pace of camels scarcely arrive there in 30 days. But this Province, being extremely hot in this time of summer, and we being scanted of money for our long journey, all mention of longer staying was most unpleasing to us. Moreover Master George Dorington, (never to be named by me without mention of love and respect), did at this time send a Caravan, (that is, camels loaded with goods) of his own to Constantinople.

And being to make a present to a Cadi returning from his government to Constantinople, that he would take his Caravan into his protection, and to pass in his company, and lovingly making offer to us, to recommend us in like sort with his goods to the same Cadi, we were easily persuaded to take this journey presently, in the company of his servants, and of a courteous English merchant called Master Jasper Tyant, being then to go for Constantinople. This our conclusion proved greatly to the loss of Sir John Spencer, Merchant of London, whose goods these were which Master Dorington sent with us. For my brother, dying by the way, and the Great Turk being heir to all Christians and strangers dying in his Empire, the Turks either thought, or fraudulently pretended that these goods belonged to my brother; and so took them into the Great Turk's storehouses, and kept them there till they had unjustly extorted good sums of money from Master Dorington, besides the great loss which was sustained by the servants and camels hired in vain.

Being now to enter this journey, we hired, for 71 piastres, a camel to carry our victuals, an ambling mule for my brother, and a horse for myself, and so much we presently gave into the hands of our muccaro, with covenant that he should pay for the meat of the meats of the beasts. Moreover we presently laid out 120 piastri for several necessaries: namely, 2 long chairs like cradles, covered with red cloth, to hang on the two sides of our camel, which chairs the Turks use to ride in, and to sleep upon camels' backs. But we bought them to carry victuals, for biscuit, and a tent wherein we might sleep; and for like provisions. But behold! When all this money was laid out, and the very evening before the day in which we were to begin our journey, my brother Henry fell sick of a flux. Being amazed by this sudden chance, we stood doubtful for a time what to do, till the considera-tion of the great sums of money we had laid out, and of the difficulty get more, made us resolve to take this fatal journey. Yet with this purpose [that] when we came to Scanderone, some 4 days journey distant, to go no further, except [unless], in that he [had] recovered his health; propounding this comfort to our miserable estate – that there we might have commodity of convenient lodging with an Englishman there abiding, Factor for our merchants.

On Thursday the last of June, (that I may now follow the old style, taken here from the English, and generally used in Turkey among the very Christians – howsoever hitherto I have followed the New Style, taking it from the Venetian ship in which I came, and from the Friars at my abode in Jerusalem); I say the last [day] of June we went out of Aleppo, passing over stony hills, and by the village...where the Jews say the Prophet Jeremiah was buried. Then, riding forward all night, at last we sat down at 8 o'clock in the morning, and pitched our tents near a village, where I saw a pillar erected to Pompey. And here we rested and refreshed our selves the heat of the day.

This kind of journeying was strange to us, and contrary to our health. For we began our journey at 4 in the afternoon to shun the heat of the day past; and rode all night. So, as we not used to this watching, were so sleepy towards the sun rise, that we could not abstain from nodding, and were many times likely to fall from our horses. To which mischief we could find no other remedy than to ride swiftly to the head of the Caravan; and there dismounting, to lie down and slumber, with our horses' bridles tied to our legs. One of us, by course walking by us, to keep us from injuries, and to awaken us when the last camel passed by, lest we should there be left a prey to thieves. And we, having some 200 camels in our Caravan, did in this sort pass the sleepy hours in the morning, till 7 or 8 o'clock; at which time we used to pitch our tents, and rest. Moreover this greatly afflicted us: that, spending the morning till 10 or 11 of the clock in pitching our tent [and] preparing meat, and eating, we had no time to rest. But the extreme heat of the noonday, which so pierced our tents that we could no more sleep, than if in England upon a summer's day we had lain near a hot sea-coal fire. And howsoever we lessened this heat, by flinging our gowns over our tent, between the sun and us, yet, for my part, I was so afflicted with want of sleep and with this immoderate heat that I feared to fall into a lunacy. What then, should a man think, would become of my sickly brother in this case?

Antioch – death of brother Henry

...we came to Antioch, a city...famous for the Patriarchate; and by histories, sacred and profane. On the east side, and upon the top of a high mountain lie great ruins of the old walls and houses, from where the seat of the city declines to the plain on the west side. In which plain our Caravan rested the heat of this day, near the pleasant and large fountain of water wherein the Scriptures record so many to have been baptised together: since, [it was] first, in this place, [that] the faithful had the name of Christians. This fountain has fair building, and seems, of old to have been very stately; and here we pitched our tents in the midst of the gardens of this plain within the walls. For howsoever the ruins of the walls show that of old the circuit of the city was very large, yet scarce the hundredth part thereof was now filled with houses....

Here, first wretched, I perceived the imminent danger of my most dear brother's death; which I [had] never suspected till this day, much less had any just cause to fear it. A Turk in this Caravan, troubled with the same disease of a flux, went to the ground more then 20 times each night's journey, and yet lived; whereas my brother only 3 or 4 times descended from his mule to that purpose – which filled us with good hope. But here first I learned, by miserable experience, that nothing is worse for one troubled with the flux, than to stop, or much restrain, the course thereof. For my brother, stopping this natural course by taking red wine and marmalade, experienced attributed (all too late) his death to no other thing. I could not hire a horse-litter by any endeavour of our muccaro: not for any price, though I offered an incredible sum for that (or like commodity) to carry him. And we thought it very dangerous to stay here among the Turks after our Caravan [had] departed, especially since Scanderone was but 25 miles distant, where we should have the commodity to lodge with an Englishman; and so to get all necessaries for his recovery.

Therefore, on Sunday in the evening, we put all our provisions in one of the aforesaid covered chairs or cradles, carried by the camel; and made my brother a bed in the other cradle, where (as we thought) he might commodiously rest. And I promised the muccaro half a piastre for every time my brother should descend from the camel to ease himself. For we were to ride ahead, with the horsemen, and he was now to come behind, with the Camels. So we set forward, and I, twice in the night, and once towards morning, left the horsemen, and rode back to my brother, to know how he fared. And when he gave me no answer, I returned to the horsemen, thinking that he slept. Then, towards morning I was so afflicted with my wonted desire of sleep, that I thought an hour's rest worth a King's ransom. Therefore myself and Master Jasper Tyant, our loving consort, rode a good pace to the village Byland [Belen?] where we were to pitch our tents, that we might make all things ready to receive him.

But within short space our muccaro running to our tent, and telling me that he had left my brother ready to give up his last breath in the first house of the village, seemed to say to me 'Go quickly and hang yourself'. With all possible speed I ran to this house, embraced my dying brother and, confounded with sorrow, understood from his mouth, how far the events of our night's journey had been contrary to our hope. For whereas I [had] advised him to leave his mule, and lie in the chair upon the camel's back, he told me that he was shaken in pieces with the hard pace of the camel. And whereas I had offered the muccaro half a piastro, for each time he should alight to ease himself, he told me that he had often asked this favour of the muccaro, but could never obtain it – he excusing himself by fear to be left behind the Caravan, for a prey to thieves. And whereas the camel's hinder parts being higher then the foreparts, I had laid my brother's head towards the hinder parts, and raised it as high as I could with pillows and clothes, for his better ease, it happened (which I being ignorant of the way could not foresee) that we all the night ascending mountains, his feet were far higher than his head. Whereupon, he told me, that most part of the night he had lain in a trance, which was the cause that he could not answer me, at such times as I came to inquire of his health. Thus mischief lighted upon mischief, to make my wretched state most miserable. Why should I use many words in a case, from the remembrance whereof my mind abhors? Therefore I will say, in a word: 'My most dear brother Henry, on Monday 4th of July, (after the old style) in the year of Our Lord 1596, and of his age the 27th, died in my arms, after many loving speeches, and the expressing of great comfort in his Divine Meditations'.

Covetouness of the Turks

The Turks presently snatched all things that were his, as belonging to the Great Turk; yea, myself cast his shirts, with many other things of good value, and whatsoever I could see that was his, out of the tent into the Turks' hands; and, as a man half out of my wits, could endure to see nothing that might renew the bitter remembrance of him. The Turkish officers, in the Great Turk's name seized upon all the goods of Sir John Spencer, which Master Dorington sent with us, as if they had belonged to my brother. Neither could they be released, without great bribes, after the contrary was proved. Presently I sent for the English Factor lying in Scanderone: who scarcely obtained, with the paying of 5 zechines, to have my brother's body buried in the open fields. Besides, the janissaries, Turks, and Moors, came in several swarms to me in this miserable case, threatening to hinder his burial, or to dig him up after it was buried, except [unless] I would satisfy their insatiable extortions. And had not the aforesaid English Factor taken [it] upon him to satisfy these people, and taken up my purse full of zechines, which I cast among them in a rage, [then] surely, for my part, I had willingly given myself and all that I had with me, to them for a prey. One thing above measure afflicted me, (which I think Job himself could not have suffered), namely, that while myself and my brother were in our last embraces, and mournful speeches, the rascal multitude of Turks and Moors, ceased not to grin and laugh at our sighs and tears. Neither know I why my heartstrings break not in these desperate afflictions. But I am sure [that] from that day to this I never enjoyed my former health; and that this hour was the first of my old age.

Scanderone [Eskenderun]

Towards the evening the same 4th July, we descended with the said English Factor (taking care to have our baggage carried), from the mountains towards Scanderone, little distant from this place, in the furthest northern part of the valley upon the seashore. From there Jasper Tyant, our loving consort in this misery, returned back to Aleppo. But myself, not knowing what to resolve, nor having power to think of disposing myself, remained at Scanderone in the English Factor's house.

The next night, while I lay waking, I heard multitudes of wolves, (as I thought) howling upon the mountains...and, in the morning I understood, from the English merchant, that a kind of beast little bigger than a fox, and engendered between foxes and wolves, vulgarly called Jackal, used to range upon these mountains in troops; and many times to scratch the bodies of the dead out of their graves. Whereupon I hired an ass to carry me, and a janissary to accompany me, and went to see the place of my brother's burial: from which part I thought to hear those howlings: And there beyond my expectation, I found that they had scratched up the earth almost to his body, and the Turks made no doubt, but that these beasts hiding themselves from day light, would according to their

136

manner, return the next night to devour his body. Therefore I hired many poor people to bring stones, whereof I made such a pile round about his body, that I preserved that prey from their cursed jaws. Which done, I returned to Scanderone (so called by the Turks), which the Christians call Alexandretta.

This is a poor village, built all of straw and dirt, excepting the houses of some Christian Factors, built of timber and clay in some convenient sort; and it lies along the seashore. For the famous city of Aleppo, having other harbour, the merchants here unload their goods, but themselves make haste to Aleppo, staying little here as possibly they can, and committing the carrying their goods thither upon camels to the Factors of their nation continually abiding here. The pestilent air of this place is the cause that they dare not make any stay here. For this village…is encompassed on three sides with a fenny plain; and the fourth side lies upon the sea. On the way to Aleppo I remember (as I remember)…there is, in this plain, a fountain of clear water….And howsoever all other waters falling out of the fen are most unwholesome, yet the goodness of this fountain is so much prized, so that merchants carry their meat there, and eat there under a pleasant shade. Not far from this fountain there stands an old castle at the foot of the mountains, which they call the Castle of Penthesilea, Queen of the Amazons. On the same side, beyond the fen, is a most high mountain, which keeps the sight of the sun from Scanderone; and, being full of bogs, infects the fenny plain with ill vapours. And beyond this mountain, dearest brother lies buried. On the other side, towards the north, (as I remember) on the way leading to Constantinople, the like fenny plain lies, and the…boggy earth, yielding ill vapours, makes Scanderone infamous for the death of Christians….

Shortly after I came to this unhappy village…the grief of my mind cast me into a great sickness, so that I, who in perfect health had passed so many kingdoms of Europe, at this time in the very flower of my age, first began to wax old. This sickness brought the first weakness to my body. And the second, proceeding from another grief after my return into England, took from me all thought of youthful pleasures; and demonstratively taught me that the Poet most truly said: 'Care makes grey-headed'.

While I languished here in a lasting sickness, it happened that, upon occasion, I looked upon the two testimonies given to my brother and myself at Jerusalem, of our having been there. And I was not a little astonished to see that they being both at the same time cut out of the same skin of parchment, and written with the same hand and ink, yet that of my brother was in all parts eaten with worms, while mine was altogether untouched. And after[wards] I did more wonder that, to this day, the same testimony given to my brother is no more eaten with worms than at that time it was: and mine still remains unperished.

My aforesaid sickness was so vehement and so long that at all men doubted I would never recover, so that my friends in England, after they had heard of my brother's death, were advertised within few weeks that myself also was dead. But for my part, though my nightly dreams that I was walking in the caves and sepulchres of Italy, might have some-what discouraged me, and though I had no other physician than the barber-surgeon of a ship, yet could I never doubt of recovering my health. But my mind still presaged that I should return home, when several times I began to recover. And presently, by the heat of the clime and ill air of the place had been cast down again, I resolved to follow their counsel, who persuaded me to try if the air of the sea would strengthen me. Therefore my dear friend Master George Dorington, having sent me 100 zechines for my expenses, (the great sums of money which I had, being all spent, by the accidents of my brothers death, and my sickness – the particulars of which expense I omit, because in this grief and weakness I had no mind to note them; only, for a taste remembering, that I paid a piasto each day to a poor man who continually cooled my heat with a fan); Master Dorington, I say, having sent me money, and I having provided all necessaries on my journey, at last on Thursday 10 October (after the new style) 1596, was carried aboard a French ship from Marseilles: partly by the help of porters; partly in a boat, being so weak that I could not stand. This ship was called *John [the] Baptist*, and the Christian name of the Master was Simon: with whom I had covenanted that I pay him 30 piastri (or ducats) for myself and my servant, [that] he should set us on land in some good harbour on the island Candia [Crete] – and if it were possible, in the chief city thereof, called Candia [Iràklion] and lying on the north side of the island; [from] where, I was now resolved to take my journey to Constantinople, leaving all thought of going by land.

On Friday 11th October, we sailed prosperously. But after, the winds grew so contrary that we were driven to the south of Candia. Therefore, the French mariners murmuring against us, as heretics causing their ill passage, and there being no hope left, with those winds, to set us on land at Candia...the Master of our ship sent us in his boat with some few mariners whom he least esteemed, that we might sail to land, being 50 miles distant. Thus on Thursday 23rd October, having sailed [for] 8 hours in great danger, towards the evening we landed under a promontory of Candia, where there was neither city, village, house, nor cottage. So, as plenty of rain [was] falling that night, we were forced to lie in an open boat, where my companion (or servant), not knowing our danger, slept soundly; but myself durst never close mine eyes, fearing lest these mariners (being Marseillians who, at that time, little loved the English), should offer us violence to gain our goods.

This consort (or servant of mine) was an Englishman, and by profession a cook, and was come into these parts to serve Master Sandys who, being sent from London to be the English Consul at Aleppo, as he passed from Constantinople thither, died in Asia Minor, of the same disease whereof my brother died, and in the same month. This servant being (after his Master's death) to return into England, I took to attend me, that I might by his company avoid solitude, and mitigate some part of my sorrow. He had no sooner entered into the French ship, but he presently fell sick. And not able to serve himself, could not give me the expected comforts, much less do me any service. But greatly increased my charge, spending all upon my purse, and much troubled me, having not the least skill in any foreign language. So, as he recovering not till we came to Venice, (where being among Christians, I had small use of his help), he was rather a burden than a comfort to me.

When I was to enter the French ship, I laid in provisions of hens, eggs, Damascus prunes, and other things. But my languishing stomach, not desiring nor being able to digest any other than salt meat, these provisions fell to the share of my sick servant. And my self, being nothing but skin and bone, as one that languished in a consumption, my blood and humours renewed with these salt meats, could not but weaken my future health, so that I, having been always very lean, after (by decay of natural heat) became very fat. And having lost the retentive faculty of my stomach, so that I continually cast all that lay upon it, so soon as in the morning I came into the air, I had no remedy against this weakness but the taking of tobacco.

The French mariners who brought us to the shore...parted from us on Friday 25th July (after the new style) early in the morning. And when I had well rewarded them for their pains; then first [only?] they showed me, above the wild rocks...a monastery of the Greeks, some 3 miles distant....We being left alone, and staying there fasting till noon, at last espied, and called to us two men passing by upon the mountains. But they, thinking us to be pirates, fled away as fast as they could. Presently behold, my man coming out of the wood, and bringing with him an ass which he [had] found there – who persuaded me to lay my baggage on that beast, and so to walk softly towards the monastery, I willingly tried my strength. And leaning upon our two swords for want of a staff, (and yet often falling) went forward like a snail: till, despairing of going forward, I fell upon the ground. After an hour's space, a shepherd passing by, and I showing him gold, and naming [the] monastery (which word he understood) he swiftly ran to the monastery. And, telling the monks...our state and condition, they presently sent a servant to us; who, in the Italian tongue telling us the great danger wherein we should be, if we stayed upon those mountains till night, advised us to make haste to the monastery.

Thus, driven with fear, and encouraged by his company, I tried again to go forward; and, with great trouble, passed one mile over the mountains. For leaning (as I said) on two swords and upon the passage of any steep mountain, by reason of the lightness of my head, creeping upon hands and feet, with great difficulty I went so far. And now, being not able to go any further, no not to save my life; behold! a boy, who came to water his ass at a fountain adjoining, to whom the servant of the monks gave a piastro. And so, whether he would or no, took his ass and set me upon it, and so at last we passed the other 2 miles (longer than 3 English miles) and came to the monastery.

The...monks received us courteously, and gave us such victuals as they had, namely, pomegranates, olives, bread, and sharp wine: which were no good meats for sick men, having fasted almost 2 days. Also they conferred lovingly with us. But still desiring us to keep aloof from them, at bed time they gave us a straw mat to lay upon a plastered floor for our bed. But we were better provided with mattresses and quilts of our own; and though lying upon the ground, yet slept soundly because we were in safety.

[Omitted: journey from Crete to Constantinople]

Comments on Constantinople

Having cast anchor (as I said) in the Port of Constantinople, behold, as soon as day began to break, many companies of Turks rushing into our Bark; who, like so many starved flies fell to suck the sweet wines, each rascal among them beating with cudgels and ropes the best of our mariners, if he durst but repine against it; till, within short space, the Candian merchant having advertised the Venetian Ambassador of their arrival, he sent a janissary to protect the ship and the goods. And as soon as he came, it seemed to me no less strange, that this one man should beat all those Turks, and drive them out of the ship like so many dogs: the common Turks daring no more resist a soldier (or especially a janisssary) than Christians dare resist them.

And the Sergeant of the Magistrate having taken some of our Greek mariners (though subject to the State of Venice) to work for their Ottoman [masters?] in gathering stones, and like base employments, this janissary caused them presently to be released, and to be sent again into their ship. Such is the tyranny of the Turks against all Christians (as well as subjects of others) that no man sails into these parts, but under the banner of England, France, or Venice: who, being in league with the Great Turk, have their Ambassadors in this city, and their Consuls in other harbours, to protect those who come under their banner, in this sort sending them a janissary to keep them from wrongs, as soon as they are advertised of their arrival.

Myself, lodged in the house of Master Edward Barton, the English Ambassador, who gave me a janissary to guide and protect me, while I went to view the City, round about the whole circuit whereof I went on foot and by boat in 4 hours' space, the form of the city being triangular, and containing 9 miles by sea towards the north and east, and 5 miles by land towards the west. I profess myself to have small skill in the art of geography, yet will I adventure (though rudely) to set down the form and situation of this City as plainly as I doubt not but [that] the reader may easily understand it. Howsoever in the same (as in other cities formerly described) I acknowledge that I use not the rule of the scale in the distance of places (or other exquisite rules of that Art) having no other end but to make the reader more easily understand my description.

The situation of Constantinople

This city (as Rome) is said to contain Seven Hills, or mounts, within the walls: whereof some to me seemed imaginary; but I will reckon them as they do. And first begin with the hill, upon which stand the ruins of Constantine's Palace. The second has the stately Mosque (or Turkish Church) built upon the Palace, which of old belonged to the Greek Patriarch. Upon the third stands the stately mosque and most richly built Sepulchre of Muhammad II, with a hospital built by the same Emperor, where all Turkish Pilgrims have their lodging and diet freely for 3 days. And it has 150 chambers built for the poor of the city; and the yearly rents thereof are valued at 200,000 zechines. Yea, the Court or Seraglio of the Great Turk pays each day 100 Aspers to this hospital. The Sepulchre of Selimus takes up the fourth hill, and the Sepulchre of Bajazet, the fifth hill. Between the fifth and the sixth hills, is the old Palace of the Great Turk, (which the Italians call 'Seraglio Vecchio'): where the concubines of the deceased Emperor, and the present Emperor's sisters and a great number of his concubines, (for the fairest and dearest to him are taken to live in his Court), are kept by eunuchs within this old Seraglio; which is of great circuit, containing many houses and gardens compassed within one wall. Upon the sixth hill stands the aforesaid wonderful mosque and Sepulchre of Suleiman....Lastly, the seventh hill contains the chief palace of the Great Turk, and the Church Saint Sophia, now made a mosque.

The tops of the Sepulchres and mosques, being of a round form and covered with brass, and the spacious gardens of cypress and fir trees, make show of more beauty and magnificence to the beholder from any high place, or outside the walls than indeed the City has. The Sepulchres are, without doubt, very stately built, having upon one or two or more round globes covered with lead or brass. On the inside they seem like lightsome chapels with many windows. And they being built in a round form, the dead Emperor is laid in the midst or centre of the Sepulchre, in a chest or coffin raised some three foot from the ground, having the turban which he wore upon his head in his life time laid upon his Tomb; being set forth with the jewels he most esteemed (which turban is made of some 20 or more yards of pure and fine white linen, folded in many folds, the form of a half a globe). Next the Emperor lies the Sultana, or Empress, in her coffin – (So they call his concubine, mother of his heir and successor) – provided always that she has had a letter of dowry by which she is made his wife. For otherwise she is not buried with him. And round about the Emperor and Empress, in coffins lower than theirs, lie the bodies of his male children, which (according to their manner) are strangled by his successor as soon as he was dead. And upon their coffins, likewise, their turbans are laid severally. These children are laid in little coffins of cypress; and this middle part wherein the dead bodies lie, is compassed with a grate, so that between the bodies and the windows there is a gallery round about, which is spread with Turkey carpets. And upon them the priests who keep the Sepulchre, lie by night, and sit cross-legged by day. Neither is the room, at any time, without some of these Keepers, so that the Emperors are attended even after death.

The buildings of the city have no magnificence; being partly of a matter like brick, but white, and (as it seems) enhardened by fire, partly of timber and clay, excepting some few palaces which are of free stone – but nothing so stately built as might be expected from the pride and riches of the Great Turk's chief servants. And these houses (as those of the adjacent territories of Europe) are built only 2 stories high, with a low roof without any windows, after the manner of Italy; whereas the houses of Asia have a plain and plastered roof to walk upon, especially in Asia the Greater.

The streets of this city are narrow, and shadowed with pentises[8] of wood; and upon both sides the way is raised some foot high – but of little breadth – and paved for men and women to pass, the middle of the street being left low and unpaved, and no broader than for the passage of asses or beasts loaded. In many places of the streets lie carcasses. Yea, sometimes the bodies of dead men, even till they are putrified. And I think this uncleanliness of the Turks, who otherwise place religion in washing their bodies, and keeping their apparel, especially their turbans pure and clean, is the chief cause that this city, though most pleasantly seated, yet above all the cities of the world is continually more or less infected with the plague.

The worthy English Ambassador, Master Edward Barton, most courteously entertained me with lodging and diet as long as I stayed in this city: so, as for them, I spent not one asper. But I pass over the due praises which I owe to the memory of this worthy Gentleman. Being hereafter to speak more of him, I will only add that I attended him once to the Great Turk's Court. And when I had nothing satisfied my curiosity in viewing the city by occasions casually happening, that he commanded a janissary to guide me round about the same, till I had taken full view thereof....

And, by the way, as we passed by land, an old woman meeting us, and taking me for a captive to be sold, demanded my price of the janissary; who, for mirth, entertained her offer to buy me and another Gentleman, servant to the Ambassador, whom he had sent to bear me company. But because I was very slender and lean after my long sickness, he could not induce her to give more than 100 aspers for me – though she offered 400 aspers for the other gentleman in my company: as the janissary told me in the Italian tongue, when he had entertained this discourse with her to pass away the time in our long walk.

Of the geographical description of Turkey, the situation, fertility, traffick [trade], and diet

The fertility of the soil generally through this Empire is exceeding great; and the goodness and variety of the fruits equals (and in some places passes) Italy. The wines of Greece, of Mount Lybanus, and especially of...Anatolia, are exceedingly rich and good. Yet have the Turks less plenty of all things than Europe. For the people, being wasted with wars, (and they who remain having not free fruition of their own goods in the great tyranny under which they live as well of the Emperor as of under-governors changed at least once a year) and the general rapacity and licentiousness of the soldiers. Hence it is that there are vast solitudes and untilled deserts on all sides; where yet the ground, of itself, brings forth many wild fruits without tillage. They have several kinds of grain: wheat; the grain called millet; barley; oats; rye; peas; and all kinds of pulses which, for their kinds, are like those of Europe....There is good abundance of rice, flax, and cotton growing in the fields. They have good plenty of all kinds of cattle; yet are no more industrious in grazing and feeding herds than in sowing or planting. And so they have eggs, hens, rice, honey (which, in a composition, they drink), fruit and bread for daily food. They desire no other dainties or greater riches since they can neither enjoy their goods while they live, nor yet bequeath them at death; and nothing is more dangerous than to the accounted rich....

In Syria they have sheep of strange bigness, whereof many have tails weighing 20 (and some 30) pounds, bearing wool, and being wrethed[9] to their heels more than the rams of horns are. And let no man think this incredible, since the same is reported of sheep in Africa; and this is confirmed by consent of all who have been in those parts. Mules are somewhat rare, but they have innumerable camels; a beast most apt to carry burdens, and lying patiently down to receive them, and most able to bear hunger, and especially thirst. When the male and female engender, they lie low down on their bellies, with tail to tail, and their heads many ells distant one from the other. And in the time of the year when they are naturally prone to generation, they are fierce with a kind of madness. So then their masters take heed of any violence they may do them.

The Turks also have many dromedaries, a kind of beast not unlike the camel; but far passing horses in swiftness, and very camels' patience in labour. Their horses are rather fair than strong, and they make their skin shine by laying them upon their own dung, dried. These horses either run (which often they put them to for spurts, and in bravery) or go a foot pace (as they follow loaded camels in journeys): but they are not taught either to trot, or to amble, as ours are, and are good for short journeys, but not able to endure long journeys, as ours do. Therefore the Turkish cavalry, for war, is of more swiftness than strength; and the German horses, being heavy, they easily overtake them flying, and as easily fly when they are beaten.

The Turks have great plenty of sea and freshwater fish, and of birds and all fowl. And for Christian buyers (whereof are great multitudes, especially at Constantinople) they furnish their markets therewith. And in truth, at Constantinople there is a great variety and goodness of these kinds as can be wished. Only the oysters, though plentiful, yet have not the delicate taste that ours have; the Mediterranean Sea being nothing so salt as the Ocean. But in general the Turks (because of their aforesaid tyranny, and of their temperance in diet) little use fishing, or fowling, or any like exercise.

Yet, by reason of the same tyranny of the Emperor, governors, and soldiers, the Turks carelessly and coldly exercise trade with the merchants. I grant that they trade in Anatolia and other parts of their own Empire after a cold manner, but they make no voyage by sea into foreign parts; excepting some few that come to Venice. For they do not labour in any kind more than necessity forces; and are so far from the insatiable desire of riches that they avoid nothing more than the opinion to be rich. So, as the Jews, the Greeks subject to the Turks, and other confederate Christians exporting their commodities, they themselves have very few ships – the Emperor only having some 12 ships, well armed, to bring him necessaries from Egypt to Constantinople. In like sort they have few marines;[10] and those, inexperienced and fearful, using the Greeks (their vassals) and other slaves taken in war, to that purpose. And they much esteem (that is, gently treat) captives skilful in navigation. Some towns keep, at their private charge, a few small galleys and barks to rob the Christians, and the Great Turk's Navy consists all of galleys [but] nothing comparable to those of Venice;[11] and they winter at Constantinople, and another harbour in Greece, whereof I shall write more largely in the discourse of the Turk's Commonwealth.

Among other cities of trade they have two very famous: one in Asia; the other in Africa. That of Asia is called Aleppo; and it being inland, the port thereof is called Scanderone by the Turks and Alexandretta by the Christians – [from] where the commodities of merchants are carried upon camels, and (on the fifth day) arrive in Aleppo; whither the commodities of Persia are brought by the River Euphrates, and upon camels' backs, from the city of Taurus (of old, subject to the Persians, but bin our age subdued by the Turks). The Indian commodities are brought there via the Red Sea and the Gulf of Arabia....

The Venetians bring into Turkey woollen cloth, which they call 'broad',[12] being dyed scarlet, violet, and of all colours. And they are so strong and well-made that they will last very long; so that the Turks prefer them before our English cloths. And because the Venetians furnish them in great quantity, they use few other cloths of that kind. And also the Venetians bring them satins and damasks (made in Italy, from Dalmatian silk), and great quantity of gold and silver [in order] to buy the precious commodities of Turkey; whence they carry out raw silk. For, by reason of the aforesaid tyranny, as the Turks are negligent in husbandry and trade, so are they in manual arts: not drawing their silk into threads, nor weaving the same into clothes. And although they have infinite numbers of silkworms (especially at Tripoli; and in most parts of Asia), which make great quantities of silk...yet they sell this silk raw and unwoven, and buy from the Venetians the aforesaid cloths made from their own silk. So that the silkworms may well be said to be more diligent, and more to promote the public good, than the inhabitants. For they, swarming in all gardens, diligently finish their web, while the idle inhabitants yield the commodity thereof to strangers. The Venetians also export from Turkey spices and apothecary wares, and great quantity of the dye called Indigo. They export galls,[13] cotton, wool, cotton thread, chamlets or grograms, made from the finest hairs of goats (not sheared, but pulled from their backs; and woven in Galatia...). They export Turkey carpets [and] goatskins wrought, and dyed into many colours.

The English bring to the Turks kerseys[14] brought, and dyed, of several colours and kinds. But they bring little broad-cloth; wherewith they [the Turks] are abundantly furnished from Venice. They also bring to them tin, and black cony-skins in such quanti-ties that the Turks, admiring the same, a Frenchman (merrily taxing our women's affability) said that in England there was such plenty of coneys – and they so tame – that they were taken into the taverns. The English export from the spices and apothecary[15] wares (for the trade into the East Indies was not then set up). The merchants coming to Constantinople hardly find there any commodities to export. Therefore the English ships, having unloaded there, sail empty to Alexandretta; and there receive the commodities from Aleppo. Again, the Italians who bring much gold and silver to Aleppo for the commodities there to be sold, again receive gold and silver for such commodities as they bring to Constantinople; and carry the same back to Venice. The English, lying at the islands of Zante and Cephalonia (subject to the Venetians) and at Petrasso (seated in the Gulf of Corinth, and subject to the great Turk), export currants....

The swords of Damascus are famous for their metal: piercing iron, and cutting a nail in pieces. But the exportation of them is forbidden [even] though our Christians supply the Turks with all warlike munitions: which they might shame to particularly named in this discourse of trade. The precious Oriental commodities of Persia and the East Indies has made the trade of Turkish cities to be famous: namely, their spices, and rich dyes, and jewels; which notwithstanding, the Turks have a part of their own. For I formerly said that Arabia yields frankincense, myrrh, cinnamon, and jewels; and Egypt yields balsam and opobalsam (the more precious gum of the balm-tree) in great quantity; omitting many commodities which, besides, they have of these kinds....

All the precious trade of Turkey, by reason of the inhabitants' slothfulness, is in the hands of Jews and of Christians. And was long in the sole hands of the Venetians; but the French in the age past, and the English in our age, have had (as I may say) a trading league with the Turk; and so partake that trade. And these 3 states only (not to speak of the Germans who, at this time had war with the Turks, and never fail so far to exercise trade) among so many States of Christians, have their Ambassadors at the Turkish Court. And if any other Christians arrive in that Empire (as the Flemings often do) they used, at this time, to come under the banner of these three nations. The reader must understand that when I was in Turkey the English and the Flemings had not yet begun their trade in the East Indies; which is likely to destroy the trade in Turkey, bringing many rich commodities from the well head.

For their diet, the Turks live sparingly. I had said 'slovenly', but then I remembered their frequent bathings and washings, and the careful cleanliness of the linen, and all other clothes which they wear. But I will be bold to say [that] they feed negligently; and without any pomp or magnificence. The richer sort sit at meat like tailors, with their knees bent, upon carpets; or upon the grass, when they eat by riversides and in gardens – as they do more frequently than in the house. And their table is so low that they may not well reach to it, sitting upon the ground. Around this table they cast a long towel to wipe their hands; but passengers by the highway, and generally the ordinary sort of Turk, use grass instead of this towel. Others carry about [with them] a table of leather, coloured red or yellow – which table shuts and opens like a purse. And upon it they can set but one dish at once, it hanging hollow on certain kinds of buckles. Commonly they eat by the highway, on the ground; and always with their knees bent like tailors. They seeth[16] their meat until it is very tender, so that they may break it with their fingers; for they have no knives. Neither have they variety of dishes set before them; but all, sitting in a circle, fall upon one dish.

Taking meat they, all together, say a short prayer or grace, and talk not while they eat; but silently fall hard to their work. They have abundance of all things, for food: as well of flesh (excepting swine's-flesh) as of birds and other meats; but they abstain from fish. They have plenty of corn (at least, sufficient for their temperate diet), which is exceedingly good, and far better than ours. They are ignorant of the arts of birding, fowling, hunting, or cookery; and, having no lascivious appetite provoking them to gluttony, are content with simple meats. Their sobriety in that kind cannot be sufficiently commended. And since their greatest men can be content to feed on rice, and drink water, it is no marvel that, with ease, they keep great armies in the field.

All the Turkish householdstuff is contained in one poor pot to seek meat in, one spoon of wood, one cup of leather or wood to drink in, a poor bed or mattress; yea, often a single coverlet alone – and the earth serves them for bedstead, table, and stools. They have no need of a troop of cooks and scullions to dress meat, and to make clean dishes. They willingly eat curds turned sour, and mingled with bread and water, commonly called mish-mash,[17] and free cheese or curds; and have plenty of milk, as well of cows as of goats. Instead of bread, they eat unleavened cakes, baked on the cinders, which commonly are mingled with a kind of seed. They feed commonly on hens, and rice (either sod[18] alone, or with a hen or mutton, in a vessel full of holes, without any liquor put in when set on the fire; so that, there being no other juice but that of the meat, the rice is made very thick). Within these narrow bounds is their most costly feeding restrained. In times of the year they feed much upon fruits; and keep grapes all winter, so you would judge them fresh. They abhor from swine's flesh, as the Jews do. For the rest, they I never saw, nor hear by relations of others, that the richest of them did affect any other variety of meat than I have named; and I have often seen men of the better sort eating out of the seething pot, without any dish set before them. The above-named flesh of muttons is very savoury; and the sheep of Syria and the adjoining parts of Asia are of such greatness than, many times, a tail of them, hanging to their heels, and very woolly and fat, and close-woven in many plaits, weigh 30 or more pounds. They also have venison. For, in the woods, there are many wild goats dispersed. And I have seen a kind of fallow deer in Syria, called 'gazelle'; of which kind I have seen some brought out of Barbary[19] into England.

And they, much delighting in fruit, have excellent [fruit] of many kinds, and in great quantity: namely; apricots and muskmelons, and several kinds of pumpions, whereof one called 'angouria', as big as our pumpions; is exceedingly full of a very cold juice, being most pleasant for the coolness in any great heat – which coolness (though I take to be unwholesome for one sick of the ague) yet myself, almost wasted with the burning of that dread disease, vehemently desired to eat this fruit, and found it nothing hurtful (or rather, healthful) to me.

In the harbour of Alexandretta (or Scanderone) a Greek, the Master of a Venetian ship, gave me a present of 4 or 5 apples; which he called (as they vulgarly do) the Apple of Adam[20] – and I never, in my life, tasted so delicate a fruit. It was, of form, like a long pear; or rather, for the crookedness, like a cucumber of the lesser sort. And it had the most thin skin, of colour like a peach's skin – the last part whereof, being opened, the juice was easily to be sucked out: which was very pleasant, and not much unlike to the juice of the fig newly pulled from the tree. If I should particularise all the kinds of pleasant fruits, I might be infinite therein.

The Turks, when they have eaten, [but?] not while they eat, go like good fellows together, and (like horses) at once drink for that meal as if the water were turned into wine: which kind of drink those who are zealous of their Law and those who journey by the highway more specially, and all Turks in general most commonly use. For which cause, those who journey pitch their tents upon the banks of pure fountains or running waters, which they no less know, or as carefully search out, as we do the best inns or taverns. Besides, commonly they have a cup (or, if I may so call it, being a purse of leather) hanging at their horse's saddle or pommel which (as they sit on horseback) they put down into the fountains, and draw water to drink – not omitting to taste a good spring of water, no more than would a piece of rare wine. Their water, especially in provinces lying near the sun is, in this property, contrary to ours that it loosens the body no less than the rice binds it.

In cities, several kinds of drinks are sold; some esteemed as much as wine with us. One kind I remember presented to us in Palestine by the Sub-Pasha of Ramma [Ramallah?], which was made of medicinal herbs to purify and cool the blood. And they drink it hot, so that it seems a very physical potion. They drink sugar, or honey mingled with water, and water sodden with grapes, rosewater, and honey. And they have whole tons of the juice of limes and lemons; which they willingly drink. And all these kinds are [to be found] sold in their cities.

145

Wine is forbidden by Muhammad's Law; which permits *aqua vitæ*,...which *aqua vitæ* they drink, even to drunkenness. And whether it is out of the common error of mankind to desire forbidden things, or out of the licentiousness of soldiers (which every day grows greater than other), in idleness they obey their Law in not planting vines. Yet not only the janissaries, but even the religious men, will drink wine largely – even to drunkenness: with Christians, as well as Ambassadors. Yea, if Christian passengers carry wine on the way for their own drinking, and have a janissary to protect them, yet will they familiarly come to drink with them. And if they have no protector, they will take their wine (and whatsoever they have else) at their pleasure. So that their false Prophet has only provoked vice, by forbidding it....

The Turkish soldiers, being to fight, if they can find no wine, drink the juice of black poppy, called 'opium', to raise their spirits to a kind of fury, thinking themselves more valiantly made thereby. For although we think this herb, especially to be taken largely, to be dangerous for the health, yet there is no a Turk (from the highest to the lowest) who does, as it were, daily use it; nothing being more frequently sowed, nothing more plentifully growing (especially in Anatolia), nothing more easily finding a buyer. Yea, if their camels and dromedaries fall by the way, or upon necessity must go further than they [are] used to go on the journey (as sometimes it falls out in armies and [on] other journeys), then they give them this herb: by which they report their spirits so stirred up that they will go until they fall down dead.

No inns in Turkey

In this vast Empire I saw no inns. No, not in their cities. And a man shall rarely find any beds among Christians. And if he does, yet the sheets are made of cotton, intolerable for heat. For in Turkey they generally lie upon tapestry carpets; and sometimes, in cities, upon a mattress, with a quilt to cover them. And by the highway they lie upon straw, hay, or grass. And in all places near Palestine they either, by night, lie upon the housetops on a plastered floor, or in yards, upon the earth and in open air, having the spangled Heavens for their canopy. And not only passengers, but all Turks daily wear linen breeches, so that in these provinces not subject to cold a man may better endure this kind of lodging.

Hospitals

But the Turkish passengers, instead of inns, have certain hospitals, built of stone, with cloisters after the manner of monasteries, where (by charitable legacy of alms) all passengers may have meat for certain meals or days – especially the Pilgrim towards Mecca; for whose sake they were especially founded. And these houses are vulgarly called 'kawne' (or as others pronounce, 'cain'). And the covered cloisters of them (built, after their manner, but one roof high) are common, as well to Turks as any other passengers to lodge in openly; and, like good fellows all to lie together, upon such mattresses as they carry; or upon the bare ground, if straw is not to be had. For Christian passengers carry such mattresses and necessary victuals: which failing, they supply them in cities. And every day in villages may buy fresh meats. But they must dress their own meats. Neither is the art of cookery greater in Turkey than with us in Wales. For [the] toasting of cheese in Wales, and [the] seething of rice in Turkey, will enable a man freely to profess the art of cookery.

Of travel in Turkey

No stranger travels in Turkey without a janissary or some other guide to him; who knows the places where most commodious lodging is to be had. But passengers on the way do not go into cities – but only to buy fresh meats. Which done, they return to the tents of their caravan, which is pitched in some field adjoining. In hot climates near the sun...the Turks there dwelling [are] used to begin their journeys towards the evening; and to end them 2 or 3 hours after the sun rising; resting in their tents all the rest of the day. Christian passengers shall do well to go to the Italian friars and to merchants (their countrymen); or (at least) to Christians in trade; and to the Ambassadors or merchants of their own country, at Constantinople who (being themselves strangers) and no ignorant of the evils incident to strangers, will no doubt, in courtesy, direct them to get convenient lodgings and other necessaries.

NOTES

1 Muccaro: probably corruption of Mokkadam, mukaddim: headman.
2 The English (French, German, etc.) name for a small Turkish coin (*OED*).
3 Zechine. Zecchin: gold coin of Venice and Turkey (*OED*).
4 Calivers: apparently (in weight) the lightest kind of portable firearm, except for the pistol; capable of being fired without the need to make use of a rest. Introduced in the sixteenth century.
5 Pope's new style. In 1582, Pope Gregory XIII succeeded in instituting a replacement of the Julian calendar, a method based upon Egyptian and Roman antecedents, but by then wholly discredited as being inaccurate. Crucially, by this time one key date for measuring the vernal equinox (a date set in the fourth century) had accumulated so much surplus time that it had shifted from 11 March to 21 March. Gregory and his advisors solved that by suppressing ten days in 1582, and further ordained that unless they were divisible by 400, that years ending in hundreds should not be leap years. While the reform was readily accepted in most Catholic countries, most Eastern Orthodox countries retained the use of the Julian calendar into the twentieth century. The reforms were not accepted in England until 1752, by which time there was a difference of eleven days between the two; further complicated by the fact that what became known as new style dating has the year as beginning on 1 January, whereas the year in old style began on 25 March.
6 Bill of Exchange: a written order to pay a specified sum of money on a certain date to a drawer or to a named payee; a promissory note (*New Shorter Oxford Dictionary*).
7 Turkey Company: founded 1581. It amalgamated with the Venice Company (founded 1583) to become the Levant Company (1592).
8 Pentis; pentice: earlier form for 'penthouse' – a subsidiary structure attached to the wall of main building, and serving as a shelter, a porch, a shed, an outhouse, etc. (*OED*).
9 Wrethe: support; hold up.
10 Marines: sailors (Fr. Marin).
11 But see Palmira Brummett, *Ottoman Seapower and Levantine Diplomacy in the Age of Discovery*, New York, 1994.
12 Broadcloth: defined by an Act of Parliament of 1482 as being, in quality, 'fine, plain wove, dressed, double width black cloth', used chiefly for men's garments. Double width required that it was 2 yards wide (as distinct from 'straight', half that width).
13 Galls: gall – an excrescence produced on a tree (esp. the oak) or other plant by the action of a fungus, bacterium, an insect, etc. (*New Shorter Oxford Dictionary*).
14 Kersey: a kind of coarse narrow cloth from long wool and usually ribbed (*OED*).
15 Apothecary: Moryson's usage here is still probably that of the name given for someone who kept a store of non-perishable commodities (spices, preserves, drugs, etc.) rather than the meaning

into which it later evolved, as referring to someone who prepared and sold drugs for medicinal purposes; a development recognized by the creation (1617) of separate societies for grocers and apothecaries. From about 1700 onwards the term gradually came to be applied to general medical practitioners.

16 Seeth: to prepare or produce by boiling.
17 Mishmash: a confused mixture, a medley, hodgepodge, jumble (*OED*).
18 Sod: boiled; prepared by boiling (*OED*).
19 Barbary: Barbary States of North Africa (including present-day Morocco, Tunisia, Algeria) were autonomous provinces of the Ottoman Empire. Their defences against being conquered by Spain were led by the Turkish corsair Barbarossa. After the failure (1451) of the Holy Roman Emperor Charles V to wrest the region from Turkish hegemony, piracy joined to increasing commercial and mercantile exploitation of the region, marked by conflict between Muslims and Christians, but also within Christian ranks: English vs French vs Spanish vs Italians.
20 Adam's apples: a variety of lime.

OTHER EDITIONS

An Itinerary... 4 vols, Glasgow: James Maclehose, 1907.

An itinerary, a facsimile of the 1617 edition, Amsterdam: Theatrum Orbis Terrarum/New York: Da Capo Press, 1971.

Charles Hughes (ed.), *Shakespeare's Europe. Unpublished chapters of Fynes Moryson's 'Itinerary'. Being a survey of the condition of Europe at the end of the sixteenth century. With an Introduction and an account of Fynes Moryson's career*, London: Sherratt & Hughes, 1903.

8

WILLIAM LITHGOW

The totall discourse, of the rare aduentures, and painefull peregrinations of long nineteene yeares trauayles, from Scotland, to the most famous king-domes in Europe, Asia, and Affrica. Perfited by three deare bought voyages, in surueighing of forty eight kingdomess ancient and moderne; twenty one rei-publickes, ten absolute principalities, with two hundred ilands. The particular names whereof are described in each argument of the ten diui-sions of this history: and it also diuided in three bookes: two whereof, neuer heretofore published. Wherein is contayned, an exact relation, of the lawes, religion, policies, and gouernment of all their princes, potentates, and peoples. Together with the grieuous tortures he suffered, by the Inquisition of Malaga in Spaine, his miraculous discouery and deliuery thence: And also of his laste and late returne from the Northere Isles. Caelum non animum.

By William Lithgovv. Imprinted at London by Nicholas Okes, and are to be sold by Nicholas Fussell and Humphery Mosley at their shops in Pauls Church yard, at the Ball, and the White Lyon. 1632.
Reprinted Glasgow: James MacLehose, 1932.

BIOGRAPHY

Born Lanark about 1582, d. 1645? Son of a merchant burgess. Walter Scott (without adducing evidence) describes him as a tailor. This is disputed by James Maidment (the editor of Lithgow's poems) who suggests that the confusion might have arisen because of a settlement made by Lithgow's mother to one of her 'overseers', who was a tailor. His inheritance from his mother (through whom he claimed remote connection with the Montrose nobility) was sufficiently large to enable him to indulge his desire to travel – perhaps hastened, as well, by the consequences of what was seen as an 'indiscreet affair' with the daughter of a local laird. Her brothers, apparently not too pleased at the atten-tions of someone they regarded as a social inferior, cut off Lithgow's ears. According to Maidment, he was forever afterwards known as 'cut-lugged Willie'.

As the title page of the *Totall Discourse* makes clear, Lithgow travelled extensively on three continents. The one that concerns us begins with a visit to Paris in the Spring of 1608. Having spent ten months there to learn the language, he went to Rome, where he says he saw 'nothing but abomination, profanation, and irreligious living'. It is an anti-Catholic animus that will not only be regularly repeated but also invariably be his yardstick for comparison with Islam. Penrose, however, notes that it has been inferred, from two stanzas in Lithgow's poem 'The Conflict between the Pilgrim and his Muse', that the traveller had heard Mass in St Peter's, prostrated himself at the elevation of the Host, received the 'Holy Blessing' and even kissed the Pope's foot, adding 'Let us hope that he did so in the interests of his travels rather than through hypocrisy'. From Rome, he went to Naples, then via the Apennines to Loretto and Venice, from where, via Dalmatia and Corfu, to Athens and Thessalonika (where he comments favourably about the benefits arising from Turkish rule) and from there to the Dardanelles in the company of merchants from Marseilles.

Arriving in Constantinople, he spent the winter (1610) living in the house of the English Ambassador, Sir Thomas Glover, and his successor, Sir Paul Pindar. Having spent three months in Constantinople he travelled to Rhodes and Cyprus, then to Tripoli, later to Aleppo, in the hope of going on to Baghdad. But, missing the caravan, he travelled, instead, to Damascus (which place he adored) and then on to Jerusalem, where he arrived on Palm Sunday 1612. From there he joined a caravan for Cairo, where he spent twelve days, before returning home via Alexandria, Malta, Sicily, France and England, where he visited the English Court and presented gifts and relics he had carried from Jerusalem and Jordan to King James, Queen Anne and the Prince of Wales.

The size of these caravans might be judged from the following details he supplies: the one from Aleppo to Jerusalem consisted of some 900 Armenian pilgrims, 600 Turkish merchants, and 100 soldiers; that between Jerusalem and Cairo of some 800 Copts plus six German Protestant and four French Catholics. Three of the Germans were to die of thirst and sunstroke on the journey; the others were to drink themselves to death on strong Cyprus wine within a week of arriving in Cairo – but not before one left Lithgow as heir to all his money: which (even after having been forced to surrender a third to the Venetian consul) was a substantial sum. He was less lucky with the French: when they died on the voyage back from Alexandria he felt that, since they were 'Papists', he could not really lay claim to their possessions, but then, as he explains, they had very little. In 1614 Lithgow made a journey via Calais, the Netherlands, Germany and Italy, to Tunis, and from there to Algiers and Fez. On his return journey, via Rome, Vienna, Transylvania and Moldavia, he was set upon, and robbed of 60 ducats by six men who also stripped him of the Turkish clothes he was wearing and left him tied, stark naked, to an oak tree. Released, and recompensed by a Protestant nobleman, he returned via Cracow, Warsaw and Stockholm.

In February 1620 he left St Malo, from where he travelled to Spain, where he arrived in June, visiting several of the key cities and indulged in '20 days of fastidious climbing'. On arrival in Malaga, he was arrested as a spy, robbed of all his money by the local governor, and later severely tortured on a rack in a winepress house for six and a half hours. Refusing to 'confess', he was eventually returned to prison, where his survival against cold and vermin was with the assistance of a Turkish slave and an Indian cook. In the meantime his books and notes were being translated by an English seminary priest and a Scots cooper then working in Malaga. Given the nature of the comments he made about the Spanish monarchy and Spanish Catholicism (some of which are included towards the end of this selection) it is not difficult to see that his interrogators would not have been best pleased with him. Given eight days in which to recant, after which he would first be tortured and then burned to death at Granada, he was fortunate that the governor's relation of his story to a friend was overheard by the friend's Flemish servant, who rushed to tell the story to the English consul, who arranged for him to be released and carried on board an English naval vessel. On arrival in England, he publicly displayed his 'martyred anatomy'. While the king twice arranged for him to visit the spa at Bath, he could not gain redress from the Spanish Ambassador, Gondomar. In April 1622 that led to an altercation between the two. Though it was unclear who had started it, Lithgow was sent to the Marshalsea prison for nine weeks – where another prisoner was his 'fellow-poet', George Wither. There is evidence that he was sent to prison again in February 1623, but that seems to have to do with his finances.

* * *

[Constantinople: description of the city: omitted – repeats earlier stories]

Slave market. A French palliard. The Dalmatian widow relieved

I have seen men and women as usually sold here in markets as horses and other beasts are with us, the most part of which are Hungarians, Transylvanians, Carindians, Istrains, and Dalmatian captives; and of other places besides, which they can overcome. Whom, if no compassionable Christian will buy, or relieve, then must they either turn Turk, or be addicted to perpetual slavery.

Here I remember a charitable deed, done for a sinful end, and thus it was; a ship of Marseilles, called the *Great Dolphin*, lying here forty days at the Galata, the master gunner, named Monsieur Nerack[1] and I, falling in familiar acquaintance, upon a time he told me secretly that he would gladly, for conscience and merit's sake, redeem some poor Christian slave from Turkish captivity. To the which I applauded his advice, and told him [that] the next Friday following I would assist him to so worthy an action. Friday comes, and he and I went for Constantinople where, the market of the slaves being ready, we spent two hours in viewing, and reviewing, 500 males and females. At last I pointed him to have bought an old man or woman, but his mind was contrary set, showing me that he would buy some virgin, or young widow, to save their bodies un-deflowered by infidels. The price of a virgin was too dear for him, being a 100 ducats; and widows were far under, and at an easier rate.

When we visited and searched those who we were mindful to buy, they were stripped stark naked before our eyes: where the sweetest face, the youngest age, and whitest skin was in greatest value and request. The Jews sold them, for they had bought them from the Turks. At last we fell upon a Dalmatian widow, whose pitiful looks and sprinkling tears struck my soul almost to the death for compassion. Whereupon I grew earnest for her relief; and he, yielding to my advice, she was brought and delivered unto him, the man being 60 years of age, and her price 36 ducats. We left the market and came over again to Galata, where he and I took a chamber for her; and leaving them there.

The next morning I returned early, suspecting greatly the dissembling devotion of the gunner to be nought but luxurious lust. And so it proved. I knocked at the chamber door, that he had newly locked, and taken the key with him to the ship, for he had tarried with her all that night. And she, answering me with tears, told me of all the manner of his usage, wishing herself to be again in her former captivity. Whereupon I went shipboard to him and, in my grief, I swore that if he abused her after that manner, and not returned to

151

her distress her Christian liberty; I would first make it known to his master the Captain of the ship, and then to the French Ambassador, for he was mindful also, his lust being satisfied, to have sold her over and over again to some other. At which threatening the old palliard became so fearful that he entered in a reasonable condition with me, and the ship, departing hence six days thereafter, he freely resigned to me her life, her liberty and freedom; which, being done, and he gone, under my hand, before several Greeks, I subscribed her liberty, and hired her, in the same tavern for a year, taking nothing from her, for as little had she to give me, except many blessings and thankful prayers. This French gunner was a Papist; and here you may behold the dregs of his devotion. And what seven nights of lechery cost him, you may cast up the reckoning of 36 ducats....

[Entry into mosques; Constantinople the 'Paradise of the earth']

It is not licensed here (nor elsewhere in all Turkey) that any Christian should enter in their mosques, or churches, without the conduct of a janissary; the trial whereof I had when I viewed that glorious and great Church of Saint Sophia; once the beauty and ornament of all Europe, and now the chief place to which the Great Turk, or Emperor, goes every Friday, their Sabbath day, to do his devotion, being accompanied by 3000 janissaries, besides pashas, chauses and hagars. Truly I may say of Constantinople, as I said once of the world, in the lament of my second pilgrimage:

> A painted whore, the mask of deadly sin,
> Sweet fair without, and stinking foul within.

For indeed outwardly it has the fairest show; and inwardly (the streets being narrow, and the most part covered) the filthiest and deformed buildings in the world. The reason of its beauty is because, being situate on moderate prospective heights, the universal textures afar off yield a delectable show, the covers being erected like the back of a coach after the Italian fashion, with guttered tile. But, being entered within, there is nothing but a stinking deformity and a loathsome contrived place, without either internal domestic furniture, or external decorations of fabrics palatially extended. Notwithstanding that, for its situation, the delicious wines and fruits, the temperate climate, the fertile circumjacent fields and for the sea (the Hellespont) and pleasant Asia on the other. It may be truly called the Paradise of the earth.

[The Christian ambassadors at Pera]

Pera is over against Constantinople, called...by the Turks, Galata....It is the place at which Christian ships touch, and where the Ambassadors of Christendom lie. The number of the Christian Ambassadors who then lay there, and now do, were these: first, the Roman Emperor's; then the French; thirdly, the English; fourthly, the Venetian; and, lastly, the Holland Ambassador's, with whom often for discourses I was familiar, although with noble Sir Thomas Glover I was still domestic for 12 weeks,[2] whose secretary for that time was my countryman, master James Rollock...he was the last Scotsman I saw till my return to Malta, after my departure from Constantinople....

[The Duke of Moldavia turned Turk]

And, by the way, I cannot but regret the great loss Sir Thomas Glover received by the Duke of Moldavia, who chargeably entertained him [for] 2 years in his house, and furnished him with great monies, and other necessities fit for his eminence. This Duke, or Prince of Bugdonia, was deprived of his principalities by Ahmed, and fled hither to the Christian Ambassadors, for relief. To whom, when all the rest refused acceptance, noble Sir Thomas received him, maintained him, and seriously wrought with the Grand Seignior and his council to have him restored again to his lands; but could not prevail.

In the end, Sir Thomas Glover's 5 years time of Ambassadry being expired, and the Duke hearing privately that Sir Paul Pindar was to come in his place (as indeed he came soon) this Moldavian prince stole early away one morning over Constantinople; and long before midday turned Turk, and was circumcised, contenting himself only, for all his great dukedom, with a palace, and a yearly pension of 12,000 chickenoes of gold during his life. When we heard, the Ambassador and we were all amazed and discontented. He was indebted to the Ambassador [for] above 15,000 chickenoes of gold. Yet, on my leaving Galata, I went twice over with Sir Thomas, and saw him, and found attended on by a number of Turks; who, when he saw me, took me kindly by the hand, for we had been [for] two months familiar in the Ambassador's house before.

The English Ambassador, within half a year, recovered the half of his monies; the other half he was forced to forgo for several importunate respects. Nay, I must say one thing for this knight: he relieved more slaves from the galleys, paid their ransoms, and sent them home, freely, to their Christian stations, and kept a better house, than any Ambassador did, that ever lay at Constantinople; or ever shall, to the world's end. His mother was Polish; who, coming from Danzig to London, was delivered of him upon the sea. Afterwards, he was brought up at Constantinople from a boy, and spoke and wrote the Slavonian tongue perfectly. And thence, returning to London, he was the first Ambassador [that] King James, of blessed memory, sent to Constantinople, after his coming to the Crown of England. And this much for this worthy and ever-renowned knight, whose praise and fame I cannot too much celebrate.

[Turkish prayers]

The Turks have no bells in their churches – neither [for] the use of a clock, or the numbering of hours. But they have high, round steeples for their contrafact, and contradict all the forms of the Christians. When they go to pray, they are called together by the voice of crying men, who go upon the bartizings[3] of their steeples, shouting and crying with a shrill voice:...'God is a great God, and Muhammad is his Prophet', or otherwise, 'There is but one God.'

In Constantinople, and all other places of Turkey, I ever saw 3 Sabbaths together, in one week: the Friday for the Turks; the Saturday for the Jews; and the Sunday for the Christians. But the Turks' Sabbath is worst of all; for they will not spare to do any labour on their Holy Day. They have meetings at their public prayers every day, several times. The first is before the rising of the sun; the second is a little before midday; the third is at 3 o'clock in the afternoon; the fourth is at the sun setting (summer and winter). Fifthly, the last hour of prayer is always 2 or 3 hours within night. Many of them will watch till that time, and not sleep; and others, sleeping, will awake at the voice of the crier, and go to church.

In sign of reverence, and in superstitious devotion, before they go into their mosques, they wash themselves in a lavatory; beginning at the privy members, next their mouths, faces, feet and hands. And entering, they incline their heads downwards to the earth and, falling on their knees, do kiss the ground 3 times. Then...their chief priest mounts upon a high stone, [from] where he makes many orations to Muhammad; and the rest, to assist him, continue a long time shaking their heads, as though they were out of their natural understanding...and sometimes will sing the Psalms of David in the Arabic tongue; but to no sense, or verity of the Scriptures.

And at their devotions they will not tolerate any women in their company, lest they should withdraw their minds and affections from their present zeal. But the men observe their turns and times, and the women theirs; going always when they go, either of them alone, to their devotions. The like custom (but not after the same manner) have I seen observed amongst the Protestants in Transylvania, Hungary, Moravia, Bohemia, and Silesia who, when they come to church on the Sabbath day, there is a taffeta curtain drawn from the pulpit to the church wall over against it, the men sitting on the right hand of the preacher, the women on the left; whose eyes and faces cannot see [each] other during Divine Service, save only the minister who overtops both sides. And truly I thought [that] this was a very modest and necessary observance....

Turkish Pilgrims

I have seen sometimes 2000 Turks travelling to Mecca in pilgrimage (which is in Arabia Felix); where many, in a superstitious devotion (having seen the Tomb of Muhammad) are never desirous to see the vanities of the world again. For, in a frantic piety, they cause a smith to pull out their eyes. And these men are called 'Hoggeis' [Hadjis], holy men; whom the Turks much honour and regard, and are always led about from town to town by men's hands, and fed, and regarded like unto princes. Or, like the Capuchins,[4] who scour themselves on Good Friday, [they are] met and homaged at every passing street, with prayers, gifts, and adorations.

Muhammad had broken his promise

Some write that Muhammad, in his youth, was a soldier under the conduct of Heraclius who, employing certain Arabians in an expedition to Persia, not only denied them their wages, but told them that that was not to be given for dogs, which he provided for the Roman soldiers. Hence, some mutinies arising in the army, he [Muhammad], with certain Arabians, his countrymen, by faction separated themselves, and revolted. Whereupon Muhammad, encouraging them in their defection, was chosen their captain. And so, for a certain time, they continued – rebellious runagates, thieves, and robbers of all people. The subtlety of this dissembler was admirable. Who, knowing that he was destitute of heavenly gifts to work miracles, feigned that God [had] sent him with the sword. He also promised, at the end of 1000 years, to return, and bring them to Paradise. But he has falsified his promise; for the time is expired 40 years ago. And they, imagining that he is either diseased, or become lame in his journey, have ascribed to him another 1000 years to come. But long may their wicked and faithless generation gape before he comes. Until such time that there is a general convocation, they will be partakers of his endless damnation in Hell – unless it pleases the Lord, in His mercy, to convert them before that time.

Muhammad chiefly prohibited, in his Qur'ān, the eating of swine's flesh and the drinking of wine; which indeed the best sort do. But the baser kind are daily drunkards. Their common drink is sherbet, composed of water, honey, and sugar – which is exceedingly delectable in the taste. And the usual courtesy they bestow on their friends who visit them is a cup of coffee, made out of a seed called coava, and [is] of a blackish colour; which they drink so hot as possibly they can, and is good to expel the crudities of raw meats and herbs, so much by them frequented. And those who cannot attain to this liquor must be content with the cooling streams of water.

Oppression of the Turks

It is incident to Turks who have not the generosity of mind to temper felicity, to be glutted with the superfluous fruits of doubtful prosperity. Neither have they a patient resolution to withstand adversity, nor hope to expect the better alteration of time. But by an infused malice in their wicked spirits, when they are any way calamited, [they] will impose compulsion, cause the poor slavish subjected Christians [to] surrender all [that] they have: the half, or so forth – sometimes with strokes, menacings, and sometimes death itself. Which plainly illustrates their excessive cruelty, and the poor Christians' inevitable misery. And yet, being complained upon, they are severely punished, or else put to death, for committing of such unallowable riots; being expressly against the imperial law of the Turk, concerning the quietness and liberty of the Christians.

I have often heard Turks brawl one with another most vilely. But I never saw, or heard, that they either in private or public quarrels durst strike one another. Neither dare they, for fear of punishment imposed to such quarrellers. But they will injure and strike Christians: who dare not say it is amiss, or strike again. It is a common thing with them to kill their servants for a very small offence; and when they have done, [to] throw them, like dogs, in a ditch. And oftentimes (if not so) will lay them down on their backs, hoisting up their heels, bind their feet together, and fasten them to a post, and with a cudgel give them three or four hundred blows on the soles of their feet. Whereupon, peradventure, some ever go lame after.

Their servants are bought and sold, like brute beasts, in the markets. Neither can these miserable drudges ever recover liberty, except they buy themselves free, either by one means or other. Their wives are not far from the like servitude, for the men (by the Qur'ān) are admitted to marry as many women as they will, or their ability can keep. And if it shall happen that anyone of these women (I mean either wife or concubine) prostitutes herself to another man besides her husband, then may he (by authority) bind her hands and feet, hang a stone about her neck, and cast her into a river. Which by them is usually done in the night. But when these Infidels [are] pleased to abuse poor Christian women against their husbands' will, they little regard the transgression of the Christian Law; who as well deflower their daughters as their wives. Yet the devout Mohamedans never meddle with them, accompting themselves damned to copulate (as they think) with the offspring of dogs. The Turks generally, when they commit any copulation with Christians, or their own sex, wash themselves in a south-running fountain, before sunrise, thinking thereby to wash away their sins.

The Turks' justice

If a Turk should happen to kill another Turk, his punishment is this. After he is adjudged to death, he is brought forth to the marketplace; and a block being brought forth hither of four foot high, the malefactor is stripped naked and then laid thereupon, with his belly downward. They draw in his middle together so small with running cords that they strike his body in two with one blow. His hinder parts they cast to be eaten by hungry dogs kept for the same purpose, and the forequarters and head they throw into a grievous fire made there for the same end. And this is the punishment for manslaughter.

But for murder or treason he is more cruelly used. For, being convicted and condemned, he is brought forth before the people where, in the street there is an exceedingly [high?] stripad erected, much like unto a maypole. Which tree, from the root till it comes almost to the top, is all set full of long, sharp iron pikes; and their points upwards. The villain being stripped naked, and his hands bound backwards, they bind a strong rope about his shoulders and cleavings. And then, hoisting him to the pillar (or top) of the tree, they let the rope fly loose. Whence down he falls, with a rattle, among the iron pikes; hanging either by the buttocks, by the breasts, by the sides, or shoulders. And there, sticking fast in the air, he hangs till his very bones rot and fall down, and the body is devoured, being quick [dead], by ravenous eagles, kept to prey upon his carcass for the same purpose.

Turkish marriages

But now I come to their nuptial rites. Their custom, and manner of marriage, is thus. If a man affects a young maid, he buys her off her parents, and gives a good sum of money for her. And after she is bought, he enrols her name in the Cadi's book, witnessing [that] she is his bound wife, bought off her father. Lo; this is all the form of their marriage! This being done, the father of the woman sends household stuff home with the bride; which is carried through the streets on mules, or [on] camels' backs. The two married folks marching before, are conveyed with music, their own acquaintances and friends, into the house.

The Turks in general, whensoever they loathe or dislike their wives, sell them in markets, or otherwise bestow them on their men-slaves. And although their affection was never so great towards them, yet they never eat together: for commonly the women stand, and serve their husbands at meat. And after that they eat apart, by themselves, without admittance of any mankind in their company, if they are above 14 years of age. They seldom go abroad [outside] unless it is each Thursday night, when they go to the graves to mourn for the dead – always covering their faces, very modestly, with white or black masks, which are never uncovered until they return to their houses. Many other ceremonies they have which would be too prolix for me to recite. And notwithstanding of all this external gravity amongst these hirelings, yet there are in Constantinople more than 40,000 brothel-houses, Turkish or Libertine,[5] in any of which, if a Christian (especially Franks) is apprehended, he must either turn Turk or slave all his life. But the women, by policy, apply a counter-poison to this severity. For they accustomably come to the chambers of their benefactors and well-wishers, or other places appointed secretly, whereso they learn either a French 'syncope' or Italian 'bergamask'.[6]

Figure 2 A Turkish woman

Source: George Sandys (1615) *A Relation of a Journey begun in An-Dom 1610*, London: printed for W. Barrett, p. 68. By permission of the British Library (ref. 1297m26)

The Emperor's concubines

As for the Great Turk's concubines, they are in number 800; being [for] the most part Emir's, Pasha's and Timariots' daughters. The third, and innermost part, of the Seraglio, is allotted for their residence; being well attended, at all times, by numbers of eunuchs, and other gelded officers. Every morning they are ranked [arranged] in a great hall, and set on high and open seats. Where, when he comes (and selecting the youngest and fairest) he touches her with a rod. And immediately she follows him into his cabin of lechery where, if any action is done, she receives from the Head Clerk her approbation thereupon: which ever afterwards serves her for a conditional dowry to her marriage, with much honour and reputation besides. And if any of them conceive, and the child born, it is suddenly despatched from this life.

The oldest hundred, every first Friday of the month, are turned out, and another new hundred come in to make good the number. Their entry and issue is always at one of the postern gates of the park, towards the seaside adjoining the palace, whence, crossing [the]

Bosphorus in an appointed barge, they both go and come in one day, from and to Galata; which I myself saw several times. The oldest and last hundred who are dismissed every month depart from Galata, home to their parents and [their] several countries, rejoicing that they were counted worthy to be chosen and entertained to be their Emperor's concubines.

The custom of the Great Turk is [that] every Friday, being their Sabbath, after Divine Service and dinner, to run at the glove, in an open place, before all the people, with some Hagars (or young striplings) who accompany him; who have the glove hanging as high on a stick as we have the ring with us. And truly, of all the Turkish Emperors who ever were, this Ahmed was the most gentle and favourable to Christians; who rather, for his bounty and tenderness, might have been entitled the Christian Emperor than the pagan king. For he disannulled all the exactions that had been inflicted by his predecessors upon his tributary subjects, and cancelled the custom of tithe on their male children, abrogating also that imposition on their female dowries.

The Turks' Paradise

The Lent of the Turks is called Bairam; which continues the space of one month, once in the year. In which time, from the sun rising to his setting, they neither eat nor drink. And at their prayers (especially in this fasting) they often reiterate these words:…'He, he, he, alone is God'; or 'There is but one only Supreme Power' – which they do in derision of Christians who (as they say) adore 3 Gods. They also have this sinister opinion that, at the Day of Judgement, when Muhammad shall appear, there shall be displayed 3 banners, under which all good people shall be conveyed to Paradise: one of Moses, under which the Children of Israel shall be; the second, of Jesus, under which the Christians shall be; the third, of Muhammad, under which shall be the Arabs, Turks, and Muslims – all of whom, they think, shall be elevated to several honours. And they, in promotion, shall be discerned from the rest, by chambers made [out] of resplendent light, which God will give them, wherein they shall banquetings, feastings, dancing, and the best melody [that] can be devised; and that they shall spend their times with amorous virgins (whose mansion shall be near by), the men never exceeding the age of 30 years, and the virgins 15. And both shall have their virginities renewed, as fast as [it is] lost.

They hold also this, as a confident article of their belief: [that] there are 7 Paradises in Heaven, the pavements whereof are laid with gold, sliver, pearls, precious stones, and garnished with stately buildings and pleasant gardens wherein there are all sorts of fruit; and princely palaces, through which run rivers of milk, honey, and wine….

The Turks' Lent

Their Lent lasts 30 days, called Bairam, some name it also Ramadan, during which time they [neither] eat nor drink nothing from [the] sun rising to its setting down. But when night comes they gourmandise at their self pleasures. Their month of Lent is our January, where (every day, after their devotions) they go to solemn plays, and all kind of profane pastimes; counting that best devotion which is most suitable to their dispositions, allotting fancy to follow their folly and blindness to overtop the ignorance of nature, drawing all their drifts within the circle of destruction. But indeed, as they are blind in the true way of sacred worship, yet are they masked with a wonderful seal to their devoted blindness, surpassing far in show and observations the Professors of Christianity, and all the ceremonies [that] can be annexed thereunto. Their running on with the floods of ignorant affection, and ours distracted with the infantile novelties of School questions, which indeed do more distemper the truth than render God to be rightly glorified.[7]

The Turks' opinion of Hell

As concerning their opinion of Hell: they hold it to be a deep gulf between two mountains, from the mouth whereof [there] are dragons which continually throw fire, being large 8 leagues; and has a dark entry where the horrible fiends meet the perplexed sinners, conveying them till they come to a bridge which is as narrow as the edge of a razor, whereon those who have not committed heinous offences may pass over to Hell. But those who have done buggery (as the most part of them do) and homicide, shall fall headlong from it, to the profoundest pit of Hell, where they shall sometimes burn in fire, and sometimes be cast into hot boiling waters to be refreshed. And, for the greater part of the wicked, they say, God has planted a tree in hell named...'The Head of the Devil', upon the fruit of which the damned continually feed. Muhammad, in one of the chapters of the Qur'ān, calls this tree the Tree of Malediction.[8] They also think [that] the tormented souls may one day be saved, providing [that] they endure the scorching flames of Hell patiently. Thus, as briefly as I could, have I laid open the opinions of the Turks concerning their Heaven and hell before the eyes of those who, peradventure, have never been acquainted with such a ghostly discourse.

[Omitted: 'The number of all the Emperors in the East and the West; the beginning of the Turks']

The Turks' complexion

The Turks who are born and bred in the Lesser Asia [Asia Minor] and east parts of Europe are generally well-complexioned, proportionably compacted, no idle or superfluous talkers, servile to their Grand Seignior, excessively inclined to venery, and zealous in religion. Their heads are always shaven, reserving only one tuft on the top above, by which they think one day to be caught to Heaven by Muhammad; and covered on all sides, counting it an opprobious thing to see any uncover his head. They wear their beards long, as a sign of gravity; for they esteem to be wise men, who have long beards. The women are of a low stature, thick and round of growth, going seldom abroad (unless it is each Thursday, at night, when they go to mourn upon the graves of their dead friends) and then they are modestly masked. They are fearful and shamefast abroad, but lascivious within doors; and pleasing in matters of incontinency. And they are accounted most beautiful who have the blackest brows, the widest mouths, and the greatest eyes.

The other Turks, who are born in Asia Major and Egypt (I speak not of the Moors of Barbary) are of a greater stature, tanny, cruel; a barbarous and uncivil people. The better sort use the Slavonian tongue; the vulgar speak the Turkish language which, being originally the Tatarian speech. They borrow from the Persian their words of state; from the Arabic their words of religion; from the Greeks their terms of war; and from the Italian their words and titles of navigation.

The puissance of the Great Turk is admirable. Yet the most part of his kingdoms in Asia are not well inhabited, neither populous. But those parts which border with Christians are strongly fortified with castles, people, and munitions. If Christian princes could concord and consult together it were an easy thing, in one year, to subdue the Turks and root out their very names from the earth. Yea, moreover I am certified that there are more Christians (even slaves, and subjects to the Great Turk) who inhabit his dominions than might overthrow and conquer these Infidels, if they had worthy captains, governors, and furniture of arms, without the help of any Christian of Christendom. And yet again I think it not amiss to discourse more particularly of the Turkish manners, of their riches and of their forces of war and the manner of their conducements.

The Turks are Tatarians

The Turks, being naturally descended from the Scythians or Tatars, are of the second stature of man, and robust of nature, circumspect and courageous in all their attempts, and no way given to industry or labour, but are wonderfully avaricious and covetous of money above all the nations of the world. They never observe their promises, unless it is with advantage, and are naturally prone to deceive strangers, changing their conditional bargains as time gives occasion to their liking. They are humble one to another, but especially to their superiors, before whom they do not only great homage, but also keep great silence, and are wonderfully coy during the time of their presence. They are extremely inclined to all sorts of lascivious luxury, and generally addicted (besides all their sensual and incestuous lusts) unto sodomy, which they count as a dainty to digest all their other libidinous pleasures.

They hold that everyone has the hour of his death written on his forehead, and that none can escape the good or evil hour predestinated for them. This ridiculous error makes them so bold and desperate (yea, and often) to run headlong in the most inevitable dangers.[9] They are not given to domestic pastimes, such as chess, cards, dice, and tables; but abroad and in travel they are exceedingly kind disposers of their meat and drink, to any stranger, without exception. The better sort of their women are sumptuously attired, and adorned with pearls and precious stones. And some of them are accustomed to turn their hands and hair into a red colour: but especially the nails of their hands and feet, and are wont to go to bathe themselves in stoves twice a week, as well as men.

The true Turks wear on their heads white turbans (except a few who are esteemed to be Muhammad's kindred, and they wear green sashes, being most part of them priests). The better part of the Turks in Asia care not for fish, but those Turks who remain in Europe love fish better than flesh; especially at Constantinople, where the best fishes and most abundant of them are taken that are in the world; and that, in the Black Sea.

They are ever desirous to seek advantage of their neighbours; which, if they cannot by force, they will under colour of truce accomplish it with perfidiousness. And if their enterprises find no happy event, they are never a whit ashamed to take the flight. Yet are they generally good soldiers, and well taught in martial discipline. Their armies, in marching or camping, (notwithstanding infinite multitudes) keep modesty and silence, and are extremely obedient unto their captains and commanders. When the Grand Seignior is abroad with his army at wars the Turks at home within the towns use great prayers and fasting for him and them. They ingeniously describe the victories of their ancestors, and joyfully sing them in rhymes and songs, thinking thereby that fashion in recalling the valiant deeds of their predecessors to be the only pleasure to encourage their soldiers to be hardy, resolute, and desperate in their enterprises.

They are not much given to contemplation, not study of letters or arts. Yet they have many fair schools where the public lecture of their laws are professed, and Muhammadanism, to the intent that their children, being elected to be brought up for a nones,[10] may be instructed to be profitable expounders of their Qur'ān, and judicious judges for the government of the Commonwealth. It is seldom and rarely seen that a Turk will speak with a woman in the streets; nay, not so much as in their mosques one to be in sight of the other. And yet they are lords and masters of their wives and concubines, from whom they receive as great respect, service and honour as from their bond and bought slaves.

[Economics and commerce]

The Great Turk's revenues are no way answerable to his great and large dominions. The causes arising hereupon are many; of which I will select three or four of the chief reasons. First, the Turks being more given to arms, to conquer, to destroy and ruin, and to consume the wealth of the people they overcome, leaving them destitute of noriture, rather than any way to give course for their increasing and stabilising of trade, out of which should flow the royal advantages. And the reason why they keep their subjects poor, and frustrate themselves of their profits, is only to weaken and enfeeble them, whereby they should not therewith to move insurrection or rebellion against them. And, on the other part, the Greeks are as unwilling to be industrious in arts, trade or cultivation, seeing [that] what they possess is not their own, but is taken from them at all occasions, with tyranny and oppression. For what gains the sower, if another reap the profit? So, in the Ottomans' state there are great forests and deserted countries, proceeding [out] of the scarcity of people to inhabit there; the multitudes being drawn from Asia to strengthen the frontiers of his dominions in Europe.

And besides, there is another reason for the dispopulosity of these parts, to whit [that] when the Great Turk's army is to march to a far country to make wars, then must their vulgar subdued peasants (perhaps 20 or 30 thousands) go along with them, to carry their victuals, and all manner of provision; being taken from the plough and constrained to this servitude. And notwithstanding [that] the half of them do not return; partly because of the change of food and air, and partly because of their long travel and insupportable service, both in heat and cold. And to these of the first reason there is another perpendicular cause, to whit: that the whole commerce of all commodities in Turkey is in the hands of Jews and Christians (to wit: Ragusans, Venetians, English, French and Flemings) who so warily manage their business that they enjoy the most profits of any trading there, disappointing the Turk's own subjects of their due and ordinary trade.

The last and most principal reason is (which is a great deal of more importance than his revenues): to wit, the great number of his timars. For the Turkish Emperors, being immediate masters of the lands they overcome, they divide the same in timars or commandments, leaving little or nothing at all to the former inhabitants. They dispose these proportions to valorous soldiers who have done good service. And with this condition: that they maintain, and have always in readiness, horses for the wars – which is an excellent good order for the preservation of his empire. For if these timariots were not rewarded with such absolute possession of parcels [of] ground, the state of his power would suddenly run to ruin; for the profit of which lands, maintaining themselves, their horses and their families, makes them the more willing to concur in the infallible service of their Emperor. These timars...entertain, through all his dominions, about 250,000 horses

161

which are ever in readiness to march at the first advertisement, without any charges to the Grand Seignior, being bound to maintain themselves in during the wars. And yet these timariots and their horses cannot yearly be maintained under the value of ten millions in gold; the consideration whereof makes me astonished when I recall the relations of some ragged authors who compare the Great Turk's revenues unto [that of] our petty princes of Christendom.

Policies of Turks

The establishment of timars, and the by-past election of...young children to be made janissaries have been the two strong foundations that supported so inviolably the Turkish Empire. The Roman Emperors for a long time used the self-same manner for the assuring of their persons and state, in election of young males to be their guard. They were called the Prætorian Army.[11] And this taxation of children was the first thing that moved the Flemings to revolt against the Romans. As for the Turkish cavalry, they sustain two important effects. First they keep under awe and subjection the Great Turk's subjects, who otherwise perhaps would revolt. And next they are ordained for any dependent enterprise for field garrisons; yea, and the principal sinews of the wars. And yet, the election of the Grand Seignior lies most in the hands of the janissaries; who cannot perfectly say [that] he is Emperor before they confirm him in his throne.

The Turks have three things in their armies which are very fearful, to wit: the infinite number of men, great discipline, and force of munitions. As for discipline, they are not only governed with great silence and obedience, but they are ruled also with signs of the eye; and being made tractable, they are tied to maintain conducements. And although their multitudes have often bred confusion in them, so that little armies have broken and overcome them, yet in their flight they are so cautelous[12] that a small number can do them no absolute violence nor final overthrow. For, as they assail, so they fly without fear....

The Turks have a custom when they are masters of any province, to exterminate all the native nobility; chiefly those of the blood-royal of the country. And, nevertheless, they permit to all and everyone of theirs to live and follow his own religion, as he pleases, without constraint. Among the Turks there is no gentility or nobility; but are all as ignoble and inferior members to one main body, the Great Turk, lineally descending of the house of Ottoman; whose magnificence, puissance and power is such that the most eloquent tongue cannot sufficiently declare: his thousands of janissaries, chauses and others daily attending him, who are the nerves and sinews of the warlike body of his whole monarchy and imperial state; his hundreds (besides his queen) of concubines, hourly maintained by his means, and monthly renewed; his armies, pashas, emirs, vizier-pashas, sanzacks, garrisons and forces here and there dispersed amongst his dominions would be impossible for me briefly to relate.

The inhumane policy of the Turks to avoid civil dissension is such that the seeds of Ottoman (all except one of them) are strangled to death. Wherefore, as Augustus Caesar said of Herod, in the like case, [that] it is better to be the Great Turk's dog than his son. His daughters or sisters are not so used, but are given in marriage to any pasha whom so they affect; yet with this condition: the king says to his daughter or sister 'I give thee this man to be thy slave. And if he offends thee in any case, or is disobedient to thy will, here I give thee a dagger to cut off his head'. Which always they wear by their sides for the same purpose.

Noble Persians

The Persians differ much from the Turks in nobility, humanity and activity, and especially in points of religion; who by contention think each other accursed; and notwithstanding [that] both factions are under the Mahometical Law. Neither are the sons of the Persian kings so barbarously handled as theirs. For all the brothers (one excepted) are only made blind, wanting their eyes; and are always afterwards gallantly maintained like princes. And it has oftentimes fallen out that some of these kings, dying without procreate heirs, there have of these blind sons succeeded to the empire; who have restored again the seed of that royal family.

And now the great advantage that the Turks have daily upon the Persians is only because of their infantry, which the Persians no ways are accustomed with, fighting always on horseback. Neither are the Persians addicted or given to building forts, or fortifications; neither have they any great use of munitions; but, exposing themselves ever to the field in the extreme hazard of battle, become ever doubtful in their victories: whose courage and valour cannot be paralleled amongst all the people of the eastern world, as Baghdad in their late and last fortunes may give sufficient testimony thereof.[13]

The Turcomans' opinion of God and the Devil

After my return to Tripoli, I then departed eastward, with a caravan of Turks, to Aleppo; being 10 days distant. In all this way...I saw nothing worthy remarking, except only a few scattered villages, and poor miserable people called Turcomani, living in tents and following their flocks; to whom I paid sundry caffars, who remove their women, children and cattle whereso they find fountains and good pasturage: which, in their vagabonding fashion plainly demonstrated the necessity they had to live, rather than any pleasure they had, or could have, in their living.

They differ also in religion from all the other Mahometans in two damnable points. The one is [that] they acknowledge that there is a God, and that, of himself, is so gracious that he neither can (being essentially good) do harm, nor yet authorise any ill to be done; and therefore more to be loved than fared. The other is [that] they confess [that] there is a Devil, and that he is a tormentor of all evil-doers, and of himself so terrible and wicked, that they are contented even for acquisiting his favour and kindness, to sacrifice in fire their first-born child to him, soliciting his devilishness not to torment them too sore when they shall come into his hands. And yet, for all this, they think afterward [that], by the mercy of Muhammad, they shall go from Hell to Paradise.

A notable obedience

[In Mesopotamia] I remember of a notable obedience done to the Great Turk by the Pasha of Aleppo, who was also an Emir, or hereditary prince, to wit: the year before my coming here, he had revolted against his Emperor and, fighting the pashas of Damascus and Caraman, had overcome them. The year following (and in my being there) the Grand Seignior sent, from Constantinople, a chaus and two janissaries in embassy to him; where, as they came to Aleppo, the pasha was in his own country at Mesopotamia. The messengers made haste after him. But in their journey they met him coming back to Aleppo, accompanied by his two sons and 600 horsemen. Upon the highway they delivered their message; where he stood still and heard them. The proffer of Ahmed was that if he would acknowledge his rebellion, and for that treason committed, send him his head, [then] his eldest son should both inherit his possessions and Pashaship of Aleppo. Otherwise he would come with great force, in all expedition, and in his proper person he would utterly raze him and all his from the face of the earth.

At which expression the Pasha, knowing that he was not able to resist the invincible army of his master, and his own presence, he dismounted from his horse, and went to counsel with his sons and nearest friends; where he, and they, concluded [that] it was best for him to die, being an old man, to save his race undestroyed, and to keep his son in his authority and inheritance. This done, the Pasha went to prayer; and, taking his leave of them, sat down upon his knees, where the chaus struck off his head, putting it in a box, to carry it with him to Constantinople. The dead corpse was carried to Aleppo, and honourably buried; for I was an eye-witness[14] to that funeral feast. And immediately thereafter the chaus, by proclamation and power from the Emperor, fully possessed the son in his father's lands, offices, Pashaship, and the authority of all the eastern Syria, part of Mesopotamia, and the Assyrian country: for this Pasha of Aleppo is the greatest in commandment and power of all the other Pashas in the Turk's dominions (except the Pasha, or Beglerbeg, of Damascus). And yet the former, in hereditary power, far exceeds the other; being a free Emir, and thereupon, a prince born. The force of his commandment reaches to 18 sanzacks and 30,000 timariots; besides janissaries, and other inferior soldiers, who would make up as many more....

[Damascus]

...arriving at Damascus, we were all lodged (some in chambers without beds; and others outside, on hard stones) in a great cain..., where we stayed 3 days, having all this time given [to] us, twice a day, provision for ourselves and provender for our beasts, gratis: being allowed by the Grand Seignior to all kinds of strangers whatsoever who come to Damascus with any caravan – being a singular comfort and advantage to weary and extorted travellers.

Damascus is the capital city of Syria...and is situated on a fair plain, and beautified by many rivers on each side..., excellent orchards, and all other objects of elegancy that, for situation, artisans, all manner of commodities and variety of fruits, in all the Asiatical provinces, is not paralleled. By Turks it is called The Garden of Turkey; or rather, their Earthly Paradise, because of a fenced garden there, where a garrison of Turks lie, continually keeping that tree...whereon, as they allege, the Forbidden Apple grew, wherewith the Serpent deceived Eve, and she Adam, and from whence the Great Turk is also styled 'Keeper of the Terrestrial Paradise'.

Some hold [that] this city was built by Eleazer, the servant of Abraham;[15] and others say it was the place that Cain slew Abel – where, indeed, it is most likely to be so: for hard by Damascus I saw a pillar of brass erected there for a commemoration of that unnatural murder of Cain executed upon his innocent brother. But, howsoever I persuade you, it is a pleasant and gallant city, well walled and fortified with a strong castle, wherein the Pasha remains. The most parts of the streets are covered, so that the citizens are preserved in summer from the heat, and in winter from the rain. The like commodity (but not after the same form) has Padua in Lombardy: their bazaar, or market-place, is also covered. So are commonly all the bazaars (or bezestans) in Turkey. The best carobiers,[16] Adam's apples and grenadines that grow on the earth are here.

Near unto the bazaar there is a mosque...wherein my guide showed me the sepulchre of Ananias, and the fountain where he baptized Paul.[17] In another street I saw the house of Ananias, which is but a hollow cellar under the ground, and where the Disciples let Paul down through the wall in a basket. In the street where they fell, there Viæno, my interpreter, showed me a great gate of fine metal which, he said, was one of the doors of the temple of Solomon,[18] and was transported there by the Tatarians who conquered Jerusalem about 380 years ago[19] who, for the heavy weight thereof, were enforced to leave it here, being indeed a relic of a wonderful bigness. And I also saw such abundance of rose-water here, in barrels, to be sold, as beer or wine is rife with us.

This Paradisiat Shamma [Damascus] is the Mother City and most beautiful place in all Asia, resembling [in] every way (the architectures of her houses excepted, being platform) that matchless pattern and mirror of beauty, the city of Antwerp. The only best sabres (or short crooked swords) that are made in the world, are made here. And so are all other weapons [such] as half pikes, bows and arrows, and baluckoes [?] of steel that horsemen carry in their hands, their shafts being 3 foot long, their heads great and round and sharply guttered, wherewith they brain or known down their enemies in the field.

The Beglerbeg or Pasha of Damascus is the greatest of commandment of all the other Pashas in Asia, having under his authority (as he is under the Emperor) 22 Sanzacks; and they conducting, under all the aforesaid, 40,000 timariots, or horsemen, besides 2,000 janissaries, who are the guard of the Pasha, and garrison of the city. His Beglerbegship extends over the greater half of Syria, a part of the two Arabias (Felix, and Petrea) Phoenicia, Galilee, Samaria, Palestine, Judea, Jerusalem, Idumea, and all the northern parts of Arabia Deserta, even to the frontiers of Egypt. The means for the preservation of so great a state is only by an induced confidence upon the power and force of timariots who, as well, have they pay and local grounds of compensation, in time of tranquillity as [well as] wars to defend these countries from the incursions of the wild Arabs (who ever more annoy the Turks; and also strangers) and cannot possibly be brought to a quiet and well-formed manner of living, but are continual spoilers of the Turk's dominions. That mischief daily increases, rather than any way diminishes. They take example from the beastly Turks [and] add, by these patterns, more wickedness to the badness of their own dispositions, so that every one of these savages, according to his power, deals with all men uncivilly and cruelly, even like a wilderness full of wild beasts, living all upon rapine and robbery, wanting all sense of humanity, more than a show of appearance: whereby, being combined together, terrorise over all, even from the Red Sea to Baghdad....

A counter-buffet to Loretto

April 20th [1612], about 10 of the clock...we arrived at Nazareth, and there reposed till the evening, providing ourselves with victuals and water. In this town dwelt Joseph and the Virgin Mary; and in which also Our Saviour was brought up under the vigilant care of Joseph and Mary. After we had dined, the Armenians arose and went to a heap of stones, the ruins of an old house, before the which they fell down upon their knees, praising God. And that ruined lump (said they) was the house in which Mary dwelt when Gabriel saluted her, bringing her the Annunciation of the Salvation of the World.[20] I am fully persuaded [that] they carried away above 5,000 pounds' weight, to keep in a memorial thereof. Then I remembered of the Chapel of Loreto and told the caravan that I had seen that house standing in Italy; which (as the Romanists say) was transported by the angels.[21]

'Oh!', said he, 'we Armenians cannot believe that; neither many other assertions of the Roman Church. For certainly, we know by Christians who have, from to time, dwelt here ever since, that this is both the place and stones of the house. Let papists coin a new Law to themselves. We care not, for as they err in this, so do they err in all. Following merely the traditions of men, they run galloping post [haste] to Hell'. The Patriarch, being informed by the laughing caravan of this news, asked me in disdain (thinking that it had been an article of my belief) if I had seen the house, or believed that the Chapel of Loreto was such a thing. To whom I instantly replied [that] I did not believe it, affirming [that] it was but a devilish invention to deceive the blind-folded people, and to fill the coffers of the Roman priests. Now, thou bottomless gulf of Papistry, here I forsake thee. No winter-blasting storms Furies of Satan's subtle storms[22] can make shipwreck of my Faith, on the stony shelves of the deceitful deeps. Thus, and after this manner too, are all the illusions of their imaginary and false miracles, first invented partly by monasterial poverty, then confirmed by provincial bribery, and lastly they are faith-sold for consistorical lucre.

Libidinous lechery

In the time of our staying here, the Emir (or Lord of the town) sent 6 women, conducted by his servants, to an Armenian prince who was a pilgrim in our company, to be used by him, and others whom so he would elect to be his fellow labourers. Which, indeed, he did kindly accept. And invited me to that feast. But I gave him the refusal, little regarding such a frivolous commodity. He and some of the chief pilgrims entertained them for the space of 3 hours, and sent them back, giving to their conductors 15 piastres in reward. Truly, if I would rehearse the impudency of these whores, and the brutishness of the Armenians, as it is most ignominious to the actors, so (no doubt) it would be the very loathsome to the reader. Such is the villainy of these Oriental slaves under the Turks that, not only be conversing with them, learn some of their damnable heretical customs, but also, going beyond them in beastly sensualness, become worse than brute beasts.

This makes me remember a worthy saying of that heathenish Roman Emperor Marcus Aurelius who, in consideration of fleshly lusts, said that although he was sure that God would not punish him for the offence, yet he would forbear it, in regard of the filthiness of the fact, in itself. Indeed, of a pagan a noble and virtuous resolution when such base and beastly Christians, these wretched Armenians, committed with these Infidelish harlots a twofold kind of voluptuous abomination, which my conscience commands me to conceal, lest I frequent this Northern world with that which their nature never knew, nor their knowledge have heard hearing of the like.

A villainous plot

But God, in His just judgements, that same night threatened both to have punished the doers; and the whole company, for their sakes. For we, having resolved to travel all that night, and because the way was rocky and hard to be known, and perilous for [with] Arabs, we hired a Christian guide named Joab, and agreed with him to take us to Lydda, which was 2 days' journey. But before we had advanced to our passage, Joab had sent a private messenger before [ahead of] us, to warn about 300 Arabs (who had their abode on the south side of Mt. Carmel) to meet him at such a place as he had appointed; giving them to know [that] we were rich, and well provided with chickenoes and sultans of gold, and piastres of silver; and that he should render us into their hands for such a recompense and consideration as their savage judgements should think fit, according to the spoils and booties they should obtain, together with the miserable murder of our lives. This being done, and unknown to us, we marched along, travelling faster than ordinary pace: some on horse, and some on foot; for my pilgrimage was ever pedestrial. Which our guide, suspecting that by our celerity, we should go beyond the place appointed for his treacherous plot, began to cross us grievously; leading us up and down amongst pools and holes, whither he listed; where many of our camels and asses were lost, and could not be recovered, because we all began to suspect and fear. Which was the cause that the owners durst not stay to relieve their perishing beasts.

In the end, the captain and janissaries entreated him earnestly to bring us in the right way. But the more they requested, the more obdurate was his heart; replying [that] he was mistaken, and could not find it [the path] till daylight; upon which words the company was stayed. And in the meantime there came a Turk, one of our soldiers, unto the captain, saying [that] he had seen a guide, before our departure from Nazareth, send a Moor before him, for what respect he knew not, being long at private conference. Whereupon they straight bound him with ropes, on a horse's back, threatening him with death, to cause him to confess the truth.

A treacherous guide

In the midst of this tumult I, having got sight of the North Star (which seemed exceedingly low to me) considered thereby that the villain had led us more to the southward than to the westward; which was our way to Jerusalem. Whereupon I entreated the caravan to turn our faces northward, otherwise we should be cut off; and that suddenly. For although (said I) it may peradventure be that we are 3 or 4 miles short of the place intended for our massacre, yet they, missing us will, like ravening wolves, hunt here and there. Wherefore, if we incline to the north, God willing, we shall prevent their bloody designs. To which advice (being duly pondered) they yielded. And so I became their guide, in that dark night, till morning. For none of them knew that star, neither the nature of it. At last this desperate wretch considering that, either by our vanquishing or the enemies' victory, he could not escape since his treason was revealed, began to beg of the caravan, saying that if he could have any surety of his life, he would sufficiently inform us how to eschew these eminent dangers: for we were all in extreme peril of our lives, and not so much courage nor comfort left us as the very smallest hope of any relief.

The captain, being distracted with fear, replied [that] he would; and thereupon swore a solemn oath. So did the janissaries swear, by the head of Muhammad, for the like effect. Which being done, he was untied, and confessed that if we had continued in our way he led us, we had been all put to the edge of the sword. And falling down upon his knees, cried with tears 'mercy', 'mercy', 'mercy'. All that night we went with the star, and against morning we were in the western confines of Phoenicia, and at the beginning of Palestine....

Here, by accident, in returning to the caravan, I met with an English factor[23], named Mr. Brockess, who then lived in Sidon, 18 miles from this place, and had been down at Acre, about some negotiations; who indeed, soon, and kindly, took me into a Moorish house by the sea where, instantly, we swallowed down such jovial and deep carouses of Leatic[?] wine that both he and I were almost fastened in the last plunge of understanding.

Yet nevertheless, he conveyed me back to my company, and put me safely into the hands of the caravan; with whom afterwards I several times met with here in London. To whose kindness I celebrate the memory of these lines.

But now the sun discovering the earth, and the night banished to the inferior world, we were all encouraged – for the light of day lends comfort. The captain (sending back that false Judas, for so he was sworn to do) sent a post to Tyre for a new guide; who came forthwith, and brought us in our way to Mt. Carmel....Great are the mercies of God, for as He had man an excellent creature, so has He also endued him with two great powers in his mind: the one, a wise power of understanding; by which he penetrates into the knowledge of things; the other a strong power of dextrous resolving, whereby he executes things well understood. For we, having judged the worst, resolved the best, and by His Almighty Providence were freed from that apparent danger, although the former day's whoredom and unnatural vices deserved better punishment.

This I intimate to all travellers in general: that if they would that God should further them in their attempts, bless their voyages, and grant them a safe return to their native countries (without which, what contentment have they for all their pains?) that they should constantly refrain from whoredom, drunkenness, and too much familiarity with strangers. For a traveller who is not temperate, and circumspect in all his actions, although he were headed like that Herculean serpent Hydra,[24] yet it is impossible [that] he can return in safety from danger of Turks, Arabs, Moors, wild beasts and the deadly operative extremities of heat, hunger, thirst and cold....

['Caffar; Caffar'][25]

Leaving Samaria on our left, we entered into a fair plain adorned with fruitful trees and all other ornaments that pleasant fields afford. But we saw no village. Marching thus, about the declining of the sun from the meridian, we came in sight of 200 pavilions, all pitched in ranks, yielding the prospect of a little city by the city of a brook. Which being perceived, the captain began to censure what they might be. And immediately there came riding towards us, 6 naked fellows, well-mounted on Arabian geldings, who demanded [to know] who we were; and whither we were bound with such a multitude; and if there were Franks of Christendom in our company. To whom the janissaries replied that we were purposed to Jerusalem, and that there was but one Frank with them. Upon the which they presented sought me, demanding 'Caffar!, Caffar!' That was a tribute for my head, and caused me, perforce (notwithstanding of the resisting caravan and the janissaries) to pay them, for my life, 7 chickenoes of gold: seven times nine shillings sterling! And that was because, they said, 'Our king is resident in these tents. And therefore we have tripled his tribute'. And yet they were discontented because there were no more Franks in our company; for, from the Armenians they could not (nor would not) seek any tribute because they were tributary slaves and subjects to the Great Turk. Neither also of any Christian born in his dominions, when they shall happen to fall into their hands.

The savage Arabian King

They, returning to their prince with the malediction of my heart and the sorrow of a pilgrim's purse, we, marching on our way, that day we travelled above 34 miles, and pitched [the caravan] at a village called Adoash, being composed of threescore Moorish and Arabian houses, standing in a fruitful and delicate plain, and garnished with olive, date and fig trees, which were both pleasant and profitable. Where we found also good herbs to eat, and abundance of water to drink, and also to fill our emptied bottles.

As we lay down to sleep after a heavy supper, on the hard ground, and our guard watching us, that same King of the Arabians came (a little before midnight) with 24 well-horsed renegades and naked courtiers, armed with bows and arrows, and half-pikes pointed at both ends with hard steel, and asked for the [captain of the] caravan. Who presently awoke and went to salute him, laying his hand on his breast, bowed his head very low (which is the usual courtesy amongst the Infidels and Christians in these parts: for they never uncover their heads to any man). And after some short parley, they sat all down on the grass. The [captain of the] caravan presented his rude-like majesty with water, bread, herbs, figs, garlic, and such things as he had. As they were thus merry, at this poor banquet, the awful King took the oath of our conductor if there were any more Franks there than I. And he, having sworn the truth, the King (by a malignant informer) incontinently caused me to be brought before him. And staring me in the face, [he] asked my interpreter where were my companions; who replied [that] I none. Then said he, 'Tell that dog, of Hell's hole, [that] he must acknowledge me with five pieces of gold more, or otherwise' (making a sign to his own throat), 'I shall cut his head because' (said he) 'I will not lose this night's travel for nothing'. The which, I being informed, and knowing that by no condition there was resistance against such a sclerate prince, gave it him forth out of my own hand, having consulted with the captain before. And that presently, with a half-smiling countenance, which he remarking, told the rest [that] it seemed I gave it with a good heart and a cheerful gesture. And to recompense my outward behaviour, he drunk a great draught of water to me, thinking thereby he had done me more honour than all the chickenoes of gold I gave him now, and in the morning, would do him profit or pleasure. Pleasure they could do him none; for they were unlawfully and dishonestly got, and too delivered from the inward sorrow of my sighing soul. And no wonder, having spent two great charges in Turkey before this time, but that I should have been exceedingly penurious of money, and thereupon desolate of relief and comfort. Truly this was one of the greatest tributes I paid for one day's journey that I had in all my voyage in Asia....

A dreadful conflict

Saturday morning before the breach of day, setting forward from Lydda, though the curling plains of fat-faced Palestine, scarcely were we advanced in our way, till we were beset by more than 300 Arabs who sent us, from shrubby heights, an unexpected shower of arrows: to the great annoyance of all our company. For, if it had not been that our soldiers shot off their guns on a sudden, and stood manly also to it with their bows and arrows to our defence, we had then miserably, in the midst of their ravenous fury, perished. But the nature of the Arabs is not unlike to [that of] the jackals. For when any of them hear the shot of an arquebus, they presently turn back with such speed, as if the fiends of the infernal court were broken loose at their heels.

In that momentary conflict, on our side there were killed 9 women [and] 5 men; and about 30 wounded: which to our worthy Armenian captain and to the rest of our heathenish conductors bred no small grief, the mourning noise among the multitude being also wondrous pitiful. Till bright day came, we stayed still in that same place, expecting the dangerous mutability of our austere fortune; and, at our departure thence, we buried the slain people in deep graves, whereby jackal should not open up their graves to eat their corpses. For such is the nature of these cruel beasts that they only love to live on man's flesh. These ravenous beasts (as is thought) are engendered of a fox and a wolf....

A grievous danger

And now, about halfway between Bera and Jerusalem I and two Armenians, advancing our way a flight shot ahead of the company; we, I say, unhappily encountered with 4 Moorish fellows, driving before them 6 asses laden with roots and shrubs of wood to burn. Who seeing us (as they thought, alone) laid hands upon us [and] robbed us of our pocket monies. Whereat, I resisting, one of them pulled forth a broad knife and, holding me by the beard, thought to have cut my throat, if it had not been for one of his fellows, who swiftly stayed him.

Well, they left us, following their beasts; and, our soldiers instantly appeared unto us; whereupon, we shouting, the Moors fled to the rocks, and our footsoldiers following, apprehended two of the chiefest, and brought them to the captain: one of which had my money; which I presently received back again, but my associates' money was with those who had escaped. The captain and janissaries meanwhile carried the two Moors along with them, thinking to execute them at Jerusalem. But their friends and neighbours, following fast on horseback and on foot, relieved them from the caravan, restoring back again the two Armenians' money: whereat all the Moors were exceedingly glad, and we noways discontented. For if they had not been redeemed, certainly their friends and their followers, who were thick flocking together, would have cut us all off, before we could have attained Jerusalem.

A joyful harmony. A dear night's supper

At last we beheld the prospect of Jerusalem, which was not only a contentment to my weary body, but also (being ravished with a kind of unwonted rejoicing) the tears gushed from my eyes for too much joy. In this time the Armenians began to sing, in their own fashion, Psalms in praise of the Lord. And I also sang the 103rd Psalm[26] all the way, till we arrived near the walls of the city; where we ceased from our singing, for fear of the Turks. The sun being passed to his nightly repose before our arrival, we found the gates locked, and the keys carried up to the Pasha in the castle. Which bred a common sorrow in the company, being all both hungry and weary. Yet the [captain of] the caravan entreated earnestly the Turks within to give us, over the walls, some victuals for our money, showing heavily the necessity we had thereof. But they would not; neither durst attempt any such thing.

In this time the Guardian of the monastery of the Cordeliers,[27] (who remained there to receive travellers from Christendom); who, having got news of our late arrival, came and demanded of the caravan if any franks of Europe were in his society; and he said 'only one'. Then the Guardian called me, and asked of what nation I was. And when I told him, he seemed exceedingly glad; yet sorrowful for our misfortune.

He, knowing my distress, returned; and sent 2 friars to me with bread, wine and fishes, which they let over the wall (as they thought, in a secret place). But they were spied; and, on the morrow the Guardian paid the sub-pasha a great fine, being 100 piastres (30 pounds sterling): otherwise both he and I had been beheaded. Which, I confess, was a dear-bought supper to the Greyfriar, and no less almost, to me – being both in danger of my life for starving, and then for receiving of food: therefore suspected for a traitor. For the Turks alleged that he had taken in munitions from me and from the other Christians, to betray the city. This they often, for a lesser fault than that was, to get bribes, and other money, from the Greyfriars, who daily stand in fear of their lives.

Anno Domini 1612, on Palm Sunday in the morning, we were entered into Jerusalem. And at the gate we were particularly searched, to the effect [that] we carried in no furniture or arms, nor powder, with us. And the poor Armenians (notwithstanding [but?] they are slaves to the Turks) behooved to render their weapons to the keepers. Such is the fear they [the Turks] have of Christians. And my name was written up in the clerk's book at the port, [so] that my tribute for the gate, and my seeing of the Sepulchre, might be paid at one time together, before my final departure thence....

A turpentine rod brought from Jordan and given to King James

Considering the ancient reputation of this famous river [the Jordan], and the rare sight of such an unfrequented place, I climbed up to the top of a turpentine tree which gave within the limited flood, a little above where I left my company (even naked, as I came from swimming) and cut down a fair hunting rod of the heavy and sad turpentine tree: being 3 yards long, wondrous straight, full of small knots, and of a yellowish colour. Which afterwards, with great pains, I brought to England, and presented it (as the rare gem of a pilgrim's treasure) to His Majesty.

But I remember [that], in the choosing thereof, an unexpected incident fell out. For I, being sequestered from the company, upon this solitary tree with broad obscuring leaves, the friars and soldiers removed, keeping their course towards Jericho. But within 2 furlongs from Jordan they were beset by the former nocturnal enemies, who assailed them with a hard conflict. For I, hearing the arquebus go off, was straight in admiration. And looking down on the place where I had left my associates, they were gone. So, bending my eyes a little further in the plain, I saw them at a martial combat. Which gave me, suddenly, the threatening of despair: not knowing whether to stay entrenched within the circundating leaves to approve the events of my auspicious fortunes, or, in prosecuting relief, to be participant in their doubtful deliverance. In the end, pondering [that] I could hardly, or never, escape their hands (either there, or by the way going to Jerusalem), leapt down from the tree, leaving my Turkish clothes lying upon the ground, took only in my hand the rod, and sash which I wore on my head, and ran, stark naked, above a quarter of a mile amongst thistles and sharp pointed grass which pricked the soles of my feet. But the fear of death, for the present, expelled my grief of that unlooked-for pain. Approaching on the safe side of my company, one of our soldiers broke forth on horseback, being determined to kill me for staying behind. Yea, and three time struck me with his half-pike. But his horse being at speed, I prevented his cruelty: first, by falling down; next, by running in amongst the thickest of the pilgrims, recovering the Guardian's face. Which, when the Guardian saw, and saw my naked body, he presently pulled off his grey gown and threw it at me, whereby I might hide the secrets of Nature. By which means (in the space of an hour) I was clothed three manner of ways: first, like a Turk; second, like a wild Arabian; and thirdly, like a Greyfriar: which was a barbarous, a savage, and a religious habit.

The Captain, at last entering in parley with the Arabs, by some contributing promises, did mitigate their fury. For their compounded acknowledgement was to be sent them from Jerusalem. Whereupon we, marching towards Jericho, reposed ourselves under a cooling shade, and dined there on the wine and provision carried with us.

NOTES

1 Side note in text: 'A French palliard': a professional beggar or vagabond (who sleeps on the straw in barns and outhouses); a low or dissolute knave, a lewd fellow, a lecher, a debauchee (*OED*).

2 It would appear that, during his stay in Constantinople, Lithgow stayed at the house of the English ambassador.

3 Bartizan: a battlemented parapet at the top of a castle or church, esp. an overhanging battlemented turret projecting from an angle at the top of a tower (*OED*).

4 Capuchins: one of the largest of the Roman Catholic Orders of friars, like the Jesuits, it was founded in Italy (*c.* 1525) at more or less the time of the Counter Reformation.

5 Libertine: probably in the sense of 'Acknowledging no law in religion or morals; free-thinking; antinomian. Also *occas.* pertaining to the sects known as Libertines' (*OED*). That may be a reference to the events described in Acts 6: 9: 'Then there arose certain of the synagogue, which is called the synagogue of the Libertines, and Cyrenians, and Alexandrians, and of them of Cilicia and of Asia, disputing with Stephen', who 'stirred up the people, and the elders, and the scribes...and set up false witnesses...against the disciple' (Acts 6: 12, 13).

6 Syncopa; bergamask: kinds of dance.

7 Schoolmen: some who professed the wide variety of philosophical and theological views of Western Christendom (invariably based upon the conjunction between faith and reason) between (broadly) the ninth and fourteenth centuries. Since virtually all medieval philosophers were also theologians, for many that meant the use of reason in order to make use of the methodologies of reason in order to clarify and deepen the prescriptions of faith; and thereby, ultimately to seek to provide a rational underpinning for faith: in the famous motto of St Anselm (1033?–1109), 'Faith seeking Understanding'. The thirteenth century is generally thought of as the 'golden age' of scholasticism, marked especially by the growth, in the universities (especially in Oxford and in Paris), of the study of Aristotle, whose works, for the first time, became available in reasonably accurate translations in Latin – some out of Arabic!

8 The relevant observations in the Qur'ān are probably the following (Penguin edition; translated by N. J. Dawood):

> We have made this tree a scourge for the unjust. It grows in the nethermost part of Hell, bearing fruit like devils' heads: on it shall they feed, and with it shall they cram their bellies, together with draughts of scalding water. Then to hell they shall return.
>
> (37: 48)

> The fruits of the Zaqqum tree shall be the sinner's food. Like dregs of oil, like scalding water, it shall simmer in his belly. A voice will cry: 'Seize him and drag him into the depths of Hell. Then pour scalding water over his head, saying: "Taste this, illustrious and honourable man! This is the punishment which you have doubted"'
>
> (44: 43)

> As for you sinners who deny the truth, you shall eat of the fruit of the Zaqqum tree and fill your bellies with it. You shall drink scalding water: yet you shall drink it as the thirsty camel drinks.
>
> (56: 55)

9 It is noteworthy that Lithgow here ignores not only the debates on predestination that can be found posited in the Bible (e.g. Romans 8: 28), but especially that of the impact on, and reworkings of, Calvinist ideas in the Protestant Reformation in England. What he seems to be stressing, once again, is the parallels between Islam and Catholicism: in this case, Jansenism (after Cornelis Jansen, 1585–1638).

10 Nones: a daily office, originally said at the ninth hour of the day (about 3 p.m.), but in later use sometimes earlier (*OED*).

11 The bodyguard of the Roman Emperors, it grew out of the troop of soldiers who attended upon the general responsible for guarding Rome. Constantine disbanded the guard (312 CE).

12 Cautelous: full of cautels; deceitful, crafty, artful, wily (*OED*).

13 Marginal note: 'Babylon [Baghdad] regained by the Persians'.

14 Compare this purportedly eye-witness account with those told by Cartwright and Biddulph.

15 Strangely, Lithgow here appears to misread. The name of Abraham's servant (Genesis 24) is not mentioned. The name Eleasar occurs in the Bible as (a) one of the sons of Aaron, designated as one of the priests of the Ark of the Covenant (Exodus 7: 23; 28: 1); (b) one of the 'mighty men of David' (2 Samuel 23: 9) and (in 2 Maccabbees 6: 18–31) in the Apocrypha.

16 Carob: fruit of a leguminous tree, a native of the Levant (*OED*).

17 Acts of the Apostles 9: 10–20.

18 2 Chronicles 2.

19 A puzzling remark. Lithgow might have in mind here the retaking of Jerusalem by Saladin (who was not a Tatar) in 1187, when his armies expelled the Crusaders, who had themselves conquered it in 1099. Saladin's conquest marked one of the moments of major rebuilding and restoration of the city under Mameluke and Ottoman rule.

20 St Luke 1: 28ff.

21 Loreto, in the Marche region of Italy. Legend has it that the house of the Virgin was transported, by air, to Loreto (1294); surrounded by the Church of Sanctuario della Santa Casa (begun 1468) by Pope Paul II (1464–71).

22 Splendid mixture of the Christian religion (the Devil) and the classical (the Furies: in Greek and Roman mythology winged women with serpent hair, the three daughters of Mother Earth out of the blood of Uranus; influential divinities who were the personifications of conscience who punished murder of kindred (especially matricide). In the myth of Orestes they act as Clytemnestra's agents. Having absolved Orestes of the crime of matricide, Athena provided them with a grotto in Athens, where they became known, euphemistically, as the Eumenides (the kindly ones)).

23 Factor: one who buys and sells for another person; a mercantile agent; a commission merchant (*OED*).

24 In Greek mythology, a water serpent with several heads; which had the additional feature that, if one were cut off, it would be replaced by two new ones. The second labour required of Hercules was that he should kill this serpent – which he did by burning the neck, once he had chopped off the heads.

25 Caffar: a word meaning 'Infidel', applied by the Arabs to all non-Muhammadans; also 'one who does not recognise the blessings of God'.

26 Bless the Lord, O my soul: and all that is within me, *bless* his holy name...

27 Friars of the Franciscan Order, so known from the knotted cord they wear tied around the waists.

OTHER EDITIONS

A most delectable, and true discourse, of an admired and painefull peregrination from Scotland to the most famous kingdomes in Europe, Asia and Affricke..., London: N.Okes...sold by T. Archer, 1614; reprinted 1616; 'Newly imprinted and...inlarged by the author, with certain relations of his second and third travels', 1623; facsimile edition Amsterdam: Theatrum Orbis Terrarum/New York: Da Capo Press, 1971; edited and with notes by Gilbert Phelps, London: Folio Society, 1974.

Discourse of a peregrination in Europe, Asia and Affricke, 1632, 1640, 1682, 1692; also in S. Purchas, *Purchas his Pilgrimes*, 1625; abridged edition London: Jonathan Cape, 1928 ('Travellers Library').

Willem Lithgouws 19.Jarrige Lant-Reyse, uyt Schotlant...uy'tt Engels overgeset, 1652 (three further editions: 1656; 1661; 1669).

Travels and Voyages, 1770 (referred to as the 11th edition); 1814 (referred to as the 12th edition. Illustrated with Notes from later travellers).

The travels and adventures of W. L in Europe, Asia and Africa, during nineteen years. A chapbook. Glasgow 1816; Falkirk 1825; Glasgow 1850.

FURTHER READING

Boies Penrose, *Urbane Travellers, 1591–1635*, Philadelphia: University of Pennsylvania Press, 1942.

9

SIR HENRY BLOUNT

A voyage into the Levant. A Breife Relation of a Iourney, lately performed by Master H. B. Gentleman, from England by the way of Venice, into Dalmatia, Sclavonia, Bofnia, Hungary, Macedonia, Thessaly, Thrace, Rhodes and Egypt, unto Gran Cairo. With particular observations concerning the moderne condition of the Turkes, and other people under that Empire.

London, Printed by I. L. for Andrew Crooke, and to be sold at the signe of the Beare in Pauls Church-yard. 1636.

BIOGRAPHY

Sir Henry Blount (1602–82), born in Hertfordshire, educated at St Albans, Trinity College Oxford (BA: 1618), and Gray's Inn. Having previously paid short visits to France, Italy and Spain, Blount embarked on the voyage on which his account is based. Leaving Venice (May 1634), his galley sailed down the Adriatic to Spalato in Dalmatia. From there he crossed the Dinaric Alps and the Bosnian Plains to arrive at Sarajevo after a journey that lasted nine days. Leaving from there in the company of the Turkish Army then on the way to the war against Poland, he reached Belgrade three days later. From there, via Sofia (Bulgaria) and Adrianople, he reached Constantinople after fifty-two days of travel overland of some 1,500 miles (2,400 km) in distance. Having stayed in Constantinople for five days (for which shortness of duration, he apologies in the text) he managed to find passage with the Turkish fleet then on the way to Egypt, where he visits Alexandria and Cairo and excursions to Gizeh and to the labyrinth at Fayyum. His return journey was on board a French vessel to Palermo; then, via Rome, Florence, Bologna and Venice, back to England. Knighted by Charles I, Blount sided with the Royalists, and was one of the monarch's attendants at several battles; though that did not apparently disbar him from being asked to serve on various commissions, including one (1655) on the trade and navigation of the Commonwealth, and, once again (1669), on trade after the Restoration. Blount's *DNB* entry praises with faint damns:

> The truth seems to be that although apparently wanting in several qualities of a good travel writer [not specified], he combined with a sturdy independence of thought keen powers of observation of men and manners. The modern flavour of the latter is quite refreshing.

175

SIR HENRY BLOUNT

Blount's younger son, Charles Blount (1654–93), was a follower of Hobbes and author of texts such as *The Oracles of Reason* (1693) and *Reasons humbly offered for the liberty of unlicens'd printing* (1693).

* * *

[Introduction]

Intellectual complexions have no desire so strong, as that of knowledge; nor is any knowledge unto man so certain, and pertinent, as that of humane affairs, this experience advances best in observing of people whose institutions much differ from ours. For customs conformable to our own, or to such wherewith we are already acquainted, do but repeat our old observations, with little acquist of new. So my former time spent in viewing Italy, France, and some little of Spain, being countries of Christian institution, did but represent in a several dressed, the effect of what I knew before.

Then seeing the customs of men are much swayed by their natural dispositions, which are originally inspired and composed by the climate whose air, and influence they receive, it seems natural that, to our Northwest parts of the world, no people should be more averse, and strange of behaviour than those of the South-East. Moreover those parts being now possessed by the Turks, who are the only modern people, great in action, and whose Empire so suddenly invaded the world, and fixed itself such firm foundations as no other did; I was of opinion, that he who would behold these times in their greatest glory, could not find a better scene then Turkey.

These considerations sent me thither; where my general purpose gave me four particular cares: first, to observe the religion, manners, and policy[1] of the Turks, not perfectly, (which were a task for an inhabitant rather than a passenger,) but so far forth, as might satisfy this scruple – to wit: whether to an impartial conceit, the Turkish way appears absolutely barbarous, as we are given to understand, or rather as other kind of civility, different from ours, but no less pretending. Secondly, in some measure, to acquaint my self with those other sects which live under the Turks, as Greeks, Armenians, Franks, and Zingaraes.[2] But especially the Jews; a race from all others so averse, both in nature and institution, as glorying to single itself out of the rest of mankind, remains obstinate, contemptible, and famous. Thirdly, to see the Turkish army, then going against Poland, and therein to note whether their discipline military incline to ours, or else is of a new mould, though not without some touch, from the countries they have subdued; and whether it is of a frame apt to confront the Christians. The last and choice piece of my intent, was to view Gran Cayro [Cairo]: and that for two causes. First, it being clearly the greatest concourse of mankind in these times, and perhaps that ever was, there must needs be some proportionable spirit in the government. For such vast multitudes, and those of it so deeply malicious, would soon breed confusion, famine, and utter desolation, if in the Turkish domination there were nothing but sottish sensuality, as most Christians conceive. Lastly, because Egypt is held to have been the fountain of all science and all arts civil, therefore I did hope to find some spark of those cinders not yet put out; or else in the extreme contrariety I should receive an impression as important, from the ocular view of so great a revolution.

For above all other senses the eye, having the most immediate and quick commerce with the soul, gives it a most smart touch to the rest, leaving in the fancy somewhat unutterable; so that an eyewitness of things conceives them with an imagination more complete, strong, and intuitive, than he can either apprehend, or deliver by way of relation. For relations are not only in great part false, out of the relater's misinformation, vanity, or interest; but (which is unavoidable), their choice and frame agrees more naturally with his judgement, whose issue they are then with his readers. So that the reader is like one feasted with dishes fitter for another man's stomach than his own apprehension affects; and through that sympathy can digest them into an experience more natural for himself than he could have done the notes of another.

Wherefore I, desiring somewhat to inform myself of the Turkish nation, would not sit down with a book knowledge thereof, but rather (through all the hazard and endurance of travel), receive it from my own eye, not dazzled with any affection, prejudacy or mist of education, which preoccupate the mind, and delude it with partial ideas, as with a false glass, representing the object in colours, and proportions untrue. For the just censure of things is to be drawn from their end whereto they are aimed, without requiring them to our customs, and ordinances, or other impertinent respects, which they acknowledge not for their touchstone. Wherefore he who passes through the several educations of men, must not try them by his own, but weaning his mind from all former habit of opinion, should as it were putting off the old man, come fresh and sincere to consider them.

This preparation was the cause, why the superstition, policy, entertainments, diet, lodging, and other manners of the Turks, never provoked me so far as usually they do those who catechise the world by their own home. And this also bars these observations from appearing beyond my own closet; for, to a mind possessed with any set doctrine, their unconformity must needs make them seem unsound, and extravagant, nor can they comply, to a rule, by which they were not made. Nevertheless, considering that experience forgotten as if it never had been, and knowing how much I ventured for it, as little as it is, I could not but esteem it worth retaining in my own memory, though not transferring it to others. Hereupon I have, in these lines, registered myself whatsoever most took me in my journey from Venice to Turkey.

[Blount now provides a fairly extensive description of the voyage, marked by comments about each of the places at which he stopped. While the story he tells contains a multitude of fascinating snippets of information about places and peoples, it seems to me that the importance of his contribution to the discursive construction of early modern Orients can perhaps best be seen in his deliberate endeavour to offer some sort of general theory – especially having to do with Turks and with Jews in the Ottoman Empire. Blount informs his readers that:]

Thus have I set down such observations, as were of passage local, and naturally borne along, with the places whereon I took them. Now follow the more abstract and general concerning the institutions, of a reckoning made in haste, and thereby subject to the disadvantage of a hasty view: that is, to over-slip many things, and to see the rest but superficially. Yet usually quick glances, take in the most eminent places, amongst which there are some like the dye of scarlet, best discerned by a passing eye, than a fixed; of this nature I esteem the moral points of behaviour. A newcomer apprehends them with a judgement fresh, and sincere, which further familiarity corrupts with affection, or hatred, according as it meets a disposition conform, or contrary.

The most important parts of all States are four: arms, religion, justice, and moral customs. In treating of these most men set down what they should be, and regulate that by their own silly education and received opinions guided by sublimities and moralities imaginary. This I leave to Utopians who doting on their fantastic supposals, show their own capacity, or hypocrisy, and no more. I, in remembering the Turkish institutions, will only register what I found them, nor censure them by any rule, but that of more, or less sufficiency to their aim: which I suppose [is] the Empire's advancement. First, then, I note their arms; because in the sway of men's affairs it is found [that] in that fear is the strongest of the passions, awes all the rest. Their infantry consists of two sorts. First, such as levied upon particular cities. They are more or less according to occasion, the ability of the town, and distance from which summoned. Many of them are Christians, and are sent forth much better appointed in clothes than with us; each town in several colours, and their arms sufficient. They are lodged and exercised outside the city [for] almost a month, before they begin to march.

The other part, and chief strength, is of the janissaries, whose number, at my being in Turkey, was 440,000, which (as it says) they use to supply upon occasion, but never exceed. The manner is to reinforce these bonds thus: every now and then there are sent out officers into several provinces, (especially the northern) who, out of all the Christian children, from the age of 10 to 18 or 20, choose, without stint or exception, such as they think fit, and carry them to Constantinople. These they call Agemoglans. Then, after some observation of their persons, those of most promising parts, are selected for the Grand Seignior's Seraglio's: either that of Constantinople, or his other at Adrianople, where they are taught to write and read, to understand Arabic, to use their bow, with other weapons. Then cull they out the choicest sparks; who, as their capacities grow approved, are instructed in State affairs and, by degrees, taken into highest preferments. They are called Icholglans. The worst, and of least quality, are assigned to the drudgery of the household, to the gardens and other base offices. Some are made mariners, and galeots. The general sort, neither rare, nor contemptible are by the Aga of the janissaries distributed abroad, where without charge to the Prince, they earn their living by hard labour, till the age of 22. Then so inured to endurance befitting a soldier they are brought back, taught their arms, and prepared for service. These are enrolled [as] janissaries.

This choice and education of persons apt to each use, must needs make it excellently performed, as being more natural than the course of Christendom, where princes put arms into the hands of men neither by spirit nor education martial; and entrust their chief employments, with respects of birth, riches, or friends. Which, to the services intended, are qualities not so proper as those personal abilities, which prevail in the Turkish election. These, the sons of Christians, hate that name above all others, and are found, (as I have seen some of them) without any natural affection to their parents, as it were transplanted, acknowledging themselves the creatures of the Ottoman family; so much are the present engagements of life too strong for all formal types of blood....

The Turks rather think the Christians now as strong, as heretofore, and therefore not to need the former diminution. Experience made me of this opinion, considering that it is many years since most of his Christian countries were taken in, and how every age dyes them of a more deeper Mahometan [hue?] than other. But should he win any Christian a province of new, he would not spare this way to exhaust it, till it were sufficiently ener-vated. The mortallest corruption of this Order has happened of late years. That is, knowing their own strength, and grown saucy with familiarity at Court, they have proceeded to such insolency, as has fleshed them in the blood of their Sovereign, Sultan Osman. And in Mustapha they have learnt that damnable secret of making, and unmaking their kind at pleasure; whereby the foundation of all monarchy, that is, the due awe towards the Blood Royal, is so irreparably decayed in them as like the lost state of Innocence, can never be restored.

[Military and colonial policy]

Muhammad knowing he had not to deal with policies scholastic and speculative generation, but with a people rude, and sensual, made not his Paradise to consist in visions, and
hallelujahs; but in delicious fare, pleasant gardens, and wenches with great eyes, who were
ever peculiarly affected in the Levant. To such as die in wars for the Mahometan faith, he
promises that their souls shall suddenly have given them young lusty bodies, and set in
Paradise, eternally to enjoy those pleasures, notwithstanding any former sins. To those who
die other deaths, he assigns a Purgatory tedious, and at last not such an height of pleasure.
It is scarce credible, what numbers these hopes bring in: I have seen troops sometimes of
above an hundred together – so effectual an instrument of State in superstition, and such
deep impressions does it make, when fitted to the passions of the subject, and that useful
in those whom neither reason, nor honour could possess.

Herein their proceeding is directly contrary to [that of] the Spaniards, he not having
multitudes of his own sufficient to plant colonies, is forced in all his conquests, (if he will
have any people to govern over,) to preserve the naturals. Now they, not being assured in
affection, must be awed by fortresses – which is a way, not unsure, but so chargeable, as
makes him gain but little by his winnings. The Turk on the other side, well stored with
people; first, considers what numbers of his own, he will assign for timariots to each
province which he takes; then he destroys all its nobility, and so far of the vulgar, till there
rest only such a proportion as may till the land, and be awed by those timariots with other
ready forces. That remainder is kept to manure the land. This thus established, he needs
not the fortress for himself; nor will he leave it as a refuge for enemies, or rebels. Yet if it
be a frontier, he does not quite demolish it, but keeps it in such case, as may hold out till
he might send an army, ever supposing himself master of the field; wherefore as it stands
in more, or less danger, so is it provided. Thus in Hungary the castle of Belgrade is neither
razed, nor carefully maintained; but that of Buda is guarded with a strong garrison; all
those within the kingdom are pulled down; so is it in his other countries.

Religion

Now follows their religion, wherein I noted only the political institutions thereof; these
observations moving only in that sphere, cannot jar with a higher, though the motion
seem contrary. Muhammad, noting the outward solemnities wherewith other religions
entertained the minds of men; he judged them perhaps in part, effeminate; as those dainty
pictures, and music in churches, those strange vestures, and processions, and partly
chargeable, as those stately sacrifices, and other solemnities of the heathen, and all driven
already, to that height, as he could not out-go. Wherefore he refused to build his sect
thereon. Nor did he much affect to support it with miracles, whose credit frequent impos-
tors have rendered suspected to the world; but rather chose to build it upon the sword,
which with more assurance commands mankind.

Every novelty draws men in for a while. But where the gain is not great, they soon
grow weary, unless compulsion hold them on. Therefore in his first beginnings, when he
was asked what miracles he had to approve his doctrine, he drawing forth his scimitar, told

that God, having had his miracles so long slighted by the incredulity of men, would now plant his laws with a strong hand, and no more leave them to the discretion of the ignorant, and vain man; and that he had therefore sent him in the power of the sword, rather than of miracles. From hence it is that now their boys ride to circumcision, bearing an iron club in their hands. Nevertheless, he failed not to frame his sect so as might take human nature. Nor the intellectual part; for all superstition subsists on weak hypotheses, whose plausible reason may for a while prevail in the world, by possessing some shallow, rash, peremptory brains, but cannot hold out long, unless it has better root, than that of argument. He therefore made it comply with the main parts of our nature – hope, and fear. To the one he set out a Paradise; to the other, though not a Hell, yet a shrewd Purgatory.

His preaching of Paradise, more than Hell, favours hope above fear, thereby filling the mind with good courage; which was much to his military purpose. For he, finding the sword to be the foundation of Empires, and that to manage the sword, the rude and the sensual are more vigorous, then wits softened in a mild rational way of civility, did first frame his institutions to a rude insolent sensuality; after which education he fitted his future pretences just unto such capacities. Wherefore seeing that men's opinions are in great part complexional and habitual it is no wonder to see them taken with promises, which to us seem beastly and ridiculous. They as much despise ours; and in a more natural way. Everything is received, not at the rate of its own worth, but as it agrees with the receiver's humour; whereby, their hopes, and fears, though false, prevail as strongly as if true, and serve the state as effectually, because opinion which moves all our actions, is governed by the apparancy of things, not by their reality.

Now, to the intent that the most notable fancies of men might be entertained, there are four several orders in their religion, all very malicious against Christians. Otherwise I have not noticed them vicious, excepting their professed sodomy which, in the Levant is not held a vice. Each order upholds its reputation upon some one peculiar virtue, which alone it professes, not pretending to any other:...So dangerous are violent spirits when seconded by religion, which, being the only pretence in its way glorified to umpire sovereign authority, is to be kept within its due limits. Left in stead of co-operating with the State, it grows abused beyond that use.

All the sects are governed by one head, called the Mufti, whose authority unites, and orders them; suppressing such disorders, as the scruples, or interests of men raise. This Mufti is created by the Emperor, to whom he is held ever subordinate: which makes the Turkish theology excellently to correspond with the State, as depending thereon; and seems of reason more politic than if this head ecclesiastic were of another country, or otherwise independent upon the Prince, whereby, having interests apart, he might often make God Almighty seem to decree more conformity thereto than either to the occasions of the Prince, or common wealth. For all heathenish Gods are used like puppets. They seem to speak, yet it is not they, but the man who, in a concealed manner, speaks through them what he pleases. That part is acted by the expounders of their Qur'ān as of the Oracles, or Sibyl's books[3] of old. Hereby the Mufti serves to animate the soldiers, by colouring of public impresses with divine authority; and also to decide controversies when they are too unruly for any arbitrement not held divine. Wherefore [about which?] he frequently consults with the Grand Vizier who, as the soul of the State, inspires him to the purpose thereto.

Full of that god [which] he gives his Oracles, they pass for grounded upon the Qur'ān which is given out for the Word of God. It is written in Arabic verse, in [the] form of dialogue between the Angel Gabriel, and their Prophet. It is prohibited to be translated, which both preserves the Arabic tongue, and conceals religion. All set texts are obnoxious to several expositions. [From] thence grows distraction. So has this bred 4 different sects of Mahometans, each interpreting it according to the genius of its nation: the Tartars, simply; the Moors and Arabs, superstitiously; the Persian, ingeniously; the Turks with most liberty. Each nation scorns to yield unto the other in opinion; for honour's sake – especially the Turk and Persian who, intending the conquest of one another, do, after the old custom of Princes, disaffect their people in religion toward the enemy [so] that they may be more fierce and obstinate against him.

In this point the Turk grows disadvantaged; for of late, his people begin to be infected with Persianism. I have heard many of them in public acknowledge the Persians better Mahometans then themselves; which makes the Turks much braver soldiers upon the Christian than upon the Persian. Against the one, they are carried by zeal, malice, and disdain, but against the other, only by national emulation. This impression is made deeper by many other circumstances; insomuch that several janissaries have told me that they go to the wars of Persia very unwillingly, but to these of Poland, or Hungary as to pastimes. One of their priests told me of an old prophecy, they have: that their Emperor should win the red apple; and, in the seventh year after, if they did not defend themselves bravely, the Christians should overcome them. But, however, in the twelfth, they should, at the furthest, be overcome by the Christians. The red apple (he said) was Constantinople – though some (quoth he) hold it to be Rome. I, holding such prophecies rather cunning than true, searched after the plot thereof; wherefore I entreated him to tell me how much time was contained in those years. He answered that each year some had limited by the age of Muhammad; but (quoth he) in vain, for it is prohibited us to search into the times appointed. That clause gave me some light; for I remembered, among other causes of a State's preservation, one assigns proximity of danger. His reason is [that] because apprehension of danger causes vigilance and diligence wherein lies safety. Hereupon this Prophet, to make the Turks vigilant against the Christian, threatens them with the seventh year; yet not so inevitable that valour may resist. And, to make every year provided against as that, therefore is it prohibited to fix the time determinate. Then their fatal destruction not to pass the twelfth year makes them, in the meanwhile, use the Christians as their future destroyers, with much hostility, as revenge anticipate. Which serves right to the purpose of the State. And when all comes to all those years, as such prophetical times used [to do] are like to prove very long ones.

Amongst other qualities whereby Mahometism possesses the minds of men, one is its pleasing doctrine. I remember when their Prophet in the Qur'ān asks the Angel concerning venery, and some other delicacies of life, he tells him that God did not give man such appetites, to have them frustrated, but enjoyed as much for the gusto of man, not his torment, wherein his Creator delights not. These kind of opinions will ever be well-come to flesh and blood, when as the contrary over-great severity of Discipline would have pleased none, but some few austere complexions – and to the greater part would have seemed but a persecution of Nature, or perhaps hypocritical, whose reputation might soon have been lost in scandal.

The cunning of that seconding humane inclination appears in the different success of two politic acts of the Qur'ān. The one permits polygamy: to make a numerous people – which is foundation of all great Empires. The other, pretending a Devil in every grape, prohibits wine. Thereby it hardens the soldier, prevents disorder, and facilitates public provision. The first, as pleasing to Nature, is generally received. The other is borne down by appetite, so that more drink wine than forbear. Thus he, maintaining his institutions by seconding of humane disposition, succeeds more readily than those whose ordinances by crossing it, go as it were, against the hair. Now the greatest number of men being governed by the passions, in all people they have been entertained, for the present life, with justice, for the future, with religion. Yet there were ever found some few intellectual complexions, in whom the understanding prevailed above the passions. Those discerning wits could not receive the gross supposals upon which the heathenish superstitions relied. Wherefore, to train them in such ways as civil societies require, they were instructed in a seeming rational way, wherein they were amused about an intelligible world, stored with rewards of honour, virtue, and knowledge, with punishment of infamy, vice, and ignorance....

Before I shut up this point of Turkish religion, I must remember two principal points; one is Predestination, the other Purgatory. The first not meant in matter of salvation, but of fortune, and success in this life. They peremptory permit to [a] Destiny fixed, and not avoidable by any act of ours. I had two notable examples. One was at Rhodes, where (just as we entered the port), a French lackey of our company died with a great plague which he had taken of the gunner's mate, who with one running upon him, conversed, and slept amongst us. The rest were so far from fear at his death that they sat presently eating and drinking by him; and within half an hour after his removal, slept on his blanket, with his clothes instead of a pillow. Which, when I advised them not to do they pointed upon their foreheads, telling me [that] it was written there at their birth when they should die. They escaped: yet several of the passengers died before we got to Egypt. The other was my passage to Adrianople in Thrace. Myself, the janissary, and one more being in a coach, we passed by a man of good quality and a soldier who, lying along (with his horse by) could hardly speak as much, as to entreat us to take him into coach. The janissary made our companion ride his horse, taking the man in; whose breast being open, and full of plague tokens, I would not have him received. But he, in like manner, pointing to his own forehead, and mine, told me we could not take hurt, unless it were written there, and that then we could not avoid it. The fellow died in the night, by our sides; and in our indemnity approved this confidence to be sometimes fortunate, how wise soever....

They admit no Hell for any but those who believe not Muhammad. Their own they affright with a Purgatory which holds but till Doomsday. It is acted [out] in the grave. The pain is inflicted by a Bad Angel, whose force is lessened by a Good one, according as the party's life was led. To strengthen this Good Angel they do many works of charity. This furnishes all Turkey with excellent hanes, hospitals and mosques; this makes the best bridges and highways that can be imagined; and stores them with fountains for the relief of passengers. These fair works so caused, seemed to me like dainty fruit growing on a dunghill. But the virtues of vulgar minds are of so base a nature as must be manured with foolish hopes and fears, as being too gross for the finer nutriment of reason....

The main points, wherein Turkish justice differs from that of other nations, are three: it is more severe, speedy, and arbitrary. They hold the foundation of all empire to consist in exact obedience, and that in exemplary severity, which is undeniable in all the world, but more notable in their State, made up of several people different in blood, sect, and interest, one from another, not linked in affection or any other common engagement toward the public good other than what mere terror puts upon them – a sweet hand were ineffectual upon such a subject, and would as soon find itself slighted. Therefore the Turkish justice curbs and executes, without either remorse or respect – which succeeds better than ever did the Romans, with all their milder arts of civility. Compare their conquests with those made by the Turk [and] you shall find his to continue quiet and firm, theirs not secure for many ages: witness first Italy, then Greece, and France, always full of rebellions, conspiracies, and new troubles – which were caused by their lenity that did not humble the conquered so low as it should.

For rebellion is nothing but bold discontent. So that, as there is required discontent, so must there be also some strength of spirit, without which the discontent cannot quicken into rebellion, but faints into a stupified humility. All victory disgusts the subdued; a mild victor leaves that disgust spirit for mischief. But the remorseless way of the Turk, mortifies it by an oppression that secures him. To this effect, I have heard several of them boast that God had appointed them for an iron rod over other nations....Nor does he so much rely upon the people's affection (which would tie him to a respectful, and less absolute domination, and then also to be in their power to alter), as upon that strength which in his own hand makes him more himself, and binds with the eye of fear, whereto humane nature is ever enthralled.

The second point wherein their justice excels, is the quick despatch. If the business is present matter-of-fact, then (upon the least complaint), the parties and testimonies are taken and suddenly brought before the judge, by certain janissaries, who (with great staves) guard each street, as our night watchmen with halberds at London. The cause is ever in two hours dispatched [and] execution instantly performed unless it appears a cause so important that is allowed an appeal...where also it is as speedily decided. If it is matter of title, or right, the parties name their witnesses, who shall presently be forced to come in. For they have no old deeds, or any other reckonings, beyond the memory of man. In such cases, possession, and modern right carries it, without that odious course of looking too far backward into the times past. This expedition avoids confusion, and clears the court; whereby it becomes sufficient for many causes, and so for a great people....

The last notable point of their judicature is [that] they have little fixed law....Yet they pretend to judge by the Qur'ān, whereby the opinion of divine authority does countenance those arbitrary decisions, which without some authentic law to justify them, would hardly be endured. This Qur'ān is manifestly no book of particular law cases; wherefore they pretend its study does not inform the judge literally, but by way of illumination; which not being given to secular persons, does neatly put losers off, from referring themselves to the text. The justice, being arbitrary, makes it in their opinion, the more to the purpose of the public. For the judges, knowing themselves but instruments of State, and that in its favour is their establishment, they will ever judge by the interest thereof, if not out of honesty, yet for their own advancement.

I must eternally remember the Turkish justice for honourable to strangers, whereof I have twice had experience. First...in Bosnia, where I was forced to justice by a Christian, whom I had sore wounded for threatening to buy me for a slave. When the cause was declared by two Turks, my companions; the judge not only freed me with words, and gesture very respectful, but fined my adversary at 40 dollars, and menaced him with death, if any mischief were plotted against me. Another time at Adrianople, eleven, or twelve of us supping together, all Turks but myself; there was...an officer very eminent about the Emperor's person. He drank so beastly drunk, that, in the night, he having a lodging in the top of the house, mistook himself, tumbled off to the ground, and within few hours died. The next morning, all the company was imprisoned but I, who in the night, had escaped out at a decayed corner of the house, and hid myself under a bridge outside the city. Every man was fined as circumstance did either excuse, or aggravate: the least paid 4,000 aspers; some twice as much. The judge, by reason of my flight, suspected some extraordinary guilt in me, and had sent out janissaries for my apprehension. I, seeing the outrageous drunkenness of the Turks, had all my voyage pretended for till less than a commandment in the religion of my country, not to drink above three draughts at a meeting; whereby the respect of conscience gave me the privilege of sobriety, which no other could have obtained. Wherefore when the judge was by the rest informed of my abstinence, and that I had no hand in the excess, he called back to the officers and pronounced me free. Wherein, whether he regarded me as abstemious, or as a stranger, I could not learn.

Upon this body of their laws I will set one note concerning their head. Every State is then best fitted when its laws and governors suit with the end whereto it is framed. A State ordered only to preservation is then happy when its laws not only bid peace, for that is vain; but contrive it – and when the Prince is of Nature peaceable. But the Turkish Empire is originally composed to amplify by war, and for that purpose, keeps the soldiers in continual pay; wherefore it is best fitted with a Prince of nature violent, and warlike, of which strain the Mahometan race use to be. And when any of them hath chance to prove mild, though never so just and religious, it had been found less profitable, and glorious to the Empire than the violence of the others, although accompanied with much tyranny. Therefore the supposed errors of Sultan Murad (now reigning) being manifestly those of a stout spirit, agree with [the] violent nature of the government – wherein they are not so pernicious as the Christians imagine.

To these better parts of their justice, I must attack the main disorder which defames it; that is, their insatiable covetousness; which in a moral, or theological way, this discourse cannot lay hold off. But in respects civil, it is a thing of dangerous effect, many times disappointing commands of greatest consequence. Charles VIII of France lost the kingdom of Naples not so much by any other error than by the covetousness of his Treasurer, the Cardinal of St. Malo in detaining such disbursements as the King had appointed to the provisions thereof. Nor can there be any greater defeat of public designs than when the commands whereon they rely are, by the avarice of the inferior magistrate, made frustrate. Wherefore I noted it as a pernicious piece of government that, after the Pashas had, at Sophia made public proclamation to hang all janissaries who should be found behind them; yet did I see many very confidently stay behind, and make their peace for money with the governors of provinces. Some told me that if it should come to the Emperor's notice, he would put those governors to cruel deaths.

The fourth point proposed was their moral parts. Those I compare to glasses. The education and laws of a country are the moulds wherein they are blown to this, or that, shape; but the metal is the spirit of a man. Therefore with that I will begin. It has been maintained that men are naturally born: some to slavery; others to command; [that] different complexions make men timid, dexterous, patient, industrious, and (of other qualities), right for service. Others are naturally magnanimous, considerate, rapacious, daring, and peremptory. No man can say [that] Nature intends the one sort to obey, the other to rule. For if Nature has intentions, yet is it vanity to argue them by our model...sure: the latter are prone to invade the others – and they are as apt to bear. The different of spirit is manifest: sometimes in whole nations. As, to compare the Spanish with the Sicilian: the bravery of the one, the pusillanimity of the other, seems to mark out the one for domination, the other for bondage.

Thus, if every race of man was born with spirits able to bear down the world before them, I think [that] it would be the Turk. He is, in his behaviour (howsoever otherwise) the right son of Ishmael: every man's hand is against his, and his against every man. Between Christendom and Persia he has all the world against him. He still designs one, for his task. And that not as other princes [desire], for counterpoise with intent of peace, but with a resolution irrevocably engaged to be all or nothing. Unto the greatness of their Empire I do much ascribe the greatness of their spirits. No man can expect in Lucca or Genoa, such vastfold men, as in old Rome. For mighty Empires exercise their subjects in mighty employments. Which makes them familiar with admirable examples and great victories, whereby our minds are enlarged. Whereas petty States, with their petty employments [notion of petty and large], timid counsels, and frequent disgraces, impoverish and enfeeble men's fancies, rendering them pusillanimous: and too straight for good thoughts.

Now, as all constitutions of bodies are prone to several diseases peculiar to their frame, so have the minds of men to several abilities some proper way of error: the subtle to be malicious, false, and superstitious; the timid inclined to breach of promise, to base ways of revenge, and the like. The magnanimous are apt to be corrupt with a haughty insolence (though, in some sort, generous). This is the Turkish way – remorseless to those who bear up, and therefore mistaken for beastly. But such it is not; for it constantly receives humiliation with much sweetness. This, to their honour (and my satisfaction) I ever found. I had almost hourly experience hereof; which my unsoiled success makes me not blush to remember.

Yet, not to weary my pen, I will note only my second day's journey which, in the contrary entertainment of myself and a Ragusean, gave me the first taste. I, clad in Turkish manner, rode with two Turks, an hour ahead of our Caravan. We found 4 Spahi-Timariots by a river[side] where we stayed. They were at dinner. And, seeing by my head [that] I was a Christian, they called to me. I, not understanding what they would, stood still till they menacing their weapons, rose and came to see me, with looks very ugly. I, smiling, met them and, taking him who seemed to be of most port by the hand, laid it upon my forehead: which, with them, is the greatest sign of love and honour. Then, often calling him 'Saltanum', spoke English. Which, though none of the kindest, yet I it gave such a sound that to them, who understood no further, might seem affectionate, humble, and hearty. Which so appeased them that they made me sit and eat together. And parted loving.

Presently after, they met the caravan where was the Ragusean, a merchant of quality, who had come in at Spalatro to go to Constantinople; he being clothed in the Italian fashion, and spruce. They jostled him. He, not yet considering how the place had changed his condition, stood upon his terms; till they, with their axes and iron maces (the weapons of that country) broke two of his ribs: in which case [condition] we left him – half-dead; either to go back as he could, or be devoured by beasts.

Not two hours afterwards, I, walking alone, on the other side of the river, met 6 or 7 more who, espying a dagger in my pocket, snatched it suddenly, and set it against my breast. Wherewith one of them, speaking Italian, I won so far upon them with respective [respectful] words that they had me into a house, where we ate, drank and lodged together. And though some got very drunk, none offered me any injury; but kindly advised me to lay aside that weapon, and use such as the country permitted. Finally, after daily success in the like kind, I grew so confident of the Turkish nature that when lances or knives were often set against me, I doubted not myself: unless it were by a drunkard or a soldier volunteer. For drink makes the fancy of the one uncertain; and the other, going

185

to merit Paradise by killing of Christians, was no safe company for me. Nor were my ways framed only to receive insolence, able to entertain malice especially a malice engaged by religion.

This haughty disposition of theirs makes the fashions of other countries rather despised than imitated: so that in all inland Turkey, where Christian merchants use not [to go], if I appeared in the least part clothed like a Christian, I was tufted like an owl among other birds. At first I imputed it to barbarism. But afterwards, lamenting thereof to one of the better sort, to note how they understood it, he told me that they would have no novelties; and therefore would disgrace all new examples. Then I perceived it to be a piece, rather of institution than of incivility. For they, desiring perpetual hostility with the Christians, must estrange the people from their customs as utterly as may be....

Upon the taking of a town, the first thing they erect is public baths; which they establish with fair revenues. So that, for less than two pence, any man or woman may be bathed, with clean linen, and never attendant. It is death for any man to enter when a woman bathes: which he shall know by a bar on the door. He or she who bathes not twice or thrice a week are held [to be] nasty. Every time they make water, or other unclean exercise of Nature, they wash those parts, little regarding who stands by. If a dog chances to touch their hand, they wash, presently. Before prayer they wash both face and hands: sometimes the head and privities. Many of their customs have been in Egypt thousands of years before Mohamedanism. So necessary a thing to prevent diseases in hot countries, and to men of gross food. To this Herodotus ascribes the old circumcision in Egypt. And so do I that of Muhammad, who had no diviner warrant, and care not for bare imitation. Or the authors of superstition, when they find customs very useful, knowing that reason suffices not to hold them in practice with the vulgar, they plant them among other ceremonies, and make them conscientious: which is the only way to put them upon low capacities....

The only beastly injustice I found among the Turks was their confidence to catch or buy up as slave any Christian they find in the country. Nor can he escape, unless where he is a settled known merchant, or goes with some protector. I met with many who, in such voyages as mine, had fallen short: and prophesied the like to me. I have several times been put to defend myself, with my knife, from being shoved into houses, by those who would have kept me slave. And scarcely any day passed, but some or other cheapened me with the janissary who (if he had sold me) I had no remedy beside what disdain of life might have presented. This I held [to be] the worst part of my danger; and against which there is no preparation of assurance, except in a small resolution.

Yet, as much as in me lay, I used two ways of prevention. One was [that] when they questioned my condition and design (which was often) I gave them several accounts as I noted the place and auditory: still, in effect, to show me born rich, but fallen to poverty, without any fault of mine – my friends all dead. And that having no ability for gain, I had wagered the small relics of my fortune upon a return from Constantinople and Cairo. This, though far below my fortunes, yet passed with them for truth – and such a one that, embellished with fit circumstance, procured me esteem and compassion and which, above all, made me appear unprofitable to the buyer. For they buy more in hope of ransom, than [of] service; and therefore often required, where I had my correspondence.

My other was to note the territories adjoining, with the ways of flight; to study our company and (giving wine to some, money to others) I ever kept in secret pension some of the Caravan who understood the language, and [who] told me all that passed. Then, in each place of abode, I acquainted myself with some renegade; whose story, after he had delivered [it], I knew how to make him for my friend, as in case of danger would have helped me to flee, or conceal. Herein was the most expense and unquiet of my voyage. That accepted, the Turkish disposition is generous, loving and honest...if I had a hundred lives, I would venture them upon his word, especially if he is a natural Turk: no Moor, Arab, or Egyptian. To those I never committed myself until he had engaged wife and children for my safe delivery. They seldom travel single. But expecting till a great number are bound for the same place, go and lodge together. This secures them from thieves: unless they come in troops; and then the Governor sends against them....

The natural Turks and the renegades are not subject to those taxes and tolls of Christendom; nor is their quiet and plenty fit to be published among the adjoining Christians – only vineyards, in whose hand soever, pay the Spahis, to the guardians and others, because wine is a prohibited ware. Yet, after all those persecutions, it is much cheaper there than in Christendom; but not everywhere to be had. For though, in that point, Muhammad's wise order suffers violence, yet with the better part it prevails, and makes some drink with scruple, the others with danger. The baser sort, when taken drunk, are often bastinadoed on the bare feet. And I have seen some, after a fit of drunkenness, lie a whole night crying, and praying to Muhammad for intercession, [so] that I could not sleep near them. So strong is conscience, even when the danger is but imaginary.

This want of wine has devised other drinks to their meat, for the better sort, such as...water soaked with raisins, sometimes with honey. But above the rest they esteem sherbets made with sugar, the juice of lemons, peaches, apricots, violets or other flowers, fruits and plums, as each country affords. These are dried together into a consistency reasonably hard, and portable for their use in war, nor elsewhere; mingling about a spoonful with a quart of water. They have another drink, not good at meat, called coffee, made [from] a berry as big as a small bean, dried in a furnace, and beaten to powder, of a sooty colour, in taste a little bitterish, which they seeth, and drink [as] hot as may be endured. It is good [at] all hours of the day, but especially morning and evening when (to that purpose) they entertain themselves [for] 2 or 3 hours in coffee-houses which, in all Turkey, abound more than inns and ale-houses [do] with us. It is thought to be the old black broth so much used by the Lacedemonians; and dries all humours in the stomach, comforts the brain, and never causes drunkenness, or any other surfeit; and is a harmless entertainment of good fellowship. For there, upon scaffolds half a foot high, and covered with mats, they sit – cross-legged, after the Turkish manner – many times two or three hundred together, talking; and likely with some poor music passing up and down....

I must not forget to note their jealousy; wherein a Turk exceeds an Italian – as far as he, us. The cause is polygamy – which makes the husband guilty of insufficient correspondence; and therein fearful that his wife may seek a further satisfaction. Therefore, the women go muffled – all but their eyes. Nor are they suffered to go to church, or so much as look out at the windows of their own houses. The man may divorce when he will, with restitution of jointure, and some further satisfaction, as the judge pleases. Yet not without some reasonable pretence against the woman. I saw, at Adrianople, a woman (with many of her friends) went weeping to a judge; where, in his presence, she took off her shoe, and held it sole upwards; but spoke nothing. I enquired what it meant [and] one told me [that] it was the ceremony used when a married woman complains that her husband would abuse her against Nature: which is the only cause for which she may sue a divorce – as she then did. That delivery, by way of emblem, seemed neat: where the *fact* was too unclean for language.

There are very few beggars in Turkey, by reason of the great plenty of victuals. Only one sort I wondered at: that is, their santones; who are able, cunning rogues, much like our Tom of Bedlams[4] – ever, with some such disguise, to pretend a crazed brain. But they act no more in a grave, sublime and meek way than ours. Why these are respected I could never hear; other than their compassion. But I observed such a reverence borne them that made me think it religious. Nor is it strange that superstitions should honour all eclipse of understanding: whose light discovers them too far....

The Turkish nation cannot yet be generally abandoned to vice, having two such great enemies: the Christian on this side, the Persian on that. Were they once removed, it would be soon corrupt, like Rome after the Fall of Carthage and Antioch, or worse; for then it would be a far greater Empire than ever the Roman was. Nor is it much less already. Nor wanting so much in extent, as it succeeds in being more absolute, and better compact. It has ever been, and yet is, the vanity of nations to esteem themselves civiller and more ingenious because more curious in superstitions than other people whose moderation, diversity, or disdain of those follies they term barbarous and beastly stupidity, incapable of such illuminations. Thus, of old, the Egyptians despised the Greeks; they the Romans; the Romans all the world; and, at this day, the Papists us; the Jews them; the Mahometans all.

After this discourse of the Party Imperial, I must not forget those other sects which it has in subjection. They are generally Christians and Jews. Christian strangers they call 'Frank'; but their own subjects are either Latins, Armenians, Greeks, or of another sort, whereof I have seen infinite numbers in all that tract of Bulgaria and Serbia: who are baptised only in the name of St. John: their difference theological I enquired not. But, in faction, I noted them so desperately malicious towards one another that each loves the Turk better than they do either of the other; and serve him for informers, and instruments against one another. The hatred of the Greek Church to the Romish was the loss of Belgrade in Hungary. And is at this day so implacable that he who, in any Christian war upon the Turk should expect the least good wish from the Christians in those parts, would find himself utterly deceived.

I often was helped by Turks and renegades against the malice of their Christians....The Latins are Papists, but so few and despised as not to be reckoned. The Armenians and Chaldeans are also Christians, but have a deeper tincture of Mahometanism than the others. The Greek Church seems less little inferior in number to the Roman – for though the Catholics are thicker in France, Spain, Germany, and Italy than the others in Turkey, Muscovy and Persia, yet their provinces do so infinitely exceed those in extent that it will make the Greek Church (though in thinner plantations) more numerous than the other.

This proportion was assured clear before the loss of Constantinople: which, to Rome itself (if not considered as a co-rival) was a deep blow. Now, in all Turkey, the number of Christians is wonderfully abated. For, beside the slaughter in conquest, they are daily diminished by other arts. The Turk takes a more pernicious way to extinguish Christianity than ever the heathen Emperors did. Their hot persecutions got them the envy which follows cruelty, and made the people compassionate the afflicted cause, whereby commiseration (which is a strong piece of human nature) blew the flame of zeal, and raised more affection to the cause than terror could suppress:...the Turk puts none to death for religion; whereby none from fire or gallows, move compassion to their cause. He rather sucks the purse than unprofitable blood, and by perpetual poverty, renders them low towards himself, and heavy to one another. He turns the Christian churches into mosques, much suppressing the public exercise of religion (especially of the Romish), though not utterly –

so that each generation becomes less instructed than [the] other. In so much that, at this time (as by trial I found) many who profess themselves Christians scarcely know what they mean by being so.

Finally, perceiving themselves poor, wretched, taxed, disgraced, deprived of their children, and subject to the insolence of every rascal, they begin to consider – and prefer – this present world before that other which they so little understand. This turns so many to Mahometanism, and prevails with less scandal than fire and sword would do, in as much as it goes less harsh with a man to forget his religion than to defy it. For conscience, wrought on by education, holds the mind of man as a lace wound about the body. The Turkish course unlaces it by degrees, as it had been wound up, so bringing it off clear. But bloody persecution, striving to pull it away [at] once, at a snatch, is too sudden a violence, disordering and entangling faster than they were....

I had much converse with renegades, and had good opportunity (by their Italian tongue) to find what spirits they were, and on what motives they fell off. Generally I found them [to be] atheists, who left our [Christian] cause for the Turkish, as the more thriving in the world; and fuller of preferment. These hate us not, otherwise than in show, unless where they find themselves abhorred for their apostasy. Then take heed! For, in your ruin, they get both revenge, and reputation of zeal. But, with a more opportune behaviour, I have won much courtesy from them and, upon occasion, put my life at one of their discretions, and found him noble.

These are the voluntary renegades. There are another sort, whom hard usage and captivity brings in, rather than any ambition, or disgust, at home. These, though necessitated to hold one, yet they bear a great goodwill towards Christians – and likely, a deep grudge to the Turks. I first noticed this by a eunuch of the garrison of Belgrade [whom] I had, with money, made a friend, against any necessity of flight. I, going to visit him in his house, near the Danube river, found him alone, very drunk. He, out of that heat, and experience of my engagement, fell to railing against the Turks and, withall, showing me how they had marred his game, 'well', quoth he, 'do you see that river? There seldom has been in this city (which was half a year) but some night or other I have thrown some of their children therein'; and told me that, formerly in other places, he had done many such secret revenges, for their gelding of him. Before my experience of these apostates, I supposed that their Paradise had won many from our side. But of all that I practised, there were none taken either with that, or other, points of their doctrine; but manifestly with respects worldly. Wherefore, seeing how many daily go from us to them, and how few of theirs to us, it appears of what consequence the prosperity of a cause is to draw men upon it; and how uncertainly they judge of all other merit.

The chief sect whereof I desired to be informed was the Jews, whose modern condition is more condemned, than understood, by Christian writers, and therefore by them delivered with such a zealous ignorance as never gave me satisfaction. Their primitive profession was [as] shepherds, whose innocent kind of life had leisure for the study of that hierarchy which, in after times, their settled possession of Canaan put into act. But (as we daily see) necessity makes shifts. And nothing corrupts clear wits more than desperate fortunes and foreign conversation. For it befell them, in their frequent captivities, wherein the malice of their estate, and the corruptions of the Gentiles, did extremely debauch their old innocence; and, from shepherds, or tillers of land, turned them to what they now are: merchants, brokers, and cheaters. Hereto is added no small necessity from their religion: which, as of old, so at this day, renders them more generally odious than any one sort of men. Whereby they are driven to help themselves by shifts of wit more than others are. And so, as it were, banding their faction against the rest of mankind, they become better studied, and practised, in malice and knavery, than others are. This makes them thrive, notwithstanding all oppressions to such excessive riches as by themselves I have heard alleged as a testimony of Divine benediction.

They are generally found the most nimble and mercurial wits in the world. Which, in part, is descended from the original complexion of their forefathers, who gave notable testimonies of a subtle generation; and had been much advantaged by their Mosaical institution of diet – a thing of no small effect to refine the blood and spirits in so many descents. Yet, above all, I impute it to this incessant necessity and exercise of wit, which ever keeps it up, without growing too remiss and stupid: as usually happens when are not quickened by such occasions. Hereupon it is that every Vizier and Pasha of State keeps a Jew in his private counsel: whose malice, wit, and experience of Christendom, with their continual intelligence[5] is thought to advise most of that mischief which the Turk puts in execution against us. Nevertheless, in most of their conversation, I noticed rather the dexterity of a cheater, or mountebank, than any solid wisdom. And so, in their railings at Christ, few invade him by any staid politic way of atheism. Most of them profane Him with beastly tales or superstitious accounts. Many of them read the New testament maliciously [in order] to cavil; and elude the Miracles of Christ, wickedly imputing them to conspiracy among the actors, and partiality in the writers – as of a Legend. Above all, places in Scripture they abuse that, where it is said that when He was to go up to the Passover (but a few days before His death), his kindred, and those about Him, did not yet believe. Whereby they (not knowing Faith to be the gift of Grace, rather than that of Reason), slander his Miracles for not [being] as manifest as we conceive [them to have been].

Once, at their celebration of a Sabbath…in Serbia, I was walking with several of their Rabbis; especially one, much reverenced by the rest, who was Principal of the Synagogue in Sofia. He would needs urge a discourse of Christianity. Where (after his malice had wearied itself) I asked him whether it were not an undeniable sign of Divine Aid to our cause that, with such a meek humility as that of Christ, had raised itself over all the proudest of oppressors? He (as the nature of poison is to infect things of most contrary condition), perverting this reason, replied that Christ came when the world had been tamed by the Romans, whose cruel victories and heavy yoke had broken the spirits of most nations. Whereupon He would not build his religion, as the old heathen had ever done: upon heroic, brave acts, but on the contrary meek humility of contrite hearts. Which, being the greatest number (especially by that time they came to govern) causes it to prevail so well. This, seeming a cold atheism, he further made vain with an addition concerning the several Ages of the World, comparing the case with this microcosm of man, whose infancy is simple, youth brave, manhood firm; but his decaying age faints till the end shuts all up. Each of these periods did he pretend [was] guided by doctrine suitable: and to the latter rejected Christianity; whose humble contempt of the world he ascribed to the world's Old Age, as in man, grown weary of itself.

After answer hereto, I desired to understand somewhat of their Kabbala;[6] which I have always held [to be] the greatest secret of the Jews. I demanded whether it consisted in that arithmetical signification of letters which we suppose, telling him withal, that it seemed strange how letters, and words (which were imposed differently by the humour of man) could touch upon the reality of things in themselves, which did not acknowledge our devices. He answered that, in part, the Kabbala did depend upon letters, and words, but only in Hebrew: wherein Adam named things when he was in a State of Innocence, and understood their nature. But, in languages made since the Fall, the foundation wanted – they, as the issue of confusion, assure nothing therein. Then he added the story of it, telling me that 'Kabbala' signifies 'Tradition': which was the way in which it was transferred from one age to another; and that it was, in some measure, a reparation of our knowledge lost in the fall of Adam. And again revealed from God four times. First to Adam who (upon his ejection out of Paradise), sitting very disconsolately, God (quoth he) sent the Angel Raguel to comfort him. And finding his chief sorrow to be in losing the knowledge of that dependency, and punctual commerce which the creatures have with their Creator, and amongst one another, the Angel, for his illumination therein, instructed him about the peculiar moments of time natural and proper to each passage; wherein things else impossible might be brought to pass with felicity.

Hereat I told him that there was not, in The Bible, any mention of the Angel Raguel's comforting, or instructing, of Adam. Whereto he replied, like a cursed Jew that the Popes had (not only in that place, but in many others) clipped, amplified, and mistreated the Old Testament, the better to conform it with the New: for their institutions, civil and ecclesiastical, which depend thereon. The Kabbala, said he, held in tradition many ages, till Time, with the accidents of the Flood, and Babel, lost it. Then, once more, God discovered it to Moses in the Bush.[7] This he proved out of *Esdras*,[8] a Book highly in esteem with him, where, in the Second Book, God is brought in....Therefore Moses published those *mirabilia*, the Creation; the Law, and the Israelites' bringing forth from Egypt. But those...disclosed to none besides his 70 rulers over Israel. These traditions soon failed, in the oppressions under the Philistines. But the third time God revealed it again, it was to Solomon, in a dream....For it is said of Solomon that...by his art, he wrote many books on all things: from the cedar to the hyssop, with several others – all of which were lost in the Captivity ensuing. Therefore, the last time He pretended it restored to Esdras, (who, as he himself writes), God made to retire for 40 days, with 5 Scribes who, in that space, wrote 204 Books. The first 134 God commanded to publish for reading by all (both worthy, and unworthy). The latter 70 were to pass privately, only among the wise of the people. These latter 70 they pretend to be Kaballistic; and not yet lost.

When I considered this Art, it put me in mind of what the Prophet says to the Church of Israel 'Thy habitation is in the midst of deceivers'.[9] For although in things of inferior natures, as well as in the passions of man...they are better disposed for this or that impression than at other times, yet do not these open them to an agent that comes opportune and (in a way) naturally proper to the predisposition of the subject. Thus is fever easier cured at one time [than] another; one medicine hits one access, another the next. The like may be observed in all things. But to extend it beyond its due limits, and to ways improper (as to wishing, writing, speaking, and other charms which cannot reach the reality of things) comes to as profound a nothing as...their great Council of Sanhedrin[10] consisting of 71, in imitation of Moses and his 70 Elders, not being able to work such wonders, did nevertheless strive to continue the reputation of the old thearchy.[11]...

This device was well framed to take with the Jews, who generally are light, aerial, and fanatical brains, spirited much like our hot Apocalypse men, or fierce expounders of *Daniel*, apt to work themselves into the fool's paradise of a sublime dotage. They expect their Messiahs with an unwearied assurance. And, as all prophetical delays do easily find excuse, so have they – restoring their hope with augmentation of glory in the more perfect trial. At His coming, they expect a temporal kingdom; whereof I have heard them discourse with so much gusto as seemed to have a touch of the Sadducee,[12] whose appetite relishes a present fruition better than the state of resurrection. To discover this fully, I told them that I thought [that] it might seem but just that all those who had lived, and died, constantly expecting the Messiah should not (by untimely death) lose the fruits of their constancy, but be restored to life at His coming. This they received with much applause, and (as flattery is) it was by them held an illumination; which they, embracing me, seconded with such a 'romanzo' of their future kingdom as showed a thirst for revenging their captivities; and therewith, to enjoy the world, in that timely Resurrection. Above all blessings given by God, they prefer that of 'Increase and Multiply'. To hold it a blessing, they have reason. But why that should be thought the greatest I know not, unless because of their salacity, ever noted for....

The Jews of Italy, Germany, and the Levant (excepting the Banditoes of Spain) are of [the tribe of] Benjamin. The other 10 tribes, in the destruction of Jeroboam's kingdom by Salmanazer, were led captives beyond the Euphrates, whence they never returned. In which destruction, perhaps worse than this of their brethren, they had the happiness never to persecute Christ. Then I asked if they had there, degenerated into the race and gentilism of the heathen, as our Christians have done in the Holy Land; whom now we know not from other Turks, except by some touch of language. They, ashamed of such apostasy, told me that those 10 Tribes are not found anywhere, but either swallowed...or, as other Rabbis write, blown away with a whirlwind. So apt are light wits to imagine God less glorified in His own glorious ways of Nature, because ordinary, than in the puffs of the vain devised miracles wherein (while they affect to seem grave and profound) they become foolish and shallow, not knowing the ways of that virtue which moves all things....

They suffer no women to enter the synagogue; but appoint them a gallery outside. I imputed it to jealousy, but they told me it was because women have not so divine a Soul as men, and are a lower creation, made only for the propagation, and pleasure, of man. This doctrine humbles their wives below that fierce behaviour whereto competition, and opinion of equality, might embolden them. When they turn Turk (which is often) they must first acknowledge Christ so far as the Turk does – which is, for a great Prophet: and no more....

If they were all united, I believe [that] there would scarcely be found any one race of men more numerous. Yet, that they can never cement into a temporal government of their own I reckon two causes, besides the many disadvantages of their religion. First, the Jewish complexion is so prodigiously timid as cannot be capable of arms. For this reason they are nowhere made soldiers – nor slaves. And, in acknowledging the valour of David's worthies, so different from the modern Hebrews, appears how much a long thraldom may cow posterity beneath the spirits of their ancestors. The other is their extreme corrupt love to private interest – which is notorious in the continual cheating and malice among themselves. So that there would want that justice, and respect to common benefit, without which no civil society can stand.

Now there remains a word or two about the zinganes. They are right such as our gypsies. I yield not to those who hold them a peculiar cursed stock. Sloth and nastiness single them out from other men, so that they are the dregs of the people, rather than of several descents. Wallowing in the dirt, and [the] sun, makes them more swarthy than others. They abound in all cities in Turkey, but does not steal like ours do, for fear of the cruel severity. They tell fortunes as cheatingly as ours; and enjoy as little. Their true life use is for sordid offices: as brew-men; smiths; cobblers; tinkers, and the like; whereby the natural Turk is reserved for more noble employments. Few of them are circumcised; none Christian. They wear their rags affectedly, but wander not: their habitation is hovels, and poor houses in the suburbs. Contempt secures them. And, with that, I leave them.

By this discourse it appears that the Turkish Empire is, in effect, divided into two parts: the Turks; and other sects. Unto these are applied the two passions of men: love, and fear. So that the government is to keep the one sort so that they shall not desire mischief, and the other not to be able to effect it. To the Turks it is a sweet monarchy, maintaining them to command the rest. To the other sects it is heavy: holding them distracted with faction between themselves, disarming, rifling, taking their goods and children from them; and awing them with as much insolency as may not quite make them run away.

Nevertheless, the Grand Seignior has not the inconvenience of tyrants; which is to secure himself against the people by strangers – who are chargeable, and perfidious. For he [the Grand Seignior], without charge, is held up by plantations of his own people, who in descent, and interest, are linked with him. Neither has he the uncertainty of a civil prince, who much subsists on fickle, popular love: for he reigns by force, and his Turks are a number able to make that good. Wherefore he seems as absolute as a tyrant [and] as happy as a king. And more established than either. Yet he has danger from both parts. Love makes apt to grow insolent. Therefore his governing multitudes are that way dangerous.

NOTES

1 Policy: in the sense of the conduct of public affairs; political science.
2 Zingaraes: 'gypsy'; 'gipsy' – a member of a wandering race [sic] (by themselves called *Romany*) of Hindu origin, which first appeared in England about the beginning of the sixteenth century and was then believed to have come from Egypt (*OED*).
3 Sibyl's Books: in classical mythology the Sibyls were inspired women who lived in several places (Delphi, Iona, Cumae, etc.) and who had the gift of prophecy. Arguably the most famous was the Cumaean Sybil also known as Herophile, in Vergil's *Aeneid*. Tarquin II, to whom she offered to sell her nine volumes of Sibylline Books, refused to pay the price she asked. His refusal prompted her to start burning the texts, one by one, until he finally agreed to buy the last three at the price she had originally set for the whole lot. These (according to the myth) were kept under guard in the Temple of Jupiter, to be consulted in moments of impending calamity, in order to seek a way of averting the anger of the gods. The story goes that when the Temple of Jupiter was burnt down (83 BCE) the Books were destroyed. A fresh collection was, however, made in the time of Augustus Caesar. These were, in their turn, destroyed in a fire in 405 CE. Perhaps the most important feature – a gendered dimension that might benefit from a revisit – about these figures is that, in early Christianity, they achieved a status on a par with those of the Old Testament prophets, of which one example is the representations of five of them in Michelangelo's Sistine Chapel ceiling.
4 Tom o'Bedlam: a person who is mentally ill. Bedlam – the Bethlem Royal Hospital, the oldest institution for the confinement of the mentally ill in England – was founded (1247) by Sheriff Simon Fitz Mary at the Priory of St Mary Bethlehem, outside Bishopsgate. Treatment of 'distracted patients' (usually by shackling them to the wall and throwing cold water over those who were adjudged as being 'violent') became a major part of the work of the hospital from 1377. When the Priory was dissolved (1547), the City of London bought the site and re-established an asylum; now under the administration of the Bridewell prison. In 1675 treatment was transferred to a new site at Moorfields, at the entrance of which there were statues entitled

'Melancholy' and 'Madness', reputedly modelled on inmates. Bedlam became a regular place to which the upper classes went (until it was stopped in 1770) to look at the inmates, a practice vividly evoked in Hogarth's 'Scene in a Madhouse' in the series *A Rake's Progress*. In 1815 the site was moved to Lambeth, south of the river, of which the only remaining part (the central section) is now the Imperial War Museum. The present Bethlehem Royal Hospital is now at Beckenham, Kent.

5 Intelligence: spying.

6 Kabbala: a system of biblical exegesis claimed to have been handed down from Abraham. Although there exists a strong body of scholarly opinion that it was first formulated in France in the eleventh century, from where it spread to Spain, there are also elements which can be traced to the earlier periods: for example, Merkavah mysticism, centred around the vision of the chariot-throne (Merkavah) in Ezekiel. Kabbalist learning was of considerable interest to Christian thinkers in the early modern period, and Blount's questions highlight a commonly held view at the time that every word, letter (indeed, accent), contained mysteries which could confer considerable power on those who could decode the signs. In the present day it still has adherents, notably within the ranks of Hasidic Jews.

7 Moses in the Bush, Exodus 3: 2: 'And the Angel of the Lord appeared unto him [Moses] in a flame of fire out of the midst of a bush: and he looked, and, behold, the bush burned with fire, and the bush *was* not consumed.'

8 Esdras: (Greek form of the name 'Ezra') of books of the Apocrypha and as an Appendix in Roman Catholic Bibles.

9 Jeremiah 9: 6: 'Thine habitation is in the midst of deceit; through deceit they refuse to know me, saith the Lord'.

10 Sanhedrin: from the Greek, meaning 'council of leaders'. Reference to it in gospels is usually associated with Supreme Court of Chief Priests and elders in Jerusalem, who (it should be remembered) assembled only with goodwill of the Roman rulers: for them it was, at times, useful to enlist the support of these leaders in aspects of the administration and application of their policies. It was the Sanhedrin which conducted the preliminary trial of Jesus (Matthew 26: 59: 'Now the chief priests, and elders, and all the council, sought false witness against Jesus, to put him to death'). Blount notes that his antagonist mentions seventy plus the Chief Priest (thus 71 members), though other sources mention the figure as twenty-three. Other scholars hold the view that there were, in fact, two Sanhedrins: one political, the other civil.

11 Thearchy: rule or government by a god, or gods.

12 Sadducee: formed around the time of the Hashmonean Revolt (*c.* 200 BCE), they were a minority, drawn primarily from within the ranks of the upper classes, who argued that the only law that was valid was the written. Here they were in opposition to the majority, the Pharisees, who held the view that the oral law was no less valid than the written. They apparently eventually came to an accommodation with the majority faction that enabled them to serve as priests, but did not survive, as a group, the destruction of the Temple (70 CE).

OTHER EDITIONS

1636, 1637, 1638, 1650, 1664, 1669, 1671. Also in: *A Collection of Voyages and Travels*, Vol. 1, 1745.

A General Collection of the best and most interesting Voyages and Travels, ed. John Pinkerton, 1811.

See- en Land-voyagie van den Ridder Hendrik Blunt, na de levant. Gedaan in het jaar 1634...Uyt her Engels vertaalt Leyden, 1707, 1727.

Des edlen Hernn Henrich Blunt, *Morgenländische Reise, durch Dalmatien, Sklavonia, Thrazien und Ægypten*, Helmstädt: J. N. Gerlach, 1687.

1638 edition reprinted in facsimile, Amsterdam: Theatrum Orbis Terrarum/Norwood, NJ: Walter J. Johnson, 1977.

10

THOMAS HERBERT

Some years travels into divers parts of Africa, and Asia the Great.
Describing more particularly the Empires of Persia and Industan.
Interwoven with such remarkable occurrences as hapned in those parts
during these later times. As also, many other rich and famous kingdoms in
the Oriental India, with the isles adjacent. Severally relating their
Religion, Language, Customs and Habit: as also proper observations
concerning them. In this fourth impression are added (by the author now
living) as well many additions throughout the whole work, as also several
sculptures, never before printed...

London, printed by R. Everingham, for R. Scot, T. Basset,
J. Wright, and R. Chiswell, 1677.

BIOGRAPHY

Thomas Herbert (1606–82), born in York, in 1627 managed (via the influence of his kinsman William Herbert, 3rd Earl of Pembroke) to be included in the embassy sent by the English monarch to Shah Abbas of Persia. One reason for that embassy was to seek to establish the validity of the claims made by Sir Robert Sherley that he had been appointed by Abbas as an envoy to the European powers – a claim contested by the Persian Ambassador, Nakd Ali Beg. Sherley, his Persian wife Teresia, and Nakd Ali Beg therefore found themselves, together with the official party under the leadership of Sir Dodmore Cotton, making the voyage at the same time. The delegation departed from Deal (near Dover) in six ships on Good Friday 1626.

Herbert provides a detailed account of the journey via the Canaries, Tenerife, Angola, the Cape of Good Hope (about whose inhabitants his is one of the most egregiously racist of characterizations)[1]; then via Madagascar, 'Ethiopia' (inevitably with comments about Prester John), Goa and Surat (main 'factory' of the English East India Company, where the Exeter-born Thomas Kerridge was in charge at the time); eventually to the Court of Akbar the Great, about whom he has extensive commentaries. Nakd Ali Beg having committed suicide shortly after their arrival in India, the party visited the Court of the Mughal Emperor at Agra, before eventually travelling to Persia (as described, in part, in the extracts below).

Following upon the death of Cotton, as well as Robert Sherley, the rest of the party (having been provided with safe-conduct passes by Abbas) visited important cities such as

195

Qom and Baghdad. Travelling via India, Ceylon [Sri Lanka] and Mauritius, Herbert returned to England towards the end of 1629. With the death of his patron, the Earl of Pembroke (1630), and therewith any possible chance of preferment, Herbert spent the next few years travelling on the European continent, before settling in London in 1631. On the side of parliament in the Civil War,[2] he carried out several commissions on its behalf before (1647) being appointed to be one of the attendants on Charles I, then in prison. Later, appointed by Charles as one of his Grooms of the Bedchamber, Herbert served the monarch right up to the moment of the latter's execution and internment of the remains at Windsor. It is reported that, on the way to the execution, Charles made Herbert a present of his large silver watch and that, from the distribution of the estate, he received (among other things) the cloak which the king had worn on the scaffold on the day of his execution and a cabinet of books – one of which was a 1623 Shakespeare First Folio. With the Restoration (1660), Herbert was made baronet, but apparently lived the rest of his life quietly engaged in his antiquarian interests and writing (and rewriting) not only the accounts of his travels, but also recollections of the imprisonment of Charles I, of which the most important was probably *Threnodia Carolina*.[3]

* * *

Arabia

The 17th December [1626] we took ship in the *William* for Gombroom[4] in Persia. The *Exchange*, the *Hart*, and other gallant ships went along with us; and above 300 slaves were put aboard, whom the Persians had bought in India...whereby it appears that ships (besides the transporting of riches and rarities from place to place), consociate the most remote regions of the earth by participation of commodities and other excellencies to each other; which (besides the ease we had, especially in hot zones) by that kind of accommodation in travel, having coasted India and Arabia (where the sweetest spices and gums do grow), we found that the flowers so perfume the air when gently blowing towards passengers, as they have discovered whereabouts they were even when no land was in sight of them....

Gombroom

Gombroom...called Bandar, i.e., 'the port town' (and not unaptly, this being more valuable than all the rest the King of Persia has) is situated upon a level ground close to the sea, the country round about rising for some miles very insensibly, without any hill of note (save to the North) which, though seeming near, is said to be 15 miles distant. Near this place the Gulf is narrowest, Arabia the Happy opposing it to the West towards 10 leagues, but so visible that it seemed to us no more than Dover does from Calais....And although the town is but of small antiquity, taking its rise from the fall of Hormoz, nevertheless one Newberry,[5] an English merchant, reports that at his being here about the year 1581, it was then a town: though I believe a very small one. Since which, the Portuguese have built two castelets (or forts): the first, by Albuquerque (1513), under whose power it rested till 1612, at which time...it was wrested from them to the Persians. But, upon the destruction of Hormoz, which was in the year 1622, by the removal of most of the inhabitants, this village so increased the buildings that, for grandeur, it is now ranked with towns of best note in Persia. So that through the access of merchants from most parts: namely English, Dutch, Danes, Portuguese, Armenians, Georgians, Muscovites, Turks, Indians, Arabians, Jews and Bannians,[6] this Gombroom, from a small village, has become a great City of Commerce, by reason of that notable concourse which, in the winter season (usually both by land and sea) from the most remote places of the world resort there; raw silk, carpets, cotton, and other inland commodities being brought there by caravan against that time – and, by ship, merchandise of all sorts. So that trade here, during 3 months, appears quick: both to the enriching of the natives and exotics, in lush degree....

And first, concerning the buildings. They are, for the most part, of brick. Not burnt with fire, but hardened by the sun; which makes them so hard that they appear no less solid and useful than those the fire obdures. They are low-built; and most with small courts and balconies, terraced or flat at the top, pargetted with plaster, in hardness not inferior to that of Paris. For indeed, such is the distemperature of heat sometimes that to live there is scarcely tolerable. But when the air becomes more moderate (which is when the sun is furthest) to have more breath, they sleep upon their terraces: to which end they spread carpets aloft, for their better accommodation. This kind of building is common in all these parts....The windows are not glazed, but wooden trellised, made to shut and open as they see cause, to welcome the breeze when it murmurs. The mountain (which they say is 6 leagues away, but by its height seems not half so much), by anticipating the cool north winds, makes this place much the hotter: so hot that, in the summer season, [it] enforces the inhabitants to remove to Lar and other neighbouring villages, where cool streams, rocks, and trees give shade and cool air that, at Gombroom, is [so] insufferable that some (according to what was practised in Hormoz) used to lie naked in troughs filled with water – which, nevertheless, so parboils their flesh as makes it both exceedingly smooth and apt to take the least cold when any winterly weather succeeds the heat; by which that becomes a little less offensive. Now, their summer being no less than 9 months, during all that time it is rare if one cloud is visible in the sky – whereby the air (in the daytime especially) is not to be endured. For, by a reverberated heat which the sunbeams strike forcibly from the ground, both earth and air become intolerable to man and beast, by reason of the inflammation.

However, of late they have raised a bazaar which, in some places by reason of its narrowness (and mostly by being arched and closed at the top) checks the sun's heat when the beams dart perpendicularly; in the sides attracting what air there is to refresh such as either sit in shops for sale of wares, or those others who keep taverns, here being plenty of Shiraz wines brought in long-necked glasses, and jars that contain some gallons: the best wine, indeed, in all, Persia. Here are coffee-houses, which are also much restored to; especially in the evening. The coffee...is a black drink (or rather, broth) [which] they sip as hot as their mouth can well suffer, out of small China cups. It is made of the flower of bunny or coava-berry,[7] steeped and well boiled in water; much drunk – though it pleases neither the eye nor the taste[buds], being black and somewhat bitter (or rather, relished like burnt crusts); more wholesome than toothsome. Yet (if it is true, as they say) [it] comforts raw stomachs, helps digestion, expels wind, and dispels drowsiness; but of the greatest repute from a tradition they have, that it was prepared by Gabriel as a cordial for Muslims.

Also sherbet-houses. [It is] a drink that quenches thirst, and tastes delicious. The composition is cool water, into which they infuse syrup of lemons and rose-water; in these torrid countries the most refreshing sort of liquor that can be invented; albeit the wine there was so good that we refused not to drink with moderation. Arack[8] also (or 'strong-water') here is plentiful. Which, qualified with sugar, is cordial; and much drunk at sea and land in the hottest seasons, especially when the diet is coarse, and stomachs crude and weak through the diffusion of heat which, in cold seasons, is contracted. However, for our better entertainment, we had a variety of fruits: some growing here; but most imported from places more remote – some of which were oranges, lemons, pomegranates…figs, dates, currants, myrobalans,[9] apricots, almonds, pistachios, apples, pears, quinces, sugar; also flowers and nuts, in great quality as well as variety. Which, with that plenty we had of carabitoes[10] and mutton, hen's eggs, and rice bought very cheaply, made the place much more delectable. And for oysters and many sorts of fish, the sea being so near, furnishes them abundantly – and would do more, were the people more industrious.

The best houses in the town are the Sultan's…the English and Dutch agents' houses: ours, in memory of the good service they did the Persians at the taking of Hormoz, are privileged to wear their flags displayed at the top of their public house.[11] And, for some time, the English had half the imported customs, according to articles. At the North and South ends of the city are 2 castles, in which are planted fourscore pieces of brass ordnance, part of the spoils or trophies of ransacked Hormoz. The gunners were not very expert. For when they had to fire, I could perceive them to stand on one side of the piece and (in a fearful manner; though with a linstock[12] as long as a half-pike, which had a lighted match) to touch the powder. Which was a bad way to take aim.

The mosques for the Mohammetans and the synagogues for the Jews are few, and inconsiderable in their structure. But the hammams, or stoves[13] are more conspicuous, no less rest resorted to; and with small expense. The floors of these hot-houses are plastered; and usually sprinkled with water: which contracts the vapours, condenses the air, and preserves the heat with moderation. The streets are narrow, the town badly served with water, and without wall or graff[14] to make it defensive.

Now, although here we have abundance of camels, horses from Arabia and Persia of the best sort, and mules and asinegoes[15] in great number (which were worthy the view) yet were we not more pleased with them than offended by those troops of jackals which here, more than elsewhere, nightly invaded the town and, for prey, violated the graves by tearing out the dead, all the while ululating in offensive noises, and echoing out their sacrilege. They are the lions' informers. And for reward always have something of the prey left [for] them to pick; as at the Cape of Good Hope we observed. We have some sport in hunting them with swords, lances, and dogs. But we found them too many to be conquered, too unruly to be banished, to daring to be frightened….

But with these it is no great injury to couple those filthy prostitutes…who infect this town when seasonable weather (which is November, December, and January) makes it the rendezvous for merchants and travellers from most places. Women I mean who, as to their bodies, are most comely; but, as to their dress and disposition, loathsome and abominable. For although their hair is neatly pleated and perfumed, and about their cheeks are hung ropes of Orient pearl, about their necks carcanets of stones, in their ears many rings (some of which are headed with ragged pearl) one by another, in their noses a brooch or piece of gold 3 inches or more in length and half an inch in breadth, embellished with turquoises, rubies, spinelles, sapphires, and stones of like value: which, for all their lustre thwarting the face, makes that which is an ornament to them to us seem very deformed. And, as a supplement to all the rest, want no fucus[16] for complexion; which, agrees not with colours olivaster,[17] save for the desire they have to please white people;[18] and that their arms and legs are chained with manilios[19] and armlets of silver, brass, ivory, and the like. The rest is veiled with a thin shuddero of lawn. And upon their feet some wear sandals; though others go barefoot.

Yet this Morisco[20] dress, together with their intolerable impudence, rendered them (at least, to my view) no other than Ovid's remedy of love. For it is a pity that the Persians have not such as the Gynaecocosmi were among the Athenians: whose care it was to see that women, in their attire and behaviour, carried themselves modestly. And albeit they are as bad as they can be, they make me call in mind a Rabbi's doctrine which maintains that such as are desperately naught do not corrupt for good manners, or are so great enemies to a good life, as those hypocrites who are but half evil, or corrupted in part; persuading others that they have some seeming goodness in them, by a dissembled sanctity. No less well observed by John de Lery,[21] that the naked [Native] American women do not so much incite to wantonness, or appear as libidinous as European women do [but] by the magic of their eyes, mimic dress, painting, patching and gestures of several immodest fashions and loose inventions. However, the better sort of that sex here wear linen drawers...and want not jewels or bracelets for further ornament. But when they go abroad, they are covered with a white sheet, from top to toe, so that they are not easily known to any[body]. The men are of the same dusky complexion. Upon their heads they wear sashes; about their waists girdles of many ells of linen cloth; elsewhere, naked. And (to express Cupid's vagaries), have the impression of round circles, and pink their skins in way of bravely....

We stayed in Bandar-Gombroom for 14 days. Which, although the view and other accommodations the sea and proximity to The Happy Arabia contribute (such time especially as the temperate months make it habitable might have allured our longer stay, had pleasure been our object), [but] our Ambassadors, thinking the time long, used the best persuasions they could with the Sultan to hasten the provisions for the journey. And although horses for our riding and camels for the caravan were ready, nevertheless such was his superstition that go we must not until, upon his casting the dice, the chance proved to his satisfaction....

The Ambassador's caravan consisted of 12 horses and 29 camels. The horses were such as were not liable to exception; the camels of those better sort they call coozelba camels,[22] a beast abounding in Persia, and of great use, esteem and value in those Oriental parts. They are long-lived (often times exceeding threescore years), of disposition very gentle, patient in travel, and of great strength, well enduring a burden of towards a 1000 lb weight: content with little food – and that the meanest sort, as tops of trees, thistles, weeds, and the like. And less drink – in those countries usually abstaining [for] no less than 4 days. Which is of extraordinary advantage, seeing that oftentimes they are necessitated to pass through desert places....Our tents (which the Ambassador had bought at Surat, and was advised to carry along) afforded us our best accommodation. However...we found a very neat caravanserai (a building resembling an empty college)...buildings erected by well-minded Mahometans as works of charity; and in which they express their magnificence more than in any other sort of building: of great use, seeing [that] these parts have no inns for the reception of travellers. But here, *en passant*, they may rest sweetly and securely *gratis*. For they are set apart for public use; and preserved from violence by thieves, wild beasts, and intemperate weather. At the gate [there] is sometimes a bazaar or tent that (like sutlers in armies) for money furnishes passengers with provisions. Yet seldom is it that travellers, not daring to depend upon uncertainties, rather choose to provide and carry their necessaries along with them....

THOMAS HERBERT

Shiraz[23]

Shiraz at this day is the second city for magnificence in the monarchy of Persia....It is very pleasantly seated at the north-west end of a spacious plain, 20 miles long and 6 broad; circumvolved with lofty hills, under one of which this city is seated; defended by Nature, enriched by Trade, and by Art made lovely, the vineyards, gardens, cypresses, sudatories[24] and temples ravishing the eye and smell, so as in every part she appears delightful and beautiful....A little out of the town is interred that learned poet and philosopher, Musladini Sadi, who wrote *The Rosarium*, which is lately turned into Latin by Gentius.[25]... And indeed, Shiraz has a college wherein is read philosophy, astrology, physic, chemistry, and mathematics; so that it is the most famous throughout Persia....The gardens are many, and both large and beautiful...the earth dry, but green; the air salubrious, though sharp a little while...so that I must acknowledge it a truth that as the East is more warm, so more refreshing and pleasant than the West, and through the gentle influence of the sun and wind makes both flowers and fruits much more delicious, succulent and fair than we find in the Occidental regions....So that it must be granted that the East has pre-eminence over the West for fruits, plants, grain, spices, drugs, herbs, gems, minerals, and other things....Further, it is agreed (says Bodin), by joint consent of the Hebrews, Greeks, and Latins, that the East is better tempered than the West; and that, by the Prophets in the Holy Writ, the East seems to challenge the dignity and superiority above the West – to which truth several philosophers and historians subscribe, as...Strabo, Pliny, and others, backed with the judgement of Hippocrates, Galen, and other grave writers, who all aver that, in Asia all (or most) things are much fairer and better than in Europe; and that the Orient produces flowers, fruits, spices and other commodities, as also greater plenty of gold, silver, pearls, and precious stones than the Occident. Which may fully evince an opposite judgement. Especially seeing [that] Almighty God, in the first Creation of the world, was pleased to endow the Eastern parts of the world with the best temper. And from which...all other parts derive their origins....I may confine my commendations to a small compass, places remote being at this day sterile, mountainous, and unable (if then, as now) to make Alexander an epicure – the wine excepted, which is indeed the most generous grape of Persia; and famous all over the Orient....They revel all the night, and drink the round, / Till wine and sleep their giddy brains confound. And it is to be feared [that] Chastity is no virtue here, [but] an unseen martyrdom. For heat makes lust so outrageous that they make little defence against it, thinking pleasure to be a delightful conqueror.

The Feast of the Spring / The Duke of Shiraz

This feast...is commonly celebrated when the sun enters into Aries; for than this they cele-brate no feast more solemnly. [Now] something about...the Duke and his banquet. This man is a Georgian by descent, a Muslim by profession, and one of those Tetrarchs[26] who, under Abbas, ruled the Empire. His territories reach every way wellnigh 400 miles, and afford him the title of Archduke of Shiraz, Sultan of Lar and Jaroun, Lord of Hormoz...Prince of the Gulf of Persia and the islands there, the Great Beglerbeg; commander of 12 Sultans, 50,000 horse; slave to Shah Abbas, protector of Muslims, Nutmeg of Comfort, and Rose of Delight. He is of extraordinary descent for nobility (as honour goes in these parts), his father and grand-father having been dukes before him.

But (which is no less strange) privileged from degradation by Abbas's oath upon a good occasion....Abbas, knowing that reward is as powerful a support of State as punishment, for that good service [of extracting a treble contribution from Murad, the governor of the town of Chiulsal, for siding with the Turks in a battle in 1514] recompensed him with the Shiraz dukedom; and his son, after him, no less fortunate in his fieldservice to Shah Abbas, having quieted Georgia, subdued Lar and Hormoz, and made part of Arabia...tributary to Persia.

Some days after our being here, the Great Duke absented himself – merely to please his humour. For although Sir Robert Sherley had taken pains to ride to him to tell him how acceptable his being in town would be at the [English] Ambassador's entrance, he answered [that] it was no dishonour for any man (his Master excepted) to stay his leisure; not knowing (or not considering) that the persons of Ambassadors are sacred, and challenge high respect in all places, according to the custom and consent of all nations – both from the representation they make, and the nature of their employment. So that this would not have been endured had our Ambassador been provided with a convoy and necessary accommodation for travel; which wanting, constrained him to practice patience. After 6 days attendance, his Eminence made his entrance into Shiraz, attended by 2,000 horse; where he took his ease [for] 2 days, without the least notice of our Ambassador. At length, finding that our Ambassador would not make application to him, he sent a gentleman to invite him to his palace. Who returned with this answer: that he was weary, having come a great journey; and that his journey was to see his Master.

The Duke, not pleased with that message, thought it best to dissemble it, knowing that the King had given express command that, in his passage, he should everywhere receive honour and hearty welcome. So, after some pause, the Duke sent word [that] he purposed, next day, to visit him; yet failed in his promise. But his son, the Beglerbeg (18 years old) came, in person, to excuse him. Next day our Ambassador sent word...to the Duke's son that his visit should be retaliated....The father seemed to be displeased that he had not the honour of the first visit, and marvelled what kind of people we were, since his own little less than adored him; nevertheless made use of it to his own satisfaction. For he [the Ambassador] was no sooner alighted near the Duke's palace when...he was ushered into a long gallery, rich in communal beauties, plate, carpets, and other furniture where (contrary to expectation) the Duke himself, like a statue, at the end of the room sat cross-legged: not moving one jot until the Ambassador was almost at him. And then, as one affrighted, skipped up, embraced him, and bade him welcome, vouchsaving also (upon knowledge that his attendants were gentlemen) to...entertain us with a banquet. So, after two hours' merriment, we departed, invited to return next day to a more solemn welcome.

The entertainment our Ambassador had was wine and sweetmeats; which were of variety. And then...according to the common mode of these Eastern parts, the dancing wenches went to work...first throwing off their loose garments or vests (the other was close to their body, resembling trews; but of several pieces of satin of several colours).... Their hair was long, and dangling in curls. About their faces were hung ropes of pearl, carcanets set with stone about their necks, and about their wrists and legs were wreathed golden bracelets with bells which (with the cymbals and timbrels in their hands) made the best consort. Their dancing was not after the usual manner. For each of them kept within a small circle, and made (as it were) every limb dance, in order, after each other: even to admiration....

The Ambassador feasted by the Duke of Shiraz

Next day being come, we were conducted by a sultan through two fair Courts; from where, on foot, we were ushered into a stately banqueting-house: which was a large room, open at the sides, supported by 20 gilded pillars, the roof embossed with gold....The ground was spread with extraordinarily rich carpets of silk and gold. At one end, a State (of crimson and gold, embroidered with pearl and gold) was erected, under which the Duke was to enthrone himself. Upon one side thereof was painted his Hormoz trophies, no cost, no Art, being left out to do it to advantage. For it expressed their encamping upon the shore, their assaults, storms, batteries, entrance, plunder of the city, massacre of the Hormozians – some beheaded; some chained; some, their heads serving for girdles, and also the English sea-fights; and the like. But so to life 'As seemed indeed, / Men arm'd to fight, ward, strike, till each man bleed'. And when the green and crimson curtains, or scenes, of silk were drawn, there was a lively prospect into a great square Court which (upon this occasion, to aggrandise the invitation) was round set with the prime men of the city – as also into another adjacent Court where, I think, I told [counted] near 500 plebeians who...were invited to illustrate the Duke's magnificence.

Before this great Duke meant to display his radiance (for, as yet, he had not entered) Sir Dodmore Cotton was seated on the left hand of the State (where note that, all Asia over, the left hand being the sword hand, is most honourable). Upon the other side sat the discontented Prince of Tatary. At the Ambassador's left hand was seated the Beglerbeg (the Duke's eldest son), and next to him the captive king of Hormoz. Next to the Tatar Prince sat...a disconsolate Prince of Georgia: a gallant person, expert in arms, and a constant Christian. Opposite to the State, Sir Robert Sherley seated himself. And in the same room with such gentlemen as attended the Ambassador were placed the two Princes of Hormoz, some Sultans, and other great officers. The rest of the banqueting-room was filled with persons of note, as Sultans, merchants, and Pashas – during which entertainment, young Ganymedes arrayed in cloth of gold, with long crisped locks of hair...went up and down, bearing flagons of gold filled with choice wine, which they preferred to all the company one by one, so long as the Feast endured.

Upon the carpets were spread fine coloured pintado[27] tablecloths, 40 ells long at least. Broad, thin pan cakes fixed one upon another, served for trenchers, near which were scattered wooden spoons whose handles were almost a yard long; and the spoons so thick and wide as required right spacious mouths to render them serviceable. The Feast was compounded of several sorts of pelo[28] of various colours, and store of candied dried fruits and meats; variety also of dates, pears and peaches, skilfully conserved. Such I took notice of (I mean, it pleased me best) were...pistachios, almonds, apricots, quinces, cherries, and the like.

The Duke is not yet noticed of. The truth is, his Eminency had not yet entered. Nor were we sorry that, when our bellies were full, our eyes might have the better leisure to survey his greatness. However, the Feast was no sooner ended than the vulgar multitude strove to rend the sky with...'Ali and God be thanked'; expressing by voice and music their joy; and then...the echo being as the signal for that great Duke to enter. His entrance was ushered by 30 comely youths who were vested in crimson satin coats. Their turbans were silk and silver wreathed about with small links of gold. Some had also pearl, rubies, turquoises, and emeralds (for I do not remember that I saw one diamond). They were girded with rich hilted swords in embroidered scabbards. They had hawks on their fists, each hood set with stones of value. The Duke followed after them. His coat was of blue satin, very richly embroidered with silver, upon [over] which he wore a robe of extraordinary length, glorious to the eye. For it was so thick powdered with Oriental pearl and glittering gems that it made the ground of it inperspicable – not less rich, I thought, than the Empress Agrippina, when clothed in a robe of woven burnished gold. His turban, or mandil, was of finest white silk interwoven with gold, bestudded with pearls and carbuncles.[29] His scabbard was set all over with rubies, pearls and emeralds....His sandals had the like embroidery, so that he seemed that day to resemble Artaxerxes, whose apparel was commonly valued at 10,000 talents, as Plutarch relates. To this glorious Idol the people offered their devotion in many 'salaams', bowing, and knocking their foreheads *à la mode,* against the ground. Sir Robert Sherley, constantly wearing the Persian habit, also zind-abaded[30] very formally; and after that, in a cup of pure gold, drank His Eminence's health – and then (knowing that bit would please the Duke) put it [the cup] in his pocket, with this merry compliment: that after so unworthy a person as himself had breathed in it, it was some indignity to return it. Which the Duke amiably accepted as good satisfaction; but perceiving our Ambassador not very merry, darted him a smile, then drank the King (his Master's) health, and exceedingly civilly bad him and his company heartily welcome. And so withdrew. The truth is [that] our Ambassador was scarce well pleased at the Duke's long absence and proud carriage; yet prudently dissembled it. So, after reciprocal salaams, some Pashas attended him to his horse. And so [he] returned to his lodgings....

[The 'skirmish' at the English ambassador's lodgings]

Two days after this Feast, the Duke, with a Train or Cavalcade of 30 Sultan and Pashas came galloping...[to] the house we lodged in. And although he [had] endeavoured to surprise Sir Dodmore Cotton with a sudden visit, yet such was the seasonable intelligence he then had that, at his alighting, he found a choice shade as the first part of his entertainment, and then chambers neatly furnished: from the balcony looking into a pleasant garden where large cypresses and other trees appeared in their best apparel for his better welcome. Here the facetious[31] Duke, encamped with all his company, resolved to encounter the fury of his own wine and [that of] our English chymick-waters.[32]...And give me leave to repeat: no part of the world has better wine than Shiraz. So that, for 3 hours, the skirmish continued; charging one another with equal resolution. Many bottles and flagons were emptied; but, by stratagem from the Duke's corner, revived afresh: thundering such an alarm in the Duke's brains that, at his mounting his horse, he fell back and had not our Ambassador (who, as he was very abstemious, so was he most civil), by chance upheld him, he would have been dismounted. Mr Stodart of Caernarvon and Mr Emery, two gentlemen attending the Ambassador in his Chamber, helped them homewards. Next day the Duke, sensible of his civil treatment, returned his thanks in a present of 12 good horses, with bridles and rich saddles suiting them. By which it appeared that all were pleased, and the Ambassador (who, without such an entertainment had never satisfied them) acquired the epithet of 'a generous and well-bred person'. After other ceremonies of welcome (in which pistachios and gifts were not left out), we had leave to prosecute our travel towards the Court. I call it 'leave', [since] the Duke seemed so unwilling to part with us. The Ambassador's attendants also (pursuant to the Duke's directions) were very well mounted and furnished with fresh camels, and asingoes for our sumpters.[33]...

Great is the difference between the Turks and Persians. For the Turks, being by Law prohibited, abstain from wine; yet drink it covertly. But the Persian now (as of old) drink with freedom openly, and to excess. It was so of old because Plutarch, in his *Life of Artaxerxes*, reports [that] the Persians were liberal wine-bibbers and lovers of magic. Cyrus, craftily endeavouring to supplant his brother Artaxerxes in the Crown...being his agent in Asia Minor, the better to ingratiate himself with the Lacedemonians, wrote unto them – and (amongst other ventures) boasted that he was fitter to rule than Artaxerxes. And the reasons he gave was this: [that] he could drink more wine; and better understood Natural Magic[34] than his brother did. Peradventure the same Genius was in this great Duke we are now speaking of....

Sir Dodmore Cotton's Entrance into Esfahan

The 10th April...we were invited to a collation prepared in one of the King's gardens that was by a highway, to where the English Agent and such other merchants who were residentiaries in Esfahan came to express their civilities unto the Ambassador. A mile nearer the city the Vizier, the Sultan of Esfahan...and the Armenian Prince, in a Cavalcade of about 4,000 horse and innumerable Foot[soldiers] came to meet us. The highway, for two full miles from the town, was full of men, women and children. Here also we found the Banians in great numbers, who, all together all the way, in a volley of acclamations, welcomed us...which, with kettledrums, fifes, tabrets, timbrels, dancing-wenches, hocus-pocusses,[35] and other antics past my remembrance; but, according to the custom of those countries, ennobled the entertainment. The bridge also over which we passed into the city was, in like manner, full of women, on both sides; many of whom, equally coveting to see as to be seen, in a fair deportment, unmasked their faces.

The first place we alighted at was...a house of the King's at the west side of the Maidan; where some of the noblemen knelt down and salaamed, three times kissing the King's threshold – and as often knocked their heads in a customary obeisance....Sir Robert Sherley, who was well acquainted with the formalities of those parts (and in all places dressed like a Persian) zindabaded also: which made him the more respected. A Pasha concluded the ceremony in a panegyric [to the effect] that the excellence of Shah Abbas had attracted a Prince and other gentlemen from the extremest angle of the world to see whether Fame had been partial in the report of his magnificence. But no wonder; since his beams [had] spread over all the universe. That done, bottles of pure wine were lavished out; after which, with a continued clamour of the plebeians thereby expressing their joy, we were conducted to another house of the King's which was at the south-east of the city; through which a broad sluice of water had its course...which made our lodging the more delightful.

The fourth day after our being in Esfahan, Mr Burt (the English Agent, and a very accomplished merchant) feasted our Ambassador, expressing a very noble entertainment and hearty welcome. Where, according to the mode of Persia, there was store of coniferous flowers, and sweet water – agreeable to the old custom mentioned by Plutarch in *The Life of Artaxerxes*, where the King, entertaining Antalcidas the Lacedemonian, circled his brows with a garland of flowers wet with most sweet and precious oils, which perfumed the place. At night, a large tank of water was surrounded with lighted tapers, artificially uniting two contrary Elements: squibs also, and other fireworks, for the more honour of the feast, such as made the Persians admire.

Next day...the Armenian Prince was visited at his house....He professes himself [to be] a Christian. But (I must be bold to say) his house was furnished with such beastly pictures, such ugly postures as indeed are not fit to be remembered. For God calls not unto uncleanliness, but to holiness...which the Prophet Jeremiah declares in chapter 44, verse 4 that...'It is abominable, for the Lord hates it'.[36] Yea, Seneca (a heathen) has this excellent saying: '...If I knew that men could not see, nor the gods punish, yet would I forbear sinning for the loathsomeness of sin'. Plato has the like: that he would do nothing in secret whereof he should be ashamed in public....No, said Cicero, albeit it were possible to conceal our sins from the gods. Pity it is then that these Christians living amongst infidels are so past shame, being a powerful restraint to keep men from sin, without which they abandon themselves to all manner of debauchery. For, says Pythagoras...'Do no sordid act that either others or thyself mayest know; and principally let thy own conscience be regarded'....

Georgians and Armenians

The Georgians are the ancient inhabitants of that country, and have little intermixture with other nations. The soil is [for the] most part mountainous, much resembling Helvetia where the Switzers live. From the top of some hills they can discover [see] (at least, as they suppose) the Black and Caspian seas. They derive their name either from St. George, their patron, or from the Gordian Hills on which they inhabit....And indeed the goodness of God is herein to be acknowledged in as much as these Georgians, with their neighbours...continue their Christian profession, although they are sufficiently threatened in that respect by Turks, tatars and Persians who environ them, and [who] tell them that all Anatolia and those other countries which lie between the Black Sea and the Mediterranean sea, although they were once altogether inhabited by Christians, are now overspread with those who embrace the Qur'ān....By profession they are now...more inclinable to arms than to trading; as their neighbours the Armenians are. But, for comeliness of body, height of spirit, and faithfulness in trust are of that repute (especially with the Persians) that many of them are employed in places of command: especially against their turbulent adversary, the Turk. And, as of old the Egyptian Sultans had their Mamelukes,[37] so at this day the Persian King has the greatest number of his pashas from there, it being seldom heard that any of them are false or, having served the Persian, ever turned to the Turk. Notwithstanding which, the Persian King in our times, upon some distaste given...made war against that nation. For (as one observes) though Glory and Dominion are two excellent things if well acquired, yet are they but bad motives to commence a war, or to invade the just possessions of another. And I may not omit that Sir Robert Sherley one time, when we were travelling together, gave us the ensuring relation.

Esfahan

Esfahan, metropolis of the Persian monarchy is seated in the Parthian territory...and as [is?] umbilic to that spacious body which at this day is awed by the Persian sceptre....She is, in compass, this day about 9 English miles; including towards 70,000 houses, and of souls (as may be conjectured) contains about 200,000. For, besides natives there are merchants from several nations – as English, Dutch, Portuguese, Polish, Muscovites, Indians, Arabians, Armenians, Georgians, Turks, Jews and others drawn there by the magnetic power of gain. It has several good buildings, but the most observable are the Maidan, the mosques, the hummams and palaces; as are the gardens, monuments and the adjoining suburb of Julfa....

[Esfahan: the maidan and the garden]

The Maidan is, without doubt, as spacious, as pleasant, and as aromatic a market as any in the universe. It is 1000 paces from north to south, and from east to west above 200; resembling our Exchange, or the Place-Royale in Paris; but 6 times larger. The building is of sun-dried brick, and an uninterrupted building, the inside full of shops; each shop filled with wares of sundry sorts; arched above, in cupolas, framed terrace-wise at the top, and pargetted with new plaster. And, being the noblest part is placed (as it were) in the heart of the city. The King's Palace...conjoins it upon the west side, possessing a large space of ground backwards, but does not jut to the street further than [does] the other buildings, which are uniform to the street. So that, to passengers, it gives not any bravery – her greatest gallantry being in the outward trim. For it is pargetted and painted with blue and gold, embroidered with posies of Arabic which (after the grotesque manner) makes it show very pleasant.

Inside, the rooms (according to the common form there) are arched, enlightened by trellises; the rooms embossed above, and painted with red, white, blue and gold; the sides painted with sports [scenes?] and landscapes; the ground or floor spread with carpets of silk and gold, without other furniture, terraced above, garnish with a phare [lighthouse] overtopping many mosques; and the Garden or Wilderness behind the house made fragrant with flowers, filled with airy citizens privileged from hurt or affrights; and for which they return their thankful notes in a...melodious consort and variety....

The north isle of the Maidan has 8 or 9 arched rooms, usually hung with lamps and...candlesticks which, being lighted (as it is usual, especially at the Festival of Lights)...give a curious splendour. To there the Pasha and others frequently resort for pastimes [such] as tumbling, sleight of hand, dancing girls and painted catamites; that...are there tolerated. At the furthest end north is the Mint; where we saw one day silver coined, gold the second, and next day brass. Not far from there are cook shops, where men feed the helpful belly, after the busy eye and painful feet have sufficiently laboured....

Within the Maidan the shops are uniform, trades usually having their shops together: of which some are mercers, lapidaries some, and (not the fewest) such as sell gums, drugs and spices; showing also greater variety of simples and ingredients of medicines than ever I saw together in any one city of Europe; and such as may give encouragement to physicians both to view and judge both of their nature and quality, as well as temperatures of the climes they come from, which such as are ignorant cannot distinguish. And indeed the drugs and spices here so perfumed the place, that it made me since give the better to that monostic[38] of an old poet...'We sucked the aromatic air of Persia...'.

Hammams in this city are many and beautiful. Some are four-square, but most be globous. The stone of which they are built is for the most part white, and well polished; the windows large without, crossed and inwardly made narrow; the glass (where glass is) is thick annealed and dark; the top or outside covering round, and tiled with a counterfeit turquoise, which is perfect blue, very beautiful and lasting. The insides of these hot-houses are divided into many cells and concamerations, some being for delight, others for sweating in, all for use. For the truth is, bathing with these is (as it was with the Greeks and Romans) no less familiar than eating and drinking; yet the excess doubtless weakens the body, by making it soft and delicate, and subject to colds. However, they may better there use it than we in Europe, by reason that they drink water, eat much rice, pelo, and like food of easy digestion, which makes their bodies solid and hard, so as little fear is that bathing will make them frothy. Besides, their much sitting and little exercise makes them sweat less and need more bathing....

The Ambassador's entertainment at Court

After four days' repose, the King assigned him [the Ambassador] his day of audience. It was the 25th May, our Sabbath, and the fag-end of their Ramadan or Lent; advantageous to the Pasha, though I will not say [that] it spared him the charge of an entertainment. Sir Dodmore Cotton, our Ambassador had Sir Robert Sherley in his company, with myself and seven or eight other English gentlemen his followers. Good reason it was some Sultan or other should convoy and show him the way (the Court being a quarter of a mile distant from our house). But yet so it happened that notice was given by a courier from Muhammad Ali Beg, the favourite. So as to the Court his Lordship got, very few of the town having notice of his time of audience; it appeared by those few that came out either to see him pass, or to view the manner of his reception; which, without doubt, was the product of the favourite's envy, occasioned through the spite he causelessly bore unto our noble countryman Sir Robert Sherley. For otherwise it might be wondered at, seeing [that] Abbas, of all sorts of honours, counted to have strangers at his Court, the highest.

At our alighting an officer bade us a welcome and ushered us into a little house which stood in the centre of a large Court, wherein [there was] no other furniture except a few Persian carpets, which were spread about a white marble tank filled with water. Here we reposed and, for two hours, were entertained with pelo and wine – nothing so good as the material they were served in: flagons, cups, dishes and covers being all of gold. From there we were conducted by some Sultans through a spacious garden which was splendid to the eye and delicate to the smell; from where we were brought into another summer-house which was rich in gold embossments and painting, but far more excellent in a free and noble prospect. For, from the terrace thereof, we had a delightful horizon into the Caspian Sea, towards the north; and southward, at a distance [we] could discern the high mountain Taurus....

Round about the room were also seated several Mirzas, Sultans, and Beglerbegs who, like so many inanimate statues, were placed cross-legged, joining their bums to the ground, their backs to the wall, and their eyes to a constant object – to speak one to another, sneeze, cough, spit in the Pahsa's presence being...held [to be] no good breeding. Nor may they offend the King who, by the fulgur[39] of his eye, can dart them dead, as soon as speak a word....The Ganymede boys, in vests of cloth of gold, richly bespangled turbans and embroidered sandals curled hair dangling about their shoulders, with rolling eyes and vermilion cheeks, carried in their hands flagons of best metal; and went up and down, proffering the delight of Bacchus to such as were disposed to taste it....

At the upper end (surmounting the rest so much only as two or three mastabas[40] or white silk shags [carpets] would elevate) sat the Pasha: beloved at home, famous abroad, and formidable to his enemies. His grandeur was this. Encircled with such a world of wealth, he clothed himself that day in [a] plain red calico coat quilted with cotton; as if he

should have said [that] his dignity consisted rather in his parts and prudence than [in]...
having no need to steal respect by borrowed colours or embroideries. The Pasha sat cross-
legged. His sash was white and large; his waist was girded with a thong of leather; the hilt
of his sword was gold, the blade formed like a semi-circle – and doubtless, well tempered;
the scabbard red; and the courtiers, from the example of their monarch, but meanly attired.

The Ambassador, by Dick Williams his interpreter (Calimachi the Persians called him)
acquainted the King that, by his master's command, he had undertaken a very great
journey to congratulate [him on] his success against the common enemy, the Turk; as also
to promote trade, and to see Sir Robert Sherley vindicate himself from Nakd Ali Beg's
imputations; and withal, to desire that a perpetual league of friendship might be continued
between the two powerful monarchs of Great Britain and Persia.[41]

The Pasha, raising his body, returned this answer. To the first: [that] the Turks were a
mean people, compared with the generous Persians; as by several battles he had given them
ample proof of; and that, than the Turks, no people in the world were more inconsiderable. Nevertheless, he wished [for] unity among Christian Princes; the Ottoman grounding
his conquest upon their discord. Concerning trade, the King of Great Britain should, if he
pleases, receive 10,000 bales of silk at Gombroom every January; and, for payment would,
by way of exchange, accept of so many English cloths as should be adequate in value. For,
as he well knew, the silk was a greater quantity than he could use in his own dominions.
So were the cloths sent to him; but he would hazard the vending them by his merchants
to serve their neighbours, so that neither we nor he should need to trade or hold corre-
spondency with Turkey. It would infinitely be to his satisfaction to disappoint the Grand
Seignior of that yearly Custom [duty] he was forced to when his caravans went by way of
Aleppo or Trebizond [Trabzon] to the Venetian, Genoan, French, or other European
merchants, because the janisarries were maintained by those Customs. What was that, but
to sharpen his enemy's swords to his destruction?

Concerning Sir Robert Sherley: he had been long of his acquaintance; and expressed as
many considerable favours towards him (though a stranger, and a Christian) as to any of
his born subjects [and] that, if Nakd Ali Beg had aspersed him unjustly, he should have
satisfaction. It argued, indeed, that Nakd Ali Beg was guilty in that he chose to destroy
himself on the way [rather] than to adventure a purgation. In some sort, he [Nakd Ali
Beg] had presaged the King's rigour, for had he come and been found guilty, [then] 'By
my head (an oath of no small force), he should have been cut in as many pieces as there
are days in the year, and burnt in the open market, with dog's turds.[42] Now, touching a
League of Friendship with the King, your master. I cheerfully embrace it. And concerning
yourself, you are truly welcome. And seeing that you have done me the honour none of
my predecessors ever had before, for you are the first Ambassadors who ever came from
Great Britain, in that quantity in my county, you may deservedly challenge the more
respect. Yea; as I account your master chief of the worshippers of Jesus, so do I, of yourself, in a superior degree to any other Ambassador now present.'

This said, the King sat down. And whereas all Mohametans...knock their heads against
the ground and kiss his garment, in a friendly manner he pulled our Ambassador near him
and seated him by his side; smiling that he could not sit cross-legged. And after Audience,
in another apartment, calling for a bowl of wine, there drank his [the Ambassador's]
master's health: at which the Ambassador stood up and uncovered his head. Which, being
noted by the Pasha, the more to oblige, he lifted up his turban. And, after an hour's entertainment, dismissed him with much satisfaction.[43]

208

It is a real truth that...the King's good will soon became diverted. For, from that day till we arrived in Quasvin (albeit no offence was given) neither was the Ambassador cajoled at Court, nor saw he the King. Neither did any Sultan invite him, or visit him: all of which was imputed to the envy of Muhammad Ali Beg who, by bribery, had been made our enemy – one who, for his faculty in diving into other men's actions and informing the Pasha with his observations, made a shift to engross the royal favour; insomuch as most business of State passed through this impure conveyance. So that it came to this, at last, [that] whom he loves, the King honours; such he hates, the King crushes to pieces. To have his good opinion, each great man outvies others – insomuch that his annual comings in...was bruited to be sevenscore thousand pounds sterling. And well might have been, since...the Overseer of the King's harems had 100,000 pounds yearly: if it is true, as some who are there assured me.

Shah Abbas his cruelty

I shall give but a few instances; too many of so brave a prince, whose virtues balance his infirmities....A poor distressed wretch bestowing a long and tedious pilgrimage from Kabul to this place upon some little business, before he knew what the success would be unhappily rested his weary limbs upon a field-carpet; choosing to refresh himself rather upon the cool grass than be tormented within the town by the merciless vermin. Poor man!...For, snoring in a climacteric hour, at such time as the King set forth to hunt, his pampered jade startling, the King examines not the cause, but sent an eternal arrow to sleep into the poor man's heart; jesting (as Iphicrates did when he slew his sleepy sentinel): 'I did the man no wrong. I found him sleeping, and asleep I left him'....The courtiers also (as the Negroes in Manicongo who, when their captain receives a hurt by war or accident sympathise by voluntary maiming themselves in the like part) to applaud the fact, parasitically made him their common mark; killing him a hundred times over if so many lives could have been forfeited. The Latin poet justly reproving such tragic acts could say [that] 'Mercy is the truest conqueror'. This is not unlike the practice of Artaxerxes, his great ancestor who, riding to hunt the lion, caused...a noble youth to be beheaded for no other fault than darting a roused lion that made at him before the King [had] begun his throw...a punishment far exceeding the offence, undoubtedly. Nor like that other Artaxerxes, who is no less famous for his mercy, by ordering the cutting off of the tiaras or turbans of several men condemned to lose their heads, the Law by this his ingenious and prince-like construction being satisfied.

But how highly soever they extol their King, I prefer that noble Pagan before him who had this excellent maxim of Juvenal: 'Delay cannot be long where life's considered'. A soldier's wife, having fed too high, in a lustful bravado petitioned the King for natural help, her good-man proving impotent. A dangerous impudence! The King finds it to reflect upon himself, old at that time and master of 4,000 concubines. So, as he promises her speedy justice, [he] calls his physicians. And when phlebotomy was held too mean a remedy for her distemper, they gave an assingoe an opiate potion: which so enraged the beast [that], as by force, he basely became her executioner....

Two needy knaves were arraigned in the Divan, and condemned for stealing. Many grievous taunts the Pasha levelled, saying [that] they deserved death for daring to come so near his Court so ragged. They confess that they therefore stole that they might wrap themselves in better clothing. Abbas, not satisfied with their excuse, commands two new vests to be brought. But winding-sheets had been more proper; for the executioner forthwith dragged them away, and upon two sticks staked them up on their fundaments – an execution practised of old in Persia.

Such and such other was his inhumane pastime during our stay at the Caspian Sea. But enough, or rather too much, upon such a subject; especially relating to so great and generous a Prince, as notwithstanding these mistakes is beloved as well as feared at home, and abroad no less highly honoured. Therefore to record the variety of tortures here too much used by men-eating hags of hell, cannibal-hounds and their death-twanging bowstrings, ripping up men's guts, and the like; what could be the effect, but an odious and unnecessary remembrance? Whose image does such as are cruel bear but his, whose true title is 'The Destroyer'?

Sir Robert Sherley's epitaph, and his lady wife's distress

But [that] this bad requital of good service is no new thing in Persia, witness that which Plutarch…relates concerning Antalcidas a noble Spartan; who, while that State was paramount, no man in the Persian Court was more regarded. But, suffering an eclipse at the Battle of Leuctra[44]…the Spartans dispatched Antalcidas to the Persian King for supplies – whose reception was then as slight as formerly was honourable. And hence came those discontents, nay that arrow of death that arrested him. For upon 13th July (in less than a fortnight after our entering Quasvin) he [Robert Sherley] gave this transitory world a final farewell in his great climacteric. A family of good antiquity, that the naming serves to illustrate it without hyperbole. This gentleman made good the old proverb, that it is better die honourably than to live with obloquy. And (wanting a fitter place for burial) we laid him under the threshold of his door without much noise or ceremony….

Let it not seem impertinent if I add somewhat to the deserving memory of his wife, that thrice worthy and heroic lady, Teresia. The country she first drew breath in was Circassia.…She was of Christian parentage, and honourable descent. Her first relation to the Court was by being sent up to attend the Sultana; and by that means became sequestered to the Harem – where [there] are many hundred virgins admitted whom the King seldom, or never, sees; and for ought I could hear, to the King she was not otherwise related. He nevertheless has power to dispose of such of them as he pleases, to his officers: who esteem it no small honour to receive a wife from his royal hands. According to which custom the Emperor of Persia presented her to Sir Robert Sherley as a testimony of his respect. Which lady was a constant companion to him in all his fortunes, until death.

Such time as her beloved Lord lay dead, and she half dead through a long dysentery, to add to her affliction one John a Dutchman (rather a Jew) a painter, regarding neither her sex, profession nor disconsolate condition, complots with Mahmud Ali Beg (her husband's enemy) to ruin her, pretending an engagement her husband was in to one Croll, a Fleming. And knowing [that] he was dead, referred himself to the testimony of the defunct to witness it, having no other evidence it seems to prove the debt. She might have paid them by like sophistry: 'That if the dead man would affirm it she would satisfy it'. But the pretended creditors hastened to the Cadi for a warrant to attach her goods. However a faithful, honest gentleman of our company, Mr Robert Hedges by name, happily having notice, hastens to her house and advises her to make quick conveyance of her goods: which the poor lady readily hearkens to, and forthwith tears the satin-quilt she lay upon, showing that virtue a stronger could not have bettered. And, taking from there a cabinet which contained some jewels of value, being indeed the all was left her, entreats that worthy gentleman to safeguard them till the danger was over. He readily obeys: and was no sooner departed, when John the Boor enters with his catchpoles.[45] Who (without any apology for their rudeness, or pity to her distress), broke open her chests, and plundered her of what was valuable: for some rich vests, costly turbans, and a dagger of great price they took away. But finding no jewels (such they had seen her wear, and the rich ostrich-feather also, which they had worried in their ostrich-appetite) they were maddened at that disappointment, and made her horses, camels and asses (being all the personal estate they could then come by) bear them company, not caring if the lady starved. The gentleman, as soon as the storm was passed returned; and besides words of comfort, gladdened her heart in delivering her jewels [to her] again – of double value by that escape: without which I am persuaded her other fortune reached not to 50 pounds: a small provision for noble a lady; especially seeing money is so useful in those uncharitable regions. But God provided better for her; and beyond expectation: having, as I hear, since placed her in Rome, where of late years she lived with more freedom and outward happiness.

Sir Dodmore Cotton's death

...discontents, long conflict with adverse dispositions, and 14 days consuming of a flux (occasioned, as I thought, by eating too much fruit or sucking in too much chill air on [Mount] Taurus) brought that religious gentleman, Sir Dodmore Cotton our Ambassador, to an immortal home. [On] the 23rd July (11 days after Sir Robert Sherley's death) he bade this world adieu. Our duty commanding us to see him buried in the best sort we could, we obtained a dormitory for him amongst the Armenian graves; who also, with their priests and people, very civilly assisted the ceremony. His horse (which was led before) had a velvet saddle and cloth upon his back. His coffin was covered with a crimson satin quilt (black they account not of) lined with purple taffeta. Upon his coffin were laid his Bible, sword, and hat. Mr Hedges, Mr Stodart, Mr Emery, Mr Mowlam [and] Dick the interpreter, and such others of his followers as were healthy, attended the corpse; and Dr. Goch, His Lordship's Chaplain, buried him: where his body rests, in hope, till the Resurrection....

The burial of our three Ambassadors (you cannot otherwise imagine) was no small discouragement to the progress of our travel, being as a body without a head. For though the Pasha seemed to commiserate us, as persons left desolate in a strange country (as an assurance of his respect having sent each of us two vests of cloth of gold) yet were we convinced that he may well call himself a miserable man, whose welfare depends upon the smiles of Persia. We prepared therefore to be gone; but could not until Muhammed Ali gave his consent. Long attendance we danced before we could produce a firman for our safe travel, and that Letter we desired from Shah Abbas to our Most Gracious Sovereign. But, at length, importunity prevailed; so that we got it, wrapped up in a piece of cloth of gold, fastened with a silken string, and with a stamp of Arabic letters skilfully gilded on paper very sleek and chamletted with red and blue, agreeable to the mode of Persia.

[The Persians: Herbert's description of them]

Now concerning the natives, they are generally well-limbed, and straight. The Zone they live in makes them tawny; the wine cheerful; opium salacious. The women paint; the men love arms; all affect poetry. What the grape inflames, the law allays, and example bridles. The Persians allow no part of their body hair except the upper lip, which they wear long and thick turning downwards; as also a lock upon the crown of the head, by which they are made to believe their Prophet will, at the resurrection, lift them into Paradise. A figment: whether proceeding from Muhammad's own brain or [that of] the apostate monk, his associate, uncertain. But probable it is he had read the Scripture, and there in *Ezekiel* 8.3[46] and in the apocryphal story of Bel and the Dragon[47] finds Habukkuk so [in that manner] transported from Judea to Babylon. For elsewhere their head is shaven, or made incapable of hair by the oil...being but thrice anointed. This has been the mode of the Oriental people since promulgation of the Qur'ān, introduced and first imposed by the Arabians. But that the wearing hair and covering the head was otherwise of old, appears in history very plainly.

But not to run into extremes. As amongst the primitive Christians it was a reproach to wear long hair, so it was to be bald. Therefore, to avoid that contempt, those who had short hair wore raised caps; those who shaved wreathed their heads with rolls of linen – not only for ornament but [also] to expel the sun's piercing rays, and for defence against an enemy. For undoubtedly those large turbans the Turks wear over a flat-crowned quilted cap is a very serviceable headpiece. Those in Persia are excessively large and valuable, although commonly of calico – for the superior sort of people have them woven with silk and gold with a rich fringe or tassel of gold and silver at the end. But at feasts, entertainments and gaudy days I have seen them wreath their sashes with ropes of orient pearl and chains of gold set with precious stones, of great value. That which the King himself has on differs not in shape from others, unless it exceeds in magnitude. All the difference [that] I could observe was that he wore it the contrary way and more erect than others....

With these sashes the Persians go covered all day long, not excepting the presence of the King, nor their set times of devotion: for to bare or uncover the head is held irreverent. Now as the Europeans in their salutes usually take off their hats in presence of their betters to bare their heads, the Mahometans signify the same only by a moderate deflexion of the head and directing their head towards their heart, by which they usually express their complement....But this custom came in with the Qur'ān; before which, the Oriental people (Persians, and others) wore a sort of hat and bonnet: as yet continued in China, where unless by the late invasion of the Tartars, Muhammad is not acknowledged. Yea, both as salutations and in presence of superiors they were uncovered; a practice not only commended but commanded by St. Paul *I Corinthians* 11:4 where it is said that at the exercise of religious duty to be covered the head thereby is dishonoured; for, that a man ought not to cover his head at those time, appears by the seventh verse.[48] But as to the other sex, it is otherwise.

Now how rigid soever the Turk may seem in abhorring the moving his turban, especially towards a Christian in salutations; the Persians nevertheless have more generosity. For with them it is a maxim (and might be so with others) that singularity is discommendable, as being a humour either slighting order and degrees of men (allowed angels,) or otherwise the civil customs and good manners of countries in things indifferent and merely ceremonial, serving only to cement affection. And albeit to one another they are strict enough to that mode of custom of being covered, nevertheless...after Sir Dodmore Cotton had his audience, at which Shah Abbas was present with the Ambassador, the King his master's health being by Sir Robert Sherley remembered, the Ambassador, standing up, uncovered, the Persian King (frolic at that time, or rather in civility) took off his turban. Another time, as I heedlessly crossed the Court where the King was sitting in an open tent hearing petitions, I, according to the European mode, made my due respects, by uncovering my head and bowing reverently towards the King, who observed it, and was so well pleased therewith that he raised his turban a little from his brows, both to honour me the more and express his satisfaction; especially, as I was afterwards told because I appeared in my own country's habit; otherwise it had been a presumption punishable; but as it proved, a grace that procured me the more respect, especially with the better sort, where-ever I passed. The King indeed took great delight and esteemed it an addition of lustre to his Court to behold exotics in their own country's habit. So that the greater the variety appeared, he would say the more was the Court and country-honoured at home, and in estimation abroad. Insomuch that, upon any affront done a stranger, if in his own habit, he should be sure of reparation; but in case he went in the bit of the country where he travelled, indistinguishable when the injury was offered, it would be otherwise upon address for vindication: the emphasis it seems wanting that inclined it. Such was then the rule of Court and populous places: albeit in travel foreigners have their liberty to please themselves as to their garb, and without cause of exception to any....

Persian women

The women here (as of old, in other parts of Asia) veil their faces in public.[49] This veiling the face is very ancient both amongst the Jews and Romans. Rebecca when she approached Isaac covered her face *Genesis* 24.65.[50] Yea, amongst men it was a note of reverence, as we find by Elijah, and by the Apostle intimated *I Corinthians* 11:10.[51] Yea, by the Romans used; for the bride was commonly presented to her husband with a yellow scarf thrown over her face....

But to describe them: I observed that generally. They are of low stature, yet straight and comely; more corpulent than lean. Wine and music fattens them; the spleen is curable when passion rules no. And, as to complexion it is usually pale, but made sanguine by adulterate fucusses. Their hair is black and curled; their foreheads high, skin soft, eyes black; have high noses, pretty large mouths, thick lips, and round cheeks. Honest women, when they take the liberty to go abroad, seldom speak to any [people? men?] on the way or unveil their faces. When they travel or follow the camp, the vulgar sort ride astride upon horses; but those of better rank are mounted two and two upon camels in cages...of wood, covered over with cloth, to forbid any man the sight of them.

Agreeable to this, we oftentimes had a prospect of the travelling Seraglios, and could well perceive that their guards were pale, lean-faced eunuchs, so jealous of their charge, that as well-travelled it was the hazard of our lives if we neglected to hasten out of the way so soon as we saw them; or else by throwing our selves upon the ground to cover us with some veil or other, that the eunuchs might be satisfied we durst not, at least, were not willing to view them. In one of these, for ease and warmth I was forced to travel upon a camel above 300 miles, being so enfeebled by a flux that I was not able to ride on horseback, and to keep company with the caravan was necessitated to this kind of accommodation.

However, that the custom was otherwise, appears by that sumptuous entertainment Belshazar made [for] a thousand of his lords, (then cooped up in Babylon) where the King and his Princes, his wives and concubines, drank wine in those golden vessels Nebuchadnezzar [had] brought there from the House of God; which was at Jerusalem.

Figure 3 A Persian woman
Source: Herbert (1677). By permission of the British Library (ref. 215e12)

Daniel 5.3. And likewise, at that magic feast which Ahasuerus made for a 180 days to the nobles and princes of his empire...where it is said [that] the King, sitting on his throne...commanded the eunuchs to bring Queen Vashti with the crown royal to show the people and the Princes her beauty; which was excellent. Plutarch also...notes how that Statira the Queen usually sat with the King to meat in public, and was placed near the King in an open chariot when he took the air abroad; the beholding of which (says the author) gave great content unto the people.

But the *amorosas*, or those of the Order of Laius...are more sociable, have most freedom, and in this region are not worst esteemed of. No question but (to free themselves from jealous husbands) many there would be of that order: those therefore that are such are not admitted without suit and giving money; after which toleration none dare abuse them, being company for the best or greatest: in which respect they go no less richly habilimented....Their hair, curling, dishevels about their shoulders, sometimes plaited in a caul of gold. Roundabout their face and chin usually they hang a rope of pearl. Their cheeks are of a delicate vermilion dye – Art (oftener than Nature) causes it. Their eyelids are coloured coal black with pencil dipped in that mineral alcohol which Xenophon said the Medes used to paint their faces with: which was the old way of painting; and from the Vulgar Translation of the Bible,[52] where it is said *Jezebel* may be presumed she was so painted....

They also have artificial incisions of various shapes and forms....Their noses are set with jewels of gold, embellished with rich stones; and their ears also have rings of equal lustre. In a word, to show they are servants to Dame Flora, they beautify their arms, hands, legs, and feet with painted flowers and birds; and, in a naked garb, force every limb about them to dance after each other, elaborately making their bells and timbrels answer their turnings. Short nevertheless of the Indian courtesans...who, at 10 years of age, when their bodies are tender and flexible, will in their dances screw themselves into admirable postures. For, standing upon one leg, they will raise the other above their heads, and leisurely lay their heels upon their heads, all the while standing upon one leg, as I have heard a merchant relate he saw done at Golconda and other places in India. Their clothes (not unlike themselves) is loose and gaudy, reaching to their mid-leg; under which they wear drawers of cloth of gold, satin, tissued stuffs or costly embroidery.

This kind of creature is of no religion, save that of the last Assyrian monarch, whose doctrine was *ede, bibe, lude.* For these look temptingly, drink notably, and covet men's souls and money greedily. They scorn, nay upbraid the soberer sort with epithets of 'slave', 'rejected', 'unsociable' and unworthy their notice....But that the women have greater liberty is observed by an author of good credit...: The Queen is present with the Persian King at supper and banquets, but withdraws when the King is disposed to drink and be merry. For then they call for music and courtesans...done in regard they would not have their wives partakers of those intemperate and wanton enterprises....

[Poetry – eunuchs – circumcision]

Above all, poetry lulls them; that genius seeming properly to delight it self amongst them. However, mimographers[53] I must call them, their common ballads resounding out the merry disports of Mars and his mistress, to which saints they dedicate their amorous devotion....And albeit the men affect not to dance themselves, (though anciently dancing was in request with men, as stories tell us) nevertheless, dancing is much esteemed there. For...seeing the bells, brass armolets, silver fetters, timbrels, cymbals, and the like so revive Bacchus in this kind of dance being so elaborate that each limb seems to emulate, yea, to contend which can express the most motion; their hands, eyes, and bums gesticulating severally and after each other, swimming round, and now and then conforming themselves to a Doric stillness; the Ganymedes, with incanting voices and distorting bodies sympathising; and poesy, mirth, and wine raising the sport commonly to admiration. But were this all, it were excusable. For though persons of quality here have their several Seraglios, these dancers seldom go without wages. And in a higher degree of baseness, the pederasts affect those painted antique-robed youths or catamites...a vice so detestable, so damnable, so unnatural as forces Hell to show its ugliness before its season....And for the detestation whereof, Alexander is honoured to all posterity.

Persia continues the ancient custom of emasculating youths; practised to preserve the excellency of their voice, but principally to guard the Seraglios of great persons. Which, though it sufficiently effeminates them, yet some eunuchs have neither wanted courage nor reputation, seeing that both in Barbary and other Mahometan countries out of them they have elected generals for the field; but, in the execution of their ordinary trust about women find them mischievous enough. For, being armed with sword and target, bow and arrows, they express their jealousy too often to the prejudice of ignorant and careless travellers. They are of most ancient standing, for we read of them in Scripture in oldest times, especially in this Empire. So that…Terence and Petronius…spare not to aver that Persia made the first eunuchs. By which word is sometime understood Chamberlains, or those great officers whose nearest attendance was upon the King: But those other who wait upon the harems have their testicles cut off: which so enervates Nature, or at least the exercise, that they are utterly disabled as to procreation. And yet it is the opinion of some, that when the testicles are forced away, there is such a remainder of seed stored up in the glandules of generation which are spermatic, that it is possible for eunuchs to generate. Notwithstanding which, until a jealous Turk observed a gelding to cover a mare, the extreme now used was not practised.

Now, concerning circumcision, it is here used, and accounted so necessary that, without it, none calls himself a Mussulman. Men (and sometimes women) conform to it: the men for Paradise; the women for honour's sake. The males at Ishmael's age (whom they imagine was Abraham's best beloved) are enjoined it before 12 [years of age], hoping he may be able to speak his profession.…However, the Arabs practised it before Muhammad's time, yea, some think he himself was not circumcised; nor that he imposed, but suffered it only to please the Arabians.

A fee is paid amid the ceremony, for want of which, the poorest sort are seldom cut. The ceremony is more or less according to the difference of their degree, acted either at home or in the mosques. If son to a Mirza, Chawn, Sultan…it has more pomp; for his kindred and friends in their best equipage assemble at the parent's house, as a symbol of their joy, presenting him with gifts of sundry prices; and after small stay, mount the boy upon a courser, richly vested, holding in his right hand a sword, in his left a bridle. A slave goes on either side, one holding a lance, the other a flambeaux; neither of which are without their allegories. Music is not wanting, for it goes first; the father next, and, according as they are in blood, the rest. Others follow promiscuously. The Hadji attending at the entrance into the mosque, helps him to alight, and hallows him. To work they straightway go: one holds his knee, a second disrobes, a third holds his hands, and others (by some trivial conceit) strive to win his thoughts to extenuate his ensuing torment. The priest (having muttered his orisons) dilates the præpuce, [and], in a trice, with his silver scissors circumcises him, and then applies a healing powder of salt, date-stones and cotton-wool; the standers by to joy his initiation into Mahometry…salute him by the name of Mussulman. But if the ceremony is at home, they then provide a banquet – before which, the boy enters well attended, unclothed before them all and circumcised. And in commemoration of such a benefit (imitating therein Abraham when Isaac was weaned) continue to feast for 3 days together; at the end whereof, the child is led about in state, bathed and purged, a turban of white silk put upon his head, and all the way, as he returns, saluted with acclamations.

But such as turn apostates to swill in luxury the more, or to robe themselves with some title or advancement, (forgetting that for a base and momentary applause or pleasure they disrobe their soul of everlasting happiness, such as run parallel with the lines of Eternity) are brought before the Cadi, who upon his signification, leads him into the mosque and without much ceremony, only by cutting the fore-skin, are thereby Believers. Which done, those devils incarnate to witness their new persuasion, or rather to aggravate – and indeed accelerate – their damnation, spurn with their accursed feet the Cross, the hieroglyphic of our salvation. Which, in the primitive and purest age, was of that honour amongst Christians as not only they used it in baptism but upon their foreheads to despite the Jews and heathens; and to glory in that same thing the more which the enemies of Christ upbraided the Christian with as a calumny.

The renegade, in token of defiance, spits thrice at it, having this mis-belief, that Christ never suffered, but Judas. And then exults in the usual battology: 'God is first, praise him, and next him, Muhammad'. After which imprecation the wretch holds up one finger, thereby renouncing a Trinity. Three Mussulmen then dart three staves three times towards Heaven. And before any touch ground, his new name is imposed. Which done, he is led slowly upon an ass, his emblem, about the city that every one man may note him for a denizen and proselyte to Muhammad. But (praised be God) I have not heard of any European Christian, who in this country, of late times, has denied his Faith. Which is cause for rejoicing.

NOTES

1 See Kenneth Parker, 'Telling tales. Early modern English voyagers and the Cape of Good Hope', *The Seventeenth Century* X(1) (Spring): 121–49, 1995.

2 Penrose (1938) offers the following reason for Herbert's adherence to the parliamentary cause:

> Doubtless because of his relationship to, as well as because of his friendship for, the Fairfax family, together with the fact that his ambitions for advancement at Court had not been rewarded, Herbert inclined early to the cause of Parliament. This partisanship was further strengthened when Lord Pembroke was relieved of his post as Chamberlain to the Royal household and was in consequence driven into the camp of the rebels [*sic*].

3 'Threnodia Carolina; or, Sir Thomas Herbert's Memoirs. Printed for the first time from then original ms', in Allan Fea, *Memoirs of the Martyr King*, 1905. See also 'Mémoires de Sir Thomas Herbert (valet de chambre de Charles 1er; sur deux dernières années du règne de ce prince)', in John Price [chaplain to George Monk, Duke of Albemarle], *Mémoires de John Price, 1823; The Trial of Charles I. A contemporary account taken from the memoirs of Sir Thomas Herbert and John Rushworth*, edited by Roger Lockwood [with an] Introduction by C. V. Wedgwood, London: Folio Society, 1959.

4 Gombroom: Bandar Abbas, the port built (1623) by Abbas the Great and named after him. It replaced Hormuz as the leading commercial trading centre during the seventeenth century.

5 Newberry. John Newberry was a member of a party of English merchants who travelled to Syria, Baghdad and Basra. John Eldred, in this account of the voyage (Hakluyt, 1589 (Vol. 2): 268–80) states that they '...departed out of London in the ship called the *Tiger*...upon Shrove Monday 1583'. Might it be simply too far-fetched to suggest a connection with that well-known observation by the First Witch: 'Her husband's to Aleppo gone, master o'th Tiger' (*Macbeth* 1.3.6)? We also know that, together with Ralph Fitch, William Leeds and Ralph Storey, Newberry was caught by the Portuguese and shipped to their prison in Goa on the trumped-up accusation of being spies, from which they were eventually released, partly with the assistance of the English-born Jesuit, Thomas Steevens, then serving the Catholic community there. Accounts of their imprisonment are given by Fitch himself, as well as by the Dutchman Jan Huyghen van Linschoten (who was in Goa at that time) in Hakluyt, *Voyages* Vol. 2: 250–68, 1598.

6 Bannians: Banian. A Hindoo trader, especially one from the province of Guzerat ('many of which have for ages been settled in Arabian ports...'); sometimes applied by all early writers to all Hindoos in Western India (*OED*). Originally applied by Europeans to a particular tree under which traders had built a pagoda (*New Shorter Oxford*).

7 While *OED* has no reference for 'bunny', it gives 'coava' as variant for coffee; from the Arabic *qahwah*, in Turkish pronounced *kahveh*.

8 Arack: Arrack/Arecha/Rakia – variant forms of name for an alcoholic spirit, usually distilled from the sap of local origin, for example rice, or palm oil.

9 The astringent plum-like fruit...formerly used medically, but now chiefly in dyeing, tanning and ink-making (*OED*).

10 Probably fruit of the carob tree, a native of the Levant.

11 The 1634 edition has the (uncorroborated) observation: 'yet I believe the Pagans are by this time weary of this courtesy, and begin to deny the English that honour any more'.

12 Linstock: a staff about 3 feet (91 cm) long, having a pointed foot to stick in the deck or ground, and a forked head to hold a lighted match (*OED*).

13 Hammams: an Oriental bathing establishment; a Turkish bath (*OED*).

14 Graff: a trench serving as fortification; a dry or wet ditch; a foss or moat (*OED*).

15 Asinegoes: asinego – a little ass (*OED*).

16 Fucus: paint or cosmetic for beautifying the skin; a wash or colouring for the face (*OED*).

17 Olivaster: olive-coloured; having an olive skin (*OED*).

18 Neither the 1617 nor the 1638 editions make any mention of colour. At this place the 1634 says, about the women, that 'They are the most ugly and impudent whores in all Persia, and infect that corporation with their heathenism and numbers'. In the 1638 edition the assertion is that 'they are the most nasty, pocky whores you shall find in any place, and who very fitly comply with Ovid's remedy of love'. The phrase 'save for the desire to please white people' appears, for the first time, in the 1658 edition.

19 Manilioes: obsolete form for manilla – a ring of metal worn on the arm or wrist by some African tribes [*sic*] and used as a medium of exchange (*OED*).

20 Morisco: appertaining to Moors in Spain; here, probably 'in the Moorish fashion'.

21 Jean de Léry, *Histoire d'un voyage fait en la terre du Bresil, autrement dite Amerique, contenant la navigation...les meurs & façons de vivre...des sauvages...*, La Rochelle: A. Chuppin, 1578; reprinted Geneva 1580; Paris 1585, 1594; Geneva 1600. There are also 'Extracts out of the Historie of John Lerius, a Frenchman who lived in Brasill', in Purchas (1625: 4).

22 Herbert here probably refers to the single-humped Arabian camel (or dromedary), to be distinguished from the two-humped Bactrian camel of Central Asia.

23 This section has been much reduced – often repetition of building construction, food, etc.

24 Sudatories: sudatorium – a room in which hot air or steam baths are used to produce sweating; a sweating room; cf. sauna.

25 Musladini Sadi, *Rosarium Politicum*, translated by Georgius Gentius, Amsterdam, 1651, 1687.

26 Tetrarch: a ruler of a fourth part; a subordinate ruler.

27 Pintado: a kind of Eastern cotton cloth painted or printed in colours; chintz (*OED*).

28 Pelo: Greek *clay, mud*. Herbert's usage here is unclear.

29 Carbuncle: a red precious stone.

30 Zindabad: loud approval or encouragement for a specified person or thing (*Shorter OED*).

31 Facetious: in the sixteenth-century sense of being urbane, polished.

32 Chymick-waters: it is fascinating to speculate on the possibility that, since water from the English spa towns (especially from Epsom, noted for purgative qualities) had been on sale in bottled form in London since the early seventeenth century, the English party might have taken a supply of this commodity with them. Were that to have been so, it offers a vastly earlier date than that usually thought of with reference to the popular image of English fear of drinking water in foreign places.

33 Sumpter: the driver of a pack-horse.

34 Natural Magic: magic which does not involve the invocation of spirits.

35 Tabret; timbrel: varieties of percussion instruments; hocus-pocus: jugglers.

36 Strictly, 'Howbeit I send unto you all my servants the prophets, rising early and sending them, saying, Oh, do not this abominable thing that I hate'.

37 Mamelukes: here, in the sense of an object of possession; a slave, rather than the regime established by emancipated *white* military slaves who ruled in Egypt (1250–1517) as a military caste under the Ottomans until 1812, and in Syria (1260–1516).

38 Monostic: monostich – a poem or epigram consisting of a single line or verse.

39 Fulgur: fulgor; fulgour – splendour; dazzling brightness.

40 Mastaba: a stone bench or seat attached to a house.

41 The phrase 'perpetual League of Friendship' occurs for the first time in the 1655 edition. There is no reference to it in 1634 and in the 1638 edition it is simply 'that perpetual amity might be continued'. Furthermore, the specification 'Great Britain' is also absent in 1634.

42 Herbert records Nakd Ali Beg's death as follows:

> The same day [that] we came to an anchor in Swalley Road [harbour], Nogdi-Ally-Beg the Persian Ambassador (Sir Robert Sherley's antagonist) died, having (as it were credibly told) poisoned himself: for 4 days only eating opium. A sad exit....The *Mary* (where he died) gave him 11 great ordnance at his carrying ashore. His son Ebrahim Khan conveyed him to Surat (10 miles thence) where they entombed him not a stone's cast from Tom Coryate's grave, known but by two poor stones that speak his name, there resting till the Resurrection. Now, this tragic end of Nogdibeg was not without cause. For it seems [that] despairing of his master's favour, and conscious to himself of his abusive carriage in England, both to Sir Robert Sherley, and some other misdemeanours of which he begot himself a complaint against him from Shah Abbas, and made known by way of Aleppo after his departure out of England, he gave himself this desperate exit, well knowing that his master was at no time to be jested with in money matters, or business relating to honour and reputation. So, as neither his past service against the Turk, his alliance at court, or what else he could think upon, could animate his defence.

43 Instead of the details (to be found first in 1638), 1634 recounts that:

> The King gave him a very gracious reply, and whereas he thinks it honour enough to let the Great Turk's Ambassador kiss the hem of his coat (and sometimes his foot), he very nobly gave our Ambassador his hand, and with it pulled him down and seated him next to him cross-legged, and (calling for a cup of wine) drank to His Majesty, our famous King. At which he [the Ambassador] put off his hat; and the King seeing it, put off his turban, and drank the cup off, which our Ambassador pledged thankfully. And the people thought it a strange thing to see their King so complemental, for it is a shame with them to be bareheaded.

44 Battle of Leuctra: Thebans, led by Epaminondas, defeated the Spartans (371 BCE).
45 Catchpoles: one who arrests for debt.
46 Ezekiel 8: 3:

> And he put forth the form of an hand, and took me by the lock of mine head; and the spirit lifted me up between the earth and the heaven, and brought me in the visions of God to Jerusalem, to the door of the inner gate that looketh toward the north; where *was* the seat of the image of jealousy, which provoketh jealousy.

47 Bel and the Dragon. An extra book in Greek OT to the *Book of Daniel*; included in Apocrypha as a separate book.
48 1 Corinthians 11 (verse 4: 'Every man praying or prophesying, having *his* head covered, dishonoureth the head'; verse 7: 'For a man indeed ought not to cover *his* head, forasmuch as he is the image and glory of God: but the woman is the glory of the man').
49 It is noteworthy that Figure 3 shows the woman with her face uncovered.
50 Strictly read, it is clear that Rebecca did not normally wear a veil; neither when looking after the camels in the fields, or on the journey. It was only when she

> lifted up her eyes, and when she saw Isaac, she lighted off her camel. / For she *had* said unto the servant, What man *is* that walketh in the field to meet us? And the servant *had* said, It *is* my master: therefore she took a vail, and covered herself.

(64–5)

51 1 Corinthians 11 contains arguably the most sustained of sexist prescriptions. The relevant verses, which culminate in the one to which Herbert refers, are as follows:

> For a man indeed ought not to cover *his* head, forasmuch as he is the image and glory of God: but the woman is the glory of the man. / For the man is not of the woman; but the woman of the man. Neither was the man created for the woman; but the woman for the man. / For this cause ought the woman to have power *on* her head because of the angels.
>
> (7–10)

52 Vulgar Translation of the Bible. From Vulgate, designating or occurring in the standard accepted version or text.
53 Mimographer: writer and composer of mimes.

OTHER EDITIONS

A Relation of some yeeres travaile, begunne Anno 1626. Into Aphrique and the greater Asia, especially the Territories of the Persian Monarchie, and some parts of the Orientall Indies....Of their religion, language, habit [dress]...and other matters concerning them. Together with the proceedings and death of the three late Ambassadours, Sir D[odmore] C[otton], Sir R[obert] S[herley] and the Persian Nogdi Beg [Nakd Ali Beg]. London. W. Stansby and J. Bloome, 1634 (reprinted in facsimile Amsterdam: Theatrum Orbis Terrarum/New York: Da Capo Press, 1971).
Some Years Travel into divers parts of Asia and Afrique. Describing especially the two famous Empires, the Persian, and the Great Magull, weaved with the history of those times....Revised, and enlarged by the author. Printed by R. Bip, for Jacob Blome and Richard Bishop. London, 1638.
*Some Yeares Travel....*Third Impression, London, Printed by J. Best for Andrew Crook at the Green Dragon in St. Pauls Church-yard; and to be sold by William Crook, at the Three Bibles on Fleet-bridge, 1665.
Thomas Herberts Zee – en Lant Reyse na verscheyde Deelen via Asia en Africa...Uyt het Engels in de Nederlantsche taal overgetset door L[ambert] v[an den] B[os]. Dordrecht, 1658.
Relation du Voyage de Perse et des Indes Orientales, traduite de l'Anglais de T[homas] H[erbert]. Traduites du Flamand de J. van Vliet (par M. de Wicquefort). Paris, 1663.
Travels in Persia 1627–1629, abridged and edited by Sir William Foster. London. C. Routledge & Sons (The Broadway Travellers Series), 1928.

FURTHER READING

Norman MacKenzie, 'Sir Thomas Herbert of Tintern: a parliamentary "royalist"', *Bulletin of the Institute for Historical Research* No. 79, 1956.
Boies Penrose, *Urbane Travellers 1591–1635*, Philadelphia: University of Philadelphia Press, 1942.

11

JOHN FRYER

A New Account of East-India and Persia, in Eight Letters. Being Nine Years Travels, Begun 1672. And Finished 1681. Containing observations made of the moral, natural, and artificial estate of those countries: namely, of their government, religion, laws, customs. Of the soil, climates, seasons, health, diseases. Of the animals, vegatables, minerals, jewels. Of their housing, cloathing, manufactures, trades, commodities. And of the coins, weights, and measures, used in the principal places of trade in those parts.
By John Fryer, M.D. Cantabrig. And Fellow of the Royal Society.
Illustrated with maps, figures, and useful tables. London.
Printed by R. R. for Ri[chard] Chiswell, at the Rose
and Crown in St. Paul's Church-Yard, 1698.

BIOGRAPHY

Following upon the award of a degree in medicine (1671), John Fryer (d. 1733), who, himself, wrote his name as 'Fryer' or 'Fryar', left England (December 1672) for India and Persia, in which places he worked for the EEIC in various capacities for some ten years, before returning to England (1682). It would be another sixteen years before he could be persuaded to publish an account of his travels. The author of the entry in *DNB* claims that the reason why Fryer finally consented to publish was because he not only became 'piqued at the frequent appearance of translations of foreign, especially French, books of travel in which English industry and enterprise were decried', but also had 'more than four hundred queries now by me to which I am pressed for answers'.

* * *

[Omitted: story of journey across Persian Gulf, stay at Gombroom, Shiraz, Esphahan, etc. – in large part repetitive, particularly of statements previously encountered in Herbert. Indeed, in his Preface, Fryer writes of 'The Ingenious Sir Thomas Herbert'. So, instead of further selections about, for example, Islam and Muhammad, Georgians and Armenians, the 'cruelty' of the legal system, etc., the extracts below would appear to be of interest precisely because they deal with themes and issues hitherto either neglected or mentioned in passing by predecessor writers.]

Of their bookmen and books

[Having ended his preceding chapter with comments on the cavalry, the infantry and the navy, Fryer begins the next:] After these come the academics. For such is the civility of these regions that arms take the place of the gown, letters being in small esteem amongst them, for the incitements to study are but few, the toils and labours are many. Whereby it is no wonder that slenderness of profit, and assiduity, should be alike irksome when (on the contrary) a military condition slights these inconveniences and austerities and lives more at large, taking pleasure, and commanding all where they come: and are in a continual prospect for advancement. On which score, a learned or a noble clerk is as rare as a black swan – they being raised to that station out of the dregs of the people. The School [University] language among the Persians is Arabic, as Latin is so held among us – in which not only the mysteries of their Qur'ān, but all their other sciences, is written.

They have their grammars, dictionaries and vocabularies, in which are the roots of the Arabic tongue; which, with other books, are all written with the pen, by great industry and pain [and] not committed to the press. Wherefore they are chargeable, and less from errors – to correct which, they compare with others more correct; one reading with a loud voice, while the other takes notice of the faults. They reckon 50 letters to a verse; and for a 1000 verses of ordinary writing they give 2 abcees[1] [and] from 5 to 10 and upwards for that which is more exquisite. After this rate are their books sold and valued. An account of the character being stated, they numerate the verses on any one page and, multiplying the other pages thereby, the price of the book is produced. If there are lines of gold, silver, ochre or the like, surrounding the margin, for ornament, as is their custom, they reckon nothing for them but bestow them *gratis* on the first buyer; and only pass as a better grace to set off the book – they being mightily taken with a fair hand and good writing....They use Indian ink, being a middling sort, between our common ink and that used in printing. Instead of a pen, they make use of a reed, as in India.

Education of youth

The children of nobles, or other rich men, are brought up at home: not stirring out of their houses without a train of eunuchs and servants, for fear of sodomy – so much practised among the pestilent sect of Mahometans. Other children, of inferior rank, are taught in their public schools, for a small matter. Their childhood being passed, and they beginning to write man, they frequent the Schools and Colleges: and everyone chooses a Master where he pleases. And, having chosen him, after a few months leaves him at his own will, and goes over to another. For such a strange itch is there for learning that before they are halfway instructed in one book, they are desirous to be perfected in another. And before they have read philosophy, morality, or any other science to qualify them they leap into the Qur'ān: for here are neither public professors to examine, or public acts to be kept: either in Divinity, Law, or Physick [Medicine]. These are constituted by the Primate of their cursed fabulous doctrine without formal disputation or other approbation than the popular fame, interest of friends, and a false appearance of a pious life. And are introduced by these means into the pensions and benefices of their wealthiest mosques.

[From] whence it comes to pass that they are so inclinable to read to all comers. For he whose lectures are most frequented, stands fairest in the noisy applause of the town, and seldom misses out on promotion: though it is known that many of them consume their patrimony in purchasing disciples and, after all [that?], reap nothing but poverty for their pains. Which kind of philosopher is always attended with envy and ambition. Nor care they whom they defame, may they but extol themselves. And after a long invective, both of master and Scholar, against whoever they think fit to bespatter (or they are in danger of being outdone by) insulting in the mean while over them as the greatest dunces and asses in Nature; at length, out of a kindness to themselves, having stretched their known worth to the highest pitch (lest the swollen bladder should burst by too much wind), they feign a humble self-reprehension: which, because nothing is more practised, I will use their own phrase…'It is indecent for a man to speak his own praise. But were I silent, this is a justice you would do me; it being noting but what you know'. Whereby it is visible [that] if they abate of their own humour it is likely to be very little to the favour of him [whom] they declaim against.

Notwithstanding these tricks and disingenuous insinuations, yet this scabby herd increases, so that they are at their wit's end how to live. Some find Maecenas' amongst the noblemen, and content themselves to live slavishly, according to their humours, for a morsel of bread. Others, by saving what they have scraped up from the poor trade of scribes, and teaching in school, hire a house, purchase a horse, and a servant to run ahead of them (it being the sign of the greatest poverty to foot it through the city). And if by any good luck they get a name, and are reputed men of note for learning, then they can enlarge their stock and family. And these are they who pride themselves about being the greatest Doctors among them, and so set up Academies of their own, and teach Aristotle's Dialect[2] and the Four Figures of Syllogism.[3] Though, the question being propounded, they bind not themselves up to the strict rules thereof, but they beg the premise by way of interrogation, as a truth granted: and from there, draw conclusions.

The terms of Negation and Concession are exotic amongst the Persians, contending that Distinctions and Laconical[4] Evasions, upon which the stress of the Aristotelian Doctrine seems to be laid, are not to be held for the true solution of the Argument; but, by a long harangue, and affluence of speech, the auditors [hearers] are brought both to admire them, and to be on their side. Whereupon the greater the convention of auditors are, the most earnest will the contention is. For, to yield in such assemblies, is not at all to be expected, unless he who holds his tongue first, intends to lose both his credit and his cause.

Universals, categories, and the depending questions they often reject. Concerning the nature of a body, place, vacuum, corruption, quantities, and qualities, they inform their students after the Aristotelian way, being unacquainted with the resolution of causes of sublunary beings by atoms, according to our modern Cartesian principles, revived in honour of Epicurus….In their theology, after the contemplation of One Eternal Divinity, after its unity and attributes which they maintain to be all one with its Essence, they hold the world to be from eternity. And such a treatise of the Soul and Passions, with the other precisions of the Intellect, which is nowhere to be found in metaphysics. In these (as in their other) speculations, they cleave so pertinaciously to their Books and undoubted Authors as if it were peculiar to depart from their traditions.

They fancy to themselves a chimerical Creation of the world by 10 Intelligences; which, by the same inexpungeable Reason, passes into their Creed. And, being freighted with this notion, they say [that] from one most simple cause can proceed no more than one Effect. And therefore [that] God framed the First Intelligence (and that [one] mediating the First Heaven). And so, in their subaltern order, to the tenth. That the world was many ages before Adam and Eve our first parents education [eviction?] out of the earth, inhabited by devils; and that the possession thereof was so long entrusted in their hands till they had exterminated the true worship of God (which, at first, they had applied themselves rigidly to observe), and gave themselves up to uncleanliness and profaneness, when man was created in their room, and they cast out of any further possession; and Men took their places....They acknowledge four kinds of Causes, viz: Material, Formal, Efficient, and Final.[5] They allow not of an exemplary, but admit a Total Cause, by which they understand such a one as no condition is defective to put it into action. And upon these foundations they suppose the world's creation, from Eternity, to be enough proved.

The books of greatest vogue are those of Corge Nessir Tussi[6] of the city of Tuss, in the province of Khorassan, written 500 years ago. He (as it is credible), understood the Greek language, as well as others: from whence he has explained some ancient authors such as Euclid, Ptolemy's *Almagest* and *Optics*, and has reduced them into a compendium; as also, works of Plato. Some expositors they have of their Law, with rules of justice and morality, which they admire and extol to the skies; and rest implicitly on the *ipse dixit*[7] of their Prophet, never inquiring further. If anything happens to oppose common sense, they protract the meaning mysteriously or analogically:[8] not to the disquisition of the truth, but to defend their fopperies – among which they have, in the first esteem the Written Letter of their Prophet, as immediately prescribed by him. And these are oracular. In the second place, those which are since published by the Mahometan sectators; and these are looked upon as human – any whereof, if they appear foolish, yet they doubt not but that their Prophet uttered them [so] that he might bring himself to the capacities of his hearers; and of the Arabians, to whom he was sent to call them from idolatry to the worship of the only One God. To which the Persians make this answer: 'Should a Doctor [of Philosophy?] speak to a rustic, and speak as if he were discoursing with a Professor; and not conform himself to the apprehension of the countryman? How should he be understood?' Which course, say they, Muhammad took for the better informing of his proselytes.

[Omitted: Muhammad's revelations: version of familiar stories]

Poets

And now, having despatched this crew [Mullahs, Hadjis, Cadis], moulded up in dull clay, let us mix with those of more liberty in their own language, allowing them (at the same time) to be kept in bounds by the rigid compressures of their taskmasters in religion, so that all the strain of their wits must bias that way. And first: they have some (though few) set up as admirers of the Muses,[9] who value themselves in being called the Wits of the Age. And these are their poets: who confine themselves to rhyme and numbers; and sometimes to quantity, inferring their verses with comparisons, exaggerations, flights of ingenuity and fictions – which they repeat with gestures (both of hands and body, and mouth contorted), animating them with suitable tones and articulations, proclaiming them dead without such information.

They have romances of famous heroes and their deeds – among which are pleasant encounters, huntings, love-intrigues, banquetings, descriptions of flowers and delightful groves, emphatically set down, with cuts and pictures represented lively enough, would their colours endure. For which skill, otherwise than for hitting the life, their limners are to be reckoned defective, not knowing how to mix their colours. The exact history they have to brag on is *Rouse el Sapha*, a book of 3 or 4 volumes, in folio, which gives an account from the first habitation of men upon earth till the last two centuries.[10] Had they the era of Augustus, or the Julian period, or a faithful state of time, there might be some likelihood of truth in their histories. But they, being convicted of inadvertency in these points, the whole superstructure must fall. Which, to defend even in their Qur'ān, they are forced to forge aspersions to confront the lameness of its stories, whereby they endeavour to come off thus: 'A wicked Emperor, having obtained the rule of the world, got the Sacred Writs together by force, and burned them; after which, what occurred to the memory of the Christians, was committed to paper just as everyone could recollect or fancy. And hence arose the several mistakes and differences.'...A book like our *Aesop's Fables*, called *Emuel Sohaly* is preferred before all others, written in the Persian language. Yet their superstition is such that they dare hardly give it house-room, or afford it a place in their libraries, lest it should bring ill luck. At the same time as this was translated out of Hindustani [Hindi] into the Persian speech, there was contemporary another Persian who had composed a book of his own, but of a far inferior stile. And, being sensible [that] his work would be postponed thereby, he industriously took care to spread a rumour among the vulgar that this book of *Anwar I Suhaili*[11] was an ill thing, because it introduced creatures irrational, talking one to another, alleging for proof some texts of the Qur'ān: and at that juncture laying hold of an accident which happened to a youth sleeping while he was reading this piece, who fell down from the upper room to the ground, whereby he broke his skull and his thighs – confirming the mobile in the newly-broached opinion of this book; it ever since bearing an ill name, because they looked upon this as an exemplary judgement wherewith the prophet was pleased to forewarn others, and denounce his anger against such as should attempt the reading of it.

Alchemy

Alchemy has bewitched some of them to spend both their time and money without any other benefit than to supply them with a peculiar cant; and affected terms of their teachers who, seized with that itch, not only infect themselves, but others, with vain hopes: which, at last, together with the consumption of all their substance, vanish in smoke. These are such as cry up the transmutation of metals[12] till they have refined them to be the most excellent in Nature's cabinet, whereby they would arrive to that degree of Midas's wish, that whatever they touched should become gold: a sottish and imprudent thirst for wealth – as if it were in the power of Art[13] to outdo the design of the Creation, wherein everything was formed good in it's own right. By which these dabblers cast a scandal on the noble profession of chemistry, to which is owing the true knowledge of medicine, by an analytical separation of the parts of the compound from the gross dregs of the mixture, whereout may be sucked such particles as are applicable for the remedies of human infirmities; while they depart not from the nature first impressed on them. Here are many good writers in this honourable science, but [they] are at present unskilful and unprovided with their instruments or furnaces such as we find the learned sons of this Art use in their laboratories elsewhere.

Mathematics, being the foundation of all Arts, should have preceded. But, treating of an ingested nation, I deliver you them conformable to their own method. They understand Euclid's *Elements* and celestial phenomena, though they want [do not have] the citations and adjuncts in the demonstration of their propositions. They have the Theodosian and Autolican Doctrine of the Spheres,[14] some fragments of Archimedes, but have not the contracted proclivity. Practical geometry is common with them; arithmetic in entire numbers and fractions they exercise, performing their multiplication and division in transverse lines. The ancient algebra, a calculation by geometrical progressions, is not hidden from them, though they have no specious invention. Trigonometry of straight lines and spherical is their own, with the canons of signs and tangents: yet without secants.[15] The staff of 60 parts, with so many fractions, by a prolix reckoning they bring to 3, 4, or 5 minutes – our chemical arithmetical transmutation never entering their thoughts of the 60th number swollen into a unity by ciphers [so] that the chords may evade absolutely and entirely. No more have they any smattering of that never-enough-to-be-admired science of logarithms.[16]...

The Astrolabe[17] is the most workmanly tool among them, it being neatly framed in brass, copper, or silver, in a truly plain and familiar method, on one double square only, divided into 180 parts each, with their tangents; from the structure of which instrument, all the centres of the circles are sooner found out by steel compasses, hung in an arch with screws, than by our old way of Staefler and Regiomontaus which, though true in itself, yet it hardly is made to come right. They have tables showing the exact motion of the planets, and from there collect their ephemeris, which is two-fold: one whereof is 'cameri' [lunar], answering to our almanac, where are set forth the conjunctions of the moons, the rains, the alterations of the air; also obscure and implicit predictions to catch the believing multitude. The other is 'chamesi' [solar], in which the longitudes, latitudes, and aspects of the stars, the eclipses – sometimes agreeing, sometimes disagreeing with ours. In this book are the suspicions of war, scarcity of corn, and other incidents not discernible in human learning; but so adapted that, like the sound of bells to the fancies of some, the prognosticator may not be reproved for unskilfulness. Such an itch for knowing contingencies reigns here that no journey is undertaken, no new book read, no change of garments put on, no fresh dwelling entered, before the stars are consulted. Here is controverted when is the good, when the unlucky hour, to begin or end upon any enterprise. The Moon's (or that of other planets') ingress into Scorpio is much dreaded among them; and if that planet is retrograde, a stop is put to all business.

[From] whence comes the vulgar juggle of the oblong cubes, in which equal and unequal numbers are disposed, where they cast at adventures. [From] what figures they happen to be upon from those points they then make their judgements....These draw schemes, and are puffed with necromantic problems: if a thief has stolen anything; if a servant has run away from his master with stolen goods; if any would be acquainted about husbands or wives they betake themselves to oracles such as these. Who begin their delusion with a gypsy cant, with eyes and hands lifted up to Heaven. Then, casting the die, he observes the points and enigmatically canvasses the event: sometimes hitting the case, and sometimes as wide from it as the East is from the West. And though, by experience, they have found them tripping a hundred times, and upbraided them for cheats, they put it off as if they had not stated the thing fairly; that a minute, in the calculation, varies the truth; that this is the true profession Daniel transmitted to posterity. And if that answers not the question, it is not because the Art is defective, but because few are so happy as to attain its perfection. And thus do they willingly continue in their belief of the gull. They encourage an infinite number of these soothsayers: as many as can invent new tricks to get money by it.

When they consult for future success in matters of great consequence, they go to some learned doctor; who divines by the Qur'ān. And he, having prayed, opens the Qur'ān (that legend of Lies), and the first page he sets his eyes upon, if the first commandment happens to be in it, the augury is in force. And they have no delay allowed them, but hasten, with all speed, about their work. And if 20 or more come to the same errand, they are sent away with the same response. Which, after comparing notes, though the event may be as unfortunate as may be, yet they contentedly acquiesce in the verity of the prophecy, however contradictory to their senses: and shall repeat the same method as if it were a point of their Faith to go on in palpable absurdities, by constantly inquiring from the Qur'ān.

Astrologers

The Emperor nourishes a great many astrologers; the chief of whom is always by his side, with his astrolabe at his girdle – and dictates the good hour, or bad hour: when to rise; when to go to bed; or perpetrate any action of note. Erecting a scheme on the sand, whose advice is always followed (though some stories are on record to their disadvantage)....

Physick [Medicine]

At last I convert myself to that noble and excellent Art so beneficial to the life of man, physick [medicine]. Which, though it is here in good repute, yet its sectators are too much wedded to antiquity, not being at all addicted to find out its improvement by new inquiries; wherefore they stick to the Arabian method as devoutly as to the Sacred Tripod, which they hold as infallible as, of old, that Delphic oracle was accounted. On which score, chemistry is hardly embraced. Nor, to the pathological part do they think the anatomical knife can bring much profit. However, many of them have wealthy presents from their grandees. Whoever applies himself to this profession takes a master of that calling, who instructs him in the style and ordinary characters of medicine. Where, being thoroughly versed in the employment, and able to set up for himself, he consults where-abouts the fewest physicians are planted in the city, and the likeliest place to draw customers to him. There he joins an apothecary to him to make up his prescriptions and sell them to his patients: the half of which goes into his pocket. Thus, by degrees increasing in fame, he covets many students to read to, who are sure to spread abroad his fame, like so many speaking-trumpets and are sent about, in quest of prey, to bring in game, like so many decoys.

But the bait that takes most are those of the women crying up their man when he is found to please them by a fair carriage and a voluble tongue: who never leave off until they have rendered him gracious to all their acquaintance – who flock to him in droves, and are as full of chat as a magpie when she has found an owl in the wood at noonday. Nor wants he his lime-twigs for such sorts of birds,[18] by whose frequentings he arrives to the top of his hopes, and sucks those riches that Galen is said to offer his disciples. But, as all the eggs laid under one hen do not always prove [hatch], so many of this tribe miss their aim and (after an expense of time and endeavour) are forced to fall upon other trades to get a livelihood. Here is no precedent License of Practising; but it is lawful for anyone to exercise this function who has the impudence to pretend it.

In the matter of their medicine, extracts (or essences) of plants, roots, or minerals are beyond their pharmacy. They only use cooling seeds, and medicines of that nature; so that...the body is left in that condition that obstructions, or an ill habit, succeeds.

Although I am not ignorant that sometimes, after greatest care in chronic disorders, such things will happen, according to the experience of Hippocrates, yet in acute distempers so frequently to fall into these indispositions I cannot excuse the indiscretion of these medicasters, whose patients in Esphanan seldom pass out of this life by any other way to their graves.

Besides this abuse, their prescriptions are pancratical,[19] a salve for every sore, without respect had to difference of temperament or constitution. Nay; or even to the distempers themselves. But asking such frivolous questions, viewing the veins of the hands and feet, inspecting the tongue, they write at adventure. The apothecary dispenses the ingredients into so many papers, and leaves them to be boiled according to his directions, and given to the sick party at such and such hours of the day, by any good woman, or heedless servant, who (not attending to the quantities of the liquor more than the qualities of the ingredients) boil more or less, not as the exigency (either of the medicines, or of the patient) requires, but as if they were to make pottage – and give him to drink of this heterogeneous broth sometimes 3 or 4 pints at a time. So that, if he fails moving the belly by the excitative faculty, yet by its excessive dose it makes way for evacuation. And this they repeat most on end for a fortnight or three weeks altogether. Which, if it succeeds not, another physician is consulted. For among such store they think it hard to miss of a cure. And in that they are so opinionated that, if their own nation cannot give them remedy, they think [that] none can: though, as to surgery, they are of another mind, thinking the Europeans better at manual operations than themselves.

But, to proceed. Being severely handled by one, they fly to another. And he, from extreme cold things, runs upon the other extreme. So that between these two rocks it is no wonder [that] the patient so often miscarried; and so many concurring causes, joined with their distemper, hurries them to another world. Rhubarb, Turbith and Scammony are dreadful to them; but senna, cassia, manna, and turpentine are swallowed without any apprehension of evil.[20] Many of their physicians insist on diet's unusual elsewhere [such] as goatsflesh, horses, asses, and camel's flesh: for which reason they have distinct shambles[21] for the same purpose.

Avicenna, Averroes and Rhazes are known authors among them; and, among the most learned, Galen and Hippocrates, and some more modern, who have treated of botany, and human parts. Their Law forbids them to inspect a dead carcass. They therefore lean implicitly on what they find among ancient anatomists; and yet think themselves at no loss in that science: whence it is [that] their practice is lame, and their theory no more than the prating of a parrot. Hence it follows that they are imperfect in the surgeon's Art. They can tell how to protract slight wounds into length of time, but for things of real danger they are to seek which way to handle; especially where 'The knife is used to part the dead, and give / the Vital part occasion to live'. Yet they are bold enough with the blood, where they command phlebotomy,[22] bleeding like farriers.

The endemial diseases of this country are frenzies, pleurisies…catarrhs, distempers of the eyes, red gum (which besets our children in Europe, is pernicious to old age here)….But the fashionable malady of the country is a clap, scarce one in ten being free from it: which the unbounded liberty of women, cheapness of the commodity, and encouragement of their filthy Law, are main incentives to. And to back [up] this lewdness they bring the example of their Prophet Ali who, lying down without a female companion, is reported to be author of this doughty dialogue between the Earth and himself; wherein the Earth upbraided him by saying: 'while you lie on the ground an unfruitful log, a burden to my sides, I sweat and labour in producing vegetables, minerals and animals for your use. Why then do you not busy yourself in getting children, to transmit your offspring to posterity?' Which pleasing reproof of the venerable Prophet's recommending to his easy disciples, they embrace with both arms, while the poison creeps into the marrow of their bones: so that they are not come to maturity, before they are rotten – though, by reason of the purity of the air, it seldom or never arrives to the height of that cruelty as in Europe; inasmuch as when any are so dealt by it, they reproach it with the [name of] 'the Frank's disease'…when it breaks out into sores and ulcers after it has seized the whole mass of blood, and eats them up alive; while they wear theirs dormant almost to extreme old age: which makes them not much solicitous for remedy. Nor are there any who profess its cure.

There is another infirmity as general almost, proceeding from their ceremonial washing, when they exonerate too frequent using of baths: which causes a relaxation of the muscles of the anus, whereby the great gut of the fundament falls down. Most of them, by a fullness of body, are subject to haemorrhoids. But what chiefly vexes them, walking or riding (putting them into miserable pain, and contorted postures of the back and whole trunk of the body) is a fistula in ano,[23] which they contract from their athletic temper, and constantly being on horseback…Nor does it seldom fall out, from their aptness to venery, and proneness to make use of boys, that they are afflicted with terrible mariscæ, or swollen piles, of several forms…wherein worms, as they persuade themselves, are bred, that excruciates them with such an itch that they cannot lie without adding sin to sin. And therein they report their cure to be completed. And this brings on them a white leprosy – not incommoding the body with illness, but disgracing it with spots in the face, arms, thighs, breast, and other parts about them. Children have frequently scald heads, which makes them keep close shaved. The plague has not been known among them this 80 years and upwards, but the spotted-fever[24] kills them frequently, yet it is not contagious. The bezoar-stone,[25] in this case, is highly approved. The gout affects few here, the pox commonly securing them from it. However, as painful as that proves to their bones (or rather, membranes surrounding them), they applaud all provocatives in medicine, and will purchase them at any rates: which are sometimes so strong that they create a continued priapism to the goats and satyrs and (by their bows being always bent) are brought to an inability of reducing them.

To divert their care and labours, they are great devourers of opium and *koquenar* (which is poppy-heads boiled), which they quaff when they have a mind to be merry: for which reason, as hemp is sewn among our fens and fields, so they sow poppies; and, when ripe, make incision for the juice – which, gathering, they inspissate and eat. To do which, those unaccustomed, adventuring unadvisedly upon too large a dose, instead of the expected effect of cheering the spirits, chain up the vitals so that they are never loosed more: for they never awake from the lethargy it entrances them into; so that they begin gradually, and then arrive at great quantities: as from a grain to half an ounce,[26] without any harm, besides [except] a frolicsome drunkenness, by means whereof, without any other sustenance, they are qualified to undergo great travels and hardships. But, having once begun, they must continue it; or else they die. Whereby it becomes so necessary that if they mis-time themselves (as in their Ramadan, or on a journey) they often expire for want of it. Yet those who live at this rate are always as lean as skeletons, and seldom themselves.

But such is their love towards it, that they give themselves up to the study of infatuating themselves by all the means they can, never smoking a pipe without the leaves of the intoxicating bhang;[27] and flowers at the same time, mixed with their tobacco. Besides which, they contrive many more medicines to put a cheat upon the pungency of their cares, and drive sorrow from their hearts. Which indeed diverts them for some few small hours, till they return with a more fixed melancholy, burdensome to themselves and [to] others. While the operation of their forced mirth lasts, they are incapable, at that time, of any business; whence they proverbially say Balki tiryaq na-rasid[28] to any trifler or fiery spirit [so] that the force of your treacle you have eaten, still remains. Moreover, they have other treacles, such as are taken notice to be sold in the markets…prepared as counter-poisons, which are compounded of garlic, mother of thyme, and other herbs beaten together. That rich one, made use of only by the nobles, is adventitious,[29] and is brought by their merchants from Venice; the poor not being able to go to the price of such medicines or physicians as exceed the common rates. And therefore it is that their great towns and bazaars are full of mountebanks, charmers and quacksalvers[30] to gull them out of their cash.

NOTES

1 Abcees: Persian abbasi – coin.
2 Aristotle's Dialect. Meaning unclear. He might simply have in mind here differences between the three key figures concerning the notion of the 'Dialectic': that of Socrates being close to the term from which it is derived, as meaning 'to converse; to discourse'; that of Plato, where (in *The Republic*) the term refers to that kind of knowledge that can offer an account of everything in terms of 'the Good', but later (in *The Sophist*), it is the name given to the study of the interconnectedness of Forms and Ideas. In Aristotle, the term refers to reasoning from premises which are probable.
3 Four Figures of Syllogism. As defined by Aristotle, a discourse in which certain propositions being made (and five rules being obeyed), something other than what is stated follows of necessity. Strictly speaking, these have been considered as applicable only to propositions capable of being expressed in a categorical subject–predicate form (S, P): thus 'All S are P', 'No S are P', 'Some S are P', 'Some S are not P'. Of the three basic types of syllogism (hypothetical, disjunctive and categorical), the last named is probably the most familiar, usually expressed in the form 'All men are mortal'; 'Aristotle is a man'; 'Therefore Aristotle is mortal'. One fascinating detail of the status of Aristotelianism in medieval and Renaissance Europe was the extent to which (especially in the thirteenth century) the rendering into Latin of these texts were themselves from the Arabic translations.
4 Laconical: pertaining to the dialectic spoken by the inhabitants of Laconia (sometimes known as Lacedaemonia or Sparta). Also as that of using few words: Spartan; laconic; terse; concise.
5 Material; Formal; Efficient; Final – distinctions known collectively as Aristotle's four causes. The use of the term 'cause' in English is (at best) misleading and it might be nearer the mark to think of the philosopher's objective here as seeking to distinguish between four fundamentally different sorts of questions, from which, correspondingly, would flow their respective kinds of answers.
6 According to William Crooke, editor of the Hakluyt edition, 'Khwajah Nasir-ud-din Tusi, the famous astronomer and philosopher, born at Tus…in 1200…died AD 1274'. Crooke quotes as his source Thomas William Beale, *An Oriental Biographical Dictionary* (1881) – though Beale offers, as his source, the distinguished French traveller, Jean Baptiste Tavernier, *The Six Voyages, through Turkey into Persia and the East Indies, together with a relation of the Grand Seignior's Seraglio* (London, 1678: 227): Their books are for the most part the work of an ancient Persian author, whose name was Kodgia Nesir, in the city of Thouss, in the province of Korassan. 'Tis very probable he was skill'd in the Greek and Arabick, having translated into Persian several

books out of these two languages'. Given that the English translation of Tavernier was in 1678 and Fryer's account appeared in 1698, one cannot help but wonder if the reference by both to Nesir's skill in Arabic and Greek is yet another example of the later traveller borrowing from the former.

7 *Ipse dixit*: 'he himself said it'; thus a categorical statement.

8 Protract...analogically: extend by process of reasoning because of perception of resemblance of relations or attributes which thus become the basis for reasoning from what are parallel cases.

9 Muses. In Greek mythology, daughters of Zeus and Mnemosyne. While there remains some residual dispute about how many there were, the general consensus is that there were nine: Calliope (epic poetry; eloquence); Erato (love poetry); Euterpe (lyric poetry; music); Polymnia (sacred poetry); Melpomene (tragedy); Thalia (comedy); Terpsichore (song and dance); Clio (history); Urania (astronomy).

10 According to Crooke, *Rauzatu-s Safa fi Siratu-l Ambia wau-l Muluk wau-l Khulafa*, 'The Garden of Purity and Biography of Prophets, Kings, and Caliphs' by Mirkhwand (AD 1433–98), translated into English by D. Shea and E. Rehatsek. Crooke also quotes the following comment made by Tavernier: 'The most considerable of their historians is *Rouse el Sapha*, who wrote a Chronology from the Creation of the world to his time; wherein there are abundance of fables, but little truth'.

11 *Anwar-I-Suhaili*, 'Emanations of the star Canopus', the Persian version, by Husain Waiz, of the folktales of Bidpay (probably Sanskrit and meaning 'wise man' or 'court scholar'), the name generally given to the author of the fables known as the Panchatantra (five treasures), compiled before 500 CE. These fables (apparently manuals for the instruction of sons of royalty) appear to have entered European literary culture via an Arabic version (*c.* 750 CE), itself a translation from the Syria (*c.* 550 CE). What is of further note is that a translation into English, from the French, by Joseph Harris: *The Fables of Pilpay. Containing many rules for the conduct of humane life*, was published in London in 1699.

12 Transmutation of metals. Transmutation of other metals into gold via the assistance of the substance called the philosopher's stone was arguably the most common and ambitious objective of the alchemists, matched perhaps only by that of the search after the elixir of life by which means all diseases would be cured and youthfulness would be eternal.

13 Art: skill, learning, scholarship. In this period, term is still closely attached to some sense of 'science', perhaps the most famous example of which is in that moment when Prospero, deciding to tell Miranda about their past, asks her to help him with the removal of his cloak of office as well as power, and says 'Lie there my Art'.

14 Theodosius II, Roman Emperor of the East (408–50), reputedly preferred to study astronomy, theology and the law, leaving public affairs to the attention of his sister Pulcheria. One of the two surviving works of the fourth-century BCE astronomer and mathematician, Autolycus, is on the subject of the revolving sphere.

15 Secants. One of the fundamental trigonometrical functions. In late seventeenth century especially a straight line that cuts a curve in two or more parts.

16 Logarithms (Greek: 'relation number'): the power to which a fixed number or base must be raised in order to produce any given number; and of a series of exponents tabulated as a means of simplifying computation by making it possible to replace multiplication and division of numbers by addition or subtraction of their corresponding exponents (*New Shorter OED*).

17 Astrolabe. Instrument used for the making of astronomical measurements, especially of the altitudes of stars, their positions and movements. In its simplest form, it consisted of a disk of either wood or metal, with the circumference demarcated off in degrees, suspended on a ring. Measurement took place by means of using a pointer (Arab astronomers gave it the name 'alidade') pivoted at the centre of the disk. It was arguably the most important instrument used by navigators in voyages.

18 Lime-twigs. A method by which birds were caught – the lime acting as a kind of glue that, by acting as an adhesive on their claws, prevented them from flying off

19 Pancratic: fully disciplined or exercised in mind, having a universal mastery of accomplishments (*OED*).

20 Rhubarb; scammony; turbith (turpeth); senna; cassia, manna – all plants which have purgative, cathartic and laxative qualities.

21 Shambles: a row of covered stalls for the sale of meat or fish.
22 Phlebotomy: action of cutting open a vein in order to assist blood flow; much used in early modern European medical practice.
23 A long pipelike ulcer up the backside.
24 Spotted fever: a fever characterized by the appearance of spots on the skin. Now usually given to a form of meningitis, but at that time probably synonym for typhus.
25 Bezoar stone. A concretion with a hard nucleus found in the stomachs or intestines of (chiefly ruminant) animals; believed to be an antidote. Probably from bezoar goat, the Persian wild goat.
26 Grain: the small unit of weight in the avoirdupois, troy and apothecaries' systems of weight (originally the average weight of a grain of wheat); ounce: a unit of weight equivalent to 480 grains in the above-named systems.
27 Bhang: cannabis.
28 Balki...: perhaps the remedy will not come in time.
29 Adventitious: coming from outside; accidental.
30 Quacksalver: a person who pretends to have medical skill or knowledge; a charlatan.

OTHER EDITIONS

Negenjaarige Reyse door Oostindien en Persien. Uyt het Engels vertaalt. Gravenhage, 1700.
Travels in India in the Seventeenth Century by Sir Thomas Roe and Dr. John Fryer. Reprinted from the 'Calcutta Weekly Englishman', London: Trübner & Co. 1873.
A New Account of East India and Persia..., ed. William Crooke, Hakluyt Society, 3 vols, 1909–15.

APPENDIX 1

Key dates and events

Date	Ottoman Empire	England	Stage and publications	Elsewhere
1453	Turks capture Constantinople; end of Roman (Byzantine) Empire	End of 100 Years War between France and England		
1455		War of the Roses begins		
1456	Turks conquer Athens			
1460		Edward IV King of England		
1463	Turks conquer Bosnia			
1467	Turks take Herzegovina			
1471		Edward IV defeats Richard, Earl of Warwick, defeats Queen Margaret and kills Edward at Tewkesbury, enters London; Henry VI murdered in Tower		
1476			Caxton prints first book in English (*Recuyell of the Histories of Troy*) in Bruges	
1477			*The Dictes and Sayengis of the Philosophres* printed in England	

Date	Ottoman Empire	England	Stage and publications	Elsewhere
1481	Bayezid II Sultan (to 1512)			Beginning of Spanish Inquisition
1483		Edward IV succeeded by son, Edward V, who (with brother) disappears; conventional view is that they were killed by Richard, Duke of Gloucester, who rules as Richard III (to 1485)		King John of Portugal refuses to finance Columbus voyage
1485	Matthias Corvinus, King of Hungary (1458–90) and of Bohemia (1478–90), captures Vienna from Ottomans	Henry Tudor defeats and kills Richard III at Battle of Bosworth, rules as Henry VII (to 1509); start of Tudor dynasty		
1492	Beyazid II invades Hungary	Henry VII of England invades France after French support of Perkin Warbeck, claimant to English throne; Peace of Etaples; Warbeck expelled from France; England paid indemnity of £159,000		Spanish conquer Granada; by order of inquisition, Jews given three months either to accept Christianity or to leave country; first terrestrial globe constructed in Nurnberg by Martin Behaim; Ferdinand and Isabella of Spain finance the Columbus voyage
1493	Ottoman invasion of Dalmatia and Croatia			Pope Alexander VI publishes bull dividing New World between Spain and Portugal
1494		Parliament of Drogheda marks subservice of Ireland to England		Treaty of Tordesillas, the division of New World between Spain and Portugal

Date	Ottoman Empire	England	Stage and publications	Elsewhere
1495				Jews expelled from Portugal; about this time, Aldus Manutius begins his series of printed editions of Greek classics, incl. five-vol. Folio 'Aristotle'
1498				Vasco da Gama rounds Cape of Good Hope, establishes sea route to India
1499	War between Ottoman and Venice; Venetian fleet defeated at Sapienza, Lepanto surrenders			
1500				Pope Alexander I proclaims Year of Jubilee, imposes tithe for crusade against Ottomans; Cabral 'discovers' Brazil, claims it for Portugal
1501		Henry VIII declines papal request to lead anti-Ottoman crusade		Ismail I (1487–1524) founds Safavid dynasty in Persia (to 1736)
1502				Da Gama founds Portuguese colony at Cochin, India
1503				Zanzibar becomes Portuguese colony
1504				Venice sends ambassadors to Sultan of Turkey, proposing construction of Suez canal
1506				Jakob Fugger, Augsburg merchant, imports spices from East Indies by sea

Date	Ottoman Empire	England	Stage and publications	Elsewhere
1509	Earthquake destroys Constantinople	Henry VIII becomes King of England		Beginning of slave trade – Catholic Bishop Bartolomé de Las Casas suggests that each Spanish settler should bring certain number of slaves to New World
1510				Portuguese take Goa
1511				Portuguese at Amboyna and Malacca
1512	Selim I, Sultan (to 1520)			Shiism state religion in Persia
1513		James II of Scots defeated at Flodden		Balboa crosses Isthmus of Panama and looks down on Pacific from Darien
1514	Selim attacks Persia	Henry VIII peace with France		Pineapples in Europe for first time
1515	Selim overruns eastern Anatolia and Kurdistan			
1516	Selim defeats Egyptian forces near Aleppo, annexes Syria			
1517	Ottomans take Cairo; Mecca under Ottoman suzerainty			Coffee in Europe for first time; Archduke Charles grants monopoly of slave trade to Flanders merchants
1519				Cortez received by Aztec ruler Montezuma

Date	Ottoman Empire	England	Stage and publications	Elsewhere
1520	Suleiman the Magnificent Sultan			Pope Leo X excommunicates Luther; chocolate brought from Mexico to Spain
1521	Suleiman conquers Belgrade, begins invasion of Hungary			Cortez completes destruction of Aztec state, takes control in Mexico
1522	Suleiman takes Rhodes from Knights of St John			
1524		Turkeys from South America eaten for first time at English Court		
1525	Seven-year truce signed between Suleiman and King of Hungary	William Tyndale's translation of the NT printed at Worms		
1526	Battle of Mohacs: Ottomans defeat Hungarians; Louis II killed; Suleiman takes Buda			Babur becomes first Mughal ruler of India in Delhi
1530				Antwerp exchange founded; Portugal establishes colony in Brazil
1531		Henry VIII recognized as Supreme Head of Church of England		Halley's comet
1531	Suleiman I invades Hungary			Sugar cane first cultivated in Brazil
1535		English clergy finally abjure papal authority; Thomas More executed		Ignatius Loyola founds Jesuits
1538				First time Mercator uses name America on his maps

Date	Ottoman Empire	England	Stage and publications	Elsewhere
1540	Treaty between Venice and Ottomans signed in Constantinople			Antwerp most important commercial city in Europe
1541	Suleiman takes Buda and annexes Hungary (see 1686)			
1545	Truce of Adrianople between Charles V, Ferdinand of Austria, and Suleiman			First European botanical garden in Padua
1548	Ottomans occupy Tabriz (Persia)			
1550		William Cecil Secretary of State		
1555				Tobacco brought for first time from America to Spain
1556				Akbar the Great, Mughal Emperor of India (to 1605)
1558		England loses Calais; Queen Elizabeth I succeeds; Cecil appointed Principal Secretary of State		Hamburg exchange founded; Portuguese introduce snuff to Europe
1560	Ottoman Navy routs Spanish fleet near Tripoli			
1561				Tulips from Near East first time in Western Europe
1562		Hawkins begins English slave trade between Guinea and West Indies		
1564		Merchant Adventurers granted new charter		

Date	Ottoman Empire	England	Stage and publications	Elsewhere
1565	Ottomans forced to give up siege of Malta	Thomas Gresham founds Royal Exchange; John Hawkins introduces tobacco, sweet potatoes		
1566	Selim II Sultan (to 1574); war between Ottomans and Turkey renewed despite truce			
1568				Mercator devises cylindrical projection for charts
1569				Mercator's *Cosmographia* and map of world for navigational use
1570	Ottomans sack Nicosia (Cyprus), declare war on Venice	Pope excommunicates Elizabeth I	Thomas Preston, *Cambyses, King of Persia*	Abraham Ortelius *Theatrum orbis terrarum*, first modern atlas (fifty-three maps)
1571	Ottoman fleet beaten off Lepanto	Act of Parliament forbids export of wool		
1572				St Bartholomew's Day massacre of Huguenots
1573	Peace of Constantinople between Venice and Ottomans	Walsingham becomes Secretary of State; Drake sees Pacific for first time		
1574	Murad III Sultan; Ottomans take Tunis from Spanish			Portuguese colonize Angola, found Sao Paulo (Brazil)
1575				Akbar conquers Bengal
1578		Levant Trading Company founded		Muhammad Khudabanda becomes Shah of Persia (to 1587)

Date	Ottoman Empire	England	Stage and publications	Elsewhere
1582		Richard Hakluyt publishes *Divers Voyages touching the Discovery of America*		Gregorian calendar adopted by papal states, Spain, Portugal, France, the Netherlands and Scandinavian states (England 1752)
1583		English expeditions led by merchants Ralph Fitch and John Eldred to Mesopotamia, India, Orient		
1586				Abbas I Shah of Persia (to 1628)
1587			Marlowe, *Tamburlaine* Pt 1	
1588		Defeat of Spanish Armada; English Guinea Company formed		
1589			Hakluyt, *The Principall Navigations...*	
1590	Shah Abbas of Persia abandons Tabriz and Georgia, makes peace with Ottomans			Akbar conquers Orissa; Emperor of Morocco annexes Timbuktu
1591		First Lancaster voyage to East Indies		
1592				Akbar conquers Sind; Portuguese settle in Mombasa
1593	Rudolf II renews war against Ottomans			
1594	Ottomans take Raab (Austro-Hungarian border city)	Elizabeth sends Thomas Dallam to Turkey with an organ for the Sultan; Lancaster breaks Portuguese trading monopoly on Indian subcontinent; Fitch returns from overland journey to India and Ceylon	*First part of the tragicall raigne of Selimus*	Akbar conquers Kandahar

Date	Ottoman Empire	England	Stage and publications	Elsewhere
1595	Mehmed III Sultan (to 1603)			Dutch begin colonization of East Indies
1596	Ottomans defeat Imperial Army at Keresztes, Hungary	Tomatoes introduced into England for first time; first water closets installed at Queen's Palace, Richmond		
1600		English East India Company founded		
1602	War between Persia and Ottomans (to 1627)			Dutch East India Company founded
1603	Ahmed I Sultan (to 1617)	Elizabeth succeeded by James VI of Scotland as James 1 of England and Ireland	William Alexander, *Tragedy of Darius*	
1604	Abbas of Persia takes Tabriz from Ottomans	East India Company voyages to Java, Moluccas, Agra		
1605		Barbados claimed as English colony		Jehangir succeeds father Akbar as Mughal Emperor (to 1627)
1606	Peace treaty between Ottomans and Austrians at Zsitva-Torok	Virginia Company of London granted charter to send 120 colonists to Virginia		
1608			Fulke Greville, *Mustapha*	
1609	Blue Mosque built Constantinople (to 1616)			Tea from China shipped to Europe for first time by Dutch East India Company
1610		Skirmishes between English and Dutch traders settled in India		
1611		James I institutes baronetage as means of raising money		Building of Masjid-I-Shah, Royal Mosque, at Esfahan, Persia

Date	Ottoman Empire	England	Stage and publications	Elsewhere
1613	Ottoman armies invade Hungary	English colonists in Virginia destroy French settlement at Port Royal, Nova Scotia, and prevent French colonization of Maryland		
1614		English Virginian colonists prevent French settlements in Nova Scotia and Maine; Native American princess Pocahontas marries John Rolfe	Tobias Gentleman, *England's Way to Win Wealth*	
1615		Merchant Adventurers granted monopoly to export English cloth	Dudley Digges, *The Defence of Trade*	Dutch seize Moluccas from Portuguese
1616		Walter Raleigh released from prison to lead expedition to search for El Dorado (Guiana)		
1618	Poland signs fourteen-year truce with Ottomans	Raleigh returns to England; executed		
1619		First slaves to North America arrive Virginia		
1620	Ottomans defeat Polish Army at Jassy	'Pilgrim Fathers' found Plymouth colony		
1621			Thomas Mun, *A Discourse of Trade from England to the East Indies*	
1622				Hormuz captured from Portuguese with English assistance

Date	Ottoman Empire	England	Stage and publications	Elsewhere
1623		First English settlement in New Hampshire; Dutch massacre English colonists at Amboyna (Moluccas)	Shakespeare First Folio published	Abbas I captures Baghdad
1625		Charles I King of England and Scotland (to 1649); Colonial Office established in London; Barbados annexed		
1626		Knighthoods for all Englishmen with property valued over £40 to help royal revenues		Dutch colony of New Amsterdam founded on Hudson river
1627				Shah Jehan Mughal succeeds father Jehangir, Great Mogul (to 1658)
1628		English adventurers arrive Nevis, Leeward Isles		Dutch occupy Java and the Moluccas
1630		John Winthrop, Puritan leader, arrives Massachusetts with 1,000 settlers, 16,000 more follow		
1631			Philip Massinger, *Emperor of the East*	
1632		First shop selling coffee opens in London; English settlements at St Kitts, Montserrat, Antigua	Thomas Goffe, *The Couragious Turke*; *The Raging Turke*	Portuguese driven out of Bengal
1633		English trading post in Bengal		

Date	Ottoman Empire	England	Stage and publications	Elsewhere
1634		English settlement at Cochin, Malabar		
1638	Murad IV recovers Baghdad from Persia			
1639		English settle in Madras		
1640	Ibrahim Sultan (to 1649)			
1641		Cotton goods begin to be manufactured in Manchester		
1642		Civil War begins	Public theatres closed	
1646		English occupy Bahamas		
1647			Robert Baron, *Mirza*	
1649	Sultan Ibrahim deposed, killed; succeeded by son Mehmed IV	Charles I beheaded; Cromwell invades Ireland, sacks Drogheda and Wexford		
1650		Tea drinking begins in England; first coffee house in England opened in Oxford		
1651		Navigation Act, directed against Dutch, gives English ships monopoly of foreign trade		
1652		Cromwell becomes Lord Protector, first London coffee house opens		Dutch settle at Cape of Good Hope
1654				Portugeuse finally expel Dutch from Brazil

Date	Ottoman Empire	England	Stage and publications	Elsewhere
1655		English capture Jamaica		
1657			Lodowick Carlell, *Osmond, the Great Turk*	
1658				Aurungzeb imprisons his father. Shah Jahan, succeeds him as Mughal Emperor
1660	Leopold I sends army to check Ottoman advance	Charles II invited to return to England; Royal Africa Company founded; water closets arrive in England from France	Theatres reopen	
1663	Ottomans declare war on Holy Roman Empire, invade Transylvania, Hungary			
1664	Austrians defeat Ottomans at St Gotthard – truce of Vasvar		Mun, *England's Treasure by Forraign Trade*	
1665		Great Plague begins in London, kills nearly 70,000 people		
1666		English pirates capture Tobago; Great Fire of London		
1667				Shah Abbas of Persia succeeded by son Suleiman (to 1694)
1668		British East India Company obtains control over Bombay		
1669	Venetians lose Crete, their last colony, to Ottomans			Aurungzeb bans Hindu religion in India

Date	Ottoman Empire	England	Stage and publications	Elsewhere
1671	Ottomans declare war on Poland	Former buccaneer, Henry Morgan, made deputy governor of Jamaica	Edward Carter, *England's Interest by Trade Asserted*	First Bible in Arabic printed in Rome
1673		Test Act excludes Roman Catholics from holding public office		
1676			Dryden, *Aureng-Zebe*	
1678		Importation of all French goods into England prohibited		
1682			Thomas Southerne, *The Loyall Brother*	
1683	Ottoman siege of Vienna begins			
1684	Austria, Poland and Venice declare Holy League of Linz against Ottomans	Bermudas become Crown Colony		
1685		James II King of England (to 1688); French Huguenot refugees begin silk manufacture in London		
1686	Russia declares war on Turkey			
1687	Battle of Mohacs: Ottoman armies defeated; Mehmed IV deposed, succeeded by Suleiman III	Sir Hans Sloane, naturalist and physician, begins botanical collection on visit to Jamaica		
1688		William of Orange accepts invitation to rule jointly with Mary; King James escapes to France		

Date	Ottoman Empire	England	Stage and publications	Elsewhere
1689		Parliament confirms 'abdication' of James		
1690	Ottoman armies conquer Belgrade	William defeats his father-in-law James II at Battle of the Boyne		
1691	Ahmed II succeeds Suleiman II (to 1695)			
1694			Robert Boyle, *The Tragedy of Mustapha*	
1695	Mustafa II succeeds Ahmed II (to 1703); Russo-Turkish War, Peter the Great fails to take Asov			
1696	Peter the Great takes Asov	Board of Plantations founded in England	Thomas Southere, *Oroonoko*	
1697	Prince Eugene defeats Ottoman armies at Zenta			Last remains of Maya civilization destroyed by Spanish in Yucatan
1699	Peace of Carlovitz between Ottoman Empire and Austria, Poland and Venice			

SOURCES

Bernard Grun, *The Timetables of History*, New York: Simon & Schuster, 1982.

The Harper Atlas of World History (a translation of *Le grand livre de l'histoire du monde*), London: William Collins, 1987.

John Paxton and Sheila Fairfield, *Calendar of Creative Man*, London: Macmillan, 1980.

Werner Kinder and Werner Hilgemann, *The Anchor Atlas of World History*, Vol. 1: *From the Stone Age to the eve of the French Revolution*, New York: Doubleday, 1974.

J. P. Kenyon (ed.), *A Dictionary of British History*, New York: Stein & Day, 1983.

APPENDIX 2

Jesuit hymn

In his *A Letter sent from Jerusalem into England, wherein relation is made of the voyage of five Englishmen from Aleppo in Syria Comagena to Jerusalem, and what famous places and memorable matters they saw on their way thither, and in Jerusalem*, William Biddulph relates the story of an encounter, on top of Mount Tabor, between a Jesuit and a Protestant from Paris. According to Biddulph, the latter told the former

> that he had been at Rome, and both seen and heard there the manner of life which he and his fellow Jesuits lead, and that he was not ignorant of how odious they were, even unto other Papists, amongst whom one of them gave him a hymn made by a papist at Rome.

Biddulph provides the text, in Latin, together with the following translation:

This hymn the usual form does give
In which the Jesuits do live

The wealthiest cities, where the rather
They most commodities may gather
Flies every Jesuit Father.

Best wine they drink, and eat good bread
With which no stranger sees them fed,
Nor notes how long they lie in bed.

With gross beef they will never deal,
But (for it) fat and tender veal
To their full kitchens still they steal.

Indian cocks and turkeys great
Fed always with the purest wheat
Are those bits that these Fathers eat.
Saffron, pepper, nourish them,
And roses of Jerusalem,
Of which no holy man doth dream.

When prisoners for their charity call,
They say 'We are deprived of all;

248

And must to our devotion fall'.

But when their mighty friends, and rich
Require their helps, they God beseech
For them, and through all nations preach.

Th'inheritances of rich heirs
And princes' nuptial affairs
Disposes this feigned zeal of theirs.

When rich lie sick, and these men gape,
To have their riches feed their rape,
They pray God they may never 'scape.

O wild and wolvish chevisance[1]
That when they charity advance
They ravish our inheritance.

Venetian wealth they still apply,
Affect the Spanish gravity,
And build on Rome's authority.

If princely offices be sought,
By Jesuits they must be wrought,
And with rich spiritual livings bought.
In temporal state they bear the bell,
In spiritual state ease must excel.
In all state, they command. Farewell!

NOTE

1 Chevisance: resource; means of extracting oneself. Also expedient, shiftiness. 'Chevisancer': a money-lender (*OED*).

APPENDIX 3

Brief biographies of key figures whose names recur in the texts

Abbas   Abbas the Great (1557–1629; Shah of Persia 1587–1628). Keen to maintain links with European powers as part of his diplomatic and military contests with the Ottomans, he obtained support of the English in expelling Portuguese from Hormoz and later founded the port named after him, Bandar Abbas. Made Esfahan a capital city celebrated for the beauty (as well as utility) of the palaces, mosques and gardens he had erected there.

Achilles   In Greek mythology the chief hero of the Trojan War. According to one legend, his mother Thetis had attempted to make her son immortal by bathing him in the River Styx, but the heel by which she held him was not immersed, and that was the place in which, according to one story, Paris dealt him the deathblow. (Another version had it that Paris struck him from behind when he went to visit King Priam's daughter, Polyxena, with whom he had fallen in love.) Whatever version on the death, according to Homer, Achilles had been an active participant in the siege until the final year, when Agamemnon stole the captured princess Briseis from him. While, as a consequence, he withdrew from the war, he allowed Patroclus to wear his armour when the latter led his troops in support of the retreating Greeks. Filled with remorse at the death of Patroclus (who was his friend, as well as his lover) at the hand of Hector, Achilles returned to the war, defeated the Trojans and, having killed Hector, brought the dead body of his antagonist back to the Greek camp by dragging it back in what was seen as an unseemly manner. It was, in part, for the abusive manner of that act, that the Trojan, Paris, killed his Greek enemy.

Aeneas   After the defeat of the Trojans, legend has it that he carried his aged father to safety on his back. Shipwrecked on the North African coast, he encountered Queen Dido (who, after her brother Pygmalion had murdered her husband, fled to, founded and ruled Carthage). When, on the instruction of Jupiter, Aeneas left Carthage to go to Italy, where he and his descendants were the founders of Rome, Dido committed suicide by throwing herself on a funeral pyre. The story is, of course, not only the basis for Virgil's celebrated epic, but (in English literature), for instance, the subject of the collaboration between Christopher Marlowe and Thomas in the play *The Tragedy of Dido, Queen of Carthage* (1594) and references in several of Shakespeare's plays.

Agamemnon   King of Mycenae (Argos) and leader of the Greek forces in the Trojan War. In order to enlist the support of the gods to provide his fleet with a favourable wind for sailing to Troy, he sacrificed one of his daughters, Iphigenia, to the goddess Artermis, thereby incurring the hatred of his wife, Clytemnestra. As mentioned earlier, he incurred the enmity of Achilles because of the captured Briseis. After eventually returning home, Agamemnon was treacherously murdered by Clytemnestra and her lover Aegisthus – for which act, in their turn, the surviving son and daughter, Orestes and Electra, killed their mother.

Agrippina (a) the Elder (d. 33 CE), granddaughter of Augustus Caesar and wife of Germanicus Caesar, whom she accompanied on his provincial duties. Having accused the Emperor Tiberius of poisoning her husband, she was eventually exiled to an island in the Bay of Naples, where she starved herself to death. Her son Caius Caesar Germanicus became the emperor best known under the name Caligula. (b) the Younger (d. 59 CE), daughter of the above. By her first husband Domitius Ahenobarbus, she was the mother of Nero. She was accused of conspiring against her brother the Emperor Caligula in order to advance the interests of her son – which she achieved when she became the third wife of Claudius I, whom she persuaded to prefer Nero over his own son Britannicus. It is generally believed that she almost certainly poisoned Claudius, thereby bringing Nero to power; but he, eventually apparently weary of her intrigues, in his turn, had her murdered. The city of Cologne, Colonia Aggrippinensis, is named in her memory.

Ahmed I (1589–1617; Ottoman monarch 1603–17), successor to Mahmud III. Key diplomatic event of his rule was Treaty of Zsitvatorok (1606), important not only because, by it, Hungarian kings were no longer required to pay tribute to Ottomans, but by the very process of negotiation it meant recognition of other European monarchs as his equals. Key military situation was the suppression of dissent on the part of Asian dependencies by his Croation Vizier, Murad Pasha – though, after the latter's death (1611), the Persians under Abbas were able to retain control over Tabriz. Ahmed, who was responsible for the construction of the Blue Mosque in Istanbul, is also interesting in that, on accession to the throne, he did not kill (as was sometimes the habit) his siblings. The outcome was that his elder brother succeeded as Mustafa I (1591–1639?; Sultan 1617–18, 1622–3).

Akbar Akbar the Great (1542–1605, Mogul Emperor 1556–1605). He expanded his territories to include parts of present-day Afghanistan and Baluchistan. But, having conquered, he sought to conciliate by giving high positions to some of the defeated, especially to the Hindu Rajputs. Noted for the introduction of a uniform system of administration, as well as for toleration of many religions, he sought, by means of a proclamation of 1582, to replace Islam with a monotheistic but eclectic combination derived from Hinduism, Islam, Zoroastrianism and Christianity. His Courts at Agra and at Fatehpur Sikri were centres at which the arts and learning (especially influenced by Persian models) flourished.

Albuquerque Alfonso de Albuquerque (1453–1515), admiral and arguably the key figure in the making of the Portuguese Empire in the East. It was his forces that captured Hormoz (1507) but were unable to keep it because he could not build a fort there. The governor at Goa at the time, Francisco d'Almeida, not only disavowed the attempted conquest but put Albuquerque in prison when he reached Goa. It was only when written confirmation arrived from Portugal that d'Almeida agreed that Albuquerque was, in fact, to be his successor. Albuquerque thereupon set about laying the foundations for Portuguese power in the region: he conquered Goa (1510), Malacca (1511) and Hormoz again (1515). It was on his return to Goa that he heard that he had been replaced, and died as his ship entered harbour – perhaps a less spectacular death than that of his predecessor, d'Almeida, who was killed by the Khoikhoi (the so-called 'Hottentots') at the Cape of Good Hope on his return home, one of the consequences of which was that the Portuguese thereafter gave that region a wide berth.

Alexander the Great   Alexander III (356–323 BCE; King of Macedon 336–323), son of Philip of Macedon, and tutored at one stage by Aristotle. Having first suppressed revolt near home (Thrace, Illyria), he crossed the Hellespont with a combined army to do battle against the Persians. In 333 he won a famous victory against Darius III at the Battle of Issus and, having secured Persia, he next (332) entered Egypt, where he met no resistance. At the oasis of the god Amun he was acknowledged as the son of that deity, and in the winter following he created the city that bears his name. Returning to Persia, he defeated Darius for a second time. Following that, he went to Persepolis and Susa, famous cities whose palaces he looted and burned. By now in the regions beyond the Oxus river, rumours of possible rebellions invariably ended up in severe reprisals against the innocent as well as the guilty that (together with his decision to dress in the Persian style) would appear to have helped to alienate some of his supporters who saw him as transforming himself into a despot and tyrant. Still, he pressed on and eventually overran the Punjab. When his men refused to go further, he had a fleet built, which he sent off via the then unknown route to the Persian Gulf, while he himself led his army back via Baluchistan, Afghanistan and southern Iran. When they finally reached Susa (324), he found that many of the officials he had left in place had become corrupt and that in Greece there had by now developed animosity against him for executing Aristotle's nephew, the historian Calisthenes. He died, aged 33, having left his mark not only as one of the great military figures of all time, but perhaps also for his role in the spreading of Hellenism throughout the Near East and into Asia.

Ananias   (a) The man who, with his wife Sapphira, failed to hand over the whole of the gift/donation they should have made to the Jerusalem church. Fell dead when confronted with it by Peter (Acts 5: 1–6). (b) High Priest at Jerusalem, 59–47 BCE. Seen by Jews as a Roman sympathizer, he was taunted by Paul with a superb epithet 'thou whited wall' (Acts 23: 3). He was assassinated at the outbreak of the Jewish War (66 CE). (c) A Christian in Damascus who received Paul after his conversion (Acts 9: 10–20). There are also several people in the OT with the name 'Hananiah', in which, in the best-known case, the name is once again associated with being a liar: the 'false prophet' who was denounced by Jeremiah for predicting that the Babylonian exile would end after two years (Jeremiah 28: 5–9).

Anthony   Marcus Antonius (83–30 BCE). Campaigned in Syria (58–6), then in Gaul with Julius Caesar. Elected quæstor (52), then tribune (49). In the Civil War, distinguished himself at the Battle of Pharsalus (48). After the assassination of Julius Caesar he joined forces with Octavius, Julius Caesar's adopted son and heir, but they were soon at odds with each other. With the formation of the Second Triumvirate, he was made commander of Rome's Asian territories, and the combined armies of Anthony and Octavius crushed their enemies at Phillipi. Anthony had, in the meantime, left Egypt and Cleopatra and resolved his peace with Octavius following the war made by his third wife, Fulvia, a peace sealed by his marriage to Octavia, who was to become his strongest defender. Having made a costly – but ultimately politically and strategically useless – incursion into Parthia, he settled in Alexandria (37), openly living with Cleopatra, the outcome of which was that (32) the Senate stripped him of his consulship. In the war that inevitably followed, the combined forces of Anthony and Cleopatra were beaten at Actium (31). When the Roman forces under Octavius entered Egypt, first Cleopatra, then Anthony, committed suicide.

Antigonous I (382?–301 BCE), Antigonus Cyclops (the One-Eyed), one of Alexander the Great's generals. In the aftermath of the latter's death he was seen by some as perhaps most suitable to recreate the empire. He had control of Asia Minor, Syria and Mesopotamia, but in the wars that followed, in which Seleucus I and Ptolemy I were ranged against him, having first defeated Ptolemy I (306), both he and Ptolemy were killed at Ipsus.

Apollo One of the most important gods on Mount Olympus. His name is associated with (among other things) prophecy and medicine, music and poetry, and the bucolic arts. Interestingly, although he was father of several children, his attentions were not always reciprocated. Daphne, for instance, turned herself into a laurel rather than go to bed with him, while Marpessa made the even more scandalous choice of rejecting him in favour of a mere mortal. He could also be vindictive. Having given Cassandra the gift of prophecy, when she refused to be dutiful, he decreed that no one would believe her. In Roman religion he was celebrated as the epitome of beauty and of youth.

Appolonius (a) Appolonius of Perga (d. 205 BCE), Greek mathematician of the Alexandrian School. He introduced the terms *parabola, ellipse, hyperbola* into the subject. (b) Appolonius of Tyana (Cappadocia), famous for wisdom and reputed magical powers. Travelled widely, and a record of those travels, based upon a journal kept by one of his companions, Damis (written *c.* 216 CE by Flavius Philstratus), is a mixture of factual information and invention. Set up a school at Ephesus, where he died (reputedly aged 100).

Aristophanes (*c.* 448–388 BCE), Greek playwright and arguably the most influential maker of ancient comedy: a mixture of literary, political and social satire that relied on a direct attack upon persons, making use of cutting invective. Of the few plays which have survived, *The Knights* is a critique of demagoguery that was characteristic of the politics of his time; *The Clouds* an attack on Socrates as a person and on sophistry as form; *Lysistrata*, in which the women of Athens refuse to have sexual relations with their men in order to bring about an end to a war.

Aristotle (384–322 BCE), Greek philosopher who studied under Plato and later was a tutor to Alexander the Great. He opened his own school in the Lyceum in Athens (335), but after the death of Alexander he was forced to flee to Chalcis, where he died. Formidable influence rests on writing that exists mostly in form of lecture notes to students: *Organum, Physics, Metaphysics, Poetics, Nicomachean Ethics*, as well as works on biology. For Aristotle, the task of the philosopher is, by means of the systematic use of logic, as expressed in syllogisms (see note 3, p. 230), to discern the first principles of all human knowledge. Given one of the key objectives of the present collection, it is important to bear in mind not simply the extent to which 'Western' philosophy is rooted upon Aristotelian foundations, but the route by which that body of work was introduced: that is, following the collapse of Rome, through the work of Arabic and Jewish scholars which, in turn, laid the basis for Scholasticism, the philosophical and theological traditions which flourished in the Middle Ages (see e.g. Avicenna, Averroës, below).

Artaxerxes There were three: Artaxerxes I (King of Persia, 464–425 BCE) succeeded his father Xerxes. Although some historians trace later weakness of Persian Empire as dating from the time of his rule, this was also a period of warm and close cultural links between Persia and Greece. Admired in Ezra 7: 11–28 and Nehemiah 2: 1–8 for supporting their endeavours to build the temple. Artaxerxes II (King of Persia, 404–358 BCE), son of Darius II; and Artaxerxes III (King of Persia, 358–338 BCE), son and successor to Artaxerxes II, who ascended to the throne by means of a generalized extermination of his brother's family. Despite failure of a military campaign in Egypt (351), Artaxerxes III persisted until eventual success (342). His rule by means of terror ended when he was poisoned by his eunuch, Bagoas, who installed the king's son Arces on the throne (338), but then also had him deposed in favour of Darius III (336).

Augustine, Saint (354–430), Bishop of Hippo (Algeria), born Tagaste, North Africa. Brought up as a Christian by his mother, when he went to school in Carthage, he renounced it in favour of Manichaeism (religion, probably of Persian origin, founded by Mani (216–76 CE), that taught, for example, dualism of good and evil, transmigration of souls, etc.). He went to Rome and Milan, and taught rhetoric in both cities. While in Milan he was introduced to the teachings of St Ambrose, as well as to Neo-Platonism. Having converted to Western Christianity, he returned to his birthplace (387) to lead a monastic life. Ordained priest in Hippo (391), he was made bishop in 396. One of the key figures of Christian doctrine, his autobiographical *Confessions* is one of the classic texts of Christian mysticism, while his work *The City of God*, which famously argues a view of history, is probably still the most sophisticated and convincing defence of Christianity. Other works include *On the Trinity, On Baptism, On the work of Monks*.

Averroës Ibn Rushd (1126–98), Arabic philosopher, lawyer and medical doctor in Cordoba (Spain) who also lived in Morocco, where he was in great favour with the caliphate. Of enormous influence in Christian and Jewish philosophy, especially for his commentaries on Aristotle and his attempt to demarcate the terrains of faith and reason, his view being that, since they were not in conflict with each other, they need not be reconciled. His other main work was translated into English as *The Incoherence of the Incoherence*. The decision to write the commentaries on Aristotle (as well as on Plato's *Republic* and Porphyry's *Isagoge*) apparently came about as a consequence of a meeting (*c.* 1169) with Prince Abu Ya'qub Yusuf, during which they held an extensive and wide-ranging discussion on the matter of the eternity of the world.

Avicenna Ibn Sinha (980–1037), Islamic philosopher born near Bokhara (Uzbezkistan), his main works, published in Rome (1593), being (in their English translations) *The Book of Healing* (of the Soul) and *The Canon of Medicine*. Arguably not only the most distinguished name in medicine from 1100 to 1500 (he was largely responsible for fixing the classification of sciences as used in the medieval schools in Europe – which, to some extent, puts into perspective Fryer's views), but, for our purposes, important for his translation of Aristotle's *Metaphysics*.

Baldwin I   Baldwin of Boulogne (1058?–1118), Latin king (by election) of Jerusalem (1100–18), brother of Godfrey of Bouogne (Bouillon), whom he accompanied on the First Crusade. With aid of Venetians and Genoese (to whom he made many concessions) he consolidated power of Latin rulers in the region and gained control of several of the chief ports of Palestine.

Bayezid II   (1447–1513; Ottoman Sultan 1481–1512), son and successor to Mahmud II. Following war with Venice (1499–1503), which he could not win convincingly, he modernized his army and navy, and when Constantinople was destroyed by earthquake (1509) he speedily had it rebuilt. But following civil war between his two sons Selim and Ahmed (1510), he was forced by the janisarries to abdicate (1512) in favour of Selim (Selim I). In Christopher Marlowe's *Tamburlaine*, Part One (1590), 'Bajazeth, Emperor of the Turks' and his empress are locked in a cage and taunted until, in desperation, they beat out their brains against the bars. The figure also occurs in Rowe's *Tamerlane* (1702), a play of some historic interest since the name of the hero was intended to be associated with William III, while that of Bajazet was supposed to represent (wholly unfavourably) the figure of Louis XIV of France. Rowe's play was, for more than 100 years, annually revived on 5 November to coincide with the date of the arrival of Dutch William and his forces in England.

Belshazzar   Not, as stated in Daniel 5: 2, to be the son of Nebuchadnezzar, and last king of Babylon, but son of Nabonidus of Babylon (556–539) – he ruled as regent during king's absence. Story associated with him is that at the feast he gave for a thousand of his lords, a mysterious hand wrote a message of doom on the wall, and that very night Belshazzar was slain and his kingdom divided between the Medes and the Persians. The story has inspired many paintings as well as music, notably William Walton's oratorio.

Benjamin   youngest son of Jacob and Rachel (Genesis 35: 18), thus ancestor of one of the twelve tribes of Israel. Following an attack upon them by other tribes (Judges 20), the Benjaminites became dependent upon Judah. Saul was probably the most prominent figure from this tribe, but so were, for example, Shimei and Sheba, who opposed David (2 Samuel 16: 5, 20: 1). After separation, the tribe became part of the southern kingdom (Nehemiah 11: 7). Descendants recall history of the tribe, for example Jeremiah 1: 1, Philippians 3: 5.

Bodin, Jean   (1530?–96), French social and political philosopher. Appalled at conflict between Catholics and Huguenots, he argued (well before Hobbes did so) in his *Six Books of the Republic* (1576) that a well-ordered state required not only a sovereign ruler but also religious toleration. Now recognized as an influential early contributor to the theory of the modern state.

Burghley   William Cecil, 1st Baron (1520–98), chief advisor to Queen Elizabeth as her chief spokesman to parliament (1558–98), as secretary (1558–72) and as lord treasurer

(1572–98). Anglican with strong anti-Catholic bias, he was a strong advocate for the execution of Mary Queen of Scots. For our purposes it is important to draw attention to his advice to the queen to come to the aid of the French Huguenots (1567) and Dutch Calvinists (1585) but not to become involved in the European wars of religion on the Protestant side. Though that policy was eventually overturned by the Puritans led by Robert Dudley, Earl of Leicester, and Sir Francis Walsingham, Burghley's position as Elizabeth's most influential advisor was never really challenged in his lifetime – except perhaps by the monarch herself, who refused to take his advice that she should get married.

Caesar, Augustus Caius Octavius (64 BCE to 14 CE), first Roman Emperor, great-nephew of Julius Caesar, who made him his heir without his knowledge. After Julius Caesar's assassination (44 BCE), Octavius, together with Lepidus and Mark Anthony, formed the Second Triumvirate. With Anthony won a famous victory against the conspirators at Phillipi (42 BCE), and again at Mylae where he defeated Sextus Pompeius (36 BCE). Following the break-up of the Triumvirate, he defeated the combined forces of Anthony and Cleopatra at Actium (31 BCE). Made Imperator by the Senate (29 BCE), the month hitherto known as Sextilis was renamed Augustus in his honour. Having inaugurated the Pax Romana (Roman Peace) he did much to beautify Rome, to build Roman roads (primarily with a military purpose of linking the distant parts of the empire to Rome, but there was also a very great commercial and cultural spin-off) and was a keen patron of the arts: supported *inter alia* Virgil, Ovid, Livy, Horace.

Caesar, Julius (102?–44 BCE), Roman politician and military strategist. Although born into one of the most patrician families in Rome, he was always associated with the popular forces. Proscribed by the dictator Sulla (82 BCE), he had to flee Rome, but returned (78 BCE) to begin a political career while still, from time to time, engaging in wars (e.g. in Spain 68 BCE, but especially in the Gallic Wars 58–49 BCE). Having been one of the key figures in the formulation of the Julian calendar, he was also prime mover in the shaping of the coalition that with Pompey (the commander-in-chief of the army) and Crassus (the wealthiest person in Rome) became known as the First Triumvirate. Between 55 and 54 BCE he explored parts of Britain, defeating the Britons in the process. With the death of Crassus (53 BCE), and therefore the ending of the Triumvirate, increasing friction with Pompey and later with the Senate, civil war broke out when Caesar famously crossed the Rubicon stream and marched on Rome and at Pharsalia defeated Pompey (48 BCE) who fled to Rome, where he was killed. Caesar, having pursued Pompey to Egypt, there met Cleopatra, whom he helped to establish on the Egyptian throne. Returning to Rome, he not only set about improving housing conditions for the poorest, but also famously had enacted agrarian laws which regulated the disposition of public lands, much to the chagrin of the wealthy. In 44 BCE he became dictator for life, but by this stage his rule had begun to build up strong resentments in certain quarters, and on 15 March (the Ides of March) he was stabbed to death in the Senate. He was also a splendid stylist: see his commentaries on the wars, Gallic and civil.

Caiaphas Son-in-law and successor to Annas, High Priest in Jerusalem in the year of Christ's crucifixion (John 18: 13–24).

Cambyses   See Cartwright extract, note 13.

Cato   (a) Marcus Porcius Cato (Cato the Elder, also known as Cato the Censor, 234–149 BCE), Roman statesman and moralist and later served as consul as well as censor. His urgings to the Senate led to destruction of Carthage (Third Punic War). (b) Marcus Porcius Cato (Cato the Younger, 95–46 BCE, also known as Cato of Utica), great-grandson of Cato the Elder. Known for being wholly incorruptible, he opposed Julius Caesar and supported Pompey, but after the latter's defeat at Pharsalia, Cato removed himself to Africa to continue the struggle from there; but when it became clear that Caesar had triumphed, he recommended that his followers make their peace with the new rulers and then committed suicide.

Cerberus   In Greek mythology, a many-headed dog with a mane and a tail that consisted of snakes. One of the twelve tasks of Hercules was to capture this figure, which was also the guardian of Hades, the world of the dead, ruled over by Pluto and Persephone.

Charon   The avaricious boatman who rowed the newly dead across the River Styx to Hades, and who extracted payment for that task by demanding from them the coin that had been placed in their mouths when they were buried.

Chrysostom, Saint John   (*c.* 347–407 *CE*), Patriarch of Constantinople (398), until illegally deposed (403) by the Empress Eudoxia and Bishop Theophilus. Although recalled briefly, he was again sent into exile, where he died. Not only admired for his eloquence, charity and ascetic life and his attacks upon lifestyle of the imperial Court, but also his writings are celebrated for elegance of style.

Circe   In Greek mythology, an enchantress who lived on an island from where she decoyed sailors and turned them into beasts. In the *Odyssey* she transformed Odysseus' companions into swine, but he enlisted the aid of Hermes and forced her to break the spell.

Cleopatra   (69–30 *BCE*), Queen of Egypt and daughter of Ptolemy XI. Married (as was the custom) to her younger brother, Ptolemy XII, she revolted against him and succeeded to the throne by enlisting the support of Julius Caesar, with whom she lived while he was in Egypt. Though Egypt remained a vassal state of Rome (where she visited and gave rise to a powerful cult within the city), she famously later married Mark Anthony (36 BCE). Eventually defeated at Actium (31 BCE) by Octavian (later Augustus Caesar), they killed themselves – perhaps most famously evoked in the closing scenes of Shakespeare's play. See Lucy Hughes-Hallett, *Cleopatra. Histories, dreams and distortions*, London: Vintage, 1990 and Mary Hamer, *Signs of Cleopatra. History, Politics, Presentation*, London: Routledge, 1993.

Constantine   Constantine the Great (*c.* 288–337; Roman Emperor 310–37), born in Nis (now in Serbia), was left by his father at the Court of the Emperor Diocletian. Following years of complex intrigues between competing factions and shifting alliances, he eventually became absolute ruler of the empire centred upon the former Byzantium, which he renamed as Constantinople (330). Having several years before (as Eusebius of

Caesarea described the event) seen in the sky a flaming cross with the words inscribed on it 'In this sign thou shalt conquer', he had converted to Christianity (but was baptized only on his deathbed) which he sought to strengthen (e.g. at the synod of Arles in France, 314; later, more significantly, at the First Council of Nicaea, 325), after which there was an attempt to resolve the troubles over Arianism – about which he appeared to be willing to be more tolerant than most. By contrast, his political rule was marked by a tendency towards despotism, allied to and supported by a centralized bureaucracy. There is still to this day considerable difference of opinion between historians about the man and his times. Before his death he sought to provide for his three sons as well for the sons of his half-brother by division of the empire that he had united; that division led to a new round of complex struggles for power between competing figures.

Constantine XI   Constantine Paleoologus, last Byzantine Emperor (1449–53), defeated by Mehmed II in a battle in which he lost his life and which ushered in Ottoman era.

Cyrus   Cyrus the Great (550–29), probably greatest of the kings of the Achaemenid dynasty in Persia (it included Darius I, Xerxes, Artaxerxes, Darius III). He conquered Media, Lydia and Babylonia. Referred to with approval in the Bible for placing Jews in command of a buffer state he created between Persia and Egypt (which he could not force into submission) and for allowing rebuilding of the Temple (Isaiah 45: 1, 13; Ezra 1: 1–2).

Darius   Darius I (Darius the Great, d. 486 BCE), one of the ablest of the Achaemid rulers of Persia, instituted highly efficient administration. Defeated by the Athenians at the famous Battle of Marathon (490 BCE) he consolidated Persian power in the East. He also continued the policy of his predecessor, Cyrus, with regard to Jews and the rebuilding of the Temple (Ezra chs 4–6).

Darius III   (d. 330 *BCE*), defeated by Alexander the Great in several major battles during the period when the Macedonians invaded Persia, and was forced to flee to Bactria, where Alexander arranged to have him murdered. His death and the victory of Alexander marked the end of the Persian Empire and the beginning of the Hellenistic period in the eastern Mediterranean.

Diodorus   Diodorus Siculus (d. after 21 BCE), Sicilian-born historian who wrote, in Greek, a history of the world in forty books, ending with the Gallic Wars of Julius Caesar. Books that have survived (on Egyptian, Mesopotamian, Indian, Scythian, Arabian and North African history) are important texts as a source of lost works of writers whose work he cites.

Diogenes Laertius   Early third-century Greek biographer. Work on lives and theories of philosophers from Thales of Miletus to Epicurus is of great historical value.

Euclid   Greek mathematician who taught at Alexandria late fourth century BCE, famous for *Elements* (though his authorship is disputed by some) and *Optics*, but especially for propositions in geometry which are derived by rigorous logical progression from five postulates.

Gabriel One of the chief archangels. In the OT a messenger from God (Daniel 8: 15–26); in the NT announces supernatural births of John the Baptist and Jesus (Luke 1: 19, 26–36). Popularly associated with the blowing of the trumpet to announce the resurrection (1 Thessalonians 4: 16).

Galen (*c.* 131 to *c.* 201 CE), physician, of Greek parentage, born in Pergamum in Asia Minor, to where he returned after study in Greece and in Alexandria to be physician at the gladiatorial school, but from *c.* 162, lived mostly in Rome. He is credited with authorship of some 500 treatises, mostly on medicine and philosophy, of which some eighty texts on medical topics have survived. Of these, his work on anatomy and physiology – especially the demonstration that arteries carry blood not air – is very important. His virtually undisputed authority until the sixteenth century is now seen as having placed a brake upon medical research.

Ganymede In Greek mythology, a beautiful youth carried off by Zeus to be cupbearer to the gods.

Gildas, Saint (b. *c.* 570). Possibly a Welsh monk, wrote (in Latin) a history of the Roman invasion and Anglo-Saxon conquest of Britain.

Grotius, Hugo (1583–1645), Dutch lawyer and humanist. Enormously influential, especially for text translated as *Concerning the Law of War and Peace* (1625), arguably the founding text of international law in which he argues that 'natural law' lays down laws of conduct for nations as well as for private individuals, and that while war used as instrument of national policy could not be condemned, it was nevertheless criminal to wage war except for certain causes. He also devoted great attention to the notion of humane warfare. Modern critics now tend to draw attention to his indebtedness to the Italian writer on international law, Alberico Gentili (1552–1608). Imprisoned for life for supporting the losing side in Dutch political affairs, he made a daring escape (1621), fleeing to Paris, until returning to Holland (1631), from where he had to flee again the following year. From 1635 to 1645 he represented Sweden at the French Court.

Habbukuk Prophet in last years of the seventh century BCE. Probably a contemporary of Jeremiah, his chief concern was with the obligations of public worship. The Book of the OT in his name (a) announces the imminent onslaught by the Chaldeans (Babylonians), who will punish the King Jehoiakim for his evil and his tyranny, followed (b) by a prayer and thanksgiving to God. One of the Dead Sea scrolls (found 1947–8) was found to be a commentary on Habbakuk 1–2.

Hagar Abraham's Egyptian concubine and slave, mother of Ishmael (Genesis 16: 1–4) who was thrown out (with her son) by his jealous wife, Sarah, into the wilderness, where they were guided by an angel. Islamic tradition has several sites in and near Mecca associated with that journey, and a site near the Ka'bah is identified as the place where mother and son are buried. St Paul (Galatians 4: 21–31) uses Hagar as a symbol for the bondage of the Old Law.

Heraclius (*c.* 575–641; Byzantine Emperor 610–41), succeeded the tyrant Phocas, whom he executed. During his rule, the empire was under constant threat: Bulgars attacked Constantinople; Persians conquered Syria, Egypt and Palestine; and although he recovered the last named in costly campaigns (622–8), he lost them to the Muslim Arabs (629–42).

Hippocrates (*c.* 460 to *c.* 370 BCE), Greek physician, popularly referred to as 'the Father of Medicine'. Although he accepted conventional view of disease as caused by imbalance in four bodily humours (blood, phlegm, black bile, yellow bile), he thought that these were glandular secretions and insisted upon need to combine objective observation with deductive reasoning.

Horace Quintus Horatius Flaccus (65–8 BCE), Latin lyric poet and a major influence on English poetry. Famously given a farm in the Sabine Hills by his benefactor, Maecenas, he retired to write his poetry there, of which some of the most significant include *Satires*, *Odes*, *Epistles* and the work of critical theory, the *Ars Poetica*.

Isaac Only son of Abraham and the aged Sarah, born in fulfilment of God's promise of a covenant (Genesis 17: 15–21), though that was soon put to the test by God's request that the son should be sacrificed. Spared at the last moment by divine intervention and the substitution of a lamb in the place of the young man, he later married Rebecca and fathered Esau and Jacob. Ishmael was his half-brother.

Ishmael Son of Hagar and Abraham (see Hagar, above).

James, Saint (d. *c.* 43 CE), one of the twelve Apostles, called St James the Greater; son of Zebedee and brother of St John (Mark 3: 17). He was, with Simon Peter and John, probably closest to Jesus, being present at the Transfiguration (Mark 9: 2–8; Matthew 17: 1–8; Luke 9: 28–36) as well as in the Garden of Gethsemane (Mark 14: 32). James was beheaded by Herod Agrippa (Acts 12: 2).

Jeremiah A prophet who preached in Jerusalem (*c.* 628–586 BCE), demanding that the Jews reform their personal and social attitudes, prophesying doom unless heeded. When Jerusalem fell to Babylon (586), he was allowed to stay in the city with those Jews who remained behind, until they too left and took him with them to Egypt. The book of prophetic oracles that bears his name in the Bible was preserved by his secretary Baruch (Jeremiah 36: 4).

Jeroboam (a) Jeroboam I, first king of the northern part of Israel which broke away from Judah when Solomon's son Rehoboam became king (922–901 BCE). He became notorious for his encouragement of idolatry (1 Kings 11: 14; 2 Chronicles chs 10, 13). (b) Jeroboam, King of Israel 786–746 BCE, who used the excuse of fear of the Assyrians to expand the borders of Israel (2 Kings 14: 25, 28) and also to increase his own personal wealth and reward his supporters. The social injustices which followed, together with the worship of Baal, led to bitter denunciation by Amos (Amos 2: 6–8).

Jerome, Saint (*c.* 347–420). Born to Christian parents, he was not baptized until 366. After studies in Rome and Trier, travelled to the Orient where, having had a vision (375) in Antioch (Turkey), he renounced his classical learning and fled into the desert to study Hebrew and to live an ascetic life devoted to the study of the Scriptures. Returning to Antioch, he was ordained (379), and went from there to Constantinople for further study, and eventually to Rome where Pope Damasus I asked him to begin a new version of the Bible. From 386 he lived in Bethlehem (living in a monastery established for his use by St Paula, one of several ladies of noble birth who had entered into convents), working on his revisions and translations that were to become the basis for the celebrated Vulgate (common edition) that was intended as a replacement for the Old Latin version, translated from the Greek. The first Bible to be printed on Gutenberg's press, by the early Middle Ages Jerome's translation was used everywhere, and it became the basis for virtually all the earlier translations into vernacular languages. In 1546 the Council of Trent made it the official version used in the Catholic Church.

Jezebel Wife of King Ahab of Israel, and a worshipper of Baal (1 Kings 18: 19). A Phoenician princess who famously disregarded traditional laws and customs in order to expropriate Naboth's vineyard in order to further the needs of the royal estates (1 Kings 18), she was renowned for her opposition to the prophets of her time, including Elijah, who forecast her doom – which was fulfilled when Jehu grabbed power (2 Kings 9: 30–7). From here derives the notion of a Jezebel as 'a wicked woman', brilliantly rebutted by the splendid poem by Micheline Wandor, 'Eve has some gossip':

> They say
> Jezebel slew the prophets.
> It's rubbish.
> She was with me all the time.

(*Gardens of Eden. Poems for Eve and Lilith*, London: Journeyman/ Playbooks, 1984)

Josephus Flavius (37 –*c.* 100 CE), Jewish historian and soldier. Following study of the three main sects of Judaism (Essenes, Sadducees, Pharisees) he became a Pharisee. During the rebellion against Rome he was commander of the forces in Galilee, where he was taken prisoner. During the siege of Jerusalem (70 CE), he was one of the interpreters for the Emperor Vespasian (Titus Flavius Vespasianus) whose name Flavius he adopted, and later went to live in Rome, where he was apparently held in high regard by successive rulers. There he wrote, in Greek, famous and important texts which are valuable sources for a study of early Judaism as early Christianity, notably his *Antiquities of the Jews* (a history of the Jews from creation to the war with Rome) and a defence of his people entitled *Against Apion*.

Joshua Successor to Moses as leader of the people of Israel. The book of the Bible that bears his name consists of a diverse collection of materials broadly divided into three sections: the conquest of the Promised Land (1–12); the allocation of that land by tribe and family (12–22); and Joshua's farewell sermon and death (23–4).

Judah   Fourth son of Jacob and Leah (Genesis 29: 35) who gave his name to the tribe which later settled the kingdom created by the division of the Jews under Rehoboam (see below) that lasted from 931 to 586 BCE, with its capital in Jerusalem, and was ruled by the House of David, with David first becoming King of Judah (2 Samuel 2: 4) but later, with the capture of Jerusalem, uniting the tribes until the death of Solomon. In Genesis, Judah emerges as a leader: with Reuben, he intercedes for Joseph's life; in Egypt he was spokesman to Joseph; during the exodus his tribe were in the lead, and gave the name to the southern part of Palestine where they settled.

Laban   Father of Leah and Rachel, and uncle to Jacob. He not only tricked Jacob into marrying Leah, but then required him to work in his fields for fourteen years before he would allow him to marry Rachel. Laban's avarice received its come-uppance when all three fled to Canaan, taking with them the *teraphim* – the household images through which rights of inheritance were passed on.

Lactanius   Lucius Caelius Firmianus (*c.* 260–340 CE), Christian convert and apologist, born in Africa, who first taught rhetoric and later was Latin tutor to Crispus, son of Constantine. His works include *The Divine Institutions, On God's Wrath* and *On the Death of the Persecutors* (telling about the horrible deaths of emperors such as Nero, Domitian and Decius).

Laius   In Greek legend, King of Thebes, husband to Jocasta and father to Oedipus. Since Laius had been warned by an oracle that he would be killed by his own son, he abandoned the baby Oedipus on a mountainside, where he was found by a shepherd who took him to the King of Corinth, who adopted the infant. When the grown-up Oedipus, in his turn, heard the prophecy that he would kill his father and marry his mother, and unaware that he had been adopted by the king and queen he thought of as father and mother, he fled from Corinth. On that journey Oedipus meets Laius, has a quarrel with him, and kills him and then journeys on to Thebes where the Sphinx was in the process of killing anyone who could not decipher a riddle it had set. Oedipus, for providing the correct answer, is rewarded with marriage to the widowed queen, as well as being king, the prophecy being thereby fulfilled. Two sons (Polynices and Eteocles) as well as two daughters (Antigone and Ismene) are born out of the unwitting incest. Then, when a plague threatens to destroy the city, another oracle recommends that the only way to save them was to expel the killer of Laius, who was polluting the city. When Oedipus eventually learns the truth (splendidly realized by Sophocles in his play *Oedipus the King*), he blinds himself but continues to rule until killed in battle. While Homer's story has the king continuing to rule, the most common version is that he was exiled by Jocasta's brother Creon and that thereafter his sons wrestled for the inheritance of the throne. Another play by Sophocles, *Oedipus at Colonus*, has as theme the wanderings of the exiled monarch, guided by a faithful daughter, Antigone.

Lazarus   (a) Brother of Mary and Martha of Bethany who, after four days in his tomb, was brought back to life as one of the miracles Jesus performed – though Jesus deliberately delayed His response to the sisters' call for help (John 11); (b) the beggar who lay suffering and neglected at the rich man's gate. After their deaths the rich man, now in hell, pleads that the beggar be allowed to offer him a drink to cool his pains (Luke 16: 19–31).

Lucan   Marcus Annaeus Lucanus, 39–65 CE, Latin poet, b. Cordoba (Spain), nephew of the philosopher Seneca, and at first a favourite of the Emperor Nero, who nevertheless demanded that he kill himself when it was discovered that he was implicated in a plot against the tyrant – which, as a Stoic, he accomplished. Several of his epic accounts of the civil war between Caesar and Pompey (erroneously entitled *Pharsalia*) survive. His poetic skill as well as the nature of his death (seeing him as a political opponent to tyranny) made him popular with poets such as Dante, Shelley and Southey, and the critic Macaulay.

Maecenas   Caius Maecenas (d. 8 BCE), Roman statesman and patron of the arts who was born into a wealthy family and became a trusted advisor to Octavian (later, Augustus Caesar) who made use of his services as a trusted go-between on political missions. Upon retirement, he cultivated a literary circle which at various times included the like of Horace, Virgil and Propertius.

Mithridates   Mithridates the Great (*c.* 163–131 BCE), King of Pontus. In First Mithridatic War (88 BCE) he conquered most of Asia Minor, but was defeated there, as well as in Greece (85 BCE). In the Second Mithridatic War (83–81 BCE), the Romans were defeated, but in the Third Mithridatic War (76–73 BCE), he was defeated by Lucullus and driven into the Crimea, where he asked a slave to kill him. His fall is the subject of Racine's *Mithridate* (1673), and he is the hero of Mozart's opera Mithridate Re di Ponto (1770).

Moses   Probably born Egypt (thirteenth century BCE), from which country he led his people out of bondage to the edge of the Promised Land, which he was not allowed to enter – though he saw it from Mt Pisgah before he died. According to the Bible, it was by means of direct contact with Moses that God proclaimed His Law. Authorship of the first five books of the Bible (Pentateuch) traditionally ascribed to him; hence they are also called 'The Books of Moses'.

Muhammad   (*c.* 570–632), founder and prophet of Islam, born Mecca, son of Abdallah ibn Abd al-Muttalib and Amina, both of the Hashim clan of the dominant Kuraish federation. Orphaned soon after birth, he was brought up by an uncle, Abu Talib, and when 24, married Khadija, a widow many years older than himself. He had no other wives during her lifetime. At age 40 he felt himself selected by God to lead the Arab peoples to true religion. Following a vision while he was in a cave on Mt Hira, near Mecca, in which he was commanded to preach, he began to record his revelations, later to become the basis for the Qur'ān. His attempts to win followers in Mecca led to considerable hostility, and he was forced into making his celebrated *hijra* (migration or flight: later to become paradigm for any flight to Islam or Islamic lands) to Medina (622), where he set up an embryonic Islamic community. Following upon three clashes, followed by a virtually bloodless coup, he conquered his birthplace, and re-entered (630). His first converts included his daughter Fatima, her husband Ali and Abu Bakr (Muhammad's father-in-law and later to be First Caliph and successor to the Prophet).

Muhammad II (Mehmet the Conqueror, 1429–81; Ottoman Sultan 1451–81), son and successor to Murad II. It was his storming of Constantinople after a fifty-day siege (1453) that marked the completion of the conquest of the Byzantine Empire. Having taken the city and moved his capital there from Adrianople, he began to settle people from other captured cities in it. And although he turned the Hagia Sophia Church into a mosque, he granted Greeks and Armenians the right to practise their Orthodox Eastern Christianity. As a military specialist, he thereafter proceeded to conquer and annex to the empire the Balkan peninsula, Bosnia, Greece, and several of the Venetian possessions in the Aegean Sea, though his further advances northwards were later defeated at Belgrade by John Hunyadi (1385–1456), an event that staved off Ottoman conquest of Hungary for some seventy years, and in Albania by Scandebeg (*c.* 1404–68), the son of an Albanian prince who had been educated at the Court of Murad II and had become a Muslim, but who, on hearing that the Ottomans intended to attack Albania, returned home, abjured Islam and formed a league of Albanian princes with whose help (as well as with assistance from the Venetians and the Pope) he managed to force Murad to conclude a ten-year truce (1461), one which he himself broke two years later, so that eventually Albania became part of Ottoman suzerainty. A highly learned man and a great patron of the arts, Mehmet was succeeded by his son, Beyazid II.

Muhammad III (1567–1603; Ottoman Sultan 1595– 1603), son and successor of Murad III. He conducted campaigns in Hungary, but these were inconclusive; in the last year of his life he was forced to surrender Tabriz to Shah Abbas of Persia. He was succeeded by his son Ahmed I.

Murad II (1403–51; Sultan 1421–51), son and successor to Mehmet I, though his accession was opposed by a pretender, Mustafa, whom he had to defeat; after which he laid siege to Constantinople (1422) and, in a war with Venice, seized Salonika (1430) and invaded Greece, thereby proving the worth of Ottoman naval power, while in the north he had to fight off the resistance of the Hungarians under John Hunyadi until victory at Varna (1444). Murad tried several times to retire from public life, but was prevented from doing so by the political and military demands of his times, but he tried his best to make his Court a centre at which poetry and the arts could flourish. He was succeeded by his son, Mehmet II, the Conqueror (see above).

Murad IV (1612?–40; Sultan 1623–40), nephew and successor to Mustafa I. He retook Baghdad from Shah Abbas of Persia (1638). He is reputed to have sent an order to murder his brother Beyazid, as well as being responsible for the death of the Greek patriarch Cyril Lucaris (1572–1637) in the belief that he was involved in a plot against him. Murad was succeeded by his brother Ibrahim (Sultan 1640–8) and Ibrahim's son, Mehmet IV (1648–87).

Naomi Widowed mother-in-law of Ruth, who, in her turn, seeks to find a husband for her daughter-in-law, Ruth, whose husband had also died.

Nebuchadnezzar King of Babylonia (*c.* 605–562 BCE). Defeated Egyptians under Pharaoh Necho (605), thereby becoming undisputed master of western Asia. Sudden death of his father forced him to return – which enabled Necho to escape and return to

Egypt, so that three years later (601 BCE) Necho was able to defeat him. This event may have sparked off the revolt in Judaea under Jehoiakim, who died soon after the Babylonians laid siege. Having crushed the revolt, Nebuchadnezzar carried off the king's young son and many of his nobles to Babylon, placing a puppet (Zedekiah) on the throne of Judaea. Following renewal of revolt (588–587), Nebuchadnezzar proceeded to lay siege to and later destroy Jerusalem (completed 586). On the other hand, he is renowned for his interest in building, notably for the Hanging Gardens of Babylon, one of the seven wonders of the ancient world. In the book of Daniel, Nebuchadnezzar is depicted as domineering and cruel.

Nestor   In Greek mythology, the wise ruler of Pylos. In the *Iliad*, he went with the Greeks to the Trojan War; in the *Odyssey* the gods allow him to return home in recognition of his piety and prudence during his long sojourn in Troy. In Shakespeare's *Troilus and Cressida* he supports the advice offered by Ulysses and tries to energize Achilles by seeking to make him jealous of Ajax.

Nestorius   (d. 451?), Patriarch of Jerusalem, who reputedly propounded the view (regarded as a heresy by the Christian Church) to the effect that Jesus was two distinct persons – one human, the other divine – but inseparably linked. He also opposed the title of Mary as Mother of God, since (in his view) she bore Jesus as a man. Councils at Ephesus (431) and Chalcedon (451) were convened at which the orthodox position was reaffirmed. Deposed after the Council at Ephesus, Nestorius was sent to Antioch, to Arabia, and finally to Egypt. While Nestorianism had more or less ceased in the Roman Empire, missionary activities enabled it to continue to survive in Arabia, China and India for some time. Though there are still in existence Christian communities in Iraq, Iran and in parts of India who are members of a Nestorian Church, these have scant connection with the views propounded by the patriarch.

Nimrod   Son of Cush, the name of the first great king to be mentioned in the OT who ruled in Assyria and Babylonia and who was 'a mighty hunter for the Lord' (Genesis 10: 8–9).

Ortelius, Abraham   (1527–98), Flemish geographer, maker of the *Theatrum orbis terrarum* generally accepted to be the first modern atlas (1570, with 53 maps; 1587, with 103 maps – in which year he also brought out another celebrated work, *Thesaurus geographicus*). Ortelius was appointed geographer to Philip II of Spain (1575). For his particular significance for travellers' tales, see Jerry Brotton, *Trading Territories. Mapping the Early Modern World*, London: Reaktion, 1997: 169–79.

Ovid   Publius Ovidius Naso (43 BCE to 18 CE), Latin poet who was major source of inspiration for the Renaissance. Key themes included those of love, including the erotic (*Amores, The Art of Love*), mythology (*Metamorphoses*) and (after being banished to the shores of the Black Sea for reasons unknown) poems on the sorrows of exile (*Tristia*). There are several translations into English (chiefly of the *Metamorphoses*) in the early modern period, including one by the poet George Sandys (1626) who also wrote *A Relation of a Iourney begun An: Dom: 1610...Containing a description of the Turkish Empire, of Egypt, of the Holy Land, of the remote parts of Italy, and ilands adioying* (1615) for selections of which, unfortunately, there was no space in the present collection.

Patroclus In the *Iliad*, son of Menoetius, friend of Achilles, who puts on the latter's armour and fights bravely but is slain by Hector. It is in order to revenge his death that Achilles returns to the fray.

Pausanias (a) Pausanias of Lydia (fl. *c.* 150 CE), traveller and geographer, wrote a *Description of Greece* that is an invaluable (and, as existing remains confirm, remarkably accurate) source document with regard to topography, monuments, legends of Ancient Greece. (b) Spartan general (d. *c.* 470 BCE), victor at Battle of Plataea (479 BCE) in the Persian Wars; then followed that up with expeditions to Cyprus and Byzantium, from where he was called back to face an (almost certainly false) charge of treasonable negotiations with the enemy. Acquitted, some years later he was faced with a similar charge for a second time, but once again acquitted. When, later, he was charged with plotting a coup in Sparta in league with the exiled Themistocles (see below), he sought sanctuary in a temple, where he was left to starve to death.

Penthesilea In Greek mythology, Queen of the Amazons, who, in the Trojan War, led her army against the Greeks. She was killed by Achilles – who then fell in love with her dead body.

Persius Aulus Persius Flaccus, Roman satirical poet (62–34 BC).

Petronius Roman satirist (d. *c.* 66 CE), also known as Petronius Arbiter because he identified with Caius Petronius (called by Tacitus the *arbiter elegentiae* at the Court of the Roman dictator, Nero). Credited with writing a verse romance that portrays (often in colloquial terms) the habits of his times, he was highly regarded in the Renaissance for the elegance of his writing style – though also for being profligate and indolent when consul in Bithynia. When placed under arrest by a rival for Nero's favours, he slashed his wrists and bled to death, attended upon by his friends.

Philip of Macedon Philip II (382–336; ruled 359–336 BCE), seized the throne while acting as regent for his nephew Amyntas. Having reorganized the army, he embarked on a policy of expansion and annexation until Athens and Thebes were forced to make war against him in an attempt to stop him, but he crushed them at Chaerona (338), thereby becoming ruler of the whole region. He was preparing for war against Persia when he was killed, his wife, Olympia, being (almost certainly unjustly) accused of murdering him. Philip's consolidation of the kingdom as well as his creation of a powerful army laid the basis for the subsequent success of his son, Alexander the Great.

Plato (427–348 BCE), Greek philosopher, pupil and friend of Socrates, founded near Athens (*c.* 387) the Academy, arguably the most influential school of the ancient world, where he taught until his death, and where his most famous pupil was Aristotle. His extant work is in the form of epistles and dialogues on subjects such as the unity of virtue and knowledge, the rational relations between the soul, the state and the cosmos, as well as on technical problems in philosophy. Texts such as, for example, the *Republic*, *Phaedo*, *Symposium* have been some of the most influential in the intellectual and political history of the West.

Pliny (a) Pliny the Elder (Caius Plinius Secundus *c.* AD 23–79), born Gaul, whose *Historia naturalis*, in thirty-seven books, deals with the nature of the physical universe, geography, botany, anthropology, etc. Encyclopedic in scope, it is not worth much as science. (b) His nephew, Pliny the Younger (Caius Plinius Caecilius Secundus, AD 62?–113), held many positions (questor, tribune, consul) in Roman civil society, but is chiefly remembered for his oratory and his letters, written for publication and valuable for providing excellent accounts of Roman life of his time.

Plutarch Greek essayist and writer of biographies, who travelled into Egypt and Italy (where he taught philosophy in Rome), but finally returned to Greece to become a priest at the temple at Delphi. Most celebrated text is the *Parallel Lives,* arranged in pairs, in which he compares one Greek with one Roman. In England, Sir Thomas North's translation (1579) was to be a major influence on subsequent writers, of which the best known is that of Shakespeare's *Julius Caesar, Antony and Cleopatra* and *Timon of Athens.*

Pompey the Great Cnaeus Pompeius Magnus (106–48 BCE), Roman general and politician. Supporter of the dictator Sulla, he had campaigns in Spain, against the Mediterranean pirates, and against Mithridates VI. He returned to Italy (62 BCE), feted for his military success, but lacked political skill. He entered into political alliance with Julius Caesar (whose daughter, Julia, he married) and Crassus, but after the death of Crassus and the rise of Caesar, he became the champion of the Senate, being appointed sole consul. Eventually driven to fight Caesar, Pompey was defeated at Pharsalia (48 BCE), from where he fled into Egypt only to be murdered, on arrival, by supporters of Ptolemy XII.

Prester John The legend that first appeared in the twelfth century and the name given to a reputedly Christian ruler of a vast and wealthy domain that stretched from the present-day Ethiopia across the Indian Ocean into Asia, though not everyone was as impressed (or spread the story) as Edward Webbe did – witness J[ohn] P[hillips], Gent. *A New History of Ethiopia. Being a full and accurate description of the kingdom of Abessinia. Vulgarly, though erroneously called the Empire of Prester John...by the learned Job Ludolphus, Counsellor to His Imperial Majesty and the Dukes of Saxony, and Treasurer to His Highness the Elector Palatine*, London, *c.* 1684.

Pythagoras (582–507 BCE), pre-Socratic philosopher, about whose life and writings little is known, except in the form and manner in which it was handed down by his followers, the Pythagoreans, a mystical brotherhood he founded, who also appear to have worshipped him as a sort of demigod. Best remembered for his theorem which states that the square on the length of the hypotenuse of a right-angled triangle equals the sum of the squares of the lengths of the other two sides. Pythagoreans were skilled mathematicians who influenced Euclid.

Rachel Daughter of Laban and Jacob's second wife (Genesis 29: 17) and mother of Joseph and Benjamin.

Rebecca Wife of the patriarch Isaac and mother of Jacob and Esau, twin sons born after twenty years of marriage; she contrived to get her favourite, Jacob (instead of the first-born, Esau), to receive his dying father's blessing.

Regiomontanus (lit.: belonging to the royal mountain). German astronomer and mathematician (1436–76), whose original name was Johannes Müller. He went to Rome (1461) to learn Greek in order to translate classics written in that language, and in 1468 was invited to the Court of the King of Hungary to make a collection of Greek manuscripts. In 1471 he settled in Nuremberg where (with his pupil and patron Bernard Walther) he set up an observatory and a printing press on which they printed several classic texts. In 1475 he was summoned to Rome to assist with the reforming of the calendar, and was made bishop of Regensburg.

Rehoboam (Reigned probably 926–910 BCE), son of Solomon who succeeded to the throne, but of Judah only because the northern tribes rejected his tax proposals and accepted Jeroboam as their king. His failure to repel the invasion by the Egyptian Shisak (1 Kings 14: 25–8) was seen as proof of his disloyalty to God, and therefore punished by being abandoned to the invader (2 Chronicles 12: 5).

Rhazes (Rasis) (860–932), Persian physician at the Baghdad hospital, generally held to be the first medical doctor to provide first formulation and description of smallpox as distinguished from measles. Although this was only translated into English in 1848 as *A Treaty on Smallpox and Measles*, his work was in wide circulation in Arabic and in Greek versions, and in Latin from the fifteenth century. These include a textbook of medicine, *Almansor*, and an encyclopedia, *Liber continens*, compiled posthumously from his papers.

Sadi (Saadi), Musladini Persian poet (1184–1291), b. Shiraz, studied in Baghdad, but when forced to flee that city because of threat of invasion by Mongols, went on long journey to Central Asia, India, Yemen and Ethiopia via Mecca. Captured by the Franks in Syria, he was forced to do hard labour until ransomed. He returned to Shiraz (1256) after further travels in North Africa and Anatolia. His *Bustan* (fruit garden) was composed in rhyming couplets, while his (even more popular) *Gulistan* was written in rhyming prose. He is also the author of many long panygerics (*qasidas*) and love poems (*ghazals*) in Persian as well as in Arabic.

Saladin (1137–93), famed opponent of the Crusaders, was born in Mesopotamia, probably of Kurdish descent. Lived for ten years at the Court in Damascus where he distinguished himself with his knowledge of Sunni theology. Having fought campaigns against the Fatimid rulers of Egypt (1164, 1167, 1168), he eventually proclaimed himself Sultan (1169), after which he proceeded to spread his empire westwards along the northern shore of Africa, as well as into Yemen and several key cities such as Aleppo, so that he was soon recognized as the chief warrior for Islam, soon gathering about him a large force of Muslims of various kinds (but all subsumed by the Christians under the name Saracen). In 1187 at the Battle of Hattin, Saladin captured two key Crusaders, Lusignan and Reginald of Châtillon, and later conquered Jerusalem. In the Third Crusade, in order to seek to recover Jerusalem, Saladin and Richard I of England confronted each other – later to be the theme for chivalric romances, notable especially for the celebration of Saladin for his generosity towards foe as well as friend. Although the Crusaders failed in their task, Saladin, at the Peace of Ramla (1192), left the Latin Kingdom a tiny strip along the coast.

Sardanapalus In the *Persica* of Ctesias (Greek historian and physician who lived for many years at the Persian Court and who looked after Artaxerxes II when the latter was wounded at the Battle of Cunaxa) Sardanapalus is the Assyrian monarch renowned for living in great luxury in Nineveh. Besieged for two years by the Medes, he set fire to his palace and burnt himself and his Court to death. Doubt has recently been cast upon the (until now) commonly held view that Sardanapalus was the Assyrian ruler, Assurbanipal. *Sardanapalus* is also the name for Lord Byron's tragedy, based upon material taken from the 'Biblioteca Historica' of Diodorus Siculus, but reworked so that the king, confronted by revolt, shakes off his sloth, fights bravely and, when defeated, makes provision for his queen Zarina and then perishes on a funeral pyre, together with his favourite slave, Myrrha. (See Martyn Corbett, *Byron and Tragedy*, London: Macmillan, 1988: 81–115).

Scaliger, Julius Caesar (1484–1558), Italian philologist, later physician in France, who wrote books on medical and botanical writings of the likes of Aristotle and Hippocrates, as well as on the style of Cicero, but especially praised Virgil and Seneca.

Selim I Selim the Grim (1467–1520; Ottoman Sultan 1512–20) ascended the throne by forcing his father, Beyazid II, to abdicate. Because of Persian support for his brother, as well as religious conflict in Islam between Sunni and Shiite factions, Selim (a Sunni) attacked Persia. In 1514 he defeated Shah Ishmael. He later also defeated the Mamluks in Syria and Egypt (1516–17), and added these to the Ottoman Empire. Furthermore, by assuming the Caliphate (the rulership of Islam) he made himself and his successors spiritual, as well as temporal, heads of the empire, gaining thereby control over the holy cities of Mecca and Medina. It is probable that it is out of these Sunni vs Shiite contests that there developed the rivalries between Ottomans and Persians, so eagerly relayed by Protestant English travellers. Selim died while preparing an attack on Rhodes. He was succeeded by his son, Suleiman I.

Selim II (Selim the Drunkard, 1524–74; Ottoman Sultan 1566–74), son and successor to Suleiman I, during which period arguably the dominant figure was his Grand Vizier, the Albanian Mehmet Pasha Solkollu (born Bajca Sokolovic). Although during Selim's reign the Ottomans conquered Cyprus from Venice, and recovered Tunis from Spain, they also underwent their first major defeat in the naval battle off Lepanto (1571).

Semiramis Mythical queen of Assyria, renowned for her beauty and wisdom, reputed to have conquered many lands and to have been the founder of Babylon. Having had a long and prosperous reign, she departed from earth in the shape of a dove. One view is that her story is based upon that of Summuramat, who was the Assyrian regent 810–805 BCE.

Seneca Lucius Anneus Seneca, Seneca the Younger (*c.* 3 BCE to 65 CE), Roman philosopher, playwright and politician, tutor to the dictator Nero, was instructed to commit suicide when accused of being involved in a conspiracy. A Stoic in philosophy, he wrote moral and philosophical essays as well as celebrated tragedies such as *Hercules Furens*, *Medea*, *Phaedra*, *Agamemnon*, *Oedipus* and *Thyestes*. His writings were of immense influence in the Renaissance

Solomon d. *c.* 930 BCE, King of the Hebrews (*c.* 970–930), son and successor to David. His period as ruler was marked by making of alliances with other states (notably with Egypt and Phoenicia), and by the greatest extension of the territory of Israel in biblical times. While Solomon was responsible for the building of several new cities as well as for the construction of the first temple in Jerusalem, his rule alienated those living in the north to such an extent that it led to the breakaway and formation of a separate state under Jeroboam I. Known for his wisdom, The Song of Solomon bears his name; Proverbs as well as Ecclesiastes were ascribed to him, and there are other accounts (2 Samuel and 1 and 2 Kings). He was supposed to have had 700 wives plus 300 concubines.

Solon Athenian statesman (*c.* 639–559 BCE), remembered for making sweeping economic and social reforms. Elected archon (594) at a time of severe inequalities between rich nobles and the poor, he annulled all debts and mortgages and outlawed all borrowings in which a person's liberty might be pledged as collateral – by which, at a stroke, he put an end to serfdom. He not only changed the law so that immigrant craftsmen could become citizens of Athens, but generally sought to bring in a more humane legal code than the one then in existence, associated with the name of Draco, known for its harshness: even the most trivial of acts could lead to a sentence of death.

Statius Publius Papinius (*c.* 45 to *c.* 96 CE), Latin poet, favourite of the Emperor Domitian. Among his surviving works are two epics in the manner of Virgil: the *Thebaid* (on the seven Greek heroes who made war against Thebes, a subject also for Euripides' *The Phoenician Women* and Aeschylus's *Seven Against Thebes*) and the incomplete *Achilleid* – on the early life of Achilles.

Strabo (*c.* 63 BCE to *c.* 21 CE). Greek historian, geographer and philosopher whose *Geography* is based partly on personal observation but relies heavily on work of predecessors – notably Homer, to whom he attributed an accurate knowledge of the places and peoples mentioned, while disregarding the information in Herodotus, often much more reliable. He was a major influence on Renaissance travels.

Suleiman Suleiman the Magnificent (1494–1566; Ottoman Sultan 1520–66), son and successor to Selim I. During his rule the Ottoman Empire reached its height of power and prestige. He expelled the Christian knights from Rhodes (1522), defeated the Hungarians at Mohacs (1526), but was unsuccessful in his siege of Vienna (1529) and his support of John Zapolya (John I of Hungary) against Ferdinand of Hungary (later Holy Roman Emperor Ferdinand I). He also entered formal alliance with Francis I of France against the Hapsburgs (1536) and although his naval campaigns in the Mediterranean were less successful than those on land (he lost Tunis to Charles II in 1535 and failed to conquer Malta in 1565), he had several successful campaigns against the Persians. The last years of his reign were marred by intrigues on the part of his favourite wife against his eldest son, Mustafa, in preference for her two sons Selim and Beyazid. For his military, educational and legal reforms, he was given the name Suleiman the Lawgiver by Muslims.

Terence Publius Terentius Afer (b. Carthage *c.* 185 or *c.* 195 to *c.* 159 BCE), Roman writer of comedies. As a boy a slave to a Roman senator, who brought him to Rome, educated him and gave him his freedom.

Themistocles (*c.* 525 to *c.* 460 BCE), Athenian soldier and statesman. In the Persian wars he persuaded the Athenians to enlarge their navy and it was his strategy that led to the victory at Salamis (480) that forced Xerxes to retreat. Afterwards, when his rivals and opponents came to power, he was exiled and retired to Persia, where he was highly regarded and well provided for by King Artaxerxes.

Theodosius Theodosius I (Theodosius the Great) (346?–95; Roman Emperor of the East 379–5; of the West 392–5), son of Theodosius, the Roman general who under Emperor Valentin I defeated the Scots and Picts in Britain (368–9) and the Alemanni in Gaul (372–4). When his father was executed on the orders of Valetin's successor, Gratian, the son moved to Spain, where he remained until Gratian chose him to rule in the East, and later elevated to being co-augustus. During his period of rule the Roman Empire was under constant threat from invasion (Visigoths) and usurpation, most of which he managed either to resolve or repel. Baptized (380), he condemned Arianism and made a belief in the Trinity the test of orthodoxy and convened the First Council of Constantinople. He was excommunicated for ordering the massacre of citizens of Salonika who had rebelled against a garrison stationed there, and readmitted only after he had done penance at the feet of Ambrose, Bishop of Milan. It was his decision to leave the eastern part of his empire to one son, Arcadius, and the west to another, Honorius, that led to the permanent partition of the empire.

Ulysses In Greek mythology, King of Ithaca, husband of Penelope, and a Greek leader in the Trojan War. His wanderings are described in the *Odyssey.*

Virgil or **Vergil** (Publius Vergilius Maro, 70–19 BCE), arguably the greatest of the Roman poets, maker of the national epic the *Aeneid* that follows the wanderings of the hero, Aeneas, from the moment of the fall of Troy, via an affair with Queen Dido founder queen of Carthage, until the eventual founding of the Roman state. Born in Mantua, Virgil went to Rome *c.* 41, but much of his other work is still rooted to the experience on his father's farm that led to the celebration of rural life (*Eclogues, Georgics*).

Xerxes King of Persia (485–465 BCE), son of Darius I, who sought to revenge the defeat his father had sustained at Marathon (490 BCE). Successful at Thermopylae (480), he was defeated in the naval battle off Salamis by Themistocles later in the same year. He is also the King Ahasuerus in the Book of Esther, though the story as it is told there contains no references to the known historical events of his reign, and more to do with seeking to provide an account of the origin of the feast of Purim.

SOURCES

Dictionary of National Biography.

The Columbia Encyclopedia, ed. Barbara A. Chernow and George A. Vallasi (5th edition), New York: Columbia University Press/Houghton Mifflin Company, 1993.

The Penguin Companion to Literature: Classical & Byzantine, Oriental & African Literature, ed. D. R. Dudley and D. M. Lang, Harmondsworth: Penguin, 1969.

A Dictionary of Philosophy, London: Pan, 1979.

Philip Mansel, *Constantinople. City of the World's Desire, 1453–1924*, London: John Murray, 1995.

W. R. Browning, *Oxford Dictionary of the Bible*, Oxford: Oxford University Press, 1997.

BIBLIOGRAPHY

Primary sources

Unless otherwise stated, the place of publication is London. Spelling and punctuation have, in some instances, been slightly modernized.

A letter from an eminent merchant in Constantinople, to a friend in London, giving an exact relation of the great and glorious cavalcade of Sultan Mahomet the fourth, present Emperour of the Turks, as he marched out of Constantinople, for the invasion of Christendome, and the siege of Vienna, A. Jones, 1683.

Addison, Lancelot [Dean of Lichfield] (1679) *The first state of Mahumedism; or, an account of the author and doctrines of that imposture*, J. C. for W. Crooke.

Alexander, William (1603) *The Tragedy of Darius*, Edinburgh: Robert Waldegrave.

——(1616) *The Monarchick Tragedies*, William Stansby.

Andrés, Jean (1652) *The comparison of Muhamed's sect; or, a confutation of the Turkish Alcoran*, translated by I. N. [Joshua Notstock], H. Blunden.

Angelos, Christopheros (1617) *Christopher Angell, a Grecian, who tasted of many stripes and torments inflicted by the Turkes for the faith which he had in Christ Iesus. (An epistle in commendations of England and the inhabitants thereof)*. Oxford.

Ashwell, George (1686) *The history of Hai Eb'n Yockdan, an indian prince; or, the self-taught philosopher. Written originally in the Arabick tongue by Abi Jaafar Eb'n Tophail, a philosopher by profession, and a Mahometan by religion. Set forth...in the Latin version by E. Pocock...and now translated into English by G. Ashwell*, Richard Chiswell.

Barker, Andrew (1609) *A true and certaine report of the beginning, proceedings, overthrowes, and the present estate of Captaine Ward and Dansiker, the two late famous pirates...from their first setting foorth to this present time*. Printed by William Hall; sold by Iohn Holme.

Baron, Robert (1647) *Mirza, a tragedie really acted in Persia in the last age. Illustrated with historical annotations*, Humphrey Moseley; T. Dring.

Biddulph, William (1609) *The travels of certaine Englishmen into Africa, Asia, Troy, Bythinia, Thracia, and to the Blacke Sea. And into Syria, Cilicia, Pisidia, Mesopotamia, Damascus, Canaan, Galilee, Samaria, Iudea, Palestina, Ierusalem, Iericho, and to the Red Sea; and to sundry other places. Begunne in the yeere of Iubilee 1600 and by some of them finished this yeere 1608, the others not yet returned. Very profitable for the helpe of travellers, and no lesse delightfull to all persons who take pleasure to hear of the manners, gouernement, religion, and customes of forraine and heathen countries*, T. Haveland for W. Apsley.

Blome, R. (1670) *A geographical description of the four parts of the world, taken from the notes and works of the famous Monsieur Sanson...and other eminent travellers and authors....Also, a treatise of travel, and another of traffick...the whole illustrated with...maps and figures*, T. N. for R. Blome.

273

Blount, Henry (1636) *A voyage into the Levant. A brief relation of a journey lately performed by Master H. B., Gentleman, from England by way of Venice, into Dalmatia, Sclavonia, Bosnia, Hungary, Macedonia, Thessaly, Thrace, Rhodes, and Egypt, unto Gran Cairo. With particular observations concerning the modern condition of the Turks, and other people under that Empire,* I[ohn] L[eggatt] for A[ndrew] Crooke.

Boemus, Johannes (1611) *The manners, lawes, and customs of all nations. Collected out of the best writers by Johannes Boemus Aubanus a Dutchman, written in Latin, and now into English.* By Ed[ward] Astor, George Eld.

Botero, Giovanni (1601) *The Travellers Breviat, or a historical description of the most famous king-domes in the world,* translated into English...by Robert Iohnston, Edm. Bollifant for Iohn Iaggard; [as] (1603) *An historicall description of the most famous kingdomes and common-weales in the world;* [as] (1608, 1616) *Relations of the most famous kingdoms and commonweales....*

Bourne, W. (1578) *A Booke called the Treasure for Traueillers,* for T. Woodcocke.

Boyle, Robert [Earl of Orrery] (1668) *The history of Henry the Fifth. And the tragedy of Mustapha, son of Solyman the Magnificent,* for H. Herringham.

Bulwer, J. (1654) *A view of the people of the whole world; or, a...survey of their polocies, dispositions...complexions, ancient & moderne customes, etc.,* 1654; as (1653) *Anthropometamorphosis: Man Transform'd; or, the artificial changeling.*

Busbecq, Ogier Ghiselin de (1696) *Travels into Turkey.*

Carlell, Lodowick (1657) *Two New Playes. Viz. 1. The Fool who would be Favourit, or the Discreet Lover; 2. Osmond, the Great Turk; or, the Noble Servant,* for Humphrey Moseley.

Carpenter, Nathaniel (1625) *Geography, delineated...in two books...,* Oxford: John Litchfield & William Turner for Henry Cripps.

Carr, William (1695) *Travellour's Guide and Historian's Faithfull Companion,* Eben, Tracy.

Cartwright, John (1611) *The Preachers Travels. Wherein is set downe a true Iournall to the confines of the East Indies, through the great countreyes of Syria, Mesopotamia, Armenia, Media, Hircania, and Parthia. With the author's returne by the way of Persia, Susiana, Assyria, Chaldea, and Arabia. Containing a full surdew of the Kingdom of Persia, and in what terms the Persian stands with the Great Turk at this day. Also, a true relation of Sir Anthony Sherleys entertainment there; and the estate that his brother, M. Robert Sherley lived in after his departure for Christendome. With the description of a port in the Persian Gulf, commodious for our East Indian merchants; and a brief rehearsal of some gross absurdities in the Turkish Alcoran. Penned by J. C., sometimes student in Magdalen Colledge in Oxford,* Thomas Thorppe.

Coryate, Thomas (1616) *Thomas Coriate Traueller for the English Wits. Greeting. From the Court of the Great Mogul, resident at the towne of Asmere [Ajmer] in easterne India,* W. Jaggard for Henry Featherston.

[Crow, Sackvile] (1646) *Subtilty and Cruelty. Or a relation of the horrible and unparalleled abuses and intolerable oppressions exercised by Sir Sackvile Crow, His Majesty's Ambassador at Constantinople, and his agents, in seizing upon the persons and estates of the English nation resident there, and at Smyrna. Together with the barbarous and tyrannical intent to do the like upon the persons and estates in all parts of the Grand Signior's dominions, directly contrary to the trust reposed in him by His Majesty, and his owne agreement with the Company of Merchants of England trading into the Levant seas, at whose charge he is there maintained,* R. Cotes.

Daborn, R. (1612) *A Christian turn'd Turk: Or, the tragicall lives and deaths of two famous pyrates, Ward and Dansiker. As it hath beene publickly acted,* William Barrenger.

Dandini, Girolano (1698) *A voyage to Mount Libanus. Wherein is an account of the customs, manners etc. of the Turks,* J. Orme for A. Roper, R. Basset.

Day, John, Rowley, William, Wilkins, George (1607) *The Travailes of the Three English Brothers, Sir Thomas, Sir Anthony, Sir Robert Sherley, as it is now play'd by Her Maiesties Seruants,* George Eld for John Wright.

Du Mont, J. [Baron de Carlscroon] (1696) *A New Voyage into the Levant. Containing an account of the most remarkable curiousities....*

Eden, Richard (1577) *The History of Trauayle to the West and East Indies...gathered in parte, and done into Englyshe by Richard Eden*, Richard Jugge.

Elded, John (1589) 'The voyage of M[aster] John Eldred to Tripoli in Syria by sea, and from then by land and river to Babylon [Baghdad] and Balsora [Basra]', Hakluyt, R. (1589) *infra.*

Federici, C. (1588) *The voyage and travel of M[aster] Caesar Frederick, merchant of Venice, into the East India, the Indies, and beyond the Indies...for the profitable instruction of merchants and all other travellers, for their better direction and knowledge of those countries.* Out of the Italian by T. H[itchcock], R. Jones & E. White.

Fryer, John (1698) *A New Account of East India and Persia, in eight letters. Being nine years travels, begun 1672 and finished 1681. Containing observations made of the moral, natural, and artificial estate of those countries, namely of their government, religion, laws, customs; of the soil, climates, seasons, health, diseases; of the animals, vegetables, minerals, jewels; of their housing, clothing, manufactures, trades, commodities, and of the coins, weights, and measures used in the principal places of trade in those parts. By John Fryer, M. A. Cantabrig. And Fellow of The Royal Society*, R. R. for Ri[chard] Chiswell.

Goffe, Thomas (1656) *Three Excellent Tragedies, viz. The Raging Turk, or Bajazet the Second; the Couragious Turk, or Amurath the First; and the tragedie of Orestes (each in five acts and verse).*

Goodall, Baptist (1630) *The Tryall of Travell; or 1. The wonders of travell; 2. The worthies of travell; 3. The way to travell*, J. Norton for J. Upton.

Grelot, Joseph (1683) *A late voyage to Constantinople...published by permission of the French king.* Translated from the French by J. Phillips.

Greville, Fulke [Baron Brooke] (1609) *Mustapha.*

Hacke, William (1699) *A Collection of Original Voyages*, J. Knapton.

Haga, Cornelius (1613) *A true declaration of the arrival of Cornelius Haga (with others that accompanied him) Ambassadour for the generall States of the United Netherlands at Constantinople. Faithfully translated out of the Dutch copie.*

Hakluyt, Richard (1589) *The Principall Navigations, Voiages and Discoveries of the English Nation*, G. Bishop and R. Newberie, deputies to C. Baker.

——(1598) *The Principal Navigations, Voiages, Traffiques and Discoveries...*, 3 vols.

Hall, Joseph (1617) *Quo Vadis? A just censure of travell as it is commonly undertaken by the gentlemen of our nation*, E. Griffen for F. Butter.

Herbert, Thomas (1677) *Some years travels into divers parts of Africa and Asia the Great, describing more particularly the empires of Persia and Industan. Interwoven with such remarkable occurrences as hapned in those parts during these later times. As also many other rich and famous kingdoms in the Oriental India, with the isles adjacent. Severally relating their religion, language, customs and habit; as also proper observations concerning them. In this fourth impression are added (by the author now living) as well many additions throughout the whole work, as also several sculptures, never before printed...*, R. Everingham for R. Scot, T. Basset, J. Wright, and R. Chiswell.

Howell, John [Historiographer to Charles II] (1642) *Forreine Travel.*

Intreigues of the French King at Constantinople, to embroil Christendom. Discovered in several despatches past [passed] betwixt him and the late Grand Signior, Grand Vizier, and Count Teckily. All of them found among that Count's papers seiz'd in December last. None of them being hitherto seen in English. With some reflections upon them. Published by authority. Printed for Donovan Newman, 1689.

Keith, George (1674) *An account of the Oriental Philosophy, showing...particularly the profound wisdom of Hai Ebn Yokdan [Abu Bakr Ibn Al-Tufail]....Out of the Arabick translated into Latine by E. Pocok and now faithfully out of his Latine, translated into English.*

Lewkenor, Samuel (1600) *A Discourse of Forraine Cities....*

Linschoten, Jan Huyghen van (1598) *His discours of voyages into the East and West Indies. Translated by W[illiam] P[hillip]*, J. Wolfe.

Lithgow, William (1632) *The totall discourse of the rare adventures and painefull peregrinations of long nineteene yeares trauayles from Scotland to the most famous kingdomes in Europe, Asia, and Africa. Perfited by three deare bought voyages in surueighing of forty eight kingdomes ancient and moderne; twenty one republickes, ten aboslute principalities, with two hundred ilands, the particular names whereof are described in each argument of the ten diuisions of this history. And it is also diuided in three bookes, two whereof neuer heretofore published, wherein is contayned an exact relation of the lawes, religion, policies and gouernment of all their princes, potentates, and peoples. Together with the grieuous tortures he suffered by the Inquisition of Malaga in Spaine, his miraculous discouery and deliuerance thence, and also of his laste and late returne from the Northerne Isles*, Nicholas Okes for Nicholas Fussell and Humphrey Moseley.

Massinger, Philip (1631) *The Emperor of the East, a tragae-comedie*, T. Harper for I. Waterson.

M. B. (1660) *Learn of a Turk, or instructions and advise sent from the Turkish army at Constantinople to the English army at London. Faithfully and impartially communicated by M.B. one of the attendants of the English Agent there....*

Meriton, George (1671) *A geographical description of the World. With a brief account of the several empires, dominions, and parts thereof. As also the natures of the people, customs, manners and commodities of the several countreys. With a description of the principal cities in each dominion.*

Middleton, Thomas (1609) *Sir Robert Sherley sent Ambassadour in the name of the King of Persia, to Sigismund the Third, King of Poland and Svvecia, and to other Princes of Europe. His Royall entertainment in Cracovia, the chiefe citie of Poland, with his pretended coming into England. Also, the Honourable praises of the same Sir Robert Sherley, given unto him in that kingdome, is here likewise inserted*, J. Windet for John Budge.

Moryson, Fynes (1617) *An Itinerary written by Fynes Moryson Gent., first in the Latine tongue, and then translated by him into English. Containing his ten yeeres travell through the twelve dominions of Germany, Bohmerland, Sweitzerland, Netherland, Denmarke, Poland, Italy, Turky, France, England, Scotland and Ireland...*, John Beale.

Neale, T. (1643) *Treatise of Direction how to Travel safely and profitably into Forraigne Countries. Written first in Latin and since translated by the author T. Neale.*

Newes from the Sea, of two notorious pyrats Ward the Englishman and Danseker the Dutchman. With a true relation of all or the most piracies by them committed unto the sixth of Aprill 1609, N. Butter, 1609.

Nixon, Anthony (1607) *The Three English Brothers. Sir Thomas Sherely his travels, with his three yeares imprisonment in Turkie: his inlargement by his Maiesties letters to the great Turke: and lastly, his safe returne into England this present year, 1607. Master Robert Sherley his wars against the Turkes, with his marriage to the Emperor of persia his neece*, John Hodgets.

Olearius, A. (1662) *The Voyages and Travels of the Ambassadors sent by Frederick Duke of Holstein to the Great Duke of Muscovy and the King of Persia, begun in the year 1633, and finished 1639...whereto are added the travels of J. Mandelso, from Persia into the East Indies...written originally by A. Olearius....Faithfully rendered into English by T. Davies.*

Parry, William (1601) *A True Report of Sir Anthony Shirlies journey overland to Venice, from thence by sea to Antioch, Aleppo and Babilon, and so to Casbine in Persia: his entertainment there by the great Sophie: his oration: his Letters of Credence to the Christian princes: and the privilege obtained of the great Sophie, for the quiet passage and trafique of all Christian merchants, throughout his whole dominions. (Reported by two gentlemen who have followed him in the same the whole of his travaille, and are lately sent by him with letters into England).*

[Pliny] (1601) *The Historie of the World, commonly called The Natural History of C. Plinius Secundus, translated by Philemon Holland*, A. Islip.

[Pomponius Mela] (1585) *The Works of Pomponius Mela concerninge the situation of the world...translated out of Latine by A. Golding*, T. Hacket.

Porter, Thomas (1659) *A Compendius View or Cosmological and geographical description of the whole World with plain general rules touching the use of the globe. Also, a chronology...since the Creation.*

Price, John (1823) *Mèmoires de John Price*, 1823.

Purchas, S. (1625) *Hakluytus Posthumous or Purchas his Pilgrimes.*

Roberts, A. (1670) *The adventures of Mr. T. S., an English merchant, taken prisoner by the Turkes of Argiers and carried into the inland countries of Africa. Written first by the author and fitted for the publick view by A. Roberts...*, M. Pitt.

Ross, Alexander (1649) *The Alcoran of Mahomet, translated out of the Arabique into French by the Sieur Du Ryer...and newly Englished for the satisfaction of all that desire to look into the Turkish vanities. (The life and death of Mahomet, etc. – a needful caveat or admonition for them who desire to know what use may be made of, or if there be danger in reading the Alcoran.)*

Russell, R. (1678) *The works...of Geber, the most famous Arabian prince and philosopher, faithfully Englished by R. Russell, a lover of antiquity.*

Sadi, Musladini (1651) *Rosarium Politicum*, translated Georgius Gentius, Amsterdam.

Sanderson, John (1625) 'Sundry the personal voyages performed by John Sanderson of London, merchant, begun in October 1584, ended in October 1602; with an historical description of Constantinople', in Samuel Purchas, *Purchas his Pilgrimes*, Vol. 2: 1614–40.

Sandys, George (1615) *A Relation of a journey begun anno Dom, 1610, Foure Bookes. Containing a description of the Turkish Empire, of Egypt, of the Holy Land, of the remote parts of Italy, and ilands adioying*, London: R. Field for W. Barrett. [Further editions, 1621, 1627, 1632, 1637. Reprinted in facsimile Amsterdam: Theatrum Orbis terrarum/New York: Da cappo, 1973].

Sherley, Anthony (1613) *Sir Anthony Sherley his relation of his travels into Persia. The dangers and distresses which befell him in his passage, both by sea and land and his strange and unexpected deliverances. His magnificent entertainement in Persia, his honourable employment there hence as Embassadour to the princes of Christendome, the cause of his disappointment therein, with his advice to his brother, Sir Robert Sherley. Also, a true relation of the great magnificence, valour, prudence, justice, temperance, and other manifold vertues of Abas, now King of Persia, with his great conquests, whereby he hath inlarged his dominions. Penned by Sir Anthony Sherley, and recommended to his brother, Sir Robert Sherley, being now in prosecution of the like honourable imployment*, Nathaniel Butter and Joseph Bagfet.

Smith, Thomas (1678) *Remarks upon the manners, religion and government of the Turks...*, Moses & Pitt.

[Solinus] (1587) *The excellent and pleasant work of Julius Solinus, polyhistor. Contayning the noble actions of humaine creatures, the secretes & providence of nature, the description of countries...translated out of the Latin by Arthur Golding, Gent*, J. Chatterwoode for T. Hooker.

Southern, Thomas (1682) *The Loyal Brother; or, the Persian Prince, a tragedy in five acts.*

Struys, Jan (1684) *The voyages of J[an] S[truys] through Greece, Muscovy, Tartary, Media, Persia, India, Japan....Together with an account of the author's...dangers by shipwreck...slavery...torture... done out of Dutch by I. Morrison.*

Tavernier, Jean Baptiste (1684) *Collections of travels through Turkey into Persia and the East Indies. Giving an account of the present state of those countries...*, 2 vols, A. Godbid & J. Playford for Moses Pitt.

Thevenot (1687) *The Travels of Monsieur De Thevenot into the Levant. In three parts....Newly done out of the French by D. Lovell*, Henry Clark for John Taylor.

Turler, J. (1575) *The Traveiler of Jerome Turler, devided into two bookes, the first conteining a notable discourse of the maner and order of traveling oversea, or into strange and forrein countreyes....*

Webbe, Edward (1590) *The rare and most wonderfull things which Edward Webbe, an Englishman borne, hath seen and passed in his troublesome travailes, in the cities of Ierusalem, Damasko, Bethlem and Gagely [Galilee]: and in the lands of Iewrie, Egypt, Grecia, Russia, and Prester John. Wherein is set forth his extreame slauerie sustained many yeares together in the gallies and warres of the Great*

Turke, against the lands of Persia, Tartaria, Spaine, and Portugale, with the manner of his release-ment and coming into England in May last, J. Charlwood for W. Wright.

Welde, T., Hammond, S., Sidenham, G. and Durant, W. (1653) *A False Jew. Or a wonderfull discovery of a Scot, baptized at London for a Christian, circumcized at Rome to act a Jew, rebaptized at Hexham for a believer, but found at Newcastle to be a cheat. Being a true relation of the cheating of one T. Ramsey...who landed at Newcastle under the name of T. Horsley, but gave himself out for a Jew, by the name of Rabbi Joseph ben Israel...*, Newcastle.

W. K. (1642) *The Devil's Last Legacy. Or a Round-Head ironmonger made executor to Pluto. Wherein is shewed the discent of roundheads. As also the Roundheads great desire of a Crowne...composed by W.K., first a Turke, and now turned Roundhead.*

Wragge, R. (1589) 'A description of a voiage to Constantinople and Syria, begun the 21 of march 1593 [n.s., 1594], and ended the 9 of August 1595, wherein is shewed the order of deliuering the second present by Master Edward Barton, her Maiesties Ambassador, which was sent from her Maiestie to Sultan Murad Can, Emperour of Turkie', in Hakluyt, R. (1589) *infra.*

Secondary sources

Adams, Percy G. (1962) *Travellers and Travel Liars, 1600–1800*, Berkeley, CA: University of California Press.

Ahmad, Aijaz (1992) *In Theory. Classes, nations, literatures*, London: Verso.

Alderson, Anthony D. (1956) 'Sir Thomas Sherley's piratical expedition to the Aegean and his imprisonment in Constantinople', *Oriens* 5: 1–38.

Arberry, A. J. (1943) *British Orientalists*, London: William Collins.

Axton, Marie (1977) *The Queen's Two Bodies. Drama and the Elizabethan succession*, London: Royal Historical Society.

Babinger, F. (1932) *Sherleiana. I: Sir Anthony Sherleys persische botschaftsreise, 1599–1601; 2: Sir Anthony Sherleys marrokanische Sendung, 1605–6*, Berlin.

Barker, F., Hulme, P., Iversen, D. and Loxley, D. (eds) (1985) *Europe and its Others*, Colchester: University of Essex.

Beale, T. W. (1881) *An Oriental Biographical Dictionary*, Calcutta: Asiatic Society of Bengal.

Bernal, Martin (1987, 1991) *Black Athena. The Afroasiatic roots of classical civilization*, 2 vols, London: Vintage; New Brunswick, NJ: Rutgers University Press.

Bitterli, U. (1989) *Cultures in Conflict. Encounters between European and non-European cultures, 1492–1800*, trans. R. Robertson, Cambridge: Polity.

Blaut, J. M. (1993) *The Colonizer's Model of the World. Geographical diffusionism and Eurocentric history*, New York: Guildford Press.

Brotton, J. (1997) *Trading Territories. Mapping the early modern world*, London: Reaktion.

Brummett, P. (1994) *Ottoman Seapower and Levantine Diplomacy in the Age of Discovery*, Albany, NY: State University of New York.

Burian, O. (1952) 'Interest of the English in Turkey as reflected in English literature of the Renais-sance', *Oriens. Journal of the International Society for Oriental Research* 5(2): 202–29.

Calder, Angus (1981; 2nd edition, 1998) *Revolutionary Empire. The rise of the English-speaking empires from the fifteenth century to the 1780s*, New York: Dutton; Harmondsworth: Penguin.

Canny, Nicholas (ed.) (1998) *The Oxford History of the British Empire. Vol. 1: The Origins of Empire. British overseas enterprise to the close of the 17thC*, Oxford: Oxford University Press.

Cardoso, J. L. (1958) *The Contemporary Jew in the Elizabethan Drama*, New York: Burt Franklin.

Cawley, R. R. (1938) *The Voyagers and Elizabethan Drama*, Oxford; Oxford University Press.

——(1951) *Milton and the Literature of Travel*, Princeton, NJ: Princeton University Press.

——(1967) *Unpathed Waters. Studies in the influence of the voyagers on English Literature*, London: Frank Cass. Originally published in 1940 by Princeton University Press.

Chambers, Douglas (1996) *The Reinvention of the World. English writing 1650–1750*, London: Arnold.

Chew, Samuel (1937) *The Crescent and the Rose. Islam and England during the Renaissance*, New York: Oxford University Press.

Clifford, James (1988) *The Predicament of Culture. Twentieth-century ethnography, literature and art*, Cambridge, MA: Harvard University Press.

Collier, J. Payne (1863) *Illustrations of Early English Popular Literature*, Vol. 2, London.

Cooper, Anthony Ashley [3rd Earl of Shaftesbury] (1900) *Characteristics of Men, Morals, Opinions, and Times*, ed. J. M. Robertson, London.

Crooke, W. (ed.) (1909–15) *A New Account of East India and Persia...*3 vols, London.

Daiber, Hans (1994) 'The reception of Islamic philosophy at Oxford in the 17th century. The Pocockes' (father and son) contribution to the understanding of Islamic philosophy in Europe', in *The Introduction of Arabic Philosophy into Europe*, ed. Charles E. Butterworth and Blake Andrée Kessell, Leiden: Brill.

Dannenfeldt, Karl H. (1955) 'The Renaissance humanists and the knowledge of Arabic', *Studies in the Renaissance* 2: 96–117.

Davies, D. W. (1967) *Elizabethans Errant. The strange fortunes of Sir Thomas Sherley and his three sons...as well in the Dutch wars as in Muscovy, Morocco, Persia, Spain, and the Indies*, Ithaca, NY: Cornell University Press.

Dawood, N. J. (1990) *The Koran. A translation, with notes*, Harmondsworth: Penguin.

Eagleton, T. (1990) *The Ideology of the Aesthetic*, Cambridge: Basil Blackwell.

Fea, A. (1905) *Memoirs of the Martyr King Being a detailed record of the last two years of the reign of His Most Sacred Majesty, King Charles I, 1646 1648/9*, London: John Lane.

Feingold, M. (1994) 'Patrons and professors. The origins and motives for the endowment of university chairs – in particular the Laudian professorship of Arabic', in *The 'Arabick' Interest of the Natural Philosophers in Seventeenth-Century England*, ed. G. A. Russell, Leiden: Brill.

——(1996) 'Decline and fall. Arabic science in seventeenth-century England', in *Tradition, Transmission, Transformation*, ed. F. Jamil Ragep, Sally P. Ragep and Steven Livesey, Leiden: Brill, 441–69.

Frantz, R. W. (1934) *The English Traveller and the Movement of Ideas, 1660–1732*, Lincoln, NE: Nebraska University Press.

Fuller, T. (1952) *History of the Worthies of England* [first published 1662], ed. John Freeman, London: Allen & Unwin.

Gikandi, S. (1996) *Maps of Englishness. Writing identity in the culture of colonialism*, New York: Columbia University Press.

Hamer, Mary (1993) *Signs of Cleopatra. History, Politics, Representation*, London: Routledge.

Hamilton, Alistair (1985) *William Bedwell the Arabist, 1563–1632*, Leiden: Brill.

Heisch, Alison (1980) 'Queen Elizabeth and the persistence of patriarchy', *Feminist Review* 4: 47–53.

Helgerson, Richard (1992) *Forms of Nationhood. The Elizabethan writing of England*, Chicago: University of Chicago Press.

Holt, P. M. (1973) 'An Oxford Arabist. Edward Pococke (1604–1691)', in *Studies in the History of the Near East*, ed. P.M. Holt, London: Frank Cass, 3–26.

——(1996) 'Background to Arabic studies in seventeenth-century England', in *The 'Arabick' Interest of the Natural Philosophers in Seventeenth-Century England*, ed. G. A. Russell, Leiden: Brill.

Horniker, A. L. (1942) 'William Harborne and the beginning of Anglo-Turkish diplomatic and commercial relations', *Journal of Modern History* XIV(3): 289–316.

Hourani, A. (1991) *Islam in European Thought*, Cambridge: Cambridge University Press.

Howard, C. (1914) *English Travellers of the Renaissance*, London: John Lane, The Bodley Head.

Hughes, C. (ed.) (1903) *Shakespeare's Europe. Unpublished chapters of Fynes Moryson's 'Itinerary'. Being a survey of the condition of Europe at the end of the sixteenth century. With an introduction and an account of Fynes Moryson's career*, London: Sherratt & Hughes.

Kaplan, Caren (1996) *Questions of Travel. Postmodern discourses of displacement*, Durham, NC: Duke University Press.

Leed, Eric J. (1991) *The Mind of the Traveller. From Gilgamesh to global tourism*, New York: Basic Books.

Lefkowitz, Mary (1996) *Not Out of Africa. How Afrocentricism became an excuse to teach myth as history*, New York: Basic Books.

Lefkowitz, Mary and Rogers, Guy Maclean (eds) (1996) *Black Athena Revisited*, Chapel Hill, NC: University of North Carolina Press.

Levin, Carole (1994) *The Heart and Stomach of a King. Elizabeth I and the politics of sex and power*, Philadelphia: University of Pennsylvania Press.

Lockwood, R. (ed.) (1959) *The Trial of Charles I. A contemporary account taken from the memoirs of Sir Thomas Herbert and John Rushworth*, London: Folio Society.

MacKenzie, Norman (1956) 'Sir Thomas Herbert of Tintern: a parliamentary "royalist"', *Bulletin of the Institute for Historical Research* No. 79.

Mansel, Philip (1995) *Constantinople. City of the world's desire, 1453–1924*, London: John Murray.

Matar, N[abil] I. (1991) 'Islam in Interregnum and Restoration England', *The Seventeenth Century* 6(1) (Spring): 57–71.

——(1998) *Islam in Britain, 1558–1685*, Cambridge: Cambridge University Press.

Mayes, S. (1956) *An Organ for the Sultan*, London: Putnam.

McKeon, Michael (1987) *The Origins of the English Novel, 1600–1740*, Baltimore, MD: Johns Hopkins University Press.

Montrose, Louis A. (1983) ' "Shaping Fantasies": Figurations of gender and power in Elizabethan culture', *Representations* 2 (Spring).

Morgan, E. D. and Coote, C. D. (1886) *Early English Voyages and Travels in Russia and Persia*, London: Hakluyt Society.

Parker, John (1965) *Books to Build an Empire. A bibliographical history of English overseas interests to 1620*, Amsterdam: Israel.

Parker, Kenneth (1995a) 'Telling tales. Early modern English voyagers and the Cape of Good Hope', *The Seventeenth Century* X(1) (Spring): 121–49.

Parr, Anthony (1995a) 'Foreign relations in Jacobean England. The Sherley brothers and the "voyage to Persia" ', in *Travel and Drama in Shakespeare's Time*, ed. Jean-Pierre Maquerlot and Michèle Willems, Cambridge: Cambridge University Press.

——(1995b) *Three Renaissance Travel Plays*, Manchester: Manchester University Press.

Penrose, Boies (1938) *The Sherleian Odyssey. Being a record of the travels and adventures of three famous brothers during the reigns of Elizabeth, James I, and Charles I*, Taunton: Barnicotts Ltd, the Wessex Press; London: Simpkin Marshall.

——(1942) *Urbane Travellers 1591–1635*, Philadelphia: University of Philadelphia Press.

——(1952) *Travel and Discovery in the Renaissance, 1420–1620*, Cambridge, MA: Harvard University Press.

Porter, Dennis (1983) '*Orientalism* and its problems', in *The Politics of Theory. Proceedings of the Essex Sociology of Literature Conference*, ed. Peter Hulme, Margaret Iversen and Diane Loxley, Colchester: University of Essex, 179–93.

——(1991) *Haunted Journeys. Desire and transgression in European travel writing*, Princeton, NJ: Princeton University Press.

Rawlinson, H. G. (1922) 'The Embassy of William Harborne to Constantinople, 1583–8', *Transactions of The Royal Historical Society* 4th Series: 1–27.

Rosedale, H. G. (ed.) (1904) *Queen Elizabeth and the Levant Company. A diplomatic and literary episode of the establishment of our trade with Turkey*, London: published under the direction of the Royal Society of Literature.

Ross, E. D. (1933) *Sir Anthony Sherley and his Persian Adventure. Including some contemporary narratives relating thereto*, London: George Routledge [The Broadway Travellers Series].

Russell, G. A. (ed.) (1994) *The 'Arabick' Interest of the Natural Philosophers in Seventeenth-Century England*, Leiden: Brill.

Said, Edward (1978; 1995) *Orientalism. Western conceptions of the Orient*, London: Routledge & Kegan Paul.

——(1983) *The World, the Text, and the Critic*, Cambridge, MA: Harvard University Press.

Salmon, Vivian (1994) 'Arabists and linguists in seventeenth-century England', in *The 'Arabick' Interest of the Natural Philosophers in Seventeenth-Century England*, ed. G. A. Russell, Leiden: Brill.

Shapiro, James (1996) *Shakespeare and the Jews*, New York: Columbia University Press.

Shaw, S. J. (1991) *The Jews of the Ottoman Empire and the Turkish Republic*, Basingstoke: Macmillan.

Sherley, E. P. (1848) *The Sherley Brothers. An historical memoir of the lives of Sir Thomas Sherley, Sir Anthony Sherley & Sir Robert Sherley. By one of the same house*, Chiswick: Roxburghe Club.

Skilliter, Susan (1965) 'Three letters from the Ottoman "Sultana" Safiye to Queen Elizabeth I', in *Documents from Islamic Chanceries*, ed. S. M. Stern, Cambridge, MA: Harvard University Press, 129–57.

——(1977) *William Harborne and the Trade with Turkey, 1578–1582. A documentary study of Anglo-Ottoman relations*, Oxford: Oxford University Press for The British Academy.

Steinschneider, M. (1859) *Al Farabi (Alpharabius) des arabischen Philosophen Leben und Schriften, mit besonderer Rücksicht auf die Geschicte der griechishen Wissenschaft unter den Arabern*.

——(1956) *Die europäischen Ubersetzungen aus den arabischen bis mitte des 17. Jahrhunderts*, Graz [photographic reprint of original published in Vienna in 1905].

Surtees, S. F. (1888) *William Shakespeare of Stratford. His epitaph unearthed, and the author of the plays run to ground (with a supplement alleging that Sir Anthony Sherley was the author of Shakespeare's plays)*, Hertford. Privately printed.

The Three English Brothers; or, the travels and adventures of Sir Anthony, Sir Robert & Sir Thomas Sherley, in Persia, Russia, Turkey, Spaine, etc. With portraits, London: Hurst, Robinson, 1825.

Toomer, G. J. (1996) *Easterne Wisedome and Learning. The study of Arabic in seventeenth-century England*, Oxford: Clarendon.

Wolf, E. R. (1982) *Europe and the People without History*, Berkeley, CA: University of California Press.

Woodhead, Christine (1987) ' "The Present Terrour of the World"? Contemporary views of the Ottoman Empire c. 1600', *History* 72: 20–37.

INDEX

CPSIA information can be obtained
at www.ICGtesting.com
Printed in the USA
FSHW020114091118
53665FS